PRINCIPLES IN POWER

A volume in the series

The United States in the World

Founded by Mark Philip Bradley and Paul A. Kramer

Edited by Benjamin Coates, Emily Conroy-Krutz, Paul A. Kramer, and Judy Tzu-Chun Wu

A list of titles in this series is available at www.cornellpress.cornell.edu.

PRINCIPLES IN POWER

Latin America and the Politics of U.S. Human Rights Diplomacy

Vanessa Walker

Cornell University Press
Ithaca and London

First published 2020 by Cornell University Press

Library of Congress Cataloging-in-Publication Data

Names: Walker, Vanessa, 1978– author.
Title: Principles in power : Latin America and the politics of U.S. human
    rights diplomacy / Vanessa Walker.
Description: Ithaca [New York] : Cornell University Press, 2020. | Series:
    The United States in the world | Includes bibliographical references
    and index.
Identifiers: LCCN 2020017808 (print) | LCCN 2020017809 (ebook) |
    ISBN 9781501713682 (cloth) | ISBN 9781501752681 (epub) | ISBN
    9781501752698 (pdf)
Subjects: LCSH: Human rights—Government policy—United States—
    History—20th century. | Human rights—Latin America—History—
    20th century. | Human rights advocacy—United States—History—20th
    century. | United States—Foreign relations—Latin America. | Latin
    America—Foreign relations—United States. | United States—Foreign
    relations—1945–1989.
Classification: LCC JC599.U5 W285 2020 (print) |LCC JC599.U5 (ebook) |
    DDC 323.098—dc23
LC record available at https://lccn.loc.gov/2020017808
LC ebook record available at https://lccn.loc.gov/2020017809

For Adi

If human rights is to be a central factor in the policy debate, the significance of non-governmental bodies is absolutely essential. I think the important thing to say about states and about human rights is that the action of states should neither be underestimated or overestimated. They should not be underestimated; you cannot ignore them in the struggle for human rights, what they do will count for good or ill. But the significance of states should not be overestimated. Our faith in the State is always tenuous, and rightly so. Our faith in the modern bureaucratic state should be fragilely placed. They need to be contained, restrained, pressured, shaped and directed from the outside. . . . What we try to do when we attempt to impose human rights criteria on other forms of power—political, economic, military—in the foreign policy equation, is we seek to use the very fragile instrument of moral suasion, the fabric of moral sinew, to control and contain the power of the modern state.

—Father J. Bryan Hehir, Seventh Annual Letelier-Moffitt Memorial Human Rights Award Ceremony, September 20, 1983

Contents

List of Abbreviations

ADA	Americans for Democratic Action
AFDD	Agrupación de Familiares de Detenidos Deseparicidos (Association of Relatives of the Detained – Disappeared)
AI	Amnesty International
Asamblea	Asamblea Permanente por los Derechos Humanos (Permanent Assembly for Human Rights)
CALA	Community Action on Latin America
CASP	Country Analysis Strategy Plan
CCC	Commodity Credit Corporation
CELS	Centro de Estudios Legales y Sociales (The Center for Social and Legal Studies)
CIA	Central Intelligence Agency
CLC	Clergy and Laity Concerned
CNFMP	Coalition for a New Foreign and Military Policy
CNI	Centro Nacional de Información (National Information Center)

CONADEP	Comisión Nacional sobre la Desaparición de Personas (National Commission on Disappeared People, Argentina)
CONAR	Comité Nacional de Ayuda a los Refugiados (National Committee to Aid Refugees, Chile)
Comité Pro-Paz	Comité de Cooperación para la Paz (Committee of Cooperation for Peace, Chile)
DINA	Dirección de Inteligencia Nacional (Directorate of National Intelligence, Chile)
DOD	Department of Defense
ERP	Ejército Revolucionario del Pueblo (Revolutionary Army of the People, Argentina)
EXIM	Export-Import (Bank)
FASIC	Fundación de Ayuda Social de las Iglesias Cristianas (Foundation for Social Assistance of the Christian Churches)
FMS	Foreign Military Sales
FRUS	*Foreign Relations of the United States*
GOA	government of Argentina
GOC	government of Chile
HA	U.S. State Department Bureau of Human Rights and Humanitarian Affairs
HRWG	Human Rights Working Group of the CFNMP
IACHR	Inter-American Commission on Human Rights of the OAS
ICJ	International Commission of Jurists
IFI	international financial institution
IMET	International Military Education and Training
IPS	Institute for Policy Studies
JCL	Jimmy Carter Presidential Library
La Liga	La Liga Argentina por los Derechos del Hombre (The Argentine League for the Rights of Man)
Las Madres	Las Madres de Plaza de Mayo (The Mothers of the Plaza de Mayo, Argentina)
MDB	multilateral development bank

MEDH	Moviemiento Ecuménico por los Derechos Humanos (Ecumenical Movement for Human Rights, Argentina)
MIR	Movimiento de Izquierda Revolucionaria (Revolutionary Movement of the Left, Chile)
NCCSC	National Coordinating Center in Solidarity with Chile
NICH	Non-Intervention in Chile
NGO	nongovernmental organization
NSC	National Security Council
OAS	Organization of American States
OPIC	Overseas Private Investment Corporation
PRM	Presidential Review Memorandum
SERPAJ	Servicio Paz y Justicia
UN	United Nations
USG	U.S. government
Vicaría	Vicaría de Solidaridad (Vicariate of Solidarity)
WHCF	White House Central Files
WHS	Wisconsin Historical Society
WOLA	Washington Office on Latin America

PRINCIPLES IN POWER

Introduction

The Politics of Complicity

September 7, 1977, should have been a high point for the Carter administration's new approach to U.S.-Latin American relations. The leaders of the hemisphere were gathered in Washington to celebrate the signing of the Panama Canal Treaties, a signature accomplishment of Carter's foreign policy agenda. The gathering not only marked a new phase of bilateral relations with Panama but also symbolized Carter's increasingly multilateral, less interventionist approach to the region. Further, in a private meeting earlier that day, Carter had persuaded General Augusto Pinochet of Chile to allow UN inspectors into his country to survey human rights conditions for the first time. This was a substantial breakthrough and the first major human rights concession Carter had been able to elicit from Pinochet, one of the most contentious figures in the human rights politics of the 1970s. The Carter administration had spent the past nine months fastidiously cooling relations with South American dictators, signaling its intention that human rights abuses would have real, material consequences for relations with the United States. Carter and his team had prepared rigorously for the bilateral meetings accompanying the signing ceremony, drafting in-depth plans for each leader, including a focus on concrete measures to address specific human rights violations. In the private bilateral meetings, Carter genially but adamantly pressed the region's strongmen—formerly close Cold War allies with Washington—on uncomfortable human rights questions, urging them to take meaningful action, and leaving no doubt of his administration's commitment to the issue.[1]

Carter seemed understandably surprised, therefore, at the evening gala when a *Washington Post* reporter informed him that more than seven hundred protestors had gathered outside the White House. "Oh really?" he responded. "Against me?" These protestors were not the conservative opponents to the Canal Treaties, who had gathered in smaller numbers on the steps of the Capitol Building that morning. Instead, many carried placards that said "Down with Pinochet" and chanted in protest against the Chilean leader, as well as several other of the foreign heads of state.[2] Earlier that day, approximately 1,500 demonstrators had rallied in front of the Pan-American Union Building, condemning political repression by right-wing military governments in many Latin American countries. In nearby Lafayette Park, speakers denounced Carter for flouting his commitment to human rights by inviting these dictators to Washington. Sue Bornstein, a member of a Chilean solidarity group, spoke to the crowd: "From now on, Jimmy Carter, you have given us the signal of what our attitude must be towards your administration. . . . This administration is all lip, all words."[3] More formally, Rep. Ronald V. Dellums (D-CA) held a press conference to remonstrate the administration for including repressive leaders in the Canal Treaties celebrations. Standing beside Isabel Letelier—a human rights activist and widow of the former Chilean ambassador who had been assassinated in Washington, D.C., by Chile's secret police just a year earlier—Dellums denounced Carter's personal "welcome to Pinochet and other 'dictators'."[4]

Although Carter expressed surprise, these denunciations could not have been totally unexpected for him. Human rights groups and members of Congress had voiced their concerns in the weeks leading up to the ceremonies. While some criticized the administration's inclusion of the region's dictators in the signing ceremony and celebratory events, most focused on Carter's private bilateral meetings, especially with the military leaders of Argentina and Chile. Letters from prominent members of Congress, including Donald Fraser (D-MN) and James Abourezk (D-SD), expressed dismay at the legitimacy that these private, bilateral meetings would convey on these repressive regimes.[5] Congressman John Burton (D-CA) cautioned in a telegram, "These meeting[s], an important symbol of U.S. relations with these countries, appear to contradict the bold human rights stand that the President has taken, and the intent of Congress that Chile and Argentina be condemned for their flagrant denials of the most basic human rights."[6]

Carter's decision to proceed with the meetings, despite these warnings, evidenced his belief that engagement on difficult issues, including human rights, was essential to resolving them. When asked at a press conference following the meetings how he would respond to people who said the U.S. government should not be meeting with these dictators, Carter replied, "I don't feel that this should be an obstacle to my meeting with them, to describing to them the problems as I see them, to ask for their explanation in a very frank and forthcoming way and to request their plans for the alleviation of the problem or the explanation of the charges that have been made against their governments."[7] Carter perhaps felt vindicated in his approach, knowing that the yet-to-be-announced concessions he garnered from Pinochet would set in motion a significant UN fact-finding mission, one that would bring even more pressure to bear on the Chilean regime to reform its repressive practices. Moreover, the treaty summit as a whole had its intended effect of signaling the administration's serious commitment to setting relations with Latin America on a less interventionist, more multilateral footing, giving it a "new measure of high priority attention."[8]

Yet those who had cautioned him against the meetings—arguing they would undermine Carter's domestic support from the human rights community and be used by foreign leaders to bolster their own legitimacy— were also vindicated. The *Washington Post* reported the day after the ceremony that most of the demonstrations "focused on charges that Carter, by personally receiving dictators or their representatives at the White House, has betrayed his own devotion to the promotion of human rights and has given these regimes a stamp of respectability."[9] Indeed, the morning headline of Chile's *El Mercurio*—a mouthpiece for the Pinochet regime—touted "67 Minutes between Carter and Pinochet," accompanied by pictures of the two leaders smiling broadly at each other.[10] Thus, even as Carter pressed vigorously for human rights with individual leaders, his apparent support for these leaders' views confirmed advocates' suspicions that the administration's commitment to implementing a human rights policy was no more vigorous or sincere than that of past administrations. Good relations with strategic allies, it seemed, would continue to trump vigorous measure on behalf of human rights violations. In short, the administration appeared to be "all lip, all words."

Figure 1. President Jimmy Carter with General Augusto Pinochet in Washington, D.C., for the signing of the Panama Canal Treaties. A similar image was featured on the front page of the Chilean newspaper *El Mercurio*, championing "67 Minutes between Carter and Pinochet." The meeting and photo op were also widely criticized by human rights groups in the United States.

Courtesy of the Jimmy Carter Presidential Library.

U.S. Cold War policies were deeply implicated in the human rights viola-tions perpetrated by many of Latin America's governments.[11] This entangle-ment of U.S. policy and human rights abuses make the Western Hemisphere a critical site for the development and implementation of U.S. human rights diplomacy during the Ford, Carter, and Reagan presidencies. New human rights advocacy targeting Latin America in the 1970s not only sought to mitigate foreign abuses but also challenge Cold War relationships between the United States and repressive right-wing regimes, contesting presidential prerogatives over the very mechanisms of U.S. foreign policy making.[12] Latin America is essential for revealing the uniquely anti-interventionist and self-critical elements of human rights policy that took shape at this time; it was at the core—not the periphery—of both U.S. domestic policy debates and the new international policies that reached far beyond the hemisphere.[13]

The United States' human rights policies that arose in the 1970s were not only about addressing abuses taking place abroad, nor has human rights diplomacy been the exclusive purview of those who "care" about human rights. Debates about new human rights initiatives quickly moved beyond whether the United States *should* pursue such initiatives, to more complex arguments about what the purpose of such a human rights policy should be, how it fit with other national interests, and, from this, what defined an effective policy. Rather than evaluate U.S. human rights policy based exclu-sively on its ability to change the behaviors of foreign governments, or as a "feel-good" measure to appease domestic critics, this book explores it as a self-critical policy to address the failings of Cold War paradigms for domestic and foreign political power.[14] Analyzing how different groups deployed hu-man rights language to reform domestic and international power reveals the multiple and often conflicting purposes of U.S. human rights policy.

A serious analysis of the multiple meanings and objectives of human rights diplomacy requires a reassessment of the complex relationship be-tween advocates and government officials. Many works now explore the critical contributions to human rights policy made by nongovernment actors and Congress before Carter's election. Few scholars, however, have explored in depth how these essential precursors shaped the Carter administration's agenda, bilateral diplomacy, and working dynamics with the broader human rights community while in office.[15] The interactions between the U.S. ad-ministrations and human rights advocates were not only generative but also limiting, even during the demonstrably sympathetic Carter presidency. This project engages the decisive contributions of nongovernmental actors while also seeking to understand their complex relationships with government officials in advancing their agendas. By taking seriously the perspectives of both advocates and policy makers, it reveals how the effectiveness and prioritization of human rights initiatives became entangled in domestic struggles over the control of foreign policy and presidential power. Tracing this relationship across three very different presidencies, moreover, gives us greater insight into the shared dilemmas and sustained relationships of policy makers and advocates that transcend any one administration's ideological proclivities. Informal collaboration between government and nongovernment actors, a self-critical reassessment of U.S. foreign policy norms, and a power struggle between Congress and the White House for control over U.S. foreign affairs all shaped human rights policies and diplomacy during the Ford, Carter, and Reagan administrations.

This work explores the relationship between advocates and diplomats from 1973 to 1982 through an influential coalition of left-liberal human rights actors targeting U.S. policy in Latin America, or "the Movement," as one State Department official dubbed them.[16] In addition to the Movement's focus on Latin America, a sense of responsibility for abuses by U.S. Cold War allies distinguished them from advocates targeting repression in the Soviet sphere. Although the Movement's constituent actors had diverse political and strategic perspectives, they shared a common assumption that human rights abuses in Latin America could not be abstracted from larger Cold War dynamics. The United States had a responsibility to mitigate foreign repression—not because of its unique historical traditions and values but because of its recent policies and practices that facilitated abuses.

The Movement was defined by its belief that curtailing human rights abuses abroad required the reform of the U.S. government's interventionist policies that supported repressive regimes in the name of Cold War security relationships. This emphasis on U.S. complicity in foreign violations led to a strategy of reforming U.S. policy as a means to improve human rights globally. The Movement's advocacy was not an irrational effort to absolve themselves of responsibility for the costs of the Cold War. The Movement believed its strategy of targeting U.S. support for right-wing dictatorships signaled moral condemnation *and* materially affected the ability of foreign governments to perpetrate abuse against their own citizens.[17] Moreover, Washington's support for repressive, right-wing governments not only undermined human rights abroad but also revealed the antidemocratic impact of Cold War foreign policy on the United States' own government structures and practices. Human rights legislation and mechanisms advanced by the Movement evidenced a desire to mitigate repression in places such as

Chile, but also to curtail presidential power and interventionism in the name of establishing democratic oversight to the foreign policy process within the United States. Advocates' desire to devolve greater authority to the legislative branch was intimately intertwined with a broad questioning of whether the growing power of the presidency was consistent with basic democratic principles within the United States.

The politics of complicity unified the diverse coalition that constituted the Movement.[18] Political scientist Lars Schoultz observes, "By 1977, the combined interest groups concerned with the repression of human rights in Latin America had become one of the largest, most active, and most visible foreign policy lobbying forces in Washington."[19] Recent scholarship on human rights in the 1970s has given much attention to Amnesty International (AI) and its apolitical ethos of freeing political prisoners, rather than "trying to remedy oppression and injustice by targeting their sources."[20] Amnesty International certainly became an institutional behemoth of the human rights world during the 1970s, and its information and international contacts were critical to the burgeoning human rights coalition focused on Latin America. Yet the Movement's agenda was not defined by AI's scrupulously nonpartisan approach but rather by a synergy of moderate liberal groups, socialist networks, and leftist organizations that targeted U.S. Cold War policies. Established liberal organizations such as the Americans for Democratic Action (ADA) and leftist groups such as the Institute for Policy Studies (IPS) increasingly turned to human rights in the 1970s as a language to expand their concern for civil rights and social justice into the international sphere, linking U.S. domestic and foreign policies. They were joined by new groups focused specifically on human rights conditions in Latin America. Organizations such as the ecumenical Washington Office on Latin America (WOLA) and socialist grassroots solidarity networks brought new voices and priorities to these established groups, targeting the connection between human rights abuses and U.S. intervention and regional hegemony.

The Movement combined the overseas contacts and information, cultivated by groups such as WOLA and other religious groups, Amnesty International, and solidarity networks, joining it with the Washington access, government connections, policy background, and lobbying expertise of the Institute for Policy Studies and ADA.[21] In 1976 the core of the Movement formalized its collaboration through the Human Rights Working Group (HRWG), under the auspices of the Coalition for a New Foreign and Military Policy (CNFMP).[22] The HRWG was a visible site of the rich informal collaboration among the groups and individuals active in the Movement. These groups also had a fluid relationship with Congress, often working in tandem with sympathetic members to pass legislation, organize testimony from Latin American actors, and provide detailed information from advocate networks. In turn, members of Congress contributed to the governance and operation of these groups, serving as national chairs, participating in events, and speaking at protests. This close working relationship with Congress mobilized the Movement and human rights concerns in the domestic political struggles between Congress and the White House over democratic governance and distribution of political power.[23] Although they often disagreed on strategies and priorities, they shared a commitment to not only curtailing abuses but also reforming the power structures and policies that perpetuated them.[24]

The Movement's emphasis on U.S. complicity in the abuses of Cold War allies became a central component of the Carter administration's human rights policy. During the Carter presidency, human rights was part of a broader reassessment of Cold War paradigms, which diminished the centrality of the Soviet Union in its strategic thinking.[25] This is not to say that East-West relations were unimportant to the Carter administration or to the development of human rights issues in the late Cold War. The Carter administration certainly believed that human rights considerations would inform relations with the Soviets and give the United States an ideological edge over its longtime adversary, but it anticipated little in the way of substantial improvements in human rights conditions within the Soviet Union. Human rights problems within the communist sphere were a serious concern for many, but the primary instruments formulated by Congress in the mid-1970s and implemented in bilateral relations—particularly restrictions on foreign aid, international financial institutions, and State Department country reports—overwhelmingly targeted the U.S. government's alignments with and support for repressive Cold War allies.

U.S. relations with the military governments in Chile and Argentina epitomized the human rights politics of the 1970s. Although they do not represent the experiences of all Latin America, both Chile and Argentina received a disproportionate amount of attention from advocates and diplomats alike, and strongly influenced the contours of U.S. policy and debates in the 1970s. The 1973 Chilean coup was a crucial catalyst for the emerging human rights movement, bringing together criticism of U.S. Cold War foreign policy with challenges to presidential power domestically.[26] Argentina is widely regarded as one of the most successful cases of the Carter administration's human rights diplomacy, and it was certainly one of the most visible, with the military coup coinciding with the 1976 U.S. presidential campaign.[27]

Yet even with this "success story," one can see the limits faced by the administration stemming from tensions with the advocate community and competing domestic and international policy objectives. The dilemmas faced by the administration in implementing its human rights policy in Chile and Argentina reflected other high-profile crises: tensions between productive engagement and dissociation, the limits of U.S. influence to shape human rights outcomes, the legacy of U.S. intervention and support for repressive regimes, divisive domestic politics, and entrenched congressional opinion.

This book bridges the fields of U.S.-Latin American relations, human rights, social activism, and policy history, situating diplomacy in a broad social and political domestic context, and considering the influence of a wide array of actors, both in and out of government. Moreover, it emphasizes the ways in which foreign actors and issues can define the central debates of U.S. politics and identity. This study thus reveals the deep and inextricable connections between international structures and policies, and domestic dissent and reform in the 1970s. In this, it is neither an exclusively "top-down" history that focuses only on policy makers and grand strategy, nor an exclusively grassroots history of human rights that seeks to decenter the state. It instead focuses on the interchange between governments and societies, with nongovernment actors providing influential limits within which policy makers operate.

Chapter 1 traces the rise of the Movement in response to the 1973 Chilean coup, revealing the centrality of Latin America in 1970s human rights activism and formulation of human rights foreign policy mechanisms— including foreign aid legislation and bureaucratic structures in the State Department. Unlike human rights violations in the Soviet sphere, U.S. advocates viewed human rights abuses in Chile as a product of U.S. political dysfunction resulting from Cold War paradigms of national interest and excessive concentration of power in the presidency. Coming in the wake of the Watergate scandal and the failures of Vietnam, U.S. complicity in the Chilean coup and the subsequent repression underscored the antidemocratic nature of Cold War foreign policy, highlighting the connections between foreign human rights abuses and U.S. policies. Using the information generated by South American advocates, newly organized and vocal human rights groups in the United States and their congressional partners advanced a slate of legislative initiatives targeted at the nexus of foreign repression and U.S. policy, challenging the logic and substance of Cold War alliances.

The political battles in the United States over the proper response to Chile's ongoing human rights problems became a way to debate the merits of competing approaches to human rights diplomacy and the distribution of foreign policy responsibilities between Congress and the president. Under pressure from new human rights forces, the Ford administration slowly moved to incorporate the issue into its State Department structures and diplomacy, yet simultaneously balked at congressional usurpation of executive privilege in foreign affairs and the prioritization of human rights over what it viewed as more concrete security interests. The limited human rights agenda of the Ford administration never led to sweeping reconceptualization of foreign policy championed by human rights advocates or the subsequent Carter administration, but these battles created an environment that would decisively shape the Carter administration's interactions with Congress, relationship with advocates, and implementation of its human rights policy.

Chapter 2 analyzes the early development of the Carter administration's human rights agenda, built in tandem with a new approach to U.S.-Latin American relations during its first year in office. From the outset, the Carter administration envisioned a human rights policy that would simultaneously mitigate human rights violations abroad, build U.S. credibility and stature in the international sphere by reasserting a moral and ideological pole of attraction, and signify a move away from the excessive secrecy and power of the Cold War presidency at home. Carter incorporated human rights into his Latin American policy as a way to demonstrate an increased respect for sovereignty in the region and divorce the United States from interventionist legacies that had both undermined self-determination and exacerbated human rights crises. The Carter administration offered a vision of human rights based not on regime change from without but on restrained U.S. engagement in the region to empower citizens to reform their own countries from within. This conception of human rights policy—laid out in a new approach to U.S.–Latin American relations in the spring of 1977—emerged also in policy frameworks well beyond the region as the administration drafted its global human rights policy in the summer of 1977.

Although Carter largely shared the premises of the Movement's vision, differences over the implementation and signifiers of this policy in high-level diplomacy created rifts between like-minded advocates and policy makers. Carter found himself grappling with the legacies of both U.S. intervention in the region and also congressional and public distrust stemming from past excesses of the Cold War presidency. The administration's options in implementing its policy were bounded by both past regional relations and human rights advocacy itself. Carter had to prove to human rights proponents that his administration was serious about its human rights agenda, that quiet diplomacy was not simply code for inaction. Yet his own advocacy to overcome this legacy of apparent executive indifference, with statements such as "our commitment must be absolute," raised expectations he could not hope to meet and ran against the more nuanced, restrained diplomacy he thought would be most effective in light of past U.S. interventionism.[28] Early battles over incorporating binding human rights language into foreign aid legislation and backlash to the invitation of Chile's and Argentina's leaders to Washington for the signing of the Panama Canal Treaties foreshadowed problems that would plague the administration throughout its time in office.

Chapter 3 addresses U.S. relations with Chile during the Carter administration as an avenue to explore the innate tensions within a policy that simultaneously sought to promote human rights abroad and champion nonintervention. The administration, seeking to appeal to both domestic and international constituencies, sought an approach that balanced distancing the U.S. government from the Pinochet regime, maintaining pressure to improve human rights, and avoiding overt interference in domestic Chilean affairs, which could prompt a nationalist backlash. The competing demands of demonstrating to domestic audiences a cooler relationship with the Pinochet regime on the one hand, and implementing a human rights policy that would improve conditions in Chile on the other, shaped and at times undermined the Carter administration's efforts. The administration was always aware that its leverage was limited and that regime change from without was not a primary objective. The assassination of former Chilean ambassador Orlando Letelier in Washington, D.C., on September 21, 1976, highlighted the tensions between the domestic and foreign policy objectives of the administration's human rights policy. When faced with the limits of pairing human rights with a commitment to nonintervention, the administration erred on the side of restraint, choosing its commitment to supporting gradual change over a more strident policy. This approach was largely supported by human rights groups in Chile and paid dividends in the long-term stature of the United States in the region. However, it undermined Carter's standing with the Movement at home, which read the restrained but open relations between Washington and Santiago as a continuation of prior administrations' "half-hearted" policies on human rights. Criticism from disappointed human rights advocates fed into broader questioning of the costs and effectiveness of the policy across the political spectrum.

Chapter 4 explores the Carter administration's approach to Argentina, driven by a rich interaction between advocates and government officials in Buenos Aires and Washington. Argentina was the site of some of the Carter administration's most sustained and vigorous human rights efforts, yet it also revealed the limits of influence and competing priorities among administration officials and U.S. human rights groups. In Argentina tensions arose around the dual objectives of U.S. policy: to defend human rights by distancing itself from dictatorships and to engage with repressive regimes to improve specific human rights problems. The Carter administration had built its foreign policy around the premise that the promotion and support of human rights would serve the national interest by building the United States' stature and influence in the international system. With Argentina, however, its human rights initiatives increasingly appeared to conflict with other national interests, particularly economic growth and new security concerns. With a struggling economy at home, the potential loss of trade and jobs due to human rights legislation curtailing international investment led some to question how this policy served the national interest. Moreover, resurgent tensions with the Soviet Union in the second half of Carter's term increased pressure to court noncommunist allies.

By summer 1978 the Carter administration faced domestic pressure from both increasingly restrictive human rights legislation passed by a liberal contingent in Congress and more conservative voices who expressed dissatisfaction with the "costs" of human rights initiatives. The tenuous connection between economic aid and human rights abuses made the costs of the policy all the more difficult to accept. Even as it chafed against the provisions that restricted its flexibility, the administration leveraged these legislative limits to obtain concessions on human rights issues from the Argentine government, including access for the Inter-American Commission on Human Rights (IACHR). Despite the IACHR visit's crucial role in improving the domestic rights climate in Argentina, the Carter administration's resumption of aid and loans to secure the visit garnered significant criticism from the Movement, which expected greater changes before offering such substantial inducements. Carter's Argentine policies simultaneously galvanized a powerful counter–human rights block in Congress and beyond, bringing together pro-business groups with ascendant conservatives. This coalition critiqued Carter's policies as being too costly to both economic and security considerations, a formulation that would gain traction under the incoming Reagan administration.

Chapter 5 traces the dramatic reinvention of U.S. human rights policy during Reagan's first year in office. The Carter administration pursued human rights as a corrective to U.S. interventionist legacies, emphasizing pluralism and eschewing regime change. The Reagan administration, in contrast, aggressively promoted human rights within a reinvigorated but narrow Cold War framework. This construction, championing a limited range of civil and political rights, downplayed the human rights violations of pro-American governments, focusing instead on what it considered the much greater moral flaws and violations of communist regimes. The Cold War framing of human rights under Reagan empowered a pairing of military power and moral values, leading the United States to not only *not* limit arms sales to governments but also recast military aid as a critical aspect of both hemispheric defense against communism and the advancement of human rights. Examining this policy shift in the Reagan administration's first year, especially in regard to Chile and Argentina, this chapter argues that Reagan's formulation of human rights in the Western Hemisphere continued conservative formulations articulated by Sen. Henry "Scoop" Jackson (D-WA) and UN ambassador Jeane Kirkpatrick, among others, developing in parallel with the liberal construction of human rights favored by Carter.[29]

Latin America was again the crucible for new instruments and reorientation of human rights policy. The Reagan administration's efforts to bring "balance" to human rights initiatives by emphasizing violations in the Soviet Bloc reinforced, rather than diminished, the importance of Latin America in framing U.S. human rights policy. The markedly warmer relations between Washington and military governments in Chile and Argentina raised pointed questions about the Reagan administration's own even-handedness and double standards, undermining its message on communist abuses. Its approach to Latin America was central to defining perceptions of its overall human rights policy as weak and inconsistent—the very criticisms it had lodged against the Carter administration. Reagan's reinvention of human rights demonstrates that human rights diplomacy was not fixed in either its goals or its mechanisms but was continually contested and reinterpreted within a larger framework of national interests and international aims.

Michael Ignatieff has observed that human rights can be seen "as the language of a moral imperialism just as ruthless and just as self-deceived as the colonial hubris of yesteryear."[30] This sense of moral imperialism is heightened in the Latin American context by the long history of U.S. intervention there. Yet the relationship between the Movement and the Carter administration was grounded in a politics of complicity, giving rise to a uniquely self-critical, anti-interventionist vision of U.S. human rights policy in the 1970s. It was, as Robert Drinan noted in 1981, a "noble experiment," addressing the failings of U.S. Cold War policies and grappling with the limits of U.S. power. Human rights, in this context, was not an abstract moral gesture or a new form of interventionism, but rather a recalibration of U.S. policies and regional relations to support both vital national interests and democratic values.

Chapter 1

The Chilean Catalyst

Cold War Allies and Human Rights in
the Western Hemisphere

In March 1976 U.S. congressman Tom Harkin (D-IA) stood outside the gates of Villa Grimaldi, an alleged secret detention center on the outskirts of Santiago, Chile. In the coming years, reports would confirm what was only whispered about at the time: that Villa Grimaldi was the site of some of the most grotesque forms of torture and human rights abuses perpetrated by the Chilean military government under the leadership of Augusto Pinochet. With Harkin were Congressmen George Miller (D-CA) and Toby Moffet (D-CT), as well as Rebecca Switzer, a congressional aid, and Joe Eldridge, the head of a small nonprofit organization called the Washington Office on Latin America.

Villa Grimaldi was surrounded by a tall wall, and when the delegation arrived there was no visible activity. Congressman Harkin walked up and knocked on the gates, with no response. After a short time, a large covered truck drove up to the compound, and as the gates opened to let the vehicle in, the delegation followed behind. Just inside the gates, the group quickly found themselves surrounded by gun-wielding guards who were confused and not too happy to have unexpected visitors. Joe Eldridge later recalled that Tom Harkin was holding up his congressional ID as if it were bulletproof yelling, "I am a U.S. congressman. I am an official representative of the U.S. government," with Eldridge translating to Spanish as fast as he could. When asked by the guards what they were doing there, Harkin stated that the delegation had permission from the military government to inspect any place they wanted in the country. The guard briefly disappeared into a nearby building; when he returned, he told them to leave. Harkin, Eldridge, and the others were quickly deposited outside the gates. They left the site without seeing one prisoner or witnessing any unsightly behavior, aside from their less-than-friendly reception, yet their visit had reverberations throughout U.S.–Latin American relations and the emerging U.S. human rights policy framework.[1]

After the delegation returned to the United States, Harkin declared in a press conference, "Human rights in Chile is nothing short of a disaster," and he stated that they "found clear evidence of systematic denial of basic human rights and efforts by the military to stomp out all opposition." Three months after the visit, the U.S. Congress passed the Security Assistance Act of 1976, which terminated all military sales to Chile. It also contained an important amendment that generalized the link between security assistance and human rights performance.

The Chilean government, for its part, rebuked the delegation for acting unprofessionally on the visit. The Chilean embassy issued a press release stating that the U.S. delegation had been given "total freedom" and had conferred with "50 Marxist women and were falsely informed that there existed in Chile 'clandestine concentration camps' and that persons continued to be tortured." The embassy also attacked Eldridge directly for setting up these meetings, seeking to discredit him based on his well-known "support to the Allende's [sic] government and opposition to the present Chilean government."[2] A spokesman for the Chilean government told the press that Villa Grimaldi was used for "temporary detention," and "those reports, you know, on torture and things, they are not true."[3] Within months, however, the military government began to include the site on its list of detention centers— making it accountable to international agencies that would later come to evaluate human rights conditions.[4]

Despite promises from the Pinochet government that individuals who met with the congressional delegates would not be harassed, in the days after their visit the government-controlled press launched an attack on those who talked with the U.S. representatives, labeling them "anti-patriotic" and "enemies of Chile." José Zalaquett, the legal advisor to the Catholic Church's Vicaría de la Solidaridad (Vicariate of Solidarity or Vicaría), was expelled from the country a month after meeting with Harkin's group. The outcry from the human rights community over his exile in turn provoked the first public reprimand of the Chilean government from the Ford administration on human rights issues. This trip thus put pressure not only on the Chilean government but also on Washington's ongoing support of the regime, raising broader questions about the nature and costs of the United States' Cold War alliances.

The Chilean coup and subsequent military dictatorship played a uniquely catalytic role in the emergence and construction of U.S. human rights policy as a challenge to existing Cold War paradigms of national interests in the 1970s. Earlier coups and dictatorships played a crucial role in conditioning the U.S. response to Chile; U.S. intervention in the Dominican Republic and the dictatorship in Brazil were both crucial in mobilizing the early core of the human rights movement that would emerge in the 1970s.[5] Moreover, by 1973 the failure of three consecutive U.S. administrations to devise a strategy to secure any semblance of victory in Vietnam undermined a host of assumptions that underpinned Cold War foreign policy for two decades.[6] Many Americans questioned the general tenor and direction of U.S. foreign policy, including its willingness to embrace dictatorial regimes that professed anticommunist values, the overwhelming reliance on military power to meet U.S. interests abroad, and the seeming inability to distinguish between the nation's vital interests and peripheral concerns. Many saw the failures of U.S. policy in Vietnam as emblematic of mismanagement and overreach by the executive branch. The Watergate scandal further reinforced the idea of a power-drunk presidency, unable to craft policy in the best interests of the country.[7]

Fallout from Vietnam and the Watergate scandal undoubtedly attenuated U.S. public and congressional reactions to the Chilean coup. Yet Chile also had its own unique elements that made it a powerful force in U.S. politics. Salvador Allende's democratic path to socialism had captured worldwide attention—both as a symbol of hope and an object of fear. In the United States, many had seized on Chile as a way to critique U.S. policies as interventionist and neo-imperialist, especially in Latin America; this critique gained damning weight with the Chilean military coup on September 11, 1973, that ended Allende's government and his life. Congressional hearings on the coup tied the United States directly to the overthrow of a democratically elected government and the subsequent military dictatorship in Santiago.[8] Some certainly believed that Allende's Chile was a gateway for Soviet influence in the hemisphere, but the specter of the Cold War had weakened in its explanatory power. A sense of U.S. complicity in the coup—and hence the atrocities in Chile reported daily—gave the human rights agenda an urgency and weight it had previously lacked for a U.S. audience.

Galvanized by the Chilean human rights crisis, a loose coalition of groups and actors formulated a vision of human rights that sought to mitigate repression abroad by targeting U.S. government policies and challenging the strategic assumptions of Cold War diplomacy. The liberal Americans for Democratic Action and leftist Institute for Policy Studies, transnational socialist and religious solidarity networks, and new groups such as the Washington Office on Latin America and Amnesty International coalesced into what one State Department official, George Lister, labeled "the Movement."[9] Never monolithic or totally detached from the broader human rights community taking shape at this time, the Movement found common cause with congressional forces ready and eager to reconsider Cold War axioms of national security and the expanded executive power that had advanced them.

Motivated by a sense of complicity in foreign repression in places such as Chile, the Movement's focus on the U.S. government and its repressive allies was more than an altruistic gesture or emotional response to the moral vagaries of the nation's Cold War crusade. The connection between U.S. policies and foreign abuses made domestic reform of U.S. foreign policy a strategic choice. The vision of human rights catalyzed by the Chilean coup sought to realign U.S. foreign policy with domestic democratic values, but its proponents also championed it as the most direct means of effecting significant change.[10]

The reaction to the Chilean coup that unfolded in the United States under the Ford administration marked a crucial moment for establishing human rights mechanisms and legislation and also initiating dynamics and tensions that would permeate U.S. human rights politics for the next decade. In this, Latin America, particularly Chile, played a central role in defining the mechanisms and meaning of human rights as a vehicle to reform U.S. policy and rein in the power of the Cold War presidency. It was one of many constructions of human rights policy taking shape in the 1970s, but it had a disproportionate impact on emerging policy frameworks.[11] Although violations in the communist sphere were of great concern to many, the policy frameworks that took shape during the Ford administration focused overwhelmingly on U.S. policies that supported human rights violations abroad, often perpetrated by traditional Cold War allies.

Defeating the Enemy Within

The military coup in Chile on September 11, 1973, stunned the world, not just for the images of jets strafing the presidential palace or the reports of violence and human rights abuses that quickly emerged but also because of Chile's long-standing history of civilian rule. In a region marked by military governments, Chile had an exceptional legacy of democracy and stability. Before the September 1973 coup, the military had ruled Chile for only thirteen months in its 130-year history. The Chilean military was the least politicized in South America, and Chileans boasted so often of their strong political culture and law-abiding nature that Chilean exceptionalism was a byword.[12] Yet despite its relatively stable government and society, Chile was not immune to the problems shared by its neighbors and the world in the second half of the twentieth century. Growing inflation, deficits, an increasingly radical youth, and divisive Cold War alignments increased polarization within Chile throughout the 1960s.[13]

Chile—with its democratic institutions and civic discourse that defied regional stereotypes of *caudillo* politics—had become a darling of the Left internationally as it sought a new path to socialism in the late Cold War. The world watched—some in elation, others in fear—as Salvador Allende became the first democratically elected Marxist head of state in October 1970. It watched in the coming months as Allende energized both the Left and Right in a way that strained the vaunted civil confines of political debate in Chile and alarmed the staunchly anticommunist governments of the region, particularly the behemoth to the north.[14] And, some thirty months later, the world watched again as the military attacked the Chilean presidential palace and tanks rolled through the streets of Santiago, ending the hopes and fears associated with the Allende government.

Led by General Augusto Pinochet, the military leadership promised to restore the institutional structure and "character" of Chile, casting the coup as an act of duty, preventing a precipitous decline into chaos and national dissolution. Chile was undoubtedly in turmoil when its military seized power. Yet the coup was not the end of violence but rather the beginning of institutionalized state-controlled repression and terrorism against broadly defined "enemies of the state." Despite promising to uphold the Constitution, the junta made use of provisions for a time of war to announce a state of siege and gave the military power over all civilian activities by declaring the entire country an "emergency zone." Through a series of decrees issued under these emergency powers, the military disbanded all political parties and major labor unions, closed Congress, and implemented censorship laws for all media outlets, shutting down many newspapers and magazines.[15]

Although armed resistance had all but ceased within a few days of the coup, the military kept up massive raids, holding more than 45,000 people for interrogation in the week after the coup.[16] Infamously, more than seven thousand citizens were corralled into El Estadio Nacional, the national soccer stadium, on the outskirts of Santiago. There they were brutally interrogated and tortured. Some were executed on the spot, and others were transported to other detention centers and prison camps, many of them never seen again. The naval ship *Esmeralda*, anchored in Valparaíso, also became a makeshift detention and torture center. In the poorest barrios and shantytowns, military raids turned into summary executions, with dead bodies left by the side of the road or washed up on the banks of the Mapocho River, flowing through the center of Santiago. The military and police raided factories, killing some and taking others to detention centers. Similarly, in the countryside, army and police officers, aided by local landowners, brutally cleared squatters from land, seizing peasants who had participated in land reform movements and arresting local labor leaders and leftists. Members of Allende's government and prominent leftists, many of whom had extensive overseas contacts, received more cautious but still severe treatment. Cabinet ministers and party leaders, former senators and academics, were arrested as "prisoners of war" and flown to an improvised prison on Dawson's Island in the far south of the country. By the end of December the military had killed at least fifteen hundred civilians, detained thousands more, and forced, directly or indirectly, another seven thousand into exile.[17]

The military government denied any abusive treatment of unarmed civilians while simultaneously arguing that the initial crackdown was regrettable but necessary to stave off even more violence. The regime deliberately played up the image of a violent, fanatical insurgency that would stop at nothing to foist its Marxist vision on Chile. The image of an enemy without compunction rationalized military control and ongoing repression; this internal enemy had exploited democracy's very openness, manipulating politics to sow seeds of discontent and exacerbate divisions among Chileans.[18] The military junta thus purported to simultaneously root out subversion and rebuild the country's civil society in a way that would prevent its future corruption by similar forces.

To exercise the control necessary to realize its agenda, the junta established the Dirección de Inteligencia Nacional (Directorate of National Intelligence or DINA) on June 18, 1974. Ostensibly an intelligence-gathering organization, it quickly became the center of the state terror apparatus, with a string of secret detention and torture centers throughout the country. At its strongest, it had almost four thousand agents and thousands more informants and collaborators. Under the direction of Manuel Contreras, DINA "enjoyed practically unlimited power," marking a transition from the coup's spontaneous and visible violence to institutionalized repression, coordinated by a centralized government agency largely obscured from public knowledge and scrutiny.[19] Insulated from the military chain of command, DINA consolidated power under Pinochet and Contreras within nine months of the coup, buttressing their position within the military government.

The regime constructed a new order that was conservative in its ultranationalist championing of traditional bastions of power: military, church, family, and private property. It was radical in its totalizing vision of the enemy and the means used to eliminate it. Yet the junta did not only offer fear; it also held out what historian Steve Stern calls a "positive meaning of liberation." The junta espoused an intention to rebuild Chile with a healthier, stronger Christian democracy and civil society that would usher in a new, more prosperous, and harmonious era for all Chileans.[20] At the root of the military regime's legitimacy and justification of political and social repression, therefore, was a heightened sense of nationalism, defined by its adherence to "Western Christian civilization."

Even as it dismantled almost every traditional civil and political institution that could challenge the regime's repression, the junta's positive vision created openings for domestic opposition. By defining the regime as a defender of Western civil traditions and Christian society—co-opting churches, families, and legal institutions into its mission—the military government unintentionally legitimized and empowered dissent from these elements of society. At the fore of the initial response to the military regime's violence and repression was the Catholic Church, especially the archbishopric of Santiago. Trading on its privileged position within the junta's self-definition as a defender of Christianity and "traditional Western values," the church helped establish two ecumenical ad hoc committees—the Comité Nacional de Ayuda a los Refugiados (National Committee to Aid Refugees or CONAR) and the Comité de Cooperación para la Paz (Committee of Cooperation for Peace, or Comité Pro-Paz)—to aid those suffering in the immediate aftermath of the coup.

Playing on the regime's facade of legalism, the Comité Pro-Paz submitted thousands of petitions and writs of habeas corpus, testifying to the pervasive violence taking place under the leadership of the military government. Although the courts accepted fewer than 5 percent of the habeas petitions, the impact of submitting them to the court established a legal record of the regime's practices and legitimized families' experiences. Moreover, the collective impact of these cases wore at the regime's pretense of regular legal order and revealed the magnitude of violence taking place in Chilean society.[21] Legal petitions also gave rise to a systematic gathering of information about abuses, and its records quickly became the most extensive data available about the abuses perpetrated by the Chilean military government.

The Comité Pro-Paz remained the vanguard of the human rights movement in Chile until it was replaced in January 1976 by the Vicaría de la Solidaridad, a formal organization under the archbishopric of Santiago, sanctioned by the Vatican.[22] Under the protection provided by the church's social legitimacy, many other human rights groups coalesced in the years following the coup, including the Agrupación de Familiares de Detenidos Deseparicidos (Association of Relatives of the Detained – Disappeared or AFDD), Fundación de Ayuda Social de las Iglesias Cristianas (Fóundation for Social Assistance of the Christian Churches or FASIC), and the Comisión Chilena de Derechos Humanos (Chilean Commission on Human Rights).[23] Legal documents revealed the farce of judicial independence; church and family groups played deliberately on their privileged position within society through symbolic protest to undermine the junta's carefully cultivated attempts to cast itself as savior of these institutions.

The Chilean junta tried to contain the domestic human rights movement from the outset, imprisoning lawyers working for the Comité Pro-Paz, limiting media coverage of human rights issues through censorship laws, and using the press to cast human rights workers as part of a larger Marxist conspiracy against the country.[24] Yet the junta's concern about its image curtailed its ability to completely shut down human rights efforts. The regime had fashioned itself as the defender of Western civil traditions and Christian society. To allow church and family members to openly challenge the regime weakened the government's claim to be acting on behalf of these segments of society. To simply silence them with overt force, however, also challenged the regime's image as the champion of these sectors of society. This tension allowed initial human rights relief efforts to grow into more institutionalized resistance to the regime as well as gain international visibility and support.

Although most Chileans involved in early human rights efforts did not set out to target an international audience, Allende's dramatic rise and fall had focused global attention on the country and created an international audience for the repression that followed. This attention resulted in a number of fact-finding trips from international organizations such as Amnesty International and the Inter-American Commission for Human Rights (IACHR) in the months following the coup. These early visits created an awareness among Chilean advocates that there *was* an international community they could work with, that could help them. José Zalaquett, the legal director for Comité Pro-Paz, recalled that "when Amnesty International came to Chile in November '73 . . . we hadn't really heard of it." These early visits conveyed to Chileans "that there was a human rights community internationally and a whole movement developing, and that somehow they thought that we could become part of that."[25] These visits fostered robust channels of communication, with information, aid, and material support flowing back and forth between Chilean groups and the burgeoning international human rights community.[26] Comité Pro-Paz, for example, sent its reports to Amnesty International, which in turn incorporated the information into its own bulletins and circulated it to a new international audience. The UN and the Organization of American States (OAS) also amplified human rights work within Chile, spreading information to broad audiences and drawing more attention to conditions in Chile, which in turn partially sheltered human rights advocates through media coverage.[27] Further, the Chilean case catalyzed changes in international mechanisms to address human rights violations. The UN took more aggressive action on Chile than it had in previous cases, developing an ad hoc working group and mobilizing both the General Assembly and the Commission on Human Rights.[28]

The emergence of an international community deeply concerned with and invested in human rights abuses in Chile had critical implications for the domestic legitimacy and international standing of the military government in Santiago. It also challenged the governments and ideologies that supported and enabled the military junta and its repression. The Chilean coup resulted from internal Chilean dynamics but was also the product of Cold War security frameworks and U.S. covert intervention in Latin America. This dynamic gave rise to a particularly pointed and powerful critique of U.S. foreign policy and its network of Cold War allies.

The National Security Doctrine

The Nixon administration's response to Chile epitomized many elements of U.S. regional policy, particularly its historic reliance on authoritarian regimes and its promotion of the so-called National Security Doctrine that permeated South America in the 1970s.[29] Right-wing military governments, with their rabid anti-Marxism and pro-U.S. political and economic policies, met Washington's policy needs.[30] Throughout the 1960s and the first half of the 1970s, the United States time and again supported these regimes as friendly allies, crucial for regional stability and international order. Believing that communism preyed on political upheaval and economic "backwardness," U.S. policy makers sought a way to transform developing and postcolonial areas into stable liberal democratic states. Programs such as the Alliance for Progress in the 1960s had sought to do this through economic, social, and political assistance designed to move the countries along the path of development without leaving them vulnerable to the inequities and instabilities that—according to U.S. thinking—led to communist revolution.[31] At the same time, U.S. leaders' vision of democracy and development based on the U.S. liberal capitalist model led them to support strongmen who would control and direct forces of revolution in the "appropriate" direction, making authoritarian regimes an integral part of U.S. foreign policy in its promotion of development, modernization, and nation building.[32] The U.S.-sponsored School of the Americas, for example, provided authoritarian regimes with material support to train and arm militaries and police forces in the Western Hemisphere against Soviet and Cuban subversion in their own countries.[33]

In the early 1970s the Nixon administration emphasized support for military regimes as an explicit part of regional and global policy. Its reliance on dictatorships in the Western Hemisphere, while not new in U.S.–Latin American relations, reflected strategic thinking embodied in the Nixon Doctrine. The Nixon Doctrine sought to ensure stability in the developing world without utilizing direct U.S. military force. Instead, the United States would build up the military capacity of its Third World allies so they could enforce order in their own countries and provide stability in their respective regions. The United States would provide economic and military aid and training to these allies but not deploy its own military without direct provocation from the Soviet Union. This would maintain the United States' commitment to contain communism but prevent military entanglements such as that in Vietnam. Dictators able to impose order and offer the stability prescribed by this doctrine would receive U.S. support, regardless of their internal practices.[34]

Although communist threats in Southeast Asia had drawn U.S. attention away from its neighbors to the south in the past decade, Latin America's proximity to the United States heightened its importance under the Nixon Doctrine. Playing up the idea of a "special relationship" between the United States and other countries in the hemisphere, the ability of the United States to preserve order and protect its interests in the hemisphere was crucial to its image and credibility as a great power. Moreover, instability at its back door would make it harder for the United States to impose order farther away.

Nixon and his national security adviser, Henry Kissinger, sought a policy to check what they saw as the growing influence of Fidel Castro's revolutionary, anti-American influence in the region, while also avoiding direct military intervention that had marred U.S.–Latin American relations in the past.[35] The Nixon administration embraced the hemisphere's military leaders as important for regional stability and security, casting them not as repressive institutions but rather modernizing entities "moving rapidly to the forefront as forces of social, economic and political change." From this perspective, "a new type of military man is coming to the fore and often becoming a major force for constructive social change in the American republics."[36]

Fears about communism and regional instability framed Nixon's response to Salvador Allende's rise to power. In addition to the anticipated economic problems Allende's nationalization programs would pose for the United States, Nixon viewed Allende's election as a significant ideological challenge, encouraging socialist ideas of governance and exacerbating anti-Americanism.[37] Even worse, Allende had not seized power but rather was democratically elected, thereby offering legitimacy to his socialist agenda. In November 1970 Nixon warned the National Security Council (NSC) that Allende's election would give "courage to others who are sitting on the fence in Latin America." He continued, "No impression should be permitted in Latin America that they can get away with this, that it's safe to go this way. All over the world, it's too much the fashion to kick us around." So, he concluded, "We cannot fail to show our displeasure."[38]

The Nixon administration developed an extensive strategy to "show its displeasure" and destabilize the Allende government. The administration identified and implemented a range of economic measures designed to "create pressure, exploit weakness, magnify obstacles," and isolate Chile from the international community, hoping to weaken Allende's ability to implement his policies or even make "his collapse or overthrow . . . more feasible."[39] At the same time it was cutting its financial aid to Chile, the U.S. boosted its military aid from $0.5 million in 1970 to $15 million by 1973 in an attempt to foster good relations with Chilean military officers. In addition to economic pressure, the U.S. spent more than $8 million on covert operations between 1970 and September 11, 1973, targeted at bolstering internal opposition and weakening Allende's ability to govern. These programs included aid to opposition parties and groups, support for the military, and propaganda campaigns. The Central Intelligence Agency (CIA) did not directly plan the coup; however, the White House made abundantly clear its support for an overthrow of the Allende government and facilitated an environment that made the military takeover possible, including material support to opposition groups in Chile. Internal Chilean dynamics brought the coup to fruition; U.S. covert operations and economic manipulations enflamed polarizations within Chilean society and eroded support for moderate options on both sides.[40]

Although international reaction to the Chilean military coup was overwhelmingly negative, the Nixon administration welcomed it with a qualified and cautious support publicly and significant relief internally. In the days before the coup, the NSC recommended that the Nixon administration support any "new government resulting from military intervention" in Chile because it would "represent a turn toward moderation," conducive to U.S. interests and stability in the region.[41] More importantly, it removed an ideological threat from the United States' backyard, and the administration praised the coup for the "preservation of Chilean democracy."[42] In the weeks after September 11, 1973, U.S. military aid and economic support quickly began to flow again to Chile.[43] Despite a clear awareness of the human rights abuses perpetrated by the military regime, the White House shared Pinochet's general premise and goals of eradicating communism and restoring "law and order" to the country.[44] U.S. ambassador to Chile David Popper wrote in early 1974 that there was "no doubt that in terms of United States interest the September 1973 change was a change for the better. A hostile regime has been replaced by one which is avowedly friendly and which shares many of our own conceptions." Moreover, he continued, "we stand to gain substantially from a policy of sympathy and support for the present government," noting the economic improvements and increased stability and order in the nation as positive indicators. The administration, he concluded, should not distance itself from the junta or pressure it to rein in its repression. This would only undermine an important ally and "assist the internal and external conspiracy we expect to see developing" against Chile.[45]

The Nixon administration's unwavering support for its Chilean ally was a logical outgrowth of Cold War policies and reflected long-standing assumptions about U.S. national interests in the region. Yet a new competing logic was taking shape under the rubric of human rights that called into question the Cold War orthodoxy at the core of these relationships. Growing grassroots criticism of human rights abuses in Chile not only challenged the military junta's rule but the very premises of U.S. Cold War policy.

The Human Rights Challenge and the Movement

At the advent of the Pinochet regime in Chile, there were few obvious coun-
tervailing forces to the military government and its powerful U.S. ally, yet the
foundations of the human rights network were already in place and seemed
to explode onto the international stage in the 1970s.[46] Cold War frameworks
had brought together the Chilean and U.S. governments in one constella-
tion but had also created interconnections between oppositional elements in
both societies that wanted to challenge those alignments and offer an alternative basis for regional relations.[47] Partnering with human rights advocates
in Chile, a new core of U.S.-based advocates—the Movement—solidified in
the wake of the Chilean coup.[48] Historian Margaret Power notes, "Chile became a case study of the nefarious effects of U.S. intervention in another
country and an example of a people struggling to end poverty, injustice and
military rule."[49] More broadly, human rights responses to U.S. relations with
Chile challenged policies that empowered foreign intervention and alliances
with repressive governments in the name of anticommunism. Thus, the human rights movement that emerged from the Western Hemisphere—catalyzed by the Chilean coup—targeted foreign abuses by challenging the core
premises of U.S. Cold War policy and targeting the unfettered power of the
Cold War presidency.

Socialist solidarity networks were some of the earliest groups to target
U.S involvement in Chile as symptomatic of broader policy problems. In
the early 1970s, even before the Chilean coup, local grassroots solidarity
movements with Chile sprang up across the United States, particularly in
hotbeds of 1960s protests, building on existing socialist frameworks and anti-
imperialist identifications.[50] Allende captured the imagination of many leftists throughout the hemisphere who championed his government as a new
socialist vanguard. Like earlier solidarity movements with Brazil and Cuba,
Chilean solidarity groups offered a systemic critique of U.S. military and
economic power in the hemisphere as imperial and inherently repressive.[51]

In Madison, Wisconsin, for example, Community Action on Latin America (CALA) took shape in 1971 to educate local communities about "the nature and extent of U.S. involvement" in Latin America, believing that this
would lead to support for "efforts to reverse the pattern of U.S. domination
of Latin America and of Hispanic peoples." Although CALA spoke of all
Latin America, its conceptual frames and early efforts focused heavily on
Chile. One pamphlet explained that the imperial power relationship between

the United States and its Latin American neighbors oppressed people in both areas. In a pamphlet detailing Kennecott Copper's antinationalization efforts in Chile, CALA argued that "it is not at all incongruous for a community action group whose primary concern is with Latin America to be investigating multinational corporations in northern Wisconsin."[52] The same pamphlet cited ITT's recruiting efforts in Madison and its antirevolutionary actions in Chile.

Solidarity networks united local efforts into a national campaign with international connections. In April 1972 CALA sponsored a national conference in Madison, Wisconsin, bringing together scholar activists from universities around the country to promote "interest in and knowledge about recent developments in Chile." The group invited Chilean ambassador Orlando Letelier to give the opening address. Letelier responded that he was "most willing to participate" but was unable to commit in advance due to the demands of his ambassadorial duties, offering one of the embassy's "higher officials" in his place if he was unable to attend.[53] In the end the first secretary of the Chilean embassy opened the conference, but Letelier's personal response indicates the stature given to grassroots efforts in the United States by the Allende government and exemplifies the personal connections between Chileans and U.S. citizens at the heart of solidarity networks.

Solidarity groups such as CALA explicitly criticized U.S. intervention and economic hegemony in Chile. One of its newsletters asked, "Why should the U.S. government apply economic sanctions and intervene directly in the political process of a small, democratic country for the sake of a few large and powerful corporations?"[54] Solidarity networks brought economic issues into human rights discussions in the United States in an early, sustained way. One solidarity meeting in Berkeley just weeks after the coup emphasized "integrating anti-imperialist work with long-term political organizing in the US."[55] Solidarity work was thus crucial for moving beyond earlier human rights efforts focused on gross abuses such as torture to thinking about repression as imbricated in larger structural inequalities.[56]

The vision of human rights promoted by U.S.-based solidarity groups was decisively informed by their Chilean partners. These transnational networks created alternative channels for information, building personal relations, and developing a common language that challenged Cold War dynamics and alliances. U.S. citizens who had moved to Chile to be part of the movement there reinforced these connections between local efforts in North and South America. These individuals maintained their ties with U.S. solidarity networks and linked efforts in both hemispheres by sharing information about local actions with Chileans and U.S. citizens alike.[57] Frank Teruggi, for example, wrote to CALA from Santiago in May 1972, recommending a new periodical, *Hoy*, as a reliable source of information for the U.S. groups. Teruggi had also been sending packets of information he compiled about the situation in Chile, and he asked in turn for more information about the "Chile group [Non-Intervention in Chile or NICH]" discussed in CALA's May conference.[58]

Many of these U.S. expats not only expressed a sense of alliance with Allende's efforts but also disavowed their own government's policies. A letter in September 1972 to CALA from Marcial, a "compañero" in Santiago, reported the ongoing opposition to the Allende regime. "I clearly see a very intelligent and organized hand behind this action," he wrote. "It is obvious for me that this is a strategy of the fascist sectors of the right wing, deviously guided from abroad by intelligent CIA hands, building a climate by sending young people to struggle and get killed. The more chaos, the better. . . . The army is coming, I smell it." He cajoled CALA to "try to show that in Chile, the system has defended itself so strongly, that if the government falls it's not because of ineptitude, but because of the strength, the incredible strength of imperialism."[59]

These transnational connections became even more important after the September 11 coup, as did the sense of U.S. complicity and responsibility. Solidarity networks, using their transnational ties, were early to document the scale of violence taking place, challenging official reports. Personal contacts established before the coup facilitated the dissemination of information from the Catholic Church's Comité Pro-Paz and CONAR, aiding those suffering repression in the immediate aftermath of the coup. Groups such as CALA and NICH compiled testimonies and information about human rights abuses based on Chilean legal petitions, newsletters, and personal conversations to counter what they saw as inaccurate accounts of the situation in Chile.[60] The information provided by Chileans circulated through U.S. networks as evidence of the costs of U.S. power and antidemocratic nature of U.S. policies. One NICH newsletter declared in October, "Allende died to save democracy. The U.S. killed both."[61] Advocates not only circulated this information within solidarity networks but also targeted the mainstream press. Editorials in local and national papers called attention to human rights violations and ongoing U.S. government support for the junta, which belied American values of democracy and freedom.[62]

U.S. participants in solidarity networks frequently articulated a sense of obligation heightened by direct U.S. involvement in destabilizing the Allende government. A 1974 solidarity newsletter, for example, declared, "We in the U.S. have a special responsibility to support the Chilean resistance. It was 'our' government, our tax money, which helped put the Pinochet regime in power." It continued, "For this reason, real support for the Chilean struggle involves support for the battles against U.S.-backed dictatorships through-out Latin America."[63] This intimate connection between Chilean abuses and U.S. power directed solidarity efforts and strategy to reform oversight and control of U.S. foreign policy as a central component of their activism. In re-counting its early history, one solidarity group noted that in all its activities, "we have consistently attempted to uphold a position of anti-imperialism and internationalism within the Chile Solidarity movement, and have made an effort to relate Chile solidarity work closely to the movement for progres-sive change in the U.S."[64]

U.S. citizens active in solidarity networks viewed abuses in Chile, and ongoing U.S. support for the military regime that perpetrated them, as em-blematic of a larger problem with U.S. government policies. "Without the economic, financial, diplomatic, political, and technological aid from the United States, the Chilean military junta today would be totally isolated, bankrupt, and fatally weakened. Our country is that regime's lifeline: cut it and not only have we aided the people of Chile, we have rolled back those in the U.S. who see Chile, Vietnam, South Korea and other dictatorial outposts

Figure 2. Protest against the Chilean junta and U.S. government support for the regime at the University of Wisconsin–Madison, ca. 1974. Courtesy of the *Daily Cardinal.*

as models for confronting movements for independence, social justice and self-determination."[65] These solidarity groups presented repression in Chile as a product of a dysfunctional U.S. government and pressed for U.S. accountability for its role in the coup and sustaining the Pinochet regime.

Addressing the U.S. role in facilitating abuses in Chile was critical for not only advancing rights abroad but also staving off the erosion of democracy at home. At a solidarity conference in February 1974, one group declared, "We in the United States have a Special Responsibility. The men who conspired to overthrow democracy in Chile and support the fascist military regime are the very ones who, running our government, are presumably the guardians of democracy here. . . . This is more than irony: it is cause for great concern. What is to keep a government that materially organizes, morally condones and financially supports fascism abroad from practicing it at home?"[66] This was a problem much broader than U.S. relations with Chile, or even the Western Hemisphere. One NICH newsletter, published shortly after the coup, declared, "As both Vietnam and Watergate have made clear, we can preserve the democratic process at home and prevent costly intervention abroad only if we insist on knowing exactly what our government is involved in and why it is involved."[67]

U.S. expatriates who had been expelled from Chile following the coup further reinforced this connection between U.S. policies and human rights abuses, bridging U.S. and Latin American human rights efforts. On their return to the United States, these individuals became witnesses to the violence taking place within Chile and vocal critics of the U.S. policies that supported the junta, challenging the underlying Cold War structures that linked the two.[68] In October 1973, for example, two students from the University of Wisconsin–Madison, Adam and Patt Garett-Schesch, gave a report to CALA about their experiences being arrested and imprisoned at Estadio Nacional during the coup. The report, based on their testimony before the U.S. Senate Subcommittee on Refugees, highlighted "the brutality of the military repression," as well as emphasizing U.S. involvement in bolstering Allende's opposition in the lead-up to the coup, noting the "ample support from the U.S. credit blockade . . . and the large influx of U.S. dollars during the October 1972 strike." The Garett-Scheschs emphasized that the military regime "cannot survive without massive support from outside sources." CALA concluded that "we must demand an immediate cut-off of military aid and a complete moratorium on economic assistance to the junta." CALA circulated the Garrett-Scheschs' testimony in its newsletter, contrasting it with mainstream media coverage of the coup that downplayed the violence and elided U.S. involvement. Comparing it with *Le Monde*, CALA criticized the *New York Times* for its "less than adequate and one sided coverage [that] has thus meant an important gap in the public's information about the coup and its ability to exert influence on U.S. policy."[69]

An ever-growing population of Chilean exiles strengthened solidarity work and human rights efforts after the coup. Within two years of the coup, more than fourteen thousand Chileans had fled or been expelled from the country. By the end of the Pinochet era, around 200,000 Chileans were living in exile, nearly 2 percent of the Chilean population.[70] Many of these exiles had been politically active before their expulsion and continued those activities in U.S. and international circles. Among their ranks were a number of high-profile members of Allende's Unidad Popular government, as well as other politicians and activists who continued their political efforts from abroad.[71]

Solidarity groups and exiles provided an early and focused core of the Movement, joining with other diverse groups, including religious networks that had been increasingly troubled by U.S. Cold War policies in Latin America, even before the Chilean coup. Like socialist solidarity networks, U.S. clergy and laity active in Latin America relied on deep personal connections to gather and circulate information about human rights conditions and political instability in the region. The invasion of the Dominican Republic and aid to the Brazilian dictatorship were both formative moments for ecumenical groups' engagement with U.S. intervention in the region.[72] In 1973 several religious organizations had begun to coordinate an ad hoc effort to respond to concerns about the human impact of U.S. Cold War policies in Latin America, as well as South Africa and Southeast Asia.[73] This effort gave rise to the Washington Office on Latin America. The group had initially thought WOLA might focus on Cuba and Panama, as well as legislative activity, public outreach, and education more generally. The Chilean coup reshaped and energized the nascent organization and became the catalyst to get the new group off the ground.[74]

The Chilean coup also had a transformative effect on WOLA's early leader, Joe Eldridge, a Methodist minister who returned from Chile in the fall of 1974 and took over the newly formed organization.[75] Eldridge arrived in the United States "shell-shocked." He later recalled, "I couldn't believe the United States was complicit in this effort, in supporting the Pinochet initiative, or supporting the coup. So I came back, frankly, full of indignation, and wrath, and fury. And so it was . . . crystallized fury that formed WOLA, if you want to know the truth."[76] Under Eldridge's leadership, WOLA became arguably the most prominent group in Washington to address human rights issues in Latin America in the 1970s.[77] Using networks of coreligionists in Latin America and beyond, WOLA gained influence with policy makers by providing data and testimony to interested congressmen and State Department officials.[78]

WOLA was one of several ecumenical groups mobilizing on human rights at the time. Others, including U.S. Catholic Conference, Friends Committee on National Legislation, Clergy and Laity Concerned, and the National Council of Churches, built on religious communities and networks internationally to bring human rights concerns into discussions of U.S. foreign policy.[79] WOLA and its partner religious groups typified the dually focused nature of the human rights movement emerging out of the Latin American context— that is, one that sought to improve human rights in the Western Hemisphere, but in doing so primarily targeted U.S. policies and policy makers.[80]

Like grassroots solidarity and ecumenical movements, one of the most pressing questions for the Institute for Policy Studies—a left-wing think tank established in 1963—was that of U.S. complicity in human rights

Figure 3. Joe Eldridge of WOLA (left) with Argentine activist and cofounder of Servicio Paz y Justicia (SERPAJ), Adolfo Pérez Esquivel (right). Esquivel was awarded the Nobel Peace Prize in 1980. Courtesy of WOLA.

violations abroad, abetted by direct military aid and economic structures that perpetuated disparities in wealth and rights. The arrival of Orlando Letelier, Allende's foreign minister and former Chilean ambassador to the United States, in 1975 put the group at the center of the rapidly evolving human rights community in Washington. Letelier arrived at the IPS after being expelled by the junta after a year of imprisonment following the coup.[81] At the IPS, Letelier began to speak out against the Chilean military government, denouncing the brutality of the military rule and gross disregard for human rights of all kinds, and particularly the connection between liberal economic systems propagated by the United States, political repression, and gross physical violence.[82]

Letelier's arrival helped incorporate new human rights concerns into the group's traditional approach to analyzing issues of social justice and equality in a broader global context. In an op-ed piece published in the *New York Times* in 1976, Richard Barnett, one of the group's founders, wrote, "The U.S. does bear a share of the moral responsibility for the bloodshed, terror and loss of freedom in Chile because it conducted continuous and intensive intervention over many years."[83] Further, the foreign policy structures that supported human rights violations abroad also perpetuated inequalities within the United States by channeling national resources to huge military budgets rather than social needs. For the IPS, its new emphasis on human rights intrinsically tied domestic reform to the United States' international policies.

The mainstream ADA similarly engaged human rights in the 1970s at the nexus of foreign and domestic policy. The ADA, which had been responsible for the Democratic Party's first civil rights plank in 1948, was among the first groups in the U.S. to take a stand against the Vietnam War. A 1973 internal memo noted that the ADA was searching for new issues of relevance to carve out a "personality" for the organization in the current political landscape.[84] ADA championed human rights in Chile as a partner to ideals of democratic reform and liberalism within the United States. Political scientist Lars Schoultz notes that, in the 1970s, ADA lobbyist Bruce Cameron concluded that the group's antiwar position "could be refocused upon United States aid to repressive governments, especially if it were to focus initially upon relations with the extraordinarily brutal Chilean junta."[85] Its message echoed that of the socialist solidarity movements, but within a left-liberal framework. The group argued, "In the interests of the integrity of our democratic institutions, ADA advocates that the U.S. government end its complicity in the suppression of human rights and the continuation of vast economic inequalities around the world. Moreover, we urge congressional

efforts be made to discover the extent to which official U.S. government programs contribute directly to suppression of basic human freedoms."[86] For
members of the ADA, human rights was not a turn away from domestic
issues such as labor and racial equality that had marked its advocacy of the
1960s but a way for those to ramify and gain new stature and relevance.

The ADA's Bruce Cameron was instrumental in formalizing the cooperation of the Movement in 1976, establishing the Human Rights Working
Group (HRWG) under the auspices of the Coalition for a New Foreign and
Military Policy (CNFMP).[87] The HRWG, led by Cameron from the ADA
and Jacqui Chagnon of Clergy and Laity Concerned (CLC), assembled the
strengths of its constituent groups. Coming from a variety of backgrounds,
the groups that participated in the HRWG shared a common belief that
U.S. security policies had made them culpable in foreign abuses, with Chile
serving as a preeminent example. This sense of responsibility to advance
human rights abroad mandated a reformulation of the basic premises and
mechanisms of U.S. foreign policy. One pamphlet decried U.S. support to the
Chilean junta. It called particular attention to the junta's dependence on U.S.
military and economic aid to sustain its control, especially as it was increasingly isolated and opposed "by nearly every other country in the world." The
HRWG, and the Movement more broadly, argued that greater respect for
human rights in U.S. foreign policy would bring the country's foreign affairs
in line with the nation's values and provide a better life for U.S. citizens and
help the nation recapture its moral authority and leadership abroad. One
pamphlet circulated by the working group read, "When our government
supports dictators everybody pays. Foreign citizens pay with their lives. U.S.
citizens pay with their taxes, jobs, and national respect."[88]

The human rights agenda pursued by the Movement was a corrective to
the secrecy, intervention, and militarism of Cold War policies. The politics
of complicity directed advocacy toward the U.S. government as a critical first
step in targeting the structural repression that underpinned human rights
abuses in the hemisphere. Reforming U.S. policies was the most direct way
they could mitigate abuses abroad. While this approach did not include the
full spectrum of human rights groups during this period, it was by far the
largest coalition of actors concerned with these issues. The Movement promoted a positive vision for the United States in the world, with human rights
at its core, to meet both moral necessities and national interests. This vision,
however, required a reconfiguration of power within the government itself
to curtail the excesses of the Cold War presidency that, in their assessment,
led to damaging foreign interventions and support for repressive regimes

in the name of anticommunism. The Movement deployed human rights to mitigate foreign abuses, reimagine U.S. foreign relations, and reform democratic governance within the United States.

A Call for U.S. Leadership

The same forces that had galvanized U.S. human rights advocates in the Movement created powerful allies for their efforts within the U.S. Congress. The question of democratic oversight of foreign policy was central to a new reformist sentiment that had taken shape in Congress in the mid-1970s. Noting that "the Constitution invites a struggle between the political branches for control of foreign policy," political scientist David P. Forsythe observes, in the 1970s, "after largely deferring to the executive branch for two decades, Congress accepted that invitation."[89] Fallout from Vietnam energized and empowered Congress to take an expanded role in foreign policy.[90] Covert operations in Chile and the gross executive overreach demonstrated by the Watergate scandal reinforced for many in Congress the necessity of curtailing the Cold War presidency.

The same crises that spurred Congress to rethink the balance between executive and congressional branches in foreign policy making also prompted the American public to vote in a new Congress in 1974 that strengthened reformist tendencies. The "Watergate Class of 1974" moved Congress decisively to the left, giving Democrats a 290 to 145 majority in the House, including seventy-five freshman Democrats. Many of these junior members of Congress had taken part in or been influenced by the social movements of the previous decade.[91] The incoming members took advantage of recent congressional reforms that curtailed the privileges of seniority and facilitated greater autonomy at the subcommittee level to leverage their power, and their influence was felt particularly in foreign affairs.[92]

Like the Movement, members of Congress began to champion human rights as a way to reform the fundamental premises of U.S. foreign policy and challenge the executive branch's exclusive authority over foreign affairs. The Chilean coup and U.S. support for repressive regimes played an important role in organizing human rights efforts in Congress, but this was not the only factor. Critics of the Soviet Union increasingly used human rights language in the late 1960s and early 1970s to attack U.S. policies of détente as acquiescence to Soviet repression, particularly on minority and religious issues.[93] Anti-Soviet proponents of human rights envisioned the issue as a way to recapture the moral authority of the United States in its battle against global communism. Senators such as Henry "Scoop" Jackson criticized the Nixon administration's policy of détente as overemphasizing the common interests shared by the two superpowers and accepting coexistence with a regime that he saw as a fundamentally oppressive form of government.[94] Jackson and his allies believed that Nixon, Kissinger, and later Ford had surrendered to the cynicism and despair of Vietnam. Jackson promoted a vision of an ultimately triumphant United States, reinvigorated by its defense of human rights around the world, especially in communist countries.[95]

The Movement and Jackson shared a vision of human rights as a check on executive power and a positive alternative to the existing realpolitik embodied by Nixon's détente agenda. Yet there were also significant differences between human rights critiques of U.S. foreign policy stemming from the Soviet and Chilean cases. Jackson's emphasis on human rights in the Soviet Union and communist sphere fit within existing Cold War paradigms, reinforcing a sense of U.S. righteousness and Soviet depravity. For Jackson, human rights policy was not about U.S. culpability in foreign violations or a reevaluation of Cold War anticommunism. This stands in stark contrast to the Chilean case, where human rights violations were perpetrated not by an inherently flawed communist enemy but by a close U.S. ally enabled by its Cold War policies. In the Latin American context, criticism of foreign governments was inseparable from criticism of the U.S. government; reforming U.S. policy and policy making processes domestically was thus central to changing human rights conditions abroad.

The focus on U.S. responsibility for its Cold War policies was at the core of the most influential and comprehensive congressional effort to instrumentalize human rights principles to reform U.S. foreign policy, led by Congressman Donald Fraser (D-MN).[96] Using his position as chair of the Subcommittee on International Organizations and Movements under the House Committee on Foreign Affairs, Fraser launched a series of hearings in August 1973 to probe the connection between U.S. foreign policy and human rights violations. Over the next year Fraser's subcommittee held fifteen hearings to examine "the official response of the U.S. government to gross violations of human rights . . . to determine whether the U.S. response was sensitive to the plight of those subjected to government oppression, and whether the human rights aspects of these situations were taken sufficiently into account in shaping bilateral relations with the government involved." Exploring human rights as a broad principle that should supersede East-West alignments and political divisions, the subcommittee studied conditions in a diverse group of countries, including Chile, South Africa, the Philippines, and Israel.[97]

Over a five-month period, Fraser's hearings solicited input from government officials, State Department officers, lawyers, and witnesses from the United Nations, academia, and nongovernmental organizations (NGOs).[98] Fraser himself served as national chairman of the ADA from 1974 to 1976, and he had clear sympathies and ties with the Movement and their nascent human rights agenda. Moreover, Fraser's aid, John Salzberg, was a crucial link between the advocate community and Congress. Joe Eldridge later claimed that Salzberg was the "architect" behind the Fraser hearings. "We'd go to John, and we'd say, 'John, we want a hearing on this, these are the people you should invite to testify,'" Eldridge recalled. "And John would say, 'Fine.' John would make it happen."[99]

Fraser's hearings and reports not only placed the issue of human rights on the national legislative agenda; the committee's reliance on NGOs also gave those groups unprecedented exposure and credibility. These hearings allowed traditional outsiders in the policy-making process to interact directly with government officials in charge of their target areas and develop vital contacts with the State Department and members of Congress. Salzberg noted that the hearings "provided an educational forum for diplomats as well as the American public to develop an understanding and appreciation of the importance of human rights for U.S. long-term interests."[100] By inviting nongovernmental groups to testify side by side with State Department officials, Fraser highlighted the importance of their work and legitimized their perspective in this educational project.[101]

The Movement's vision of human rights was clearly evident in the emerging policy framework. The subcommittee's 1974 report, "Human Rights in the World Community: A Call for U.S. Leadership," offered twenty-nine specific recommendations to incorporate human rights considerations into U.S. foreign policy and "enunciated the enduring ethical principles of U.S. responsibility for the international protection of human rights." Like the hearings that preceded it, the report largely sought to transcend Cold War ideological alignments and left-right divides, providing a comprehensive basis for implementing human rights considerations "as a regular part of U.S. foreign policy decision making." This included the creation of an assistant secretary post to coordinate and promote human rights concerns at the State Department, detailed reporting on human rights conditions in foreign countries, and linkage of foreign aid to human rights performance. The report provided both the logic and road map for U.S. government action on human rights in the coming years, one that focused on reforming U.S. governmental procedures and policies. Moreover, although it detailed abuses in communist countries, its main policy recommendations targeted areas of U.S. policy that enabled abuses abroad, tacitly challenging Cold War constructions of national interest and underscoring U.S. complicity through alliances with repressive regimes.[102]

The most enduring statute to arise from the report was a Sense of Congress resolution attached to section 502B of the Foreign Assistance Act of 1974, which stated that "no security assistance may be provided to any country the government of which engages in a consistent pattern of gross violations of internationally recognized human rights." Fraser targeted military aid because—more than other kinds of U.S. assistance and policy—it affiliated the United States with repressive governments, implicitly sanctioning questionable practices. Moreover, foreign regimes often used U.S. military aid directly in perpetrating human rights violations. Terminating military aid, reasoning went, would not only distance the United States from such regimes and their practices but also send a strong signal that human rights violations had material consequences, increasing the likelihood that governments would modify their behaviors in response. This dual purpose of improving human rights and avoiding U.S. affiliation with repressive regimes, such as that in Chile, was unmistakable in the wording of the amendment, which directed the U.S. President "to formulate and conduct international security assistance programs of the United States in a manner which will promote and advance human rights and avoid identification of the United States, through such programs, with governments which deny to their people internationally recognized human rights and fundamental freedoms."[103] By identifying foreign aid as a primary instrument of human rights foreign policy, the Fraser committee codified a human rights vision consistent with the Movement's central premise: to have a substantial impact on human rights globally, it was necessary to reform the central operating assumptions of U.S. foreign policy. This statute inherently targeted allied countries rather than communist adversaries, curtailed executive independence in foreign policy, and challenged basic Cold War premises about national interests and security.

The work of the Subcommittee on International Organizations and Movements in 1973 and 1974 provided the framework for congressional human rights advocacy in the coming decade. Although Chile was only a small part of the Fraser committee's work, it is hard to miss the way it informed much of the committee's logic and strategy. The report anticipated the major mechanisms for reforming U.S. foreign policy to meet human rights concerns—from limits on foreign aid to detailed country reports on human rights and the reorganization of the State Department to advance new human rights considerations. Moreover, the subcommittee's collaboration with outside witnesses, particularly in the advocate community, set a pattern for subsequent hearings. From 1973 to 1978, Fraser used his subcommittee to shed light on human rights issues, holding more than 150 hearings, with testimony from more than 500 witnesses, many of whom came from the growing NGO community, in Washington, D.C., and around the world.[104]

For Fraser and many of his congressional colleagues, human rights offered a way to move beyond the debilitating divides of the Cold War that had harmed national interests and undermined U.S. principles. At the same time, it sought to hold the United States accountable for the costs of its Cold War policies. The framework constructed by Fraser and his partners in and out of Congress put pressure for reform on repressive foreign governments as well as the U.S. president and his foreign policy apparatus. Unsurprisingly, many within Congress and the White House were not so willing to set aside

Figure 4. Rep. Donald Fraser (D-MN), chair of the House Subcommittee on International Organizations and Movements, with Secretary of State Henry Kissinger in 1978. Fraser also served as president of the Americans for Democratic Action from 1974 to 1976. Courtesy of AP Photos.

existing Cold War frameworks or to embrace human rights as a core consideration of U.S. foreign policy.

Going to the Mats on Chile

On September 8, 1974, just one month after his unprecedented assumption of the presidency, Gerald Ford pardoned Richard Nixon, hoping to "heal" the nation and move the country past the scandals that had dominated the political landscape in the past year.[105] The same day as the pardon, however, an article by Seymour Hersh appeared on the front page of the *New York Times*, detailing the Nixon administration's efforts to destabilize the Allende government. The article reported, "High level officials in the State Department and White House repeatedly and deliberately misled the public and Congress about the extent of United States involvement in the internal affairs of Chile during the three-year government of Dr. Allende." Claiming that the Nixon administration had "deliberately deceived" congressional bodies responsible for oversight, one congressional counsel concluded, "the fundamental issue now is who makes foreign policy in a democracy, and by what criteria?"[106] There was no avoiding the political conflagration that arose from the reports; a battle was brewing between Congress and the executive branch over control of foreign policy, with Chile as a proxy for larger questions about U.S. human rights abroad and democratic oversight at home.

In a uniquely tumultuous time in U.S. politics, Ford placed a premium on stability and continuity, particularly in foreign affairs.[107] Yet new human rights forces in and out of Congress disrupted "business as usual" and demanded a fundamental reconsideration of the basic premises of U.S. foreign policy. Ford's initial State Department briefing papers on regional relations hinting at the growing international attention to human rights violations in Brazil, Haiti, Paraguay, Uruguay, and especially Chile placed new pressures on existing relationships. U.S. policy currently supported the OAS's Inter-American Commission on Human Rights as a vehicle to address these problems, along with "discreet bilateral approaches to governments." The briefing memorandum stated that "while favoring observance of human rights and making our own position known to governments, we refrain from telling them how to conduct their internal affairs."[108]

The State Department gave particular attention to Chile, noting that it had "become the focal point of international criticism." Despite widespread condemnation of the military government in the international community for its repressive practices, the memo was overwhelmingly sympathetic to the Pinochet regime. Acknowledging the serious human rights violations perpetrated by the Pinochet regime, the memo observed that the "Junta's heavy hand, although perhaps required under the circumstances, has produced an international reaction of opprobrium reinforced by a Marxist ideological campaign and by misconception of Allende as a champion of democratic socialism." Current U.S. policy with Chile sought to "contribute to the Junta's sense of confidence in its ability to govern and to meet the country's economic problems and defense requirements." This confidence would in turn favor the return to rule of law and eliminate the need for repression. "Quiet but steady U.S. support of the junta is the indicated strategy." The briefing report noted that European countries had terminated almost all their aid to the government, and thus the junta relied on the United States for assistance rebuilding its economy and assuring its security.

Despite its sympathetic portrayal, the Department of State clearly anticipated that Chile would become an early battleground and preeminent test case for human rights issues and the new administration's regional policy. U.S. policy was "seriously hampered by hostile Congressional attitudes," State reported, noting the pending legislation limiting aid to Chile for the coming fiscal year. In response, "we seek to persuade—not always with success—that more can be accomplished through quiet diplomacy than legislative restriction." The State Department was particularly concerned that military leaders in the hemisphere would view foreign aid restrictions as lacking "respect for their sovereignty or regard for our commitments as allies." It also raised concerns that restrictions endangered security cooperation for a hemispheric defense, detailed in the Rio Pact, as well as harming U.S. economic interests tied to military sales.

"Hostile Congressional attitudes" gained strength and support in the coming year with the Church committee investigation into U.S. covert operations reinforced the connection between U.S. involvement and Chilean human rights abuses.[109] The revelations from these hearings—detailing covert action programs to assassinate foreign leaders, destabilize the Allende regime in Chile, surveille thousands of American citizens, and mislead Congress about many of these operations—underscored congressional distrust of the White House.[110] Findings on Chile reinforced legislative efforts to distance the United States from the Pinochet government through curtailment of foreign aid. Even before the Church committee convened, Sen. Ted Kennedy (D-MA) had targeted U.S. support for the regime. Kennedy opened hearings in the immediate aftermath of the coup, and in October 1973 he had offered a Sense of Congress resolution that called on President Nixon "to deny economic or military assistance, other than humanitarian aid, until he finds that the Government of Chile is protecting the human rights of all individuals."[111] As he wrote to one CALA member in October 1973, "I fully share your concern over the human tragedy in that country, and over the ouster of its democratically elected government in a military coup." He reassured them that he would "continue to do all that I can in behalf of human rights in Chile."[112] Kennedy made good on his assurances, putting forth a $25 million cap on economic aid to Chile and an amendment curtailing military aid in the fall of 1974.

Kissinger met congressional human rights initiatives with disdain, labeling Kennedy's proposed restrictions on Chilean aid a "disaster." Kissinger saw the battle over this legislation as a standoff between executive privilege and congressional encroachment, between important strategic considerations and what Undersecretary of State Carl Maw called that "silly human rights question."[113] Kissinger was skeptical that the human rights situation in Chile merited the heightened attention it had received.[114] He berated his staff in a meeting on December 20, 1974, "My position is that I don't yield to Congress on matters of principle. . . . We've got to go to the mat on things of national interest. What else are we here for? You can't just throw the country to Kennedy just because it satisfies some ego trip that he's got."[115] Three days later, Kissinger returned to this point: "If we are going to be taken on in Congress, we will have to have a public fight about it. I intend to make a public fight about it anyway, over the aid to Chile question. I just do not think we can continue to let Congress legislate in this manner, without the most dire consequences for our foreign policy."[116] Kissinger concluded that the current legislation was "insane," and if the administration failed to make a stand now, it would encourage Congress to continue in this manner in other cases.[117] Insane or not, Rogers reminded him that "there are an awful lot of Democrats on the Hill this coming session who want to go to the mat on the issue of human rights and want to make a fight about it. It is very hard to make a national interest argument on Chile." Rogers continued a minute later, "My diagnosis of the reason they [Congress] stuck it on the Department in this case is because they didn't think we were sincere on the human rights issue. That is what they all told me."

Kissinger, however, rejected the issue of sincerity and attacked the premise that linking military aid to human rights performance would improve human rights conditions in Chile. "What is going to help human rights more in Chile—if you are really concerned with human rights—the United States copping out of it entirely and losing all position. . . . What is our leverage then?" Although Kissinger may have been right about losing leverage, his insistence on battling with Congress on principle forced the administration into a position that appeared entirely unsympathetic to human rights issues. Chile was a line in the sand for Kissinger, yet it was a hard one to defend on national interests, as even his staff recognized.[118]

Although Kissinger seemed impervious to human rights pressures from Congress and the Movement, his indifference was not universally shared within the administration. Responding to congressional demands, the State Department moved to improve reporting on human rights issues to provide Congress with more detailed reports requested by Fraser's 502B resolution. In January 1975 Deputy Secretary of State Robert Ingersoll sent a cable to all diplomatic posts requesting information regarding human rights in each country. "Facts obtained from this reporting," the cable read, "will be used in formulating our policies and in considering, country by country, what we should do to promote respect for and observance of human rights both for their own sake and in response to increasing congressional interest." Ingersoll reminded the diplomatic posts, however, that "we must at all times be as candid as possible and at the same time be sure to protect our legitimate security concerns."[119]

In the spring of 1975 the State Department named James Wilson as the newly established special assistant for humanitarian affairs (later changed to coordinator for humanitarian affairs). This position advanced "a new focus and direction for all aspects of human rights in foreign affairs," coordinating among the departments and geographic bureaus and providing advice and information at all levels of the bureaucracy, as well as advising on legislation and representing the department before Congress. In addition, the coordinator would work with the human rights officers recently appointed to each bureau, focusing particularly on "problems of special political sensitivity at home and abroad." Wilson anticipated that the new organization's mandate of inserting human rights concerns into existing policy-making mechanisms and established bilateral relations would prompt others at State to regard it as the "Department's hair shirt."[120] Still, the administration's guidance for the Organization for Humanitarian Affairs clearly sought to demonstrate to Congress that the State Department was responsive to human rights concerns and wanted to facilitate better—or at least less constricting—relations between the two branches of government.[121]

The Chilean mission's 1975 Country Analysis Strategy Plan, or CASP, exposed a growing rift within the State Department over human rights issues, as ongoing human rights violations in Chile prompted U.S. embassy staff to challenge Ambassador Popper and current U.S. policy. Popper acknowledged that although the Chilean government's progress on human rights had been "less satisfactory from our point of view," he believed that the best way to meet U.S. interests in the region was by supporting and strengthening the current regime. Popper argued that international criticism was politically motivated and that "the inequality involved in singling out Chile in a world of sinners in this regard is patently clear." Although the report noted that the United States was the "most influential single country" when it came to the potential for external pressure to change unacceptable human rights practices, Popper discouraged direct action, which might create a "siege mentality" in Santiago. The U.S. government should instead "emphasize somewhat more forcefully" its position on human rights as a central component of good relations between the two countries.[122]

In a dissenting report, four embassy officers challenged Popper's policy recommendations. "This policy of friendly persuasion," the dissenting foreign service officers argued, "has not worked and the GOC [government of Chile] has not significantly modified its human rights practices." Continuing U.S. support for the Chilean government "in effect is support for an unacceptable status quo" that was not in the U.S. interest, and the Ford administration should "take no new initiatives to assist Chile politically, economically, or multilaterally unless and until its human rights practices have reached an acceptable standard." The dissenting officers reasoned that "at this time, there are no other U.S. interests in Chile, individually or collectively which outweigh" human rights considerations. "Continued USG [U.S. government] support to a regime of the type of the present GOC, in a country of little strategic importance whose natural resources are not important to the United States, gives the appearance that the USG in practice attributes low priority to human rights considerations." This position was damaging executive relations with Congress, which in turn inhibited the administration's ability to effectively address a variety of foreign policy issues. By continuing to support the Chilean government, the Ford administration was thus "expending our influence and effectiveness with our traditional friends and world allies over an issue of relatively little vital importance to us."[123]

By July the Ford administration's Chile policy was in "disarray." The Policy Planning Staff and the Latin America bureau "strongly supported" the dissent to the CASP, while all other agencies backed the ambassador's position. This divide was carrying over into other legislative areas, including loans for housing guarantees and military sales, where the Department of Defense wanted to push through military sales to Chile while the Latin American bureau at State "wants a hold put on everything." Pinochet himself called the U.S. ambassador to "protest the run-around being given his representative in Washington" on arms sales. The administration worried that without greater coordination, the U.S. message to the Chilean regime would be "confused." Meanwhile, several departments were "annoyed" by the disruptions of loans and sales, and they sought greater guidance on how to proceed.[124]

In the coming months Kissinger sought to reassure the Pinochet regime that congressional actions on human rights did not reflect the administration's policy.[125] In a September 1975 meeting with Chilean foreign minister Patricio Carvajal, Kissinger openly disparaged human rights issues. "I read the Briefing Paper for this meeting," he greeted Carvajal, "and it was nothing but human rights. The State Department is made up of people who have a vocation for the ministry. Because there were not enough churches for them, they went into the Department of State." Kissinger continued, stating that the attacks on Chile regarding human rights were "a total injustice." By way of pressuring the Chileans to improve the situation, Kissinger reassured the foreign minister that the United States was sympathetic to the Chileans' position, and he asked the foreign minister to think about what could be "visibly" done in Chile to prevent Congress from placing "restriction upon restriction against the U.S. interest." Kissinger then moved on to guaranteeing military and economic aid—using commercial sales to maneuver around the Kennedy amendment's limitations—as well as offering assistance by opening up international loans that had been closed off during the Allende years.[126]

The Ford administration's response to Chile reveals an approach to human rights that sought to signal an attentiveness to the issue without accepting the underlying premise that such alliances were fundamentally counterproductive to U.S. interests and values. Kissinger's machinations to get around congressional restrictions and derision of concerns expressed by his own State Department were not lost on human rights advocates. Distrust of the executive, exacerbated by Ford and Kissinger's continued warm relations and aid to dictators such as Pinochet, led Congress and the Movement to seek more binding measures that would force the administration to take its human rights concerns seriously.

Foreign Aid and Presidential Prerogatives

The battle over foreign aid, particularly for Chile, had been brewing since the early days of the Ford presidency, as seen with Kennedy's early actions on Chile and Fraser's 502B resolution in 1974. For Congress and the Movement, reforming foreign aid was a critical step in dismantling U.S. foreign policy mechanisms and processes that directly enabled human rights abuses abroad, reflecting a sense of responsibility for repression in places such as Chile. The Movement and Congress identified economic and foreign aid as critical levers to influence U.S. policy, and they thus also became markers of the administration's commitment to human rights issues beyond easy rhetoric and "quiet diplomacy." For already skeptical advocate groups, the administration's intransigence on aid to Chile signaled a broader indifference to Congressional guidance on implementing human rights in foreign policy decision-making. After a year in office, the Ford administration had done little to distance itself from the Pinochet government or signal that human rights concerns were a priority in the region. In April 1975 WOLA contrasted ongoing U.S. aid with European boycotts of debt negotiations with Chile. "With all this economic support," WOLA wondered, "will Chile also receive moral support from the U.S. in the next O.A.S. General Assembly meeting," where the findings of the IACHR would be presented?[127] The Movement sought to influence evolving aid policy through public pressure on government agencies and congressional lobbying. Members of CALA and other solidarity groups, for example, wrote directly to the Treasury Department, urging it to refuse to renegotiate Chilean debt to the United States until the Chilean government improved human rights conditions. They also published editorials urging people to write to Congress to pressure the Treasury and State Departments on the same issues.[128]

The growing pressure from Congress and the Movement for meaningful action on human rights weighed on the administration's review of security assistance for the coming year. State Department guidance on Section 502B questioned the legislation's central premise linking aid to human rights performance, arguing, "It is, of course, obvious that reduction or elimination of security assistance will not necessarily advance the cause of human rights in a particular country. It is also clear that in some cases such action could produce undesired results." Kennedy, Fraser, and others, however, had made clear that the administration's response to Section 502B "will be considered an important indication of our intention. They will be looking for the reduction or elimination of security assistance in serious problem cases and/or persuasive evidence that the USG is actively pursuing other measures in support of human rights in security assistance beneficiary countries." In order to allay further restrictions, the State Department should develop "new initiatives in the human rights area (other than reductions in Security Assistance) which might demonstrate responsiveness to Congressional concerns."[129]

The State Department singled out several countries—including Chile and South Korea—as "virtually certain" to face "intensive examination" from Congress and the public as markers of the administration's commitment to human rights and fidelity to the 502B statute. This portended difficulties for the administration as both countries showed dramatic increases in funding levels from the previous year, with South Korea moving from $145 million in 1975 to a projected $176.6 million in 1976 and Chile jumping twentyfold from $0.7 million to $20.8 million. If the administration sought to signal its commitment to human rights through its compliance with 502B, its message in the two highest-profile cases was one of complete disregard.[130]

The State Department's report on Chile noted that human rights conditions remained "extremely serious" and conceded there was little reason to believe that these laws "will be administered in good faith." The Latin America bureau outlined several possible options for security assistance to Chile, the most aggressive of which eliminated Foreign Military Sales (FMS) credits and military training and increased diplomatic pressure on human rights. This approach "would avoid confrontation with Kennedy, Fraser, and others on an issue where we are likely to lose with unfavorable side effects on other Administration requests." The Latin America bureau, fearing damage to bilateral relations, instead recommended the full requested funding for approval. It anticipated that this would "elicit a strong reaction from members of Congress," and "given the continuing adverse publicity on Chile might place the administration in a difficult position domestically in the United States and in some sectors of Latin America." Regardless, the bureau believed that the administration's record on human rights in Chile was "sufficiently strong" to convince congressional critics if "properly communicated."[131]

As anticipated, the Movement viewed the Ford administration's security budget as an affirmation of continued U.S. support for the repressive regime. Advocates closely monitored and contributed to congressional hearings on new foreign appropriations, becoming increasingly outraged by the administration's seeming indifference to congressional guidance.[132] WOLA's newsletter reported continuously on security assistance and foreign aid, claiming in August 1975 that "the importance of military sales and their impact on American foreign policy [are] becoming increasingly evident as deliveries [of] arms continue to grow at the fastest rate in history. . . . What it means for the oppressed whose dictatorial governments continued to purchase the munitions remains one of the unfinished chapters in modern history."[133] Advocates followed legislation from committee to the floor of Congress, highlighting the administration's support for ongoing repression, petitioning Congress, and rallying public support.

On September 10, 1975—just one day before the second anniversary of the Chilean coup—Congressman Tom Harkin introduced an amendment to the Foreign Assistance Act, which proposed to prohibit economic assistance to "the government of any country which engages in a consistent pattern of gross violations of internationally recognized human rights . . . unless the President determines that such assistance will directly benefit the needy people in such country."[134] Although it became known as the Harkin Amendment, it had been drafted by Joe Eldridge of WOLA and Ed Snyder of the Friends Committee on National Legislation.[135] Earlier hearings on the Foreign Aid Act had led to concern among nongovernment advocates and sympathetic congressmen alike about the amount of economic aid going to gross violators of human rights, often as a means to get around restrictions on military sales and aid. One solidarity newsletter wrote that the Ford administration's proposed $195 million in aid to Chile "is particularly significant if it is seen in the light of Congress' cieling [sic] on aid to Chile of $25 million." It noted that this was indicative of an effort by Ford and Kissinger to circumvent congressional limits to aid, concluding, "It is important to begin pressuring Congress for . . . restrictions on support for the US' puppet governments." The newsletter urged readers to contact their congress members "demanding a total cut-off of aid to the Junta and a freeze on all arms sales."[136]

Borrowing 502B language, the Harkin Amendment underscored the growing belief among members of Congress and the Movement that nonbinding guidance was insufficient to elicit meaningful human rights reforms from the administration. WOLA touted the bill in its newsletter, praising it as the culmination "of a long struggle to introduce conscience into U.S. foreign policy." It argued that "the main value of this amendment is its usefulness in setting standards and providing a vehicle for Executive/Congressional dialogue on human rights." The group promoted the bill as "a responsible and meaningful way to assure the human rights considerations become an integral part of Executive Branch decisions in allocating aid."[137] The legislation clearly targeted executive decision-making and democratic control of foreign policy, as well as foreign violators. It rejected the government's rationale that these relationships served "national interests" or provided "diplomatic leverage to moderate these inhumane practices," instead advocating that both U.S. interests and Chilean rights would be better served in taking a strong public stand against abuses by military regimes by terminating aid.[138]

The close collaboration between the Movement and Congress on foreign aid issues was not lost on the State Department. In a memo to Assistant Secretary of State William Rogers in September 1975, George Lister highlighted the work of WOLA, calling Joe Eldridge "a good friend" and noting that it was Eldridge who drafted the Harkin Amendment. Lister told Rogers, "I have long preached to those in 'the movement' who would listen that they could be much more effective working inside the system, and that Congress should be a prime target"; apparently human rights advocates agreed. In his memo Lister included a copy of WOLA's September newsletter, observing that it was "typical in that it focuses on Congress, criticizes the AID reporting to Congress, hits our alleged whitewash of human rights violations, and singles out the governments of Brazil, Uruguay, Chile, Nicaragua and Argentina for specific criticism." He warned Rogers that human rights advocates would "zero in" on his upcoming congressional testimony on human rights, implying that Rogers should be prepared and target his testimony to these groups as well as Congress. Lister concluded by stating that he knew Rogers had "too much to read, but I will circulate the WOLA *Legislative Update* from now on, and will mark items of possible interest to you."[139] Lister clearly viewed WOLA and its *Legislative Update* as representative of a wider human rights movement in Washington. For his part, Lister was not dismissive of human rights advocates or their message, even as he disagreed with their emphasis on right-wing dictators. Indeed, he saw them as an important factor in the emerging new human rights policy, one that Rogers needed to be aware of in order to be effective.

A greater awareness of the Movement and its goals did not translate into support from the Ford administration for the legislation it promoted or its underlying logic that economic and military assistance implicated the United States in foreign repression. As the Harkin Amendment advanced through Congress, the administration maintained its opposition to further curtailment of aid on human rights grounds. It instead noted its accomplishment on human rights in Chile and Latin America and argued that simply cutting off aid was an imprecise and inappropriate vehicle for expressing human rights concerns. A summary of the administration's Latin American policy in fall 1975 listed human rights as an area "of greatest importance to

Latin Americans," yet the issue was not found among the six elements that "formed the basis of the administration's policy."[140] Also indicative of the low priority human rights received within the administration were ongoing staffing issues with the State Department's new Humanitarian Affairs office (HA). James Wilson, the director of the office, complained to Ingersoll in October that he had seen a recent internal report questioning "whether there should be any human rights organization [in the State Department] at all . . . questions which I had assumed were decided by you last February."[141]

In the face of executive reticence, Congress and its partners in the Movement continued to advance their human rights agenda through legislative restrictions on foreign aid. WOLA championed the bill, arguing: "The logic for such an amendment is compelling. How can development be isolated from the state of human rights in a country. Dictatorships employing terror as government policy represent a collection of vested interests fundamentally inimical to the common good. Certain elements in Congress have been cognizant of these dynamics for a long time. The Executive Branch unfortunately has been much slower in grasping this simple truth. . . . [This legislation] will require the Executive Branch to pay closer attention to these human rights considerations."[142] This logic prevailed as the Harkin Amendment passed Congress in December 1975, becoming a foundational piece of U.S. human rights policy.

The successful passage of the Harkin Amendment signaled that the Movement had become a serious player in Washington politics. State Department officials, at least those at the Latin America desk, monitored the Movement and its impact on upcoming legislation. Lister continued to circulate WOLA's newsletter and urgent action memos, noting which legislative amendments WOLA supported and highlighting its legislative priorities for Rogers and others. Lister met with exiles and attended Movement meetings and rallies, reporting back to Rogers and others at State.[143] In a memo to Rogers, Lister noted that he was in "almost daily contact" with HRWG members such as Bill Wipfler and Tom Quigley, and he told Rogers that it would be "well worth your time" to meet them.[144] Indeed, Rogers did meet with a group of religious leaders active in the human rights community in the fall of 1975, including Eldridge. After the meeting, Eldridge wrote a heartfelt letter to Rogers, thanking him for "the generous and magnanimous way you listened for two hours to the collective concerns and criticisms" of the group. "I for one was moved by the informed and sensitive analysis of the human rights situation in Chile you displayed," Eldridge continued. "The signals from Chile are frightening. The rumbles that I detect within the State

Department are more encouraging." Rogers responded to Eldridge with an equally generous letter. "George Lister," Rogers wrote, "has told me several times that you are a vigorous and articulate critic of ours, but fair. . . . I am most grateful for your encouragement. . . . Tough times lie ahead, and I am counting on the constructive criticism of the U.S. religious community. And of course I welcome and need its support, to the extent forthcoming. Keep telling George whenever you think we should be doing better."[145]

The frequent communication with the Movement at State did not close the growing divide over how to incorporate human rights concerns into foreign aid decisions. The administration violently objected to what it saw as "legislative encroachment" on executive prerogatives of foreign policy making, including the coming battle with Congress over security assistance. "Viewing the carnage thus far," Robert McCloskey wrote to Kissinger in December 1975, "I conclude that there are two main forces at work: a) one which uses the bill as a vehicle to effect fundamental revisions in U.S. foreign policy and b) another which uses the bill to create alterations in the Constitutional division of responsibility between the Executive and the Legislature." He offered a warning about the pending legislation on security assistance coming out of the House and Senate, concluding that "both versions hit us hard" on human rights. "It is clear that some sort of human rights amendment will be adopted and . . . our chance of appreciably mitigating its worst features are not good."[146] A showdown with Congress over human rights and control over foreign policy prerogatives seemed inevitable.

Indeed, in the wake of the Harkin Amendment's success, the Movement was already seeking to make binding restrictions on military aid, gearing up for the coming year's security assistance bill. As 1975 drew to a close, WOLA highlighted military requests from Latin American countries. "At least two executive departments of the United States government—State and Defense—work very hard this time of year to make sure that their friends (and even those who are not so friendly) south of the border and in the Caribbean have a very merry military Christmas," the *Legislative Update* playfully reported. "Of the 17 recipients of Uncle Sam's Yuletide largesse by far the majority are under a military dictatorship of some sort or another." It continued by noting that many human rights groups were already working with members of Congress to "trim drastically the FY 1976 Security Assistance Program" with a good chance of success.[147] In its end-of-the-year roundup, WOLA touted the success of human rights initiatives in Congress in the past year. With the passage of the Harkin Amendment and the "almost certain inclusion of similar language in the Military Assistance Authorization . . .

the question of human rights violations in Latin American countries is no longer academic and should take on new meaning in the days ahead."[148] The ADA similarly championed new legislative initiatives on human rights, arguing that "the most positive development recently has been the expansion of congressional oversight and review power to include more aspects of U.S. foreign policy." Recent congressional efforts to assert limits on aid and military sales to dictatorships "exemplify the hope of legislation which lays the basis for a truly democratic foreign policy."[149]

Even as Congress generalized its efforts linking foreign aid and human rights performance, Chile remained a critical bellwether of the administration's commitment. WOLA noted ongoing and severe human rights violations in the country, warning, "When the time of testing the new legislation comes . . . Chile is sure to be the target. Its dismal record on human rights seems tailor-made for the test."[150] Amnesty International had formed a Chile coordination group to facilitate better connections between its letter-writing campaigns, its contacts with the Vicaría, and its Washington partners to support ongoing legislative efforts.[151] It armed its partners in the Movement with new reports and testimonies of human rights violations in Chile. Solidarity networks reinforced these efforts, continuing to drum up support for the termination of U.S. aid to Chile, arguing to U.S constituencies that "it is our responsibility and moral obligation to the Chilean people and to the rest of mankind to pull the plug on Pinochet's junta."[152]

These efforts reached beyond Movement newsletters and meetings to a broader audience, with op-eds in national media ahead of congressional votes. One *New York Times* editorial, for example, stressed the connection between U.S. policy and ongoing repression in Chile. "Why should we feel any connection with the cruelty and misery in Chile?" the editorial asked. "The first inescapable reason is that we share responsibility for bringing about the situation that exists," citing Nixon's covert operations that destabilized Allende. Americans cannot feel "detached from particular outrages to human rights, in terms either of responsibility or of the ability to help." The editorial stressed that the United States' attitude was crucial for bringing pressure to bear on the Chilean regime to change its repressive practices. It noted that many private institutions such as universities and professional associations had acted on behalf of specific individuals, advocating for their release from prison or providing means for them to come to the United States through employment opportunities. "All of which makes it depressing that, the reaction of the United States Government to official terror in Chile and elsewhere, so often appears to be studied indifference."[153]

In the months leading up to the passage of the Security Assistance Act, advocates continued public and private efforts to build support for limitations on military aid.[154] CALA and other local groups held meetings to publicize the legislative debates and share information about conditions in Chile. They encouraged people to write to their representatives, supporting Senator Kennedy's amendment cutting off military sales to Chile by arguing that "the American people must not continue in this, or any fashion, to support a regime which so massively violates the human rights of the citizens of Chile. We are outraged that such sales are allowed at the present time."[155] WOLA's *Legislative Update* warned, "Whatever the outcome of this particularly controversy," Congress would persist in advancing similar legislation in the 1977 military authorization bill. This included targeted amendments to reduce or eliminate military aid, and "one will certainly address itself to Chile."[156]

The Movement's most visible impact on debates in the lead-up to votes on military aid was its support for a congressional visit to Chile in March 1976 to "determine the real effect of U.S. foreign aid dollars."[157] Congressmen Tom Harkin, George Miller, and Toby Moffett, along with Joe Eldridge of WOLA, met with government officials, human rights organizations, and business groups. The Movement had been instrumental in organizing the visit, providing contacts with Chileans active in human rights work and drafting questions for the delegation's meetings with various government officials and groups. The IPS, informed by their local Chilean contacts and exiles active in the Movement, provided the delegation with a list of proposed questions for their meetings with various officials and groups. This included a recommendation that they ask about "non-recognized prisoners" and "detentions camps," which ultimately led them to the gates of Villa Grimaldi.[158]

On their return, the delegation offered unflinching condemnation of human rights conditions in Chile and called for the termination of all U.S. military assistance. In an official press release, the congressmen asserted, "As long as U.S. aid keeps flowing through the pipeline, there is no deterrent to the military junta's repressive human rights policies."[159] Harkin charged, "There is no excuse for us to continue to aid the systemic violation of human rights by the Chilean junta by providing them with the tools to carry out their coercion."[160]

The Ford administration sought to downplay Chilean abuses and frame its opposition to pending human rights limits on security assistance as an issue of executive control of foreign policy. The visit, however, invited public scrutiny of the connections between Chilean violations and U.S. policy.

Movement newsletters made explicit the connection between the visit and the pending vote on military aid. "Harkin and others are hopeful that their visit will strengthen their case for stronger restrictions on the 1977 Military Authorization Bill," one solidarity newsletter reported, concluding, "WRITE TO YOUR REPRESENTATIVE TODAY."[161]

The trip mobilized public opposition to Cold War alliances, connecting U.S. aid to human rights abuses. Moreover, the Movement highlighted the domestic costs of these programs. U.S. security interests, it argued, were not served by supporting the Chilean government with military aid when it faced "no external threats, and is not critical to U.S. perceived balance of power interests." One newsletter argued that the United States was paying for the junta's ability to "maintain torture centers and defy world opinion." It continued, "Where does this money come from? Our schools, hospitals, social welfare programs, the hard-earned benefits for which we have struggled here, are literally being melted down into means of terror and repression." U.S. aid to Chile supported the regime's repression and undermined the rights of Chileans and Americans. "The willingness of our government to strip away millions of US taxpayer dollars during the worst economic crisis in decades and place them in the junta's hands demonstrates a mentality that can only alarm us." The real interests of Americans, and Chileans, were better served by exercising democratic restraint on U.S. foreign policy by closing "loopholes" that the Ford administration used to get around congressional prohibitions on foreign aid.[162]

The showdown over human rights restrictions on security assistance came to a head in May 1976, when President Ford vetoed S. 2662—International Security Assistance and Arms Export Control Act. The president objected to the expanded role it gave Congress in controlling foreign military sales, including the "arbitrary arms sales ceiling," and congressional veto by concurrent resolution. In his letter to Congress, Ford charged that the bill was unconstitutional. "The erosion of the basic distinction between legislative and Executive functions which would result from the enactment of S. 2662, displays itself in an increasing volume of similar legislation which this Congress has passed or is considering. Such legislation would pose a serious threat to our system of government, and would forge impermissible shackles on the President's ability to carry out the law and conduct of foreign relations of the United States." Ford expressed his administration's commitment to human rights "as a standard for all nations to respect," but he argued that "the use of the proposed sanctions against sovereign nations is, however, an awkward and ineffective device for the promotion of those policies." He particularly objected to the binding requirements in the bill:

> These provisions of the bill represent further attempts to ignore important and complex policy considerations by requiring simple legalistic tests to measure the conduct of sovereign foreign governments. . . . By making any single factor the effective determinant of relationships which must take into account other considerations, such provisions would add a new element of uncertainty to our security assistance program and would cast doubt upon the reliability of the United States in its dealing with other countries. More-over, such restrictions would most likely be counterproductive as a means for eliminating discriminatory practices and promoting human rights. The likely result would be a selective disassociation of the United States from governments unpopular with the Congress, thereby diminishing our ability to advance the cause of human rights through diplomatic means.

Ford concluded that in using his veto power, "I act as any President would, and must, to retain the ability to function as the foreign policy leader and spokesman of the Nation. In world affairs today, American can have only one foreign policy."[163]

Congress, however, was not willing to cede foreign policy prerogatives to the executive. The past two years had shown that without binding guidelines, foreign policy priorities such as human rights would be subsumed by other con-cerns. In a letter to congressional representatives, HRWG coordinator Bruce Cameron noted that the executive branch's disregard for previous congressio-nal guidance on aid to Chile necessitated more binding restrictions. He urged them to support the revised security assistance bill coming to a vote, arguing that "in the future, a much more thorough review of U.S. military commit-ments to governments which systematically violate internationally recognized human rights must be taken" but that the amendments on Chile and South Korea "represent a good first step."[164] CALA and the HRWG similarly urged citizens to write to their Congress members and members of the International Relations and Foreign Relations Committees in support of the upcoming bill and the restrictions to aid for Chile.[165] "At stake," one pamphlet declared, "is the extent to which taxpayer's money will be used to prop up these repressive regimes that brutally violate the human rights of their own citizens."[166]

Congress quickly resubmitted its security assistance authorization bills with some altered provisions, such as the veto by concurrent resolution, to address the Ford administration's strongest objections but kept the human rights language and termination of military aid to Chile. Ford signed the bill, crediting Congress with modifying human rights language to recognize "that diplomatic efforts, rather than absolute statutory sanctions, are the most effective way in which this country can seek further progress abroad in these areas of deep concern to all Americans." He noted that in order for these "efforts to bear fruit," the executive branch must preserve its flexibility.[167] The battle over S. 2662 was one of principle for both sides, but the principle was not simply human rights itself but rather presidential prerogatives, control over foreign policy, and, more abstractly, the essential nature of U.S. interests.

Staking a Claim on Human Rights

Facing new legislative restrictions on economic aid and security assistance, the Ford administration confronted the fact that human rights issues were limiting its ability to implement desired policies in other areas, and it would have to respond more aggressively to regain policy-making initiative. The Ford administration seized on the Organization of American States' General Assembly in June 1976 to stake a public claim and assert a positive position on human rights issues. The fact that the OAS meeting was held in Santiago, Chile, and that the Inter-American Commission on Human Rights was scheduled to present its findings on human rights violations in Chile made it a perfect place for the administration to address head-on the question of U.S. relations with Chile and its human rights policy more broadly.

Prior to the OAS meeting, Kissinger had warned Rogers that he was "not on the same wavelength as you guys [at the Latin America bureau]" on the question of human rights and that he was not willing to go to Santiago and "undermine" the Pinochet regime.[168] Still, Kissinger himself addressed the OAS General Assembly on June 8, offering one of his most comprehensive statements on human rights as an objective of international relations.[169] In the speech he proclaimed human rights to be "one of the most compelling issues of our time." The Western Hemisphere, he continued, had a particular burden in advancing the cause of human rights due to its unique history and "tradition of freedom," which made "our shortcomings more apparent and significant."[170]

Kissinger's speech was more than a general affirmation of human rights principles. Had he given this speech in front of a European audience, a criticism of communism would have been clear. But Kissinger was addressing the United States' hemispheric neighbors in a country that had become a symbol of the new human rights politics, and Kissinger's speech clearly had a

Chilean subtext. Kissinger advocated "access to courts, counsel and families" for political prisoners and respect for habeas corpus, arguing that it reduced "the risk and incidence of unintentional government error, of officially sanctioned torture, of prolonged arbitrary deprivation of liberty." These comments carried particular weight in Chile where human rights groups relied heavily on the courts and petitions of habeas corpus to publicize ongoing government repression and violence. "No government can ignore terrorism and survive," Kissinger observed, but he cautioned that "it is equally true that a government that tramples on the rights of its citizens denies the purpose of its existence."[171] The Chilean government responded to his statement with "stony silence."[172]

Kissinger's speech was not all subtext and allusion on the question of human rights in Chile. Kissinger walked a fine line in his speech between upholding the veracity and impartiality of the IACHR and softening criticism of Chile, the OAS's host country and U.S. ally. Kissinger lamented, "The condition of human rights as assessed by the OAS human rights commission has impaired our relationship with Chile and will continue to do so. We wish this relationship to be close, and all friends of Chile hope that obstacles raised by conditions alleged in the report will soon be removed." As he acknowledged the Chilean government's human rights problems, he also stressed the "quantitative reduction" of certain violations of rights in the country since the commission's last investigation, noting that the Chilean government had offered a "comprehensive and responsive answer" outlining a number of "hopeful prospects which we hope will soon be fully implemented." He contrasted this with the Cuban government's unwillingness to cooperate with the IACHR, to leaven his criticism of Chile. Implying that much of the criticism of Chile was politically motivated, Kissinger observed that "the cause of human dignity is not served by those who hypocritically manipulate concerns with human rights to further their political preferences nor by those who single out for human rights condemnation only those countries with whose political views they disagree."[173]

Indeed, Kissinger had met with Pinochet earlier that day and said he would mention Cuba explicitly to highlight the "hypocrisy of some who call attention to human rights as a means of intervening in governments." Kissinger reassured him that the speech was not intended to target or embarrass Chile. "My evaluation is that you are a victim of all left-wing groups around the world, and that your greatest sin was that you overthrew a government which was going communist," Kissinger told him. These were hardly the words of condemnation or pressure advocates hoped for. Yet Kissinger also did not let the human rights issue drop or simply dismiss the issue as he had in meetings with Foreign Minister Carvajal the past September. Kissinger bluntly told Pinochet, "In the United States, as you know, we are sympathetic with what you are trying to do here. I think that the previous government was headed toward Communism. We wish your government well. At the same time," Kissinger continued, "we face massive domestic problems in all branches of the government, especially Congress but also in the Executive over the issue of human rights. . . . This is a problem which complicates our relationships and the efforts of those who are friends of Chile." Kissinger indicated that whether or not he agreed personally with new legislative demands, human rights issues were not going away and the Chilean government would have to change its behaviors if it wished to maintain close relations with Washington.[174]

In a dispatch to Ford from the OAS, Kissinger reported he was pleased with the tone he had struck on human rights. Kissinger noted that the OAS meeting had overwhelmingly revolved around human rights issues, particularly the IACHR's report on Chile. "I believe I was able to strike a balance between the feelings of our host country, Chile, and the need to recognize the demand that we speak out on the issue," he reported to Ford. "This was certainly the most extensive statement we have made on the subject. Although I have not satisfied those who want us to harass this particular Chilean government, we have supported measures to strengthen protection of human rights by international organizations, and done so under circumstances that require some tact."[175] A day later, Kissinger sent a second report to Ford, which noted a new, more cooperative tone in U.S.–Latin American relations, describing it as "the warmest and most productive meeting of the Hemisphere's Foreign Ministers of any of the five I have attended." The report pointed explicitly to U.S. human rights initiatives as a key factor in bringing about this change. "We have played a leading role in bringing balance and respectability to consideration of human rights," he concluded. "Delegates were pleased at both the atmosphere of frankness on human rights and Chile's forthrightness on the issue."[176] By July Kissinger had called the meeting a "turning point" in hemispheric relations, and he counted the administration's support for human rights among the three major issues that contributed to this change. Rogers agreed, writing that "the Santiago meeting, in short, has put paid to a lot of old accounts. Historians may someday come to mark it as the end of one critical era and the beginning of another."[177]

The OAS meeting in Santiago was a turning point in the administration's rhetorical embrace of human rights, but not one celebrated by historians or contemporaries as Kissinger had hoped. Indeed, as Kissinger congratulated the administration for its stance on human rights at the OAS, it simultaneously offered a warm welcome to the new, repressive military regime in Argentina.[178] In a private meeting with Argentine foreign minister César Guzzetti at the OAS, Kissinger conveyed that the administration was "aware you are in a difficult period" and "wish[es] the new government well. . . . We will do what we can to help it succeed."[179] Its relations with Argentina in its last year in office revealed that the Ford administration continued to rely on regional strongmen sympathetic to U.S. interests, even as it became more discreet in its policy and sought to mitigate the public relations problems stemming from the human rights violations of its allies. Human rights violations posed image, not policy, problems.

In response to two years of coordinated efforts by the Movement and Congress, the Ford administration slowly moved to incorporate human rights considerations into its State Department structure and diplomacy. By the end of the Ford administration, the basic legislative frameworks and mechanisms for implementing a human rights foreign policy were largely in place. Yet the Ford administration also defended presidential prerogatives in foreign affairs, resisting congressional efforts to exercise greater authority in this area through its human rights agenda. Moreover, the administration systematically prioritized Cold War security interests over even modest human rights overtures. The evident lack of serious pressure in private bilateral talks and the administration's efforts to get around military bans also signaled to foreign governments and domestic audiences alike that new legislation did not represent the overall thrust of U.S. foreign policy and that costs of human rights violations would be minimal.

This executive indifference was not lost on the Movement. In a September 29 congressional hearing, Senator Kennedy named Chile as perhaps the "most brutal example of the Administration's distorted view of our interests and ideals," asking for "a single instance where HAK [Kissinger] or any official has spoken up about the violation of human rights in Chile and then acted to reflect that concern." This sentiment was echoed in a 1976 statement by several religious groups active in the Movement, which expressed deep concern over "the low priority which human rights now have in United States foreign policy." They observed, "We sense a worldwide trend toward totalitarian governments and we believe United States policies, especially military aid, training and sales of military equipment are contributing significantly to the trend." They concluded, "We urge a fundamental re-examination of what really contributes to United States security."[180]

The Ford administration's reluctant inclusion of human rights never fundamentally challenged or reshaped its politics in the region. Its half-hearted efforts, particularly with Kissinger's almost constant derision of human rights publicly and privately, did, however, galvanize a critical mass of actors around the issue of human rights in Washington, D.C. As Congressman Ed Koch (D-NY) wrote to one of WOLA's founders in 1976, "That 'little office' which you helped establish—this Washington Office on Latin America—has had a tremendous impact on the policy toward Latin America and is causing untold headaches to the State Department. I work with the office quite closely, and find it quite helpful."[181] Carter's successful electoral bid would usher in a sea change in U.S. human rights policy. Yet Carter also inherited Ford's power struggle with Congress and the Movement for control of foreign policy, as well as their lasting distrust of the executive branch's commitment to advancing a human rights agenda.

Chapter 2

Words Are Not Enough

Building a Human Rights Agenda in the Shadow of the Past

On October 6, 1976, Jimmy Carter and Gerald Ford met in San Francisco for the second debate of the 1976 presidential election. Carter, the Democratic nominee, had not performed well in the first debate, and the second debate focused on foreign policy, an area in which many considered Carter to be weak and lacking experience. Carter won the night, however, offering a vision of values serving national interests, of strength and principle that not only critiqued the Ford administration's tired Cold War approach but also suggested a reinvigorated role for American democracy at home as a cornerstone of U.S. power overseas. "We've lost in our foreign policy the character of the American people," Carter asserted in his opening statement, presenting Ford as a continuation of the failed Nixon administration policies. "What we were formerly so proud of—the strength of our country, its moral integrity, the representation in foreign affairs of what our people are, what our Constitution stands for has been gone [*sic*]," Carter said. He continued, "Every time Mr. Ford speaks from a position of secrecy in negotiations, . . . in supporting dictatorships, in ignoring human rights, we are weak and the rest of the world knows it." Carter asserted that America's global leadership depended on its strength at home. "And we can have that strength if we return to the basic principles. It ought not be a strength of bombast and threats. It ought to be a quiet strength, based on the integrity of our people, the vision of the constitution, and an innate strong will and purpose that God's given us in the greatest nation on earth."[1]

Carter's strong showing was aided by Ford's gaffe—asserting that "there is no Soviet domination of Eastern Europe and there never will be under a Ford administration."[2] Although Ford's slip was by far the most publicized statement of the evening, another moment caught the attention of the Movement. When asked to clarify his vision for bringing "the American people into the decision-making process," Carter denounced the secrecy "characteristic of Mr. Kissinger and Mr. Ford." He pointed explicitly to U.S. actions in Chile, arguing that "we have seen in the past a destruction of elected governments like in Chile, and the strong support of military dictatorship there. These kinds of things have hurt us very much." Carter returned to Chile again later, saying, "I notice that Mr. Ford didn't comment on the prisons in Chile. This is a typical example, maybe of others, where this administration overthrew an elected government and helped to establish a military dictatorship." In his closing statements of the debate, he invoked Chile once again, placing it alongside Vietnam and Watergate. In the aftermath of these events, he argued, "We've been hurt. Our people feel that we've lost something precious. . . . We ought to be a beacon for nations who search for peace and who search for freedom, who search for individual liberty, who search for basic human rights. We haven't been lately. We can be once again."[3]

Carter's statements, and particularly his criticism of the U.S. government's interventions in Chile, resonated across the Western Hemisphere and signaled that his thinking on human rights and foreign policy might diverge significantly from that of his predecessor. Joe Eldridge of WOLA later recalled, "I couldn't believe my ears as I heard him square off with Ford and talk about human rights [in Chile]. And that resounded all over Latin America. We immediately got echoes of his speech all over Latin America because he uttered the words 'human rights,'" in connection with U.S. policies in Chile.[4] Carter's emphasis on Chile in the debate hinted that the promotion of human rights was not simply an altruistic gesture or self-congratulatory championing of U.S. values. He tacitly acknowledged U.S. complicity in foreign abuses to argue for a move away from shortsighted policies that axiomatically supported repressive regimes in the name of anticommunism and stability.

Carter's first year in office was marked by a consistent effort to integrate human rights into the basic machinery of U.S. foreign policy, grapple with the complexities and trade-offs it entailed, and rethink many fundamental premises that had guided U.S. Cold War policy for three decades. Its policy was largely informed by Movement precepts, with a focus on U.S. allies and complicity in foreign repression, anti-interventionism, a reassessment of Cold War paradigms of national interests, and an expansive vision of human rights that included economic and social rights. For Carter, human rights was part of a national self-examination about the nature of U.S. power and the consequences of Cold War policy abroad and at home. To recapture domestic public support and regain international leadership, the incoming administration would have to reshape its own institutions, priorities, and instruments of foreign policy.

During his first year in office, as in the presidential debate, Carter turned to Latin America as an example of how his promotion of human rights would be implemented. Carter's Latin America policy became a crucible for policy pairing human rights with greater respect for national sovereignty, and for challenging traditional Cold War alignments and interests. This effort was marked by serious debate within the administration about the best strategy to meet these goals and how to balance the new emphasis on rights with other national interests. As the administration grappled internally with the complexity of implementing this new policy, it also struggled to project its commitment externally. As a result, U.S.–Latin American relations became a site to debate the relative merits of legislative approaches and policy instruments, as well as test the administration's commitment to human rights for an attentive audience, at home and abroad.

The Movement shaped not just the foundational concepts of Carter's policy but also the political environment in which the new administration operated. The Carter administration sought to distinguish itself from the Ford administration's "half-hearted" diplomacy by championing its "absolute" commitment to human rights.[5] The administration's efforts to establish credibility with the Movement and Congress, however, increasingly conflicted with the nuanced, comprehensive agenda it sought to develop. Carter convincingly argued that a policy that embodied the nation's best values could also serve its long-term interests; he was less transparent on how his administration would reconcile competing objectives. Further, the administration's emphasis on protecting "flexibility," particularly regarding congressional mandates, undermined its credibility with the Movement and clashed with congressional intentions to exercise democratic oversight of foreign policy. Early conflicts over human rights language in foreign aid and multilateral lending institutions, contrasts between absolutist rhetoric and incrementalist policy, and high-level visits with Latin American dictators highlighted these tensions. Although the Movement and the Carter administration should have been allies, residual distrusts from the Ford administration and ambivalence over how to best implement shared concerns soured relations before new human rights policies had fully formed.

Defining Carter on the Campaign Trail

The broad themes of Carter's human rights policy were present from the earliest days of his presidential campaign. Specifically, Carter's call for a new moral foundation for foreign policy echoed the Movement in its rejection of Cold War interventionism and alliances with repressive anticommunist regimes, both flowing from a secretive, antidemocratic policy-making process in Washington. In announcing his candidacy in December 1974, Carter declared, "It is obvious that domestic and foreign policy are directly interrelated. A necessary base for effective implementation of any foreign policy is to get our domestic house in order." He continued, "The time for American intervention in all the problems of the world is over." In the coming months, Carter would stress a return to core national values and democratic oversight as critical components of putting the "domestic house in order."[6]

On the campaign trail, Carter often invoked Vietnam as emblematic of the problems with established Cold War foreign policy, and he evidenced a desire to move away from a reliance on military power to advance U.S. interests internationally. In an early stump speech in May 1975, Carter reflected on the lessons of Vietnam, concluding that "we must reassert our vital interest in human rights and humanitarian concerns and we must provide enlightened leadership in the world community."[7] Carter returned to Vietnam time and again throughout his campaign, using it to pair a commitment to advancing American democratic values and national interests through promotion of human rights with a greater respect for the sovereignty of other nations. This pairing is significant and seemingly contradictory: advancing human rights seemed inherently interventionist; the codification of human rights principles in international law and norms had always been in tension with the sovereign prerogatives of nation-states.[8] Yet Carter echoed the Movement's vision of a reformed foreign policy and restrained U.S. interventionism culpable in human rights calamities around the world, including Vietnam and Chile.

Indeed, Carter frequently placed Chile next to Vietnam in his campaign rhetoric as a reference point for his human rights vision as a correction to

Cold War interventionism. Speaking to the Council on Foreign Relations in March 1976—one of the first major foreign policy addresses of his campaign—Carter's nascent foreign policy vision took form through criticisms of the Ford administration's secrecy, pessimism, and overdependence on military force. In a reference to Chile, he argued, "It is obviously un-American to interfere in the free political processes of another nation. It is also un-American to engage in assassinations in time of peace in any country." He continued, pointing explicitly to Chile, along with Vietnam, to argue that lack of democratic oversight of U.S. foreign policy resulted in policies that ran against the country's basic character, undermining the moral authority that underpinned U.S. influence internationally. "Policies that strengthen dictators or create refugees, policies that prolong suffering or postpone racial justice, weaken that authority. Policies that encourage economic progress and social justice promote it," he argued. He denounced the "traditional paternalism" in U.S. relations with Latin America and Africa, which often resulted in the support of repressive governments against the interests and desires of their citizens. The United States should instead "treat the people of other nations as individuals, with the same dignity and respect we demand for ourselves."[9]

Carter increasingly articulated a vision in which human rights was embedded in a larger multilateral framework that eschewed intervention and secrecy and embraced democratic values at home and abroad. Addressing the Foreign Policy Association in New York in June 1976, Carter argued that alliances must evolve beyond their military, Cold War foundations to engage with the current challenges of a multipolar world, including human rights.[10] In the address—which his national security advisor, Zbigniew Brzezinski, later billed as the campaign's "major statement on foreign policy"—Carter clearly identified human rights as part of a larger reconceptualization of U.S. interests, moving away from Cold War axioms and criticism of communist regimes.[11] He observed, "Many of us have protested the violation of human rights in Russia, and justly so. But such violations are not limited to any one country or one ideology." This rejection of Cold War pieties was especially evident when paired with the subsequent affirmation of ideological and economic diversity, clearly elevating human rights beyond Cold War utility to a new guiding principle for U.S. power.

Democratic processes may in some countries bring to power parties or leaders whose ideologies are not shared by most Americans. We may not welcome these changes; we will certainly not encourage them. But we must respect the results of democratic elections and the right of countries to make their own free choice if we are to remain faithful to our own basic ideals. We must learn to live with diversity, and we can continue to cooperate, so long as such political parties respect the democratic process, uphold existing international commitments, and are not subservient to external political direction.

Carter's speech also revealed an increasingly expansive vision for human rights, one that included "human needs" as well as democratic values. Moreover, he posed this vision of human rights not in opposition to security interests but rather as a reassessment of narrow understandings of national security.[12]

The Movement affected debates beyond the Carter campaign, and its influence was clearly evident in the Democratic Party platform. The platform—less than a third of which addressed foreign policy—reflected the intersection of domestic needs and foreign policy reform championed by Movement actors and their congressional allies. The platform called for a reassessment of security aims and policies, charging that "the security of our nation depends first and foremost on the internal strength of American society." It also rejected Cold War militarism and intervention, denouncing explicitly the "extensive American interference in the internal politics of Chile and other nations." It concluded, "We must make clear our revulsion at the systematic violation of basic human rights that have occurred under some Latin American military regimes."[13]

In calling for "a new American foreign policy," the platform championed recent legislation linking foreign aid to human rights performance, clearly embracing the guiding principles established by Congress in the past year. "A primary object of American aid, both military and economic, is first of all to enhance the condition of freedom in the world. The United States should not provide aid to any government . . . which uses secret police, detention without charges, and torture to enforce its power." It continued, "The United States should be open and unashamed in its exercise of diplomatic efforts to encourage the observance of human rights in countries which receive American aid."[14] The centrality of foreign aid to its human rights vision is unsurprising given the leadership of congressional Democrats in drafting the legislation. It also spoke to the utility of foreign aid policy as a marker of executive commitment to human rights and a mechanism of democratic control of foreign policy. Moreover, the platform reflected the Movement's logic broadening the definition of rights in ways that positioned military spending against social rights at home and supporting basic human needs abroad. The platform stated, "We will ensure that human needs are not sacrificed to military spending," and it affirmed that aid must work to eliminate poverty and support "the quest for human liberty and dignity." This was an agenda both to advance human rights abroad and protect rights and democracy within the United States.[15]

While the Movement's approach to human rights policies clearly shaped the party platform, it also reflected the influence of the "Jackson Democrats" and those marshalling human rights within a more traditional Cold War framework. The platform reaffirmed a commitment to the Helsinki Accords, explicitly condemning abuses by the Soviet government. "Our stance on the issue of human rights and political liberties in the Soviet Union is important to American self-respect and our moral standing in the world." The platform's vague commitment to "reaffirm[ing] the fundamental American commitment to human rights across the globe" reflected an increasingly polarized Democratic Party.[16] Carter utilized the platform's vagueness—championing rights that would be equally applicable in communist regimes and right-wing dictatorships, such as freedom of the press and right of workers to organize—to unite various party factions under the promise of human rights unmoored from specific policy prescriptions.

By the time Carter received the Democratic Party's nomination for president in July, he had a clear set of interrelated themes that forecast a new direction for U.S. foreign policy, consistent with the Movement's vision. Addressing B'nai B'rith in Washington, D.C., on September 8, Carter advocated an approach that looked beyond simple Cold War moralism and instead focused on the shortcomings and counterproductive dimensions of U.S. policies. "Often there has been a gap between the values we have proclaimed and the policies we have pursued," Carter observed. "We have often been overextended, and deeply entangled in the internal affairs of distant nations." The first step to advancing human rights, he contended, was to "support the principle of self-determination by refraining from intervention in the domestic politics of other countries." Speaking to a group of activists concerned primarily with abuses in the Soviet Union, this was an unlikely starting point. Yet Carter's emphasis on nonintervention reflected the construction of human rights championed by the Movement and targeting the U.S. policies that had contributed to abuses. Similarly, the more concrete measures he identified—leveraging foreign aid, supporting UN and private groups, ratifying international human rights treaties—all mirrored the Movement's emphasis on reforming U.S. behaviors and practices. With

Figure 5. Democratic presidential candidates Jimmy Carter and Rep. Morris Udall (D-AZ) at a dinner hosted by the Americans for Democratic Action in April 1976. Courtesy of AP Photos.

foreign aid, inherently an instrument targeting countries with which the United States had a collaborative relationship, Carter stressed the need to make sure that U.S. support was "used to benefit the people of that country," not the repressive government.[17]

Carter's electoral victory on November 2 elicited a mix of hope and skepticism from the Movement. Even as Carter's rhetoric on human rights increasingly reflected the logic and framing of the Movement, many left-leaning groups had been slow to warm to Carter, preferring established progressives such as Rep. Morris Udall of Arizona, who had been backed by the ADA in the Democratic primary. In a closed-door session leading to Udall's endorsement, even Carter's defenders were moderated in their praise, championing him as "not that illiberal."[18] Still, Carter offered human rights advocates a clear alternative to the discredited Ford administration. After Carter's election WOLA expressed enthusiasm for the new administration, contrasting Carter's campaign positions with the Kissinger State Department's "hardline realpolitik," which had stressed "political values at the expense of human values." WOLA's December newsletter asserted that President-elect Carter shared with members of Congress a "profound concern" over U.S. policy in Latin America in the face of escalating human rights violations. "We at the

Washington Office on Latin America are optimistic that the policy of overt support to military dictatorships is at an end, and that a new era of support for genuine democratic forces which oppose the military dictatorship is a strong possibility."[19]

Despite optimism among some in the Movement about the new administration, it was clear that Carter would need to earn the trust and support of human rights advocates and Congress. The White House's credibility deficit with the Movement would not be erased with sympathetic statements by a new administration, and goodwill from human rights proponents was clearly tied to expectations for immediate actions that would signal a new direction in policy. The ADA noted that throughout the campaign "many promises were made and many commitments were sought as to what would be the shape of a Carter Administration's domestic and foreign policy." Now was the time for the new government to make good on these promises. The ADA identified a "new direction" for foreign policy as one of "two critical problems that demand immediate and bold action." In an open letter in December 1976, the group called for Carter to "reshape our foreign policy" prioritizing "basic humanitarian interests" and moving away from a reliance on military force. The ADA's "laundry list" for the new administration highlighted familiar elements of the Movement's agenda, linking foreign policy reforms to domestic democratic values, including greater "public scrutiny and participation" in policy making and substantial reductions in military spending and "increases in the social programs that raise the standard of living and quality of life."[20]

Looking for early signs of the Carter administration's commitment to reorienting foreign policy, the Movement focused on high-level cabinet appointments for insight into Carter's intentions during the transition. State Department staffing was a clear priority and symbol of larger ideological changes. In a meeting with the Carter campaign in early October, a group of Movement advocates, including WOLA, stressed the importance of appointing a secretary of state who had demonstrated "a deep commitment to the cause of human rights. Such an appointment," they reasoned, "can provide a climate in which many effective, imaginative, and creative steps can be taken to advance human rights in other countries." In a letter to Carter shortly after his election, the ADA similarly stressed that a reassessment of foreign policy necessitated new leaders "unencumbered by attachments and involvements of the mistakes of past administrations."[21]

During his campaign, Carter had established himself as an "outsider" to Washington, frequently criticizing the "east coast foreign policy establishment." His announcement of Cyrus Vance as secretary of state and Zbigniew Brzezinski as national security advisor—both from traditional foreign policy backgrounds—thus raised questions about his commitment to fundamentally reshaping U.S. foreign policy. Indeed, just weeks earlier, Carter's own chief of staff, Hamilton Jordan, had said that "if, after the inauguration, you find Cy Vance as secretary of state and Zbigniew Brzezinski as head of National Security, then I would say we failed. And I'd quit."[22] Jordan's statement was clearly intended to affirm that Carter would be innovative in his foreign policy rather than relying on "establishment" figures. The press seized on the quote and circulated it widely after the appointments were announced, embarrassing the new administration and reinforcing concerns that Carter was not committed to the fundamental changes necessary to have a dynamic human rights policy.

Vance's confirmation hearing before the Senate Foreign Relations Committee on January 11 showcased the administration's efforts to establish its credibility on human rights in the face of congressional skepticism. Laying out the administration's foreign policy priorities, Vance acknowledged that East-West relations were critical. He continued, however, "I do not think that the preoccupation with these vitally important issues should so dominate our foreign policy that we neglect other critical issues which are growing increasingly important," pointing to global issues such as arms control, "economic development and the dignity of the developing world," food security, and the environment. He concluded by saying, "We must have policies based upon fundamental values. In particular, we must stand for human rights. Without being interventionist, we can make this concern a major focus of our foreign policy calculation."[23]

Sen. Frank Church (D-ID), asking the first substantive question of the hearing, picked up on Vance's embrace of human rights, stating, "I would hope that this will translate into some refusal on the part of the administration to continue to extend military and economic aid to regimes that are systematically engaged in the repression of human rights, at least in the absence of overriding considerations of national security." Vance reassured him that although "there are cases in which the security aspects are of overriding importance," the administration would give human rights "greater emphasis with respect to those decisions." Church also stressed that "the other side of the coin in the matter of human rights" was the United States' own behaviors. Pointing to covert actions in recent years, Church rejected the rationale that countering Soviet subversions required the use of "the black arts of covert operations" that the Russians used. "I don't know how we can be true to our own values as a country," Church reflected, "and continue to believe that it is our right to use such methods." A serious commitment to human rights, Church implied, required the reform of the United States' own practices and policies. Vance concurred, stating that he would support covert actions beyond intelligence gathering "only in the most extraordinary circumstances," and he supported the expansion of monitoring mechanisms in Congress and beyond.[24]

Vance and Church's discussion of covert operations and legislative guidance revealed that human rights served as both a new foreign policy objective and a symbol of a restrained executive that respected its coequal branch of governance. Several members of the committee expressed hope and enthusiasm for significant changes in U.S. foreign policy under the new administration, even as they stressed the necessity of partnering with Congress in doing so. Echoing Carter's campaign message that "American strength and leadership abroad proceeds from a strong America at home," Vance asserted that the heart of public confidence in foreign policy rested on "a close and cooperative relationship between the executive branch and the legislative branch. I do not believe that we can develop or properly implement American foreign policy without the closest cooperation between these two branches of government." Despite Vance's good-natured offer of his personal office number to members of Congress, his confirmation hearing revealed the lingering distrust in relations between the two branches of government. The staunchest advocates of human rights expected the new administration to act quickly and unequivocally if it wanted their support.[25]

Our Commitment Must Be Absolute

As he was sworn in as president on January 20, 1977, Carter took up the mantle of advocate with an uncompromising rhetorical position, declaring, "Our commitment to human rights must be absolute." Carter committed his short inaugural address—one of the briefest in history—to championing the need for humane policies and a return to the nation's core values both domestically and internationally. The United States' "unique self-definition," Carter asserted, had given the nation "an exceptional appeal—but it also imposes on us a special obligation: to take on those moral duties which, when assumed, seem invariably to be in our own best interests." He thus rejected the premise that an effective policy must choose between the nation's values and its interests. Instead, he championed the interdependence of domestic and international strength, with a commitment to the nation's most basic ideals drawing the two together. "Our nation can be strong abroad only if it is strong at home, and we know that the best way to enhance freedom in other lands is to demonstrate here that our democratic system is worthy of emulation." Strength and unity at home required a foreign policy that the American people could support as an extension of their own values. "We will not behave in foreign places so as to violate our rules and standards here at home, for we know that the trust which our nation earns is essential to our strength," he explained. A government that sacrificed its principles would create distrust and divides with its citizens and undermine the credibility it relied on in the larger world. Human rights was a way to encapsulate what the United States ought to stand for, at home and in the world, a new basis of strength that would not wholly replace traditional security interests but augment them in a changed international environment.[26]

In his inaugural address, Carter clearly sought to demonstrate to a skeptical Congress and the Movement that human rights would have a central place in his foreign policy, and early efforts to implement human rights policy targeted these constituencies. Despite the Movement's dissatisfaction with Carter's selection of Vance and Brzezinski, both men made early staffing choices that sought to foster positive relations with key congressional allies. At the National Security Council, Brzezinski recruited staff that was well connected to Congress and the Movement. This including Jessica Tuchman from Congressman Udall's office, who took the lead on human rights and global issues at the NSC, and Robert Pastor for U.S.–Latin American relations.[27] At the State Department, Vance retained George Lister, who now moved to the Latin America bureau, and sought new assistants from outside the government to develop the administration's policy, offer fresh perspectives, and distinguish Carter from his predecessors and "establishment" politics.

Patricia Derian, appointed as coordinator for the State Department's new bureau for Human Rights and Humanitarian Affairs, embodied the administration's commitment to bringing in fresh perspectives and activist sensibilities to energize its foreign policy. Derian had little experience in foreign affairs or large government bureaucracies, but she had a strong record as an outspoken advocate for civil rights and had been an early and active member of Carter's presidential campaign.[28] Derian staffed her office with people who shared her background and passion for human rights. Most influential of these was her deputy assistant, Mark Schneider, a member of Ted Kennedy's staff who had been central to the senator's efforts to advance human rights in Latin America.[29] Schneider had coordinated the numerous hearings on human rights abuses in Chile during the Ford administration, developing an intimate working relationship with members of Congress as well as deep connections to the advocate community.

As the Carter administration turned to governing, its human rights agenda was indelibly shaped by the frameworks that the Movement had established through congressional legislation in previous years, as well as its deep distrust of executive power. In a memo to Brzezinski days after Carter's inauguration, Tuchman flatly stated that her initial policy recommendation on human rights "pretty well covers the ground of those actions recommended by members of congress and by various interest groups." She admitted that "there is virtually nothing innovative in it, but it does contain enough substance so that if Administration action were taken on some or all of these options it would amount to a very major initiative on the President's part."[30]

Tuchman focused almost exclusively on measures that would affect right-wing governments, stressing U.S. material support for repressive regimes through direct aid and multilateral institutions. Only one small section toward the end of the memo was dedicated to "influencing communist nations," noting the limited leverage the United States possessed in these cases. She presented the Jackson-Vanik Amendment as unpopular in Congress, and even the Helsinki Accords, while valuable for avoiding charges of "double standards," must be approached with a "realistic appraisal of what we can in fact accomplish."[31] In short, actionable human rights policy very much rested on the agenda developed by the Movement targeting the United States' own entanglement in foreign abuses, restraining interventionism, and rethinking the fundamental nature of U.S. security and national interests.

Tuchman's memo reflected early policy planning for human rights in the Carter administration's first months. Its initial approach to human rights was part of an introspective reassessment of core values and goals of foreign policy that transcended East-West relations. High-profile events such as Carter's public exchange of letters about human rights with Soviet dissident and Nobel laureate Andrei Sakharov led many to believe that Carter's human rights policy targeted first and foremost the Soviet Union and communist adversaries.[32] The administration's early efforts, however, focused overwhelmingly on right-wing allies. In February a State Department policy outline established that supporting human rights started with self-examination "to put our own house in order," including the ratification of UN covenants and providing clearer guidelines to U.S. missions on their role in implementing human rights. Further, the U.S. government needed to "reduce symbols of US embrace of authoritarian regimes" and strengthen its support for multilateral institutions engaged in human rights concerns.[33] This would strengthen the U.S. position when it did criticize foreign governments and mitigate the appearance of hypocrisy and interventionism in its human rights efforts.

Although it had been developing as a foreign policy issue for years, there was "wide confusion" over what the new administration meant by "internationally recognized human rights" and how it intended to prioritize them.[34] Government efforts during the Ford administration had focused overwhelmingly on "gross violations." Early conversations within the Carter administration, however, made it clear that it sought a wide-ranging agenda that embraced the full spectrum of rights embodied in the UN Universal Declaration of Rights, encompassing "attention for both political/civil and economic/social rights" as well as gross violations committed by governments against the person. Patricia Derian and Anthony Lake at the State Department argued, "There is an important relation between the political/civil liberties and the economic/social rights specified in the Declaration. We cannot pursue our commitment to both economic development and political freedom if we give one set of rights priority over the other."[35] An expansive definition of rights reflected the administration's emphasis on North-South relations rather than Cold War divides in its policy framework. State and AID officials stressed that the administration's approach must include economic rights if it hoped to appeal to third world countries with its policy.[36] Tuchman agreed, urging the president to emphasize that "human rights begins at breakfast," signaling that his human rights policies would support economic and social development, not just cessation of political violence.[37] Addressing the UN General Assembly on March 17, Carter asserted "that the reduction of tension, the control of nuclear arms, the achievement of harmony in the troubled areas of the world, and the provision of food, good health, and education will independently contribute to advancing the human condition."[38] His speech integrated human rights into a wide array of foreign policy objectives from arms control to economic development, offering an appealing harmony of interests between humanitarian and security concerns.

The administration's deliberations over how to define rights necessarily intersected with questions of how to instrumentalize these concerns in foreign policy. The administration faced early and pervasive challenges in formulating a policy that went beyond moral gestures to recalibrate the nation's fundamental interests and practices of policy, prompting internal debates among government officials. The mechanisms developed by Congress thus far focused on punitive measures for gross violations. A more expansive agenda that included basic human needs and economic development would require instruments beyond the existing legislative mandates. The administration sought to increase support for programs that assisted economic development as part of its human rights agenda. This included the expansion of AID's program for "New Initiatives in Human Rights," launched in 1975, but that effort was hobbled by its lack of support from the Ford administration and hostility from some of the regional bureaus at State.[39]

The goal of developing robust policies targeting the developing world and economic rights was further complicated by the United States' legacies of interventionism. In an early policy outline, the State Department warned that a vigorous human rights policy risked "impinging on sovereignty sensitivities of individual countries." This could damage U.S. relations and interests with the targeted regime and create "opportunities for regime leaders to arouse popular nationalistic support for resistance to foreign interference." In Latin America, for example, U.S. policy must account for "historic sensitivity to [the] US penchant for interventionism" and the "need for a balanced approach to regimes of different political and ideological orientations."[40] The aggressive pursuit of human rights could draw the Carter administration dangerously close to the patterns it sought to reshape—namely, U.S. interference in internal affairs of other countries—and risked provoking nationalist backlash and counterproductive tensions.

The administration's early efforts to deploy a successful human rights policy that redefined U.S. interests and provided a check on military interventionism necessarily coincided with a reconsideration of U.S. relations with Latin America. Two high-profile reports drafted in 1976 and released in early 1977 brought Movement actors and logics into the Carter administration's efforts to reconceptualize U.S.–Latin American relations and human rights. The Institute for Policy Studies' *Southern Connection* and the Commission on United States–Latin American Relations, or Linowitz Commission, both offered the administration a new approach to hemispheric affairs and a template for how human rights and anti-interventionism could reorient Cold War assumptions of national interest.[41] Although differing in scope and vision, both reports grew out of a shared concern for a long history of U.S intervention that had exacerbated human rights violations and associated the United States with problematic military dictatorships. The authors of the *Southern Connection* stated that the "practices and assumptions that now undergird U.S. policy are outmoded, ineffectual, and morally unacceptable."

The report challenged policy makers to discard the "presumption of hege-mony" that had marred regional relations, abetted human rights violations, and undermined respect for the self-determination of the peoples in the hemisphere. The Linowitz Commission similarly encouraged U.S. policy makers to reject outdated notions of paternalism connoted by the idea of a "special relationship" and instead place U.S.–Latin American relations in a global context that respected national sovereignty.[42]

Both reports gave significant attention to foreign aid, tying it to the United States' military interventions, interference in national elections, and sales of military equipment to repressive regimes. The authors of the *Southern Connection* concluded, "The nexus of official U.S. assistance and repres-sion in recipient countries must be broken."[43] As in many IPS reports, Chile was held up as the ultimate example of the relationship between human rights violations and a program of national economic development.[44] The report noted that despite its record of oppression and congressional limits on military aid, Chile remained one of the largest recipients of U.S. support in 1975. The Linowitz Commission similarly supported the use of foreign aid as an instrument to promote human rights objectives, and it urged the new administration to support international and U.S. law prohibiting aid to coun-tries exhibiting patterns of gross violations of human rights.[45] This position both reflected the congressional agenda of recent years and reinforced no-tions of U.S. culpability in foreign abuses. Reforming U.S. aid programs and the Cold War alliances they facilitated was therefore an essential component of advancing rights and U.S. interests in the region.

Challenging fundamental Cold War precepts and interests, the reports called for U.S. policy makers to embrace, or at least tolerate, diverse ap-proaches to development and not simply dismiss more left-leaning initia-tives as Soviet or Cuban infiltration. The Linowitz Commission challenged Cold War alignments in the region, calling for policies "respectful of the sovereignty of countries of the region and tolerant of a wide range of politi-cal and economic forms." The United States, in formulating a new approach to the region, had to eschew intervention to shape foreign governments and societies to its own preferences. The *Southern Connection* similarly argued that the "new thrust of U.S. policy in Latin America should be to support the ideologically diverse and experimental approaches to development" and po-litical economies. The *Southern Connection*'s championing of "ideological di-versity"—that is, tolerance for socialist socioeconomic projects, and diverse models of development—was an implicit rejection of Cold War binaries and alliances grounded in simple anticommunist alignments.[46]

Moving beyond the focus on gross violations that had dominated the Ford administration's limited efforts, the reports included economic and social frameworks as critically relevant factors in advancing rights and improving U.S. relations with the region. The *Southern Connection*, for example, argued that "vast disparities in socio-economic opportunities obstruct the creation of a climate in which human rights can be fully respected," or more simply, "human rights are not violated in a political and economic vacuum."[47] The Linowitz Commission report focused on opportunities for development to improve regional relations and support the realization of basic human needs in the poorest countries, stressing the need to address Latin America's diversity and situate regional policy in a broader global framework. Moreover, although it advised against "automatic and absolute formulas," it recommended that economic aid should not "abet repressive actions" or associate the U.S. government "with brutally repressive governments."[48]

The reports' conceptualization of human rights embedded in a broader framework of regional interests—emphasizing nonintervention, rethinking security relations beyond Cold War binaries, and incorporation of economic rights and development—clearly influenced the Carter administration's early human rights efforts and development of its Latin America policy. Key members of Carter's foreign policy team—most notably Robert Pastor, a key strategist for U.S.–Latin American relations at the NSC—had participated in drafting both reports.[49] Sol Linowitz—joining the administration to lead the Panama Canal negotiations—sent his committee's report directly to Brzezinski and discussed its contents with Vance before the inauguration. In early February Carter wrote to Linowitz personally, praising the report and promising to give it "very careful consideration."[50]

The administration's request for a Presidential Review Memorandum (PRM) on Latin America, issued on January 26, mirrored the reports' core elements, reconsidering Cold War assumptions underpinning regional relations and questioning "whether the current assumptions underlying U.S. policy toward the region" served U.S. interests. Given the regional and global changes of the past decade, it questioned the basic U.S. interests in the region and devoted significant space to implementing human rights as a central aspect of regional relations. The review also reflected congressional guidance as it sought ways to strengthen reporting, identify "consistent patterns of gross violations," incorporate human rights into bilateral and multilateral relations, and strengthen connections with and efforts by advocate groups.[51]

By mid-March the administration was engaged in a robust internal conversation about its Latin America policy—the only region the administration singled out for a comprehensive policy review—with human rights and non-intervention occupying a central position.[52] A draft study for the PRM noted, "Our pressures for human rights and non-proliferation have raised new fears about U.S. intervention and paternalism." In the past, Latin American policy was "determined largely by the Cold War. The policies and instruments used to achieve this end were largely determined by the nature of the perceived challenge: all out resistance to Communism." This "East-West Bias" in turn drove interventions that damaged U.S. relations and reputation in the region. An emphasis on global or North-South approaches to the region did not entirely eliminate Cold War security concerns, but the policy review concluded that "we can accept more ideological pluralism in 1977 than we could in 1962."[53]

This acceptance of "ideological pluralism"—echoing the *Southern Connection*'s emphasis on "ideological diversity"—also reflected the engagement with a broad range of issues as central to a serious human rights policy in the region. Although the linkage of human rights and intervention necessarily raised questions about U.S. alliance with military governments, the report went beyond this to advocate for the inclusion of social and economic rights in regional policy. "The growing rich/poor dichotomy is the bottom line in our relations in this hemisphere. As the United States projects its values on human rights abroad, we can be more effective if we demonstrate in word and deed that we also give great weight to the egalitarian aspirations of the poor nations."[54]

Although the policy review process prompted significant debate over the relative importance of various objectives, key elements of the Movement's approach were widely accepted within the administration's policy discussions.[55] Robert Pastor, for example, disliked the Latin America bureau's framing of the issues presented by ideological diversity but still affirmed that U.S. policy should "exhibit a *greater tolerance* for regimes of widely *different political philosophies*, distinguishing only on the basis of their respect for fundamental rights." He continued, arguing, "Currently, our ability to influence events in Latin America appears greatest not when the power equation is most weighted to our advantage, but when we are cognizant and sensitive to the principal norms of the developing world—sovereignty and social justice."[56]

Even as it borrowed heavily from the Movement's reports and logic, the administration's evolving approach to regional relations challenged some of the existing mechanisms and policies supported by human rights advocates. Carter's staff was increasingly concerned with what it saw as an overreliance on punitive measures, and the March policy review emphasized the need to *"explore affirmative ways to express our policy."*[57] Although it supported the inclusion of human rights factors in decisions about foreign aid and loans, the administration feared that too much emphasis on sanctions would undermine its leverage with foreign governments over a wide array of issues, including human rights.[58] Moreover, although military aid had clear connections to foreign abuses and directly associated the United States with the repressive regimes, economic aid and multilateral lending were more complex. Mandatory cutoffs of nonmilitary aid and loans could come at the expense of social rights, food security, and economic development, penalizing the vulnerable populations their policy sought to aid. A March 14 draft of the PRM noted the tension between the broad range of rights the policy sought to advance and the instruments currently in use, stating that "the Harkin Amendment symbolizes to many our overriding stress on political as opposed to economic rights."[59] A policy review committee in late March agreed that the administration should utilize aid as a way to "improve human rights conditions in very poor countries," rather than relying on it solely as a punitive sanction for gross violations.[60]

Figure 6. President Carter presents his administration's new approach to U.S.–Latin American relations in an address to the Organization of American States General Assembly, April 14, 1977. Courtesy of the Jimmy Carter Presidential Library.

An invitation for Carter to address the general assembly of the Organization of American States offered an opportunity for the administration
to present its vision for human rights embedded in a new regional policy.
Addressing the OAS General Assembly on April 14, 1977, the administration
set out two seemingly contradictory objectives as the backbone of hemispheric relations: respect for the "individuality and the sovereignty" of the
nations of the region and wide support for human rights. Early drafts of
the speech made it clear that the focus on sovereignty was a clear rejection
of past U.S. interventions and covert operations in the region, as well as an
effort to signal that this administration would be more tolerant of diverse
modes of governance and development. By pairing it with sovereignty, the
administration was trying to make clear that human rights was not simply a
cover for imposing U.S. values and order on the region, but rather an attempt
to realign regional dynamics in a way that was more responsive to the needs
of a diverse population and communities.[61]

Carter's speech echoed the Linowitz Commission and *Southern Connection* reports in its linkage of human rights and a broad agenda of structural
challenges in regional relations and a move away from Cold War security
concerns. "Our values and yours," Carter argued, "require us to combat
abuses of individual freedom, including those caused by political, social, and
economic injustice." By emphasizing disparities in development and economic and social inequality, Carter tacitly broadened the scope of human
rights issues that his administration's policies would address. This approach
reflected the administration's emphasis on multilateralism and its "desire to
press forward on the great issues which affect the relations between the developed and the developing nations."[62] Strikingly, Carter's address made little
direct mention of traditional security threats; instead, his vision for human
rights and national sovereignty was embedded in a larger reorientation of
policy goals that highlighted economic cooperation, normalization of relations with Cuba, and a treaty for the Panama Canal.

The administration's Latin America policy revealed its desire to integrate
human rights into the fabric of its foreign policy, breaking with the more superficial approach of past administrations. Rather than treat it as an isolated
issue, the administration inserted human rights considerations into every
key area, from security to economic development and cultural/educational
programming. This approach carried well beyond the Western Hemisphere.
At the end of March, the State Department circulated an action memorandum on human rights that reveals the all-encompassing nature of the
administration's efforts to incorporate human rights into its foreign policy

apparatus. The State Department noted that the Carter administration had "moved fast to establish its *bona fides* on human rights," detailing structural changes under way to better integrate human rights concerns into the foreign policy apparatus. This included enlarging the staff in the new Human Rights Bureau, and expanding the scope and efficacy of consultation with other parts of the executive branch relevant to human rights concerns, including Defense, Treasury, CIA, USIA, and AID.[63]

The administration's early guidelines and priorities were deeply intertwined with recapturing the trust and support of Congress and domestic constituencies, without which any new initiatives would surely fail. In late March a State Department review of the administration's preliminary efforts concluded, "Present U.S. policy is in tune with what most on the Hill want. The *next step*—since some Congressmen fear that we have a helter-skelter approach that could dissolve in the face of *Realpolitik*—is to demonstrate to the Congress that our human rights program is serious, coordinated, and related to other U.S. national interests."[64] Indeed, just a week before, Brzezinski reported to Carter that the administration's early efforts had fostered a new appreciation of human rights issues domestically. "However, I do not believe that at this stage the larger design of what you wish to accomplish has emerged with sufficiently sharp relief." He recommended that Carter express a "more coherent vision of what we aim to accomplish, of what our priorities are," as well as "convey to the public your awareness of the complexity of the problems that we confront." He continued, "The effort to build a more cooperative world framework will be tedious, painful, and frequently disappointing."[65] Carter's rhetoric championing human rights, he feared, was increasingly at odds with the nuanced, complex work of crafting specific policies that would both advance U.S. interests and improve repressive conditions abroad. Indeed, even as the administration moved to integrate human rights into its policy mechanisms, foreign aid became a flashpoint for tensions within the competing objectives of U.S. human rights policies.

The Foreign Aid Battle Ground

In early February the *Guardian* reported that foreign aid and State Department country reports had become the president's "first foreign policy hot potato," placing the administration "on a collision course with the growing 'human rights lobby' on Capitol Hill."[66] From its first days in office, disputes with Congress over security assistance and mandated country reports presented the Carter administration with a divisive, complex issue with Latin America once again serving as a central testing ground. During the Ford administration, foreign aid had become a key marker of both the underlying logic of human rights and democratic oversight of foreign policy. Congress's approach to the Carter administration on country reports and foreign aid reflected its more assertive role in policy making and the residual distrust of the executive from the Nixon-Ford years. Similarly, many human rights advocates approached the Carter administration with both hope and skepticism, believing that binding legislation was the only way to guarantee that the new administration would prioritize human rights beyond rhetoric.

The Security Assistance and Arms Export Control Act of 1976—signed by President Ford in June 1976—expanded the reach of the 502B legislation linking foreign aid to human rights performance to include all recipients of military assistance. The statute required the State Department to "consider in their status reports the 'relevant findings of appropriate international organizations.'"[67] This gave the Movement an important point of leverage within the State Department. The annual reports on human rights conditions in recipient countries not only created a demand within the government for NGO information and reporting; it also gave groups a yearly opportunity to scrutinize government evaluations of human rights conditions in target countries, comparing them with their own.

Shortly after the Security Assistance Act passed in July 1976, Bruce Cameron of the HRWG and lobbyist for the ADA met with several legislative aids, including John Salzberg and Mark Schneider from Fraser's and Kennedy's staffs, to develop a strategy to pressure the Ford administration to declassify the country reports before the end of the congressional session. On August 30, under the guidance of Cameron, the HRWG presented a letter to Sen. Hubert Humphrey (D-MN), chair of the Senate Foreign Assistance Subcommittee, urging him to request the declassification of State Department country reports for South Korea, the Philippines, Argentina, Indonesia, Ethiopia, Haiti, Peru, and Uruguay. Accompanying Cameron's letter was detailed human rights information on the eight target countries drawn from Amnesty International, WOLA, and other Movement networks. The letter cast the Ford administration's commitment to human rights as "half-hearted and very much tied to outside pressure, especially from Congress." Making the reports public would put foreign governments "on notice that continued violations of human rights will jeopardize its relationship with the United States." Moreover, the compilation of data in these reports provided the basis for a "comprehensive review of specific U.S. security relationships with specific countries."[68] The 502B country reports were a beginning, not an end, of security assistance and foreign policy reform.

Even as it criticized Ford's lackluster performance on human rights issues, Cameron's letter reflected a strategy that transcended the current administration, arguing that the reports served as a "potent tool for Congress to influence U.S. foreign policy." These reports would raise awareness within the State Department that "concern for human rights is an integral part of U.S. foreign policy" and underline Congress's concern with the issue. Cameron observed that "the democratic nominee [Jimmy Carter] has made some strong statements on the importance of human rights as a major factor in foreign policy." Despite this promising rhetorical position, Congress should still move ahead with its efforts to make the reports public: "The issuance of the Secretary of State's reports . . . would lay the groundwork for a comprehensive review of the entire U.S. security assistance program. And because these reports would be produced in accordance with the 502B procedure as required by Congress, a new administration would be more likely to consult with Congress not only on broad policy issues, but also on the appropriateness of security assistance to specific governments." The Movement clearly envisioned these reports as part of a more active role for Congress and the public in guiding foreign affairs, regardless of the election's outcome.[69]

Shortly after receiving Cameron's letter, Senator Humphrey—joined by Congressman Fraser—sent a letter to Kissinger, requesting the specified country reports be declassified. The Ford administration remained staunchly opposed to releasing the reports publicly, fearing they would both damage relations with the target countries and infringe on executive prerogatives of policy making. Ford's failed presidential bid prevented a "long and possibly acrimonious battle" between the Movement and the State Department but left the issues of the reports' accuracy and declassification unresolved for the incoming Carter administration.[70]

The country reports, partially declassified in a congressional presentation document on December 30, 1976, generated a heated response from the Movement. On January 14, just days before Carter's inauguration, the HRWG released a detailed report critiquing much of the information and conclusions presented in five of the State Department's country reports. With Argentina, for example, the HRWG report questioned the number of political prisoners documented in the State Department report and its conclusion that torture was "rare," offering contrasting figures from Amnesty International. The HRWG took particular offense at the State Department's

assertion that "U.S. military credits have little or no bearing on the counter terrorist capability of the armed forces." This statement, the HRWG
responded, was in direct contradiction with a congressional presentation
document from March 1976 that stated, "The FMS credits being proposed
for Argentina will support their program of armed forces modernization,
particularly their counterinsurgency and sea control capabilities." The
HRWG observed that the State Department's rationale for continuing security assistance to the Argentine government cited no "vital U.S. interests" or
external threats to the country. The HRWG concluded, "They are the kind
of flimsy reasons that have caused the U.S. Security Assistance Program to
come into such disrepute among the American people."[71]

In a letter to President-elect Carter, the HRWG expressed an "urgent
concern" about the "superficial treatment of human rights violations" by
the State Department in these reports, citing the discrepancies between the
State Department's figures on political prisoners and those of international
organizations. It characterized the State Department's logic for continued
security assistance as "simplistic," stating that such assistance "gives an appearance of legitimacy to repressive governments and their activities they
otherwise would not enjoy" and was "just one more indication of the Ford
administration's insensitivity to human rights." WOLA's January newsletter
echoed the HRWG critiques of the State Department report, arguing that "a
cutoff of security assistance to Argentina would have an important symbolic
effect on the Argentine government, even though it would not substantially
effect [*sic*] the junta's financial situation. It would indicate to all political
leaders, including civilians, that the US government was not fully backing
the military junta, as is generally assumed to be the case at the present." It
continued, "If the opposition to Videla has coalesced into a non-communist
nationalist resistance, then imaginative policy makers should begin to entertain the costs of continued identification with Videla."[72]

Following a line of reasoning that had become familiar for the Movement
in recent years, the WOLA and the HRWG both advanced the idea that national interests were better served by supporting democratic governments.
Not only would this engender greater support from people abroad but "the
confidence of the American people in our public institutions will continue to
erode" if the new administration failed to return the nation's foreign policy
to "the principles of our Constitution and the Declaration of Independence."
The HRWG urged the Carter administration to make the country reports
public in their entirety, to require the State Department to review and reis-
sue the country reports with greater attention to the link between human

rights violations and U.S. security assistance, to reevaluate the criteria for granting security assistance, and to voluntarily cut aid to governments that consistently violated human rights. In a press release accompanying the letter, Jacqui Chagnon of the HRWG stated, "We are confident that President-elect Carter will convey his wishes to the State Department that full texts of reports will be declassified and released to the public," but she noted that the group was prepared to "use the appropriate legal remedies to compel their release" if the new administration was not forthcoming.[73] Foreign aid was clearly going to be the first litmus test for the new administration, and its response would set the tone for relations with the Movement and Congress.

The legacy of distrust and the symbolic importance of foreign assistance for its human rights agenda was not lost on the incoming Carter administration. Even before the inauguration, Brzezinski charged his staff with "giving some thought to how we might inject, in a realistic fashion, greater concern for human rights into our foreign policy initiatives. I do not want human rights to become merely a slogan or a contentious issue between the Executive and Legislative branches." In a February memo to Brzezinski, Tuchman identified human rights guidance on foreign aid as the center point of fraught relations between the two branches. She noted that the Ford administration's apparent indifference to human rights legislation had provoked a great deal of frustration among certain Congress members and resulted in increasingly restrictive legislation. The current human rights legislation, she observed, was the result of what happens "when congressional concern met executive disdain—with results that satisfy no one."[74]

Tuchman believed that the incoming administration's commitment to human rights was one of its "best opportunities to radically improve executive-congressional relations," but it required early action on upcoming military and economic aid to signal a break from the Ford administration's intransigence. "The content of these budget requests will be taken as the *single most important* signal of this Administration's policies on human rights." A week later she argued that "for better or worse, the President must recognize that *the individual country by country budget items for security assistance will be taken by Congress and the press as the real signal of whether this Administration really means to get serious over human rights,* or whether the President's campaign talk was just more rhetoric." She warned that if the Carter administration submitted the budget for security assistance to Congress unchanged from the proposals made by the Ford administration, it would prompt a hostile response from Congress, likely in the form of new legislative restrictions.[75]

In light of the attention given to the security budget requests by Congress, the administration focused on cutting aid to Latin America as a signal of commitment to human rights measures. With aid to Chile already terminated, the administration cut aid to Argentina by half of the level proposed by the Ford administration and terminated aid to Uruguay. Many in the administration—including both Tuchman and Derian—urged further cuts at the beginning of February, arguing that the current levels *"will not meet Congressional expectations for evidence of a human rights policy different from that of the past Administrations."* After consulting with key congressional staffers, Tuchman warned "that the message was clear. . . . While no one expects a complete turn-around on this issue, if Carter comes up with a 'full Ford-type platter' there will be loud and angry protests."[76]

The administration—including leadership at both State and NSC—was reluctant to implement additional cuts outside a comprehensive strategy. The administration largely embraced the logic of tying security assistance to human rights performance, stating that it had a "special responsibility to respect human rights in countries receiving security assistance or buying arms from the US," even as it stated that this responsibility must be weighed against other American national interests.[77] The question of what that balance should be and who would make that decision, however, was still unclear. Even with additional cuts, the administration feared that Congress would regard changes as "tokenism" rather than a sincere commitment to reevaluate security assistance programs.[78] Brzezinski instead recommended waiting for the development of a PRM on the issue for a "serious policy."[79] Although it expressed a clear commitment to complying with congressional mandates, early policy guidelines hinted at the new administration's growing dissatisfaction with the current legislation, questioning its efficacy for improving human rights in target countries. Policy guidance for the Department of State in early February tasked it with "identifying more effective means to pursue" the administration's human rights objectives beyond foreign aid.[80]

The administration sought to reassure congressional members that it was acting to build a policy framework and develop "rational criteria" that could be "applied across the board."[81] Despite being less than a month into the administration's tenure, key members of Congress were "becoming increasingly restive about not being consulted."[82] In an early February meeting, State Department staffer Lucy Benson told Congressman Fraser that Vance was "serious [about human rights] and would make certain the word reached both our Ambassadors and our people at all levels at State." Benson pointed to cuts in security assistance to Argentina, Uruguay, and, "of course,

Chile" as an indication of the administration's commitment to complying with congressional guidance, reassuring him that they "were no longer faced with a situation where the Secretary of State was unresponsive on human rights matters." Fraser acknowledged that the administration was "making a good start," but he clearly remained skeptical of its progress developing alternative mechanisms to supplement congressional guidance. Fraser recognized that military aid was an imperfect instrument, but he added that "quiet diplomacy had proved ineffective (if it had ever been used), and no cuts had ever been made except at the Congress' insistence."[83]

The Movement was also advancing its agenda to codify human rights concerns through the reform of security assistance. On February 14 the ADA released "Human Rights and Security Assistance: A Proposal for Reform," linking security assistance to a fundamental reassessment of Cold War security assumptions. "To contribute constructively to the search for solutions to the world's major problems," the report asserted, "the United States not only must possess economic and military strength, but also the political strength that comes from adherence to moral principles." Of central concern was the United States' traditional support for military dictatorships. "Third world military dictatorships are not reliable allies or linchpins of regional stability," it argued. "Giving arms to an authoritarian government, especially one guilty of major rights violations, always will have the effect of allowing the recipient government to rely less on the support of its own people." U.S. support for these regimes damaged its international leadership, eroded domestic support for foreign policy objectives, and rarely met specific security interests. Moreover, repressive regimes also undermined economic stability and prosperity. Pointing to the military coups in Argentina, Chile, and Brazil, the report argued that "each of those governments embraced economic policies which severely depressed the real wages of low-income workers." Political repression and economic inequality were inseparable.[84]

Presenting his report to the Senate Subcommittee on Foreign Assistance on March 4, Cameron framed the issue as one of democratic oversight of foreign policy. "We have learned from the Vietnam era that the American people no longer will give uncritical support to U.S. foreign policy," he informed committee members. To build a policy that the American people would support, the U.S. government must reduce its "identification with and support of foreign dictatorships." Human rights "must play a determining role, not just a rhetorical role, in deciding who is to receive U.S. arms. Only vital and strategic U.S. interests should be permitted to override human rights considerations." Although he praised Carter's human rights advocacy,

Cameron noted that aside from cuts to Argentina, Uruguay, and Ethiopia, all other assistance programs from the Ford administration remain unchanged. Congress must therefore take the opportunity to "take another step in its continuing efforts to reform the security assistance program," establishing its own authorization levels in response to human rights conditions and establishing ceilings on FMS credit programs.[85]

The Carter administration met the Movement's proposals and congressional pressure with significant attention, if not complete agreement. Hoping to regain initiative and craft policy free from further legislative encumbrance, the administration sent both Vance and Deputy Secretary of State Warren Christopher to testify before Congress in a three-week period. Speaking before the Senate Subcommittee on Operations, Vance called for a "process of self-examination and cooperative dialogue" with Congress, imbricating human rights in a larger reorientation of U.S. policies to emphasize "the increasingly important North-South dialogue," multilateralism, and conflict resolution, as well as national security. In outlining the administration's objectives for foreign aid, Vance highlighted "compassion for the poor and dispossessed," creating incentives for conflict resolution, fostering "constructive cooperation" in North-South issues, and "social progress and human rights for individuals wherever they might be." Particularly striking was Vance's emphasis on economic justice as part of a human rights agenda for foreign aid.[86] Moreover, Vance clearly accepted the premise that aid to governments that systemically violated human rights did not serve U.S. security interests.

Although he called for Congress's help in making "new directions" a reality, Vance's testimony was also a plea for patience and legislative restraint. "The Carter Administration," he reassured them, "accepts the challenge that Congress has posed" and was "working to fulfill both the letter and the spirit of current legislation relating human rights concerns to foreign assistance." He also, however, requested flexibility, noting that these human rights principles must be balanced against other national interests. "No formula can resolve the larger conflict of commitments," he argued, "but prudent and dedicated attention to both the basic objectives and the day-to-day operations of our programs can make specific problems tractable." Moreover, Vance highlighted the challenges of advancing human rights as a critical response to U.S. interventionism. "Our task," Vance noted, "is to achieve those ends without interfering in the internal affairs of other countries, mindful of the fact that there are limits to what we can achieve no matter how noble our motives."[87]

In his own testimony before the Senate Subcommittee on Foreign Assistance just three days after Cameron, Christopher sought to reassure Congress that "the concern for human rights will be woven into the fabric of our foreign policy." He also acknowledged that Congress had "a unique role to play" in strengthening U.S. human rights initiatives, including "reflecting public concern for human rights in the laws it passes" and "assuring that our domestic law is in conformity with our international obligations." Although he validated congressional guidance, Christopher, like Vance three weeks prior, made the case for patience and flexibility, arguing, "If we are to do justice to our goals, we must act always with a concern to achieve practical results and with an awareness of the other demands on our diplomacy." Christopher's call for pragmatism was obviously directed toward the complexities of linking human rights considerations to economic aid, including the new IFI's proposals taking shape. "[Give] the present legislation with human rights provisions a chance to work," Christopher requested, and then the administration and Congress could consider *together* any new legislation deemed necessary.[88]

Even with the concentrated attention paid to human rights in its first months in office, and sympathy for Movement logic, the Carter administration struggled to publicly distinguish its agenda from the more conservative approach of its predecessor.[89] WOLA, for example, praised the administration's inclusion of human rights considerations in foreign aid requests—particularly the elimination of FMS credits to Argentina and termination of security assistance to Uruguay—calling it "a welcome departure from the policies of the Nixon/Ford Administrations." It noted, however, that Congress had taken the lead on these efforts, and it criticized the administration's emphasis on "flexibility over legislative rigidity." Moreover, WOLA was critical of the FMS and economic credits still flowing to repressive regimes, noting the "increasingly large amounts of economic aid and loans from multilateral lending institutions and private banks." These funds, WOLA argued, were in effect enabling governments to acquire weapons commercially.[90]

Indeed, international financial institutions, or IFIs, had become the new front in Movement and congressional efforts to enact human rights through legislative guidance. Despite the administration's direct appeals for patience, Congress was unwilling to cede its leadership on human rights, nor was it confident that the White House intended to pursue human rights with the vigor many on the Hill wanted. On April 6 the House passed the Badillo Amendment, the stronger of two human rights amendments to the authorization bill for international financial institutions (H.R. 5262), much to the delight of the Movement. This amendment required U.S. representatives to vote against loans in international financial institutions to governments designated as human rights violators.[91]

In a letter to representatives in advance of the vote, the ADA urged Congress members to support the Badillo Amendment, arguing it would close the loophole that allowed repressive regimes to get funding for weapons when security assistance had been terminated on human rights grounds. Advocates who supported the legislation dismissed the concerns that binding amendments would unduly politicize these institutions. Cameron, for example, argued that often "banks' 'non-political,' technical criteria for granting loans . . . have subverted democratic forces," citing the increase in lending to Chile, Argentina, and the Philippines when their democracies were replaced by military dictatorships. A newsletter from the Chile Legislative Center, a solidarity group, similarly supported the Badillo Amendment and stressed it would have a "serious impact on those governments which consistently and grossly violate human rights." Chile, they noted, had "taken the edge off lost U.S. direct aid" by relying on international loans.[92]

For Congress and the Movement, this issue was about reforming governance in the United States as well as advancing human rights internationally; the two objectives clearly intertwined in the logic that underpinned these legislative proposals since Fraser's 502B amendment. The ADA letter argued that without the "enforceable language" offered by Rep. Herman Badillo (D-NY), "Congress would merely be stating policy not expressing its will. It would be, in fact, taking a step backward, against the direction of the past three years in which Congress has moved to bring human rights to the forefront of foreign policy objectives. It also is a retreat from hard-fought battles to increase the role of Congress in foreign policy affairs." The Chile Legislative Center newsletter noted that the Badillo Amendment had passed the House "in the face of lobbying efforts by State Department officials," noting the Carter administration had, "so far, opposed strong human rights language." Battle lines were being drawn, and the Carter administration and the Movement found themselves on opposing sides.[93]

The Carter administration had indeed sought to avoid amendments with binding language that required the United States to vote against loans based on human rights criteria. An internal memo following the House vote noted that "recent Congressional actions have placed the Administration in a difficult position on human rights."[94] As with security assistance, the administration was caught between wanting to demonstrate its commitment to Congress while also protecting its autonomy to integrate foreign aid into a comprehensive policy that was still taking shape. The administration was also concerned about the "many pitfalls" tying loans from multilateral institutions to human rights performance. Brzezinski had warned Carter in early March that "such a highly interventionist approach is directly contrary to the reason we have supported multilateral aid—in order to insulate economic development from politics." He continued, noting a "serious conflict of values," in leveraging loans from IFIs in the same way as military aid. "Do we deprive people of jobs and economic progress because their governments suppress human rights?" he questioned.[95] The administration viewed the Badillo Amendment, which *required* the United States to vote against loans to any country with a consistent pattern of gross human rights violations, "too wooden an approach to the problems it addresses."[96]

Although the administration questioned the efficacy of binding measures, it was also concerned that its resistance to legislative efforts would "undermine much of our credibility in our espousal of human rights as a fundamental cornerstone of our foreign policy." In an effort to signal support for the principles at the core of this legislation while still maintaining its flexibility, the administration worked with members of Congress—specifically Sen. Humphrey and Rep. Henry Reuss (D-WI)—who offered what the administration saw as moderate and workable amendments with nonbinding language and broad executive discretion in implementing human rights concerns. Vance presented the Humphrey Amendment as "a positive approach which permits us to maximize our influence for human rights within the banks and with the recipient governments." Concerned that support for the more flexible Humphrey proposal would be interpreted as an effort to "*avoid* action on human rights," the administration needed to "spell out how we intend to implement our overall policy on human rights including what we would do in the IFIs." The administration had to make clear the concrete actions it would take to "(a) disassociate the US from the offending governments and (b) influence changes in their practices," and not just leave human rights concerns at a rhetorical level.[97] In order to do this, however, the administration needed to solidify its broad human rights framework, a time-consuming task taking place behind the scenes.

In the absence of a guiding policy, the administration took a "wishy-washy" position on foreign aid in its first months. Unwilling to respond to its first congressional test by opposing human rights initiatives, but also reluctant to "shoot from the hip" and commit to policy precedents that might restrain its autonomy in the future, the administration's half measures on legislative initiatives reflected the tension between establishing domestic public credibility and retaining the flexibility necessary for the nuanced policies it wanted to develop.[98]

This tension enflamed congressional and Movement distrust of the White House, even as the administration worked to build a serious policy that shared many of their priorities. WOLA, for example, reported that the administration's approach to legislation incorporating human rights provisions into foreign aid policy had been "confused and tortuous," pointing to internal divisions and inconsistencies within the State Department. The administration's signals to "Congress regarding policy toward specific countries are unclear at best, contradictory at worst. Faced with a variety of signals from State, even a cooperative Congress had difficulty knowing how to express its support for the new administration's stand on human rights."[99]

Debate over foreign aid and IFI legislation revealed the persistent uncertainty about Carter's policy approach to human rights and his administration's commitment to the issue. Moreover, it demonstrated that the administration's early rhetoric designed to signal commitment to a skeptical Congress and public had raised unrealistic expectations about what the policy could accomplish and how it would implement its policy. Seeking to regain the initiative on human rights, Vance used his address to the University of Georgia Law School's Law Day on April 30 to lay out the administration's rationale and approach to the issue, presenting human rights as serving both U.S. interests and values. "Our own well-being, and even our security, are enhanced in a world that shares common freedoms and in which prosperity and economic justice create the conditions for peace," Vance proclaimed. His speech, consistent with the administration's early statements and policy guidelines, championed a broad range of interdependent rights that went well beyond "gross violations" to include economic and social justice issues, as well as basic human needs. "There may be disagreement on the priorities these rights deserve," he acknowledged, "but I believe that, with work, all of these rights can become complementary and mutually reinforcing."[100]

Echoing the self-critical tone foundational to the Movement's approach, Vance reminded the audience that the United States' "record is not unblemished." He added, "Let us remember that we always risk paying a serious price when we become identified with repression." Moreover, "we must always keep in mind the limits of our power and of our wisdom. A sure formula for defeat of our goals would be a rigid, hubristic attempt to impose our values on others. A doctrinaire plan of action would be as damaging as indifference." Vance also sought to avoid unrealistic expectations on what the U.S. policy could achieve. Although he believed U.S. policies could help bring a "rapid end" to some of the most egregious cases of torture and abuse, he cautioned that "the promotion of other human rights is a broader challenge," and that by undertaking the improvement of human rights in a complex international environment, the nation had "embarked on a long journey." Although the government would be diligent in its promotion of the issue, "we can nourish no illusions that a call to the banner of human rights will bring sudden transformations in authoritarian societies." Instead, a sustainable human rights policy would take patience and compromise.[101]

In his memoirs Vance explained that he wanted the address to "make clear the shape and substance of our human rights policy, and the fact that it was universal in application, yet flexible enough to be adapted to individual situations."[102] Yet his emphasis on flexibility and limits, combined with the administration's resistance to the Badillo Amendment, reinforced growing concerns among the Movement about Carter's commitment to human rights. An internal ADA report on the administration's first one hundred days in office was "pleased and proud" of the administration's human rights stance. "Nevertheless," it continued, "we must be careful to make sure that our actions do balance our rhetoric." It expressed disappointment that, with the exception of Argentina and Ethiopia, the administration had largely left Ford's security assistance budget untouched. Moreover, it presented Vance's recent calls for balance as a retreat from legislative mandates. The report concluded, "We hope that the genuine concern expressed by this administration in human rights will finally end those supports to governments which permit them to oppress their own people. . . . This is the only way that the U.S. can disassociate itself from human rights violations, and thus encourage a more open political process" in target countries. In a press release assessing the administration's first hundred days, the ADA "strongly applauded Carter's forthright statements regarding international human rights." It continued to caution, however, that "words are not enough," and it called on the administration to "end all assistance that makes the United States a party, even indirectly, to violations of human rights."[103]

A Fundamental Tenet

Vance's Law Day speech sought to clarify policy not only for the public but also for the administration itself. Internal debates over the proper response to Congress on the IFI issue in April raised concerns within the administration about the lack of consensus on the purpose and application of its human rights policy. Despite its extensive engagement with the intricacies of the issue from its first days in office, the administration still lacked explicit criteria for making decisions or assessing human rights conditions in foreign countries. Debates over IFI legislation had highlighted the internal demand for greater clarity on decision-making criteria. The administration's approach to making human rights a "fundamental tenet" required the reorganization of decision-making processes and creation of new procedures internally. Inserting these changes into a complex bureaucracy was time-consuming and often provoked debate over policy applications, as well as highlighting tensions between its multiple objectives.

Writing to Brzezinski in late April, Tuchman argued, "At this time my judgment is that the Administration's policy on human rights amounts to: 'The President is deeply committed to promoting human rights wherever possible'—and nothing more. There is no agreed conception of how human rights fits into the fabric of foreign policy, its trade-off vis-à-vis other issues . . . no idea of how to present and defend a policy that is not 100% moralistic." Tuchman lamented the absence of specific criteria and policy guidance for IFI loans and expressed frustration with the lack of an overarching policy vision.[104] This, she believed, pushed the administration to rely too heavily on punitive legislation to enact its commitment to human rights, with diminishing results. Without clearer frameworks, "we will in the interim be making ad hoc decisions which may set precedents for further decisions. While flexibility is important, we have to be careful not to make arbitrary decisions, justified in the name of human rights or basic human needs. If that happens, Congressional support will surely dwindle."[105]

Tuchman's concerns were widely but not universally shared. Significantly, Mark Schneider and Patricia Derian at the Human Rights Bureau argued that early policy action memos provided sufficient guidance for the time being and that many of the targeted issues were in fact already being addressed.[106] They instead expressed the need for flexibility and recognition of human rights conditions specific to each case. Moreover, where Tuchman continued to question the fundamental purpose of the policy, Derian and others at State pointed to Carter's public rhetoric, including his addresses to the United Nations and OAS, as well as Vance's recent Law Day speech. Indeed, in a State Department cable, Christopher circulated Vance's speech to all diplomatic posts, calling it a "comprehensive administration statement of the President's determination to place human rights considerations at the center of U.S. foreign policy." It reiterated that the administration's policy definition of human rights was not limited to "governmental violation of the integrity of the person" and included "such vital needs as food, shelter, health care and education," as well as "civil rights and political liberties." Promoting these rights, Christopher noted, "will be implemented on a case-by-case basis, according to the criteria and questions spelled out in text."[107]

The administration's statements over the first one hundred days offered a clear philosophical expression of the goals of integrating human rights into a broader reorientation of U.S. policy and interests that transcended old Cold War paradigms. Carter's address to the graduates of Notre Dame on May 22 underscored the core logic of its human rights policy for both the general public and his own staff.[108] Carter's endorsement of human rights as "a fundamental tenet of our foreign policy" evidenced the mix of national reform and international appeal at the heart of his administration's human rights agenda. He laid out his vision for a new U.S. foreign policy guided by human rights, articulating a vision that united moral strength and influence with national interests. "We can no longer separate the traditional issues of war and peace from the new global questions of justice, equity, and human rights," Carter argued. Vietnam had demonstrated the moral and strategic bankruptcy of containing communism at any cost. Now, Carter asserted, the United States was "free of that inordinate fear of communism which once led us to embrace any dictator who joined us in that fear." He continued, "For too many years, we've been willing to adopt the flawed and erroneous principles and tactics of our adversaries, sometimes abandoning our own values for theirs. We've fought fire with fire, never thinking that fire is better quenched with water. This approach failed, with Vietnam the best example of its intellectual and moral poverty." Onstage with Carter during his speech was Father Theodore Hesburgh of Notre Dame—a strong and early supporter of human rights in foreign policy—as well as Bishop Donal Lamont, Paul Cardinal Arns, and Stephen Cardinal Kim, clergy and human rights advocates from Rhodesia, Brazil, and South Korea, respectively. Carter praised their efforts to advance human rights around the world, even in the face of harsh repression. Notably, none of these advocates were from communist states but rather traditional Cold War allies.[109]

Carter's Notre Dame speech—along with his addresses to the UN and OAS, and Vance's Law Day speech—presented a coherent purpose for human rights in foreign policy, one that moved the country away from traditional Cold War security relationships and intervention that undermined human rights abroad and democracy at home. Like Vance's address a month earlier, it was intended to clarify the meaning and purpose of the administration's policy and demonstrate its commitment to a robust, nuanced human rights policy that reflected a larger reorientation of U.S. foreign policy.[110] This included a new understanding of national interests that prioritized stability and peace as essential for long-term U.S. prosperity and security, and presented a wide array of issues as germane to human rights, including basic human needs and economic development.

Although the Notre Dame address underscored key themes, it offered little on actual policy application that Tuchman and others at the NSC had sought. A "brief and somewhat confused" interagency meeting at the end of May brought these concerns to a head, exposing divides between those who wanted to discuss the instruments of implementing the policy and others who wanted to establish more clearly its overall objectives. Derian identified Vance's Law Day speech as "a major policy directive" and detailed the initiatives including country action plans for each country to provide a basis for strategies and decisions on IFIs. Tuchman responded that it was "a great speech, but not a policy."[111] Warren Christopher weighed in, arguing that although a comprehensive policy review memorandum was being written to solidify the policy apparatus, the administration had a clear policy "recently amplified" by the president in his Notre Dame address and "premised upon comprehensive statement" in Vance's Law Day speech, which "specifically defined the human rights which are the subject of our policy, set forth in detail the questions to be conserved," and detailed a range of possible instruments available to implement the policy.[112]

Debates over policy mechanisms reflected a growing rift between NSC and State about the meaning and implementation of human rights. Indeed, NSC staff frequently voiced their frustration with the State Department, particularly the Human Rights Bureau. In the midst of the IFI debate in April, Deputy National Security Advisor David Aaron wrote Brzezinski, "I am increasingly concerned that we are all over the lot on this issue [human rights]." Aaron pointed to State as a source of confusion, noting that "they don't know what they are talking about half the time." Derian in particular was often mentioned dismissively or contemptuously by NSC staff as being "unpredictable" or "talking to all the fanatics in Congress and in the NGOs, and has therefore absorbed a pretty lopsided view of things."[113]

Despite these internal rifts, there was a broadly shared commitment within the administration to bringing human rights considerations to bear on a wide array of foreign policy issues. Although some of the disagreements were driven by personal animus and bureaucratic parochialism, the debates over *how* to implement a serious human rights policy reflected the dilemmas of reconciling competing objectives and the trade-offs implicit in building human rights into the machinery of U.S. foreign policy. This shared vision, and its inherent contradictions, were evident in the PRM on human rights taking shape over the summer of 1977. The administration's human rights policy, as envisioned by the PRM, was never a freestanding objective pursued simply for its own ends, nor did it have a singular purpose in U.S. foreign policy. The PRM did not present human rights as inherently in conflict with other foreign policy objectives—such as national security, economic interests, alliances, and military strength—but the priority that one would necessarily take over the other would certainly result in tensions at times. The PRM did not dictate how the administration would strike that balance when there were competing interests; it did stress, however, that "the clear implications of making the promotion of human rights a fundamental tenet of our foreign policy is that there will henceforth be fewer instances when promotion of human rights will be viewed as a marginal objective."[114]

The PRM presented human rights as an alternative to Cold War paradigms of national interests and strategic concerns. Although effective human rights policies would "assist in the philosophical debate with the Soviet Union as to the type of society worth developing, thus helping us in those European states with competitive communist parties and in much of the Third World," this was not the primary emphasis of the policy. Instead, most of the space was devoted to developing a new framework with which to engage "non-communist" countries, replacing "a standard based on governmental behavior toward people for an increasingly outmoded Marxist–non-Marxist standard." By reestablishing the United States' commitment to freedom and democracy in the international system, it would strengthen U.S. influence among like-minded nations and serve as a pole of attraction in the developing world. Moreover, the administration intended a vigorous human rights policy to strengthen its relations with both Congress and the American public. "By permitting the moral and ethical values of our people to be reflected in that policy," human rights would engage an American public disappointed and disillusioned by Vietnam in a policy that envisioned a positive role for their country in the world.

The PRM revealed sophisticated and complex thinking about human rights issues, their role in U.S. foreign policy, and the potentials and difficulties in implementing such a policy. Like its Latin America policy, the administration's human rights framework reflected an acute awareness of the history of U.S. intervention, particularly in the Global South. It revealed a particular concern with avoiding provoking an unproductive backlash from foreign governments: "Our pressure for human rights may prompt a greater degree of repression by a government, either because it fears our criticism will encourage dissident groups to act with more strength or because it wants to demonstrate its refusal to buckle to our demands." It may also enable the target government to "wrap a banner of national sovereignty around itself," thereby gaining popular support from negative reactions to U.S. interference.

Although it did not eschew public criticism altogether, the memo cautioned that "critical public statements ought to be used sparingly, or they will lose their effectiveness: a constant stream of criticism of foreign governments may cause the United States ultimately to be ignored as a tiresome and ineffective international scold." Public advocacy, while important for raising the profile and building support for human rights in the public sphere, must be employed with discretion if it was "to retain its potency." Engagement, not alienation, was the first step to addressing particular human rights problems, with the PRM stressing that "our action with respect to the human rights conditions ought to begin with a diplomatic demarche." This strategy, however, left unanswered how to reconcile this approach with the objective of improving the nation's image by distancing it from repressive regimes it had formerly supported. Quiet diplomacy, while perhaps effective at engaging with reticent foreign leaders and mitigating charges of imperialism, also countered the administration's goals of building credibility and support for its foreign policy with key domestic constituents.

Discussions about quiet diplomacy revealed a broader challenge, that of punitive sanctions and disassociation versus engagement with repressive regimes. This debate had emerged early on in questions over foreign aid and IFI legislation. Legislative mechanisms tying foreign aid to human rights performance provided the U.S. government with some of its most tangible levers to influence change in human rights conditions abroad. Moreover, as debates earlier that year had highlighted, it also served as a measure of executive commitment to human rights concerns and democratic oversight of foreign policy. Echoing the Fraser committee's rationale codified in the 502B language, the PRM noted that "more than any other factor, U.S. security assistance implies U.S. support for the recipient regime. . . . To be perceived as supporting a repressive regime necessarily and substantially impeaches the credibility of our human rights policy." The PRM noted that the value with which other governments regarded U.S. economic and military aid provided the administration with a clear point of pressure.

Although linking foreign aid to human rights behaviors could underscore the administration's seriousness on the issue and make the costs of human rights violations tangible to offending governments, it could also damage vital U.S. security and economic interests. Punitive sanctions could prompt backlash from the targeted government, punishing disproportionately vulnerable populations the policy sought to aid. The PRM noted the difficulties of extending the "gross violators" language to IFIs without undermining a broad agenda of rights beyond political violence, especially basic human needs and economic development. The effectiveness of withholding or granting aid was qualified by a number of factors, particularly whether the target country could get similar aid and support from other sources. Even if it could obtain support from other sources, the administration should still consider the symbolic value of limiting aid, particularly security assistance, to offending regimes. At the same time, it should consider basic human needs as its own form of rights that foreign aid could support and advance.

The PRM revealed that the administration, for all its dedication to implementing human rights into the very core of its foreign policy, was better at recognizing conflicts in the policies' multiple objectives than resolving them. By calling for flexibility and the need to decide on a case-by-case basis, the PRM largely deferred the hard choices on these trade-offs. It sidestepped the contradictory demands for a visible commitment to demonstrate credibility to advocates and the subtler policy responsive to the complicated legacies of U.S. interventionism.

Slipping from Center Stage

Internal debates and inconsistencies inherent to the administration's policy between dissociation and engagement played out publicly in a series of high-profile engagements with Latin American countries in the summer and fall of 1977. As the administration worked slowly behind the scenes to put its policy framework in place, advocates increasingly looked for evidence of a policy that transcended rhetoric. The Movement applauded a visit by Rosalynn Carter to Latin America in June, which deliberately omitted the region's worst offenders, including Argentina and Chile. WOLA reported that the two-week trip was "designed to make believers even out of the staunchest critics" of the administration. It praised the administration's efforts to "convey new trends in U.S. thinking toward Latin America," first presented in the president's OAS speech. "In each of the countries visited, the human rights theme was thoughtfully expressed as a touchstone affecting the overall shape of U.S. policy."[115]

Vance's staunch defense of human rights at the OAS meeting in June, just after Mrs. Carter's return, also garnered praise from the Movement. WOLA reported that human rights concerns "completely dominated discussions" at the annual meeting, with the secretary of state standing strong against the Southern Cone's efforts to frame human rights abuses as an unavoidable response to terrorism. "In dry and measured form," the newsletter recounted, Vance argued that "'if terrorism and violence in the name of dissent cannot be condoned, neither can violence that is officially sanctioned. Such action perverts the legal system that alone assures the survival of our traditions.' The impact of his message was not lost on the assembled delegates." Moreover, the United States defended the OAS's Inter-American Commission on Human Rights "with a firmness bordering on insistence."[116]

Closer to home, staffers at NSC and the State Department regularly met with Movement groups, attending events and soliciting feedback. Shortly before Mrs. Carter's tour, Robert Pastor attended an IPS event to discuss the *Southern Connection* and Linowitz Commission reports and the president's Pan American Day speech at the OAS. Pastor reported to Brzezinski that the reception of the administration's new policy was "somewhat critical but overall quite favorable," unsurprising given the reports' influence on the shape of administration policy.[117]

Mark Schneider similarly participated in a June luncheon hosted by the IPS, attended by a number of prominent human rights groups to discuss the administration's policies, particularly the pending IFI legislation. At the event, Schneider reiterated that the administration's definition of human rights policy was "clear," pointing to Vance's Law Day and Grenada speeches. Moreover, he affirmed that the administration considered that "economic and social rights are of equal importance" to rights of the person. Although the administration believed that human rights had to act in concert with other U.S. interests, he reassured them that "since the advent of the new administration, in no case has the [State] Department made the decision to abandon human rights in favor of other considerations," pointing to the administration's recent decision to not support five IFI loans based on human rights considerations. In an attempt to underscore the institutional priority given to human rights within the State Department, he recounted recent changes in the department's organization and programming, including a full-time human rights officer in every regional bureau, the Christopher committee's coordination of interagency decision-making on foreign aid, and Patricia Derian's impending promotion from coordinator to assistant secretary. He encouraged patience, saying that "high human rights standards" may take a long time to achieve in some areas, despite the U.S. government's best efforts. Schneider painted a picture of an administration engaged, concerned, and active on human rights on a number of fronts, including IFIs and foreign aid.[118]

Despite the administration's efforts to position itself as acting in concert with Movement interests and goals, rifts emerged throughout the summer. Differences over the binding language for human rights conditions in the IFI legislation divided the administration and human rights proponents. The Movement continued to push for the more restrictive legislation as an essential component of guaranteeing executive adherence to their human rights vision; the administration's resistance to more stringent legislation raised questions as to its commitment to the issue beyond rhetoric. For advocates, this language was not just about guaranteeing the Carter administration's fidelity to legislative principles; they also believed it was strategically important as a mechanism to signal to foreign governments the material consequences of continued repression. An ADA letter to senators supporting binding legislation pointed to a recent *Washington Post* article that reported, "Encouraged by President Carter's opposition to legislation barring U.S. approval of multilateral loans to human rights violators, Latin America's military governments are awaiting an indication of where the Administration's human rights policy is heading."[119] By resisting binding legislation in the name of flexibility, the administration was thus undermining its own credibility with the targets of its policy.

A July memo of the HRWG meeting made clear that foreign aid legislation continued to be a critical litmus test of administration policy. Cameron reported to the group that the Badillo Amendment "will probably be compromised to give more flexibility to the Administration to support loans to repressive regimes even when the loans are not for projects which benefit basic human needs." He thus suggested the group focus on some country-specific legislation, such as an amendment barring military training for Argentina and cuts in military aid to the Philippines. Given the ongoing disagreements with the administration over legislation advancing human rights, the HRWG established four major subcommittees, including one to monitor pending legislation and an "Executive Watch-Dog to monitor the Executive Branch implementation of existing legislation and to develop HRWG proposals for impacting on IFI loan decisions, 502(b) reports, and country-by-country aid allocations."[120] This organizational move clearly signaled its ongoing dissatisfaction with the administration's approach. WOLA's August newsletter reported that "this year's foreign assistance legislation has been a sort of testing ground for implementation of human rights legislation." The newsletter acknowledged that the administration had "begun a process of institutionalization of the human rights 'machinery' in the Departments of State, Treasury, and Defense. But," the newsletter continued, "the Administration also gives mixed signals on human rights, has not been consistent within itself, backs away from criticism of specific countries, resists legislation for the sake of 'flexibility,' and lobbies against some human rights legislation." WOLA lamented recent congressional willingness to cede initiative to Carter "to execute the law *as he sees fit*."[121]

The Movement's dissatisfaction with the administration's desire for flexibility was evident in the ADA's letter to representatives before the final vote on IFI legislation in September, which it labeled "the most important vote of this legislative session." The letter was dismissive of the administration's policy thus far, calling it simply "rhetoric," and argued that without binding measures, it was unlikely the U.S. government would prompt any real progress on human rights conditions or changes in its foreign policy. "In speech after speech," Cameron reported, "officials have made it clear that the Administration does not believe in 'negative sanctions'[;] in other words it favors with rare exceptions, the continuation of military aid, Export-Import Bank loans, and a 'yes' vote on every loan project in the international banks." The current amendment included greater executive discretion than earlier amendments; given its depiction of the administration's human rights stance, it was not surprising that the ADA presented the bill's human rights provision as "worthless" in its current form. The ADA urged Congress to vote down the measure and send it back for revision.

The Movement presented the clash with the administration over the Badillo Amendment as more than just extending human rights provisions to multilateral lending bodies, or as differences in strategy. The letter argued that this vote would define *"the very substance of the United States human rights policy"* and Congress's role in policy making. The central issue, the ADA explained, "is whether Congress will accept a growing role in foreign economic policy and put teeth into the human rights policy of the United States, or acquiesce to the rhetoric of the Administration's policy."[122] Despite the administration's votes in favor of human rights in IFIs over the past months, its position on binding legislation was a litmus test for fidelity to the human rights issue. The Movement and its congressional allies were unwilling to simply wait and see how Carter officials resolved inconsistencies. Implementation of a serious, sustainable human rights policy required the curtailment of executive autonomy and greater congressional oversight.

Congressional legislation was not the only place where divides over strategy emerged between advocates and the administration. The final debates on IFIs overlapped with Assistant Secretary of State for Latin America Affairs Terence Todman's visit to Latin America. This visit, unlike Mrs. Carter's two months prior, included a series of talks with the military governments in Chile and Argentina. After his meetings, Todman praised the progress on human rights in both countries over the last year.[123] Although Todman had pressured both governments quite vigorously on human rights in the meetings, his seemingly unhesitant praise muddled perceptions of the administration's position and cast it as unsympathetic to the vast ongoing human rights problems. In a letter to President Carter, the U.S.-based Argentine Commission for Human Rights called Todman's statements "misleading" and argued, *"These misrepresentations can only favor the resurgence of a U.S. policy conciliatory with the repressive military regimes of Latin America—a policy thoroughly discredited among the peoples of the world and the people of the United States."*[124] If dissociation was a marker of the administration's sincerity on its new human rights initiatives, the message Todman gave the public was one of indifference, where concern for human rights remained at a rhetorical level.

The Todman incident was closely followed by an even greater affront in the eyes of the advocate community: the official invitation to Washington of Generals Pinochet and Videla, along with the other heads of state in the region, for the signing of the Panama Canal Treaties in September 1977. It was a gala event, celebrating the capstone achievement of the administration's first year. Carter saw these treaties as an important symbol of respect for regional sovereignty and self-determination, a key goal and component to the nation's larger policy objectives and interests in the region. The treaties signaled a new relationship with the region as a whole, not just Panama, and as such, the administration believed it was important to have all the region's leaders present. Interestingly, some of the event's strongest critics, such as the IPS, had promoted the treaty as a top priority for regional affairs, arguing that a willingness to turn control of the Canal over to Panama was a symbol of a change in U.S.–Latin American relations.[125] The administration planned to use the visit not only to emphasize a greater respect for national sovereignty in the region but also to press leaders on human rights in private meetings—two goals that went hand in hand in the administration's Latin America policy. A memo from Brzezinski to Carter in advance of the bilateral meetings noted that they provided a "unique opportunity to make genuine progress on a number of important issues." He continued, "The Southern Cone leaders will need to hear directly from you of your commitment to human rights, your willingness to recognize *real* improvement (as opposed to announcement of intention)."[126]

The administration's attempt to promote human rights while also signaling greater respect for sovereignty and regional governments confused many outside of the administration and fostered misunderstandings and distrust with the Movement. In the same letter to Carter that criticized Todman's statements on Argentina, the Argentine Commission for Human Rights expressed dismay over the upcoming meetings. The organization noted that in recent weeks, the military government had launched a massive, international public relations campaign to improve its image. "In this context, your upcoming meeting with General Videla acquires special significance," they warned. "Interested parties in the U.S. and particularly in those countries ruled by discredited and diplomatically isolated regimes, will attempt to portray your hosting and meeting with the Latin American dictators as an expression of tacit support for their past and current policies, as well as a departure from your stated intention on human rights." Moreover, the press in Argentina was already portraying the scheduled meeting between Carter and General Videla as a "significant diplomatic achievement" on the part of the Argentine military government. "We fear, Mr. President, that unless you explicitly and publicly disassociate yourself from the dictator and brutal practices of some of your guests you may, in the eyes of the world, be lastingly identified with them."[127]

Many in the Movement expressed similar concerns over the upcoming meetings and Pinochet's invitation to Washington. One solidarity newsletter observed that the twenty-seven leaders of the Western Hemisphere nations "share more than language and a common interest in the Panama Canal; for the most part, they are right-wing military dictators united in their fervent belief that socialism is evil and must be suppressed at all costs. Ultimately, this has meant stripping their citizens of their most basic civil and political liberties. In most countries this has been accomplished by means of brutal repression." In Chile, the newsletter pointed to the continued state of siege, in effect since the 1973 coup, including the absence of political freedoms, economic impoverishment, and media censorship. By extending invitations to these leaders, the Carter administration "simultaneously shows a lack of sensitivity and political wisdom. An Administration committed to making human rights an integral part of its foreign policy can only lose credibility and respect when its actions appear hypocritical."[128] For those who had been skeptical from the beginning about the sincerity of Carter's human rights policy, this invitation reaffirmed their doubts.

In an open letter to the president published in the *Washington Post* on the first day of the meetings, a number of human rights advocates wrote that they "condemned the Pinochet visit with the full weight of our moral consciousness." The letter focused on the 1,500 disappeared people in Chile and urged Carter to demand of Pinochet answers as to their whereabouts. It also asked Carter to state publicly his views "on the human rights situation in Chile, Argentina, Uruguay, and other countries of the Americas where arbitrary rules and repression are the institutions of daily life. Bestowing on these dictators the same honors reserved for genuine representation of democratic nations serves only to cast doubt on the true meaning of your human rights policy and to lessen the moral prestige of the nation in the world community."[129]

Members of Congress mobilized on human rights were equally disturbed by the meetings, particularly those with Pinochet and Videla. In the week before the meeting, Senator Abourezk wrote to Carter, urging him "as strongly as possible, that because of the human rights situation in Chile, that you not meet with General Augusto Pinochet." Such a meeting, Abourezk argued, would only further empower Pinochet and continue the dire human rights violations taking place under his leadership. "As a clear demonstration of our deep concern," the senator concluded, "I hope your contact with General Pinochet will be solely at the signing of the Treaty . . . and that you will not hold private conversations with him."[130] Brzezinski wrote to Abourezk, noting that these meetings were important for advancing a whole host of concerns in the administration's new regional policy. He reassured the senator that human rights was a key topic of discussion, and that the administration was "hopeful that the President's discussions will have the effect of encouraging the observance of human rights throughout Latin America." In response to a similar entreaty from Representative Burton, the administration acknowledged his concerns but explained, "Our feeling is that even though we disagree with [Pinochet's and Videla's] human rights policy, it is always better to talk with them than to refuse to meet with them. Only by discussion can we hope to persuade them to change their actions."[131]

Carter's meetings with Pinochet and Videla did, in fact, put human rights front and center. In a clear break from the "quiet diplomacy" of the Ford administration, Carter utilized the bilateral meetings to press them on specific human rights concerns. In his talk with Pinochet, Carter prompted a discussion on human rights, stating that "he wished to ventilate the matter in a frank and positive way . . . and invited President Pinochet to analyze the Chilean situation to help him understand the situation." Carter did not

Figure 7. Flyer for a solidarity rally protesting Carter's invitation of Augusto Pinochet and other Latin American dictators to Washington, D.C., for the signing of Panama Canal Treaties in September 1977. Courtesy of Rubenstein Library, Duke University.

challenge Pinochet's assertions that the Chilean government "was the victim of a vast and successful Marxist propaganda campaign" but instead urged him to come up with "Chilean solutions" that would also be acceptable to the international community. Carter utilized Pinochet's assertion that there was no serious human rights problem to push him to accept two UN observers to verify that this was, in fact, the case. In a significant breakthrough, Pinochet agreed to this proposal, after having previously blocked such UN access. Although it would take more than six months to finalize arrangements, Carter, by engaging in direct talks, was able to secure entry for international human rights observers.[132]

Although quiet diplomacy did secure access for UN inspectors, Carter's talk with Pinochet would have been ineffective had public opinion not made human rights violations a liability for the Pinochet regime. Massive protests in Washington disproportionately focused on Pinochet as a symbol of abuses perpetrated by U.S. allies and abetted by U.S. policies. The pressure created by advocates and Congress necessitated action by the Chilean government to address its human rights problem. It also created pressure on the Carter administration itself. Not being privy to the private conversations, advocates relied on public statements to gauge the administration's efforts. Pinochet undercut the administration's credibility by announcing publicly after the meeting that he and Carter agreed on human rights issues. The seeming goodwill between the two men further exacerbated the growing distrust of the administration's commitment and sincerity, and it reinforced suspicions that Carter, like Ford, was more interested in optics than real changes in human rights conditions.[133]

At the heart of the Movement's disaffection with the administration were tensions, anticipated but unresolved in the PRM, particularly the use of quiet diplomacy as a legitimate instrument of human rights policy. "Words are action," Carter had declared in his Notre Dame address, and the administration had built its credibility and policy on forceful rhetoric in its early months. WOLA's October newsletter stated, "In the early days, the Administration distinguished itself as the human rights rhetorician par excellence," and it praised the administration for giving human rights "central billing" in its speeches, laying aside "standard prescriptions in favor of a new respect for human rights and ideological diversity." Symbolic actions such as Mrs. Carter's visit to the region and the "sensitive messages he conveyed to many governments [were] similarly persuasive." At the end of Carter's first year, however, WOLA expressed concern that human rights "has slipped from center stage." The article noted that administration officials were speaking about the issue less frequently, "and when they do speak, especially Assistant Secretary Todman, it is often to cite with satisfaction even the slightest hint that a regime is improving its human rights record."[134]

Indeed, a critical corollary to the perceived change in rhetoric was the question of positive engagement versus punitive sanctions. WOLA noted that the administration increasingly resisted withholding aid. "Besides, as they never tire of saying, there must also be some 'carrots.'" While the Movement was ready to acknowledge that a purely punitive policy would not be effective, the critical question remained, "What constitutes improvement?" Where the administration sought to encourage incremental improvements, advocates saw cosmetic changes designed to appease international critics. "While such 'improvements are salutary' they are but minor behavioral modifications which leave untouched the institutional mechanisms of repression." The administration, by praising such inconsequential changes, lost both its leverage with the regimes and its respect from the Movement.[135]

An article in the *Washington Post* in late October captured the administration's tenuous position with the Movement. The article reported, "Nagging fears that the Carter administration is going soft on human rights are being voiced on Capitol Hill and in some private organizations concerned with the issue." Although the administration remained firmly committed to its human rights policies and agenda, its change in tone in recent months had fostered doubts among human rights leaders. The article contrasted Carter's assertions in his inaugural address that "our commitment must be absolute" with the quieter public stance the administration had taken in recent months. Ed Snyder of the Friends Committee on National Legislation argued, "With regard to giving military aid to repressive regimes, I see little difference between this administration and the Nixon-Ford approach." The article also quoted Joe Eldridge of WOLA, who observed, "Rhetorically, the administration has modified its position. Such a pulling back is bound to affect the whole momentum. . . . We don't wonder about their basic commitment, but about their implementation. Competing interests are going to play a much greater role."[136]

Ironically, even as they doubted the administration's commitment to human rights, not all advocates viewed the more restrained government rhetoric as a negative. Cameron, speaking on behalf of the HRWG, approved of the administration taking a quieter approach. "All those high-level statements didn't do a damn thing to improve the situation for dissenters or political prisoners or emigration." Perhaps advocates' ambivalence about the administration was best captured by Rep. Fraser, who told the *Post*, "I think

the quieter approach was what was required. Once the issue moves into quieter channels, the question is: what is happening?" In those two sentences,
Fraser expressed both the support and distrust that marked the Movement's
relationship with the Carter administration as it approached the one-year
mark.[137]

On February 17, 1978—more than a year after taking office—the Carter administration released its long-awaited presidential directive on human rights.
The final draft clearly affirmed human rights as a "fundamental tenet" of
U.S. foreign policy, reflecting a broader reorientation of national interests
away from Cold War national security imperatives of containment, and it included a broad range of rights as relevant to U.S. policy and interests.[138] Like
the Movement, Carter's human rights agenda was also grounded in an effort
to restrain U.S. interventionism and tacitly acknowledged U.S. complicity in
foreign abuses, particularly in Latin America. His administration sought to
develop a policy that would legitimize human rights principles in international relations, address violations around the world, and change both the
United States' image and behavior in the international sphere and engender
trust in the government domestically.

In a review of the administration's first year, Brzezinski reported to
Carter that its early foreign policy was "a relative success." U.S. foreign policy,
Brzezinski stated, had been "clearly in need of broad renovation" breaking
from "a heavy concentration on the U.S.-Soviet relationship, with most other
aspects of foreign policy being derivative of that relationship." He noted that
"the administration has not gone for quick success or band-aids; on the contrary, it has undertaken responses which are potentially of a more structural
enduring kind." Brzezinski pointed to the Panama Canal Treaties, "a new
maturity" in U.S.–Latin American relations, and wide-ranging negotiations
with the Soviet Union even while "deemphasizing the primacy of U.S.-Soviet
relations" in U.S. foreign policy. Among its strengths was identification of
U.S. foreign policy with human rights for both domestic and international
audiences, "generating some genuine progress regarding human rights."
The administration's commitment to the issue was not merely symbolic; it
had made structural changes so that "human rights has been woven into the
bureaucracy."[139]

Even as he lauded these changes, he noted that they had created some
uncertainty about the administration's vision. "Except for the Notre Dame
address," there had been "inadequate articulation of our broad foreign
policy assumptions and priorities." For human rights specifically, this led

to difficulties with Congress. "The leading human rights advocates on the Hill," Brzezinski noted, "are still not convinced that the administration is serious." This resulted in part from a muddled public message, as well as dissent within the administration over its approach to adding human rights criteria to IFIs. The administration's attempt to find a middle ground between absolute denunciation of foreign governments and "business as usual" with a more subdued public advocacy and calls for flexibility alienated some of its strongest supporters in the human rights community.[140]

The Carter administration's initial efforts, both public and private, were colored by the legacies of the Ford administration's engagement with human rights. Carter's uncompromising advocate vision of human rights policy in his early days in office quickly collided with the more quiet and subtle policy mechanisms needed to promote actual change in conditions abroad. Moreover, the policy frameworks it developed left unresolved some of the tensions innate in the administration's conceptualization of its human rights policy. This reflected the complexities and context-specific nature of human rights problems, but it made it all the more difficult to communicate with an energized but skeptical advocate community and Congress, and it opened the administration to charges of inconsistency and hypocrisy. As with the Nixon and Ford administrations, Chile, and later Argentina, became the place to test the United States' commitment to human rights and measure both the administration's effectiveness and sincerity.

Chapter 3

A Special Responsibility

Human Rights and U.S.-Chilean Relations

"The tyranny of the Pinochet government has now been extended to Washington," declared Senator James Abourezk.[1] Two days earlier, on the morning of September 21, 1976, former Chilean ambassador to the United States Orlando Letelier was killed, along with a young coworker named Ronnie Moffitt, when a bomb exploded under his car as they drove to work along Embassy Row in Washington, D.C. As the investigation unfolded, evidence pointed to the complicity of Chile's secret police (DINA) and the highest levels of Chile's military regime; only ten days before his death, this same regime, under the leadership of General Augusto Pinochet, had stripped Letelier of his citizenship for "gravely endangering the essential interests of the state."[2] Letelier had been one of the most visible and outspoken opponents of the Pinochet government and its human rights violations. Exiled from Chile after the 1973 coup, he arrived in Washington, D.C., as a senior fellow at the Institute for Policy Studies in the fall of 1975. His assassination further disrupted already tense relations between the United States and Chile, strained by widespread reports of Chilean human rights abuses, congressional hearings, and pressure from human rights groups.[3] By 1979, conflicts over Letelier's assassination brought relations between the two countries to their nadir after the Chilean supreme court refused to extradite to the United States three high-level Chilean officials implicated in the assassination.

During the Carter presidency, human rights issues dominated U.S. relations with Chile, culminating in the failed extradition request in the Letelier case. In the years since the September 11 coup, Chile had become a potent symbol for the Movement of the failures of U.S. Cold War alliances, and the preeminent test case for the new human rights policy mechanisms. The unique history of U.S. intervention in support of the military coup loomed large in debates about human rights abuses in the country and regional policy more broadly. Chile was exceptional in the public attention it garnered and the degree to which the United States' own policies were implicated in the abusive regime. Yet precisely because of its unique aspects, U.S.-Chilean relations became the terrain to debate and assess the Carter administration's human rights agenda in Latin America and beyond.

The Carter administration's approach to Chile revealed the tension between two key dimensions of its human rights objectives: distancing the United States from dictators such as Pinochet and the Cold War alliances he symbolized, and advancing tangible improvements in human rights conditions. In Chile these two objectives became increasingly embedded in opposing strategies—isolation of the regime, which supported the former, and bargaining to advance the latter. The Carter administration pursued a policy that balanced the two, dramatically cooling bilateral relations but maintaining diplomatic channels to push for changes that would empower Chilean actors to reform their own government. The administration's strategy was based on its recognition that the Pinochet government sought international legitimacy, but not at the expense of its internal control. Eschewing overt regime change, the administration pursued an agenda of pragmatic, incremental changes, responsive to local conditions and leaders, that recognized the limits of U.S. influence but remained true to its human rights vision.

Carter sought to use human rights to move U.S. policies toward a greater respect for sovereignty and ideological diversity in the Western Hemisphere in the shadow of U.S. hegemony and paternalism. Yet the public criticism of human rights conditions in Chile, vocal support of U.S. advocates, and aggressive pursuit of Letelier's assassins drew the Carter administration perilously close to the patterns it sought to reshape—namely, U.S. interference in internal affairs of Latin American countries. An aggressive human rights policy risked provoking a nationalist backlash to perceived U.S. intervention in Chile's judicial system and infringement on its sovereignty. Not wishing to mirror the interventionism it critiqued nor back away from its commitment to human rights, the Carter administration sought a course of action that would promote human rights in Chile without compromising the change in U.S. behavior that Carter's human rights policy promised.

Although the Carter administration, often working in tandem with the Movement, was able to secure some modest improvements in human rights in Chile, its policies resulted in a serious rift between the administration and some of the staunchest human rights supporters within the United States. Distrust of the executive's commitment to human rights fostered in the Nixon-Ford years, paired with the Pinochet regime's inconsistent and unreliable response to diplomatic pressures, undermined Movement support for Carter's moderate strategy. The administration's reliance on a flexible approach that simultaneously engaged and marginalized the regime looked inconsistent at best and a return to Cold War "business as usual" at worst. Yet more aggressive approaches invited criticism of intervention, potentially rallying a counterproductive nationalistic backlash without necessarily advancing human rights or national interests. Pinochet himself had become such a polarizing figure that the Movement saw any effort by U.S. officials to praise him for positive developments in Chile's human rights conditions as a betrayal of its human rights policy. Dissatisfied with the slow, grudging concessions offered by the Pinochet regime, the Movement instead pushed the White House for more vigorous public diplomacy, isolating and perhaps

Figure 8. A September 26, 1976, rally in Washington, D.C., protesting the killing of Orlando Letelier and Ronnie Moffitt. Letelier and Moffitt had died five days earlier when a bomb planted under their car exploded as they drove to work along Embassy Row in Washington, D.C.
Courtesy of AP Photos.

even destabilizing the Chilean leadership. Pinochet, in turn, rallied a nationalist defense to U.S. human rights pressures, condemning them as intervention in Chile's internal affairs. The Carter administration consistently rejected a Cold War basis as a rationale for repression or a foundation for relations for the two countries, even as it failed to convince its own public of its commitment to human rights there or bring Letelier and Moffitt's assassins to justice.

A Special Responsibility

The Carter administration's initial approach to Chile reflected its twin desire for an effective human rights agenda and a less interventionist policy. Further complicating the desire to improve human rights was the equally strong necessity of distancing Washington from its previously close relations with the Chilean military leadership. The Carter administration had to cool relations with Santiago to demonstrate its seriousness on its human rights program yet maintain relations sufficient to exert influence. At first these goals proved to be mutually reinforcing as a distant and critical posture demonstrated a commitment to human rights to the public and the Chilean government.

During his campaign, Carter had not shied away from criticizing both the Chilean government and past U.S. policies in the country.[4] He came to office with a clear rejection of the warm Nixon-Ford relations with the regime, symbolizing a fresh approach to human rights and foreign policy more broadly. In a press conference two weeks after his election, Carter pointed specifically to Chile as an example of the pervasiveness of human rights problems in the world and their interconnection with misguided Cold War policies. "I think here again the attitude of our nation's people and our government toward another foreign government like Chile's would be very seriously affected by an absence of concern for human rights," Carter stated. He continued noting that in the past year, Chile had received almost 80 percent of the U.S. Food for Peace allocations in the region, concluding, "I think the allocation of foreign aid and the normal friendship of our country would be determined or affected certainly by the attitude of those countries toward human rights." Food aid, like other forms of economic assistance, had become a sensitive point for the Movement as it had become a means for the Ford administration to circumvent congressional restrictions on military aid to Chile. Solidarity newsletters circulated Carter's news conference statements, calling them "encouraging" and "a sharp contrast to the Nixon-Ford Administration."[5]

The Chilean government had been cavalier about Carter's campaign rhetoric, saying, "It is very difficult to maintain that which is said before the election, because in that moment, one doesn't have responsibilities."[6] Pinochet himself declared the day after Carter's victory, "Chile will never double over before any type of pressure or threats."[7] Despite its public bluster, the Chilean junta faced the unavoidable conclusion that its human rights record was becoming a serious liability to its international standing and its domestic legitimacy. A newsletter by the solidarity group Chile Committee for Human Rights reported that "the atmosphere in Santiago was nervous before the election," noting that "Carter's statements during the campaign had been carefully analyzed by the [pro-government] press." An internal report of the Vicaría de la Solidaridad (Vicaría) stated in October 1976 that the upcoming U.S. elections, and the apparently strong support from Congress and the U.S. public for the termination of foreign aid to governments with systematic violations of basic human rights, were indeed creating pressure on the regime to act. "In this context, the detentions and disappearances are reduced," the Vicaría reported.[8]

Two weeks after the U.S. elections, and the day after Carter's November 15 press conference in which he specifically targeted Chile's human rights record, the Chilean government announced its decision to release 302 political prisoners. Pinochet asserted that this action was undertaken in the spirit of "Christian humanity" and "absolutely sovereign and free from considerations of foreign pressure." The prisoner release was followed by a decree relaxing internal political restrictions and easing limitations placed on Chileans in "internal exile," allowing them to travel around the country. At a press conference following the announcement of the prisoner release, Pinochet insisted that this was not a response to Carter's election and that he had already decided on these measures in September. He declared, "I do not let anyone influence me."[9] Carter's election did not singularly prompt these actions by the Chilean government, but his successful candidacy emphasized the growing costs of human rights violations for Chilean relations with the United States and the international community.

The U.S. press hailed the prisoner release as a response to Carter's public statements on human rights, and U.S. embassy sources in Santiago and intelligence reports cast these actions by the Chilean government as an effort to deal with new international pressures on human rights issues.[10] The Movement shared this sentiment and also lauded the change in tone in Washington.

At the same time, Movement actors were quick to qualify this "victory" as primarily superficial and cautioned against undue optimism. An op-ed by Mary McGrory, a journalist sympathetic to Movement objectives and views, credited Carter's election with the release, writing, "He has had a rather dazzling demonstration of how he can make tyrants quake. The question is, will he require them to do more." She cautioned, "If Carter thinks that the junta's sudden, cosmetic mercy is enough, of course, it will be a propaganda victory for the rulers of the police state we helped to create in Latin America's oldest democracy." Joe Eldridge shared McGrory's assessment, expressing concern that the prisoner release "may be taken as a signal by progressives here that the Junta is serious about reform. It's Carter's first diplomatic coup. I hope he won't be led astray."[11] The Chile Committee for Human Rights newsletter similarly reported that "this limited gesture by Pinochet is a clear response to the Carter election. . . . Mr. Carter's tough statements during the campaign have clearly worried the generals." It continued, however, to challenge the notion that the Pinochet regime was fundamentally recalibrating its systems of repression. "Policymakers should not harbor any illusions about the ability of the generals to reform themselves," the newsletter warned. As long as Pinochet remained in power, "human rights are and will continue to be violated." The limited prisoner release was simply a "calculated gambit" to generate positive publicity and reduce pressure for more systemic changes.[12] Movement statements about the prisoner release revealed an abiding belief that the Pinochet government was irredeemable.

Chile was a symbol of a broader commitment to a particular vision of human rights constructed by the Movement in the past three years. During Carter's first week in office, the administration's attentiveness to the Movement's agenda was evident in an emerging problem with a Chilean official— Lieutenant Colonel Jaime Lavin—currently visiting the United States on a U.S. government international visitor grant.[13] An Amnesty International report had recently identified Lavin as a torturer, and solidarity groups quickly mobilized to protest his visit in New York and San Francisco.[14] The issue escalated on January 24, when journalist Jack Anderson raised the issue on *Good Morning America*, lamenting that "the State Department invited accused Chilean torturer to the United States as a guest of the taxpayers." Anderson's appearance on morning television, detailing the conversion of Chile's Air Force War College into a "house of torture" after the coup, reinforced the image of a morally depraved regime in Santiago and called into question the Carter administration's commitment to human rights in its first days in office.[15]

The Carter administration, taking the Movement's charges against Lavin seriously, responded quickly. The next day, the State Department issued press guidance stating that it was assessing the accuracy of the claims, "but obviously we would not have invited any foreign leader when we had any reason to believe he had engaged in acts of this kind." It simultaneously sent State Department officers to Los Angles to meet with Lavin and "encourage him to cut short his visit." When Lavin resisted, arguing that to leave would be an "admission of guilt," the administration pressured the Chilean government to recall him, arguing it was in the best interest of both countries. Although it sought to minimize damage to U.S.-Chilean relations, the administration was clear that if the Chilean government did not recall Lavin, the United States would revoke his visa unilaterally. Wishing to avoid further embarrassment, the Chilean government conceded, and Lavin left the United States on January 29, almost a week earlier than scheduled.[16]

The administration's response—both public and private—evidenced a desire to avoid an ugly public relations problem in its first days in office. Vance reported, "We have strong indications from Congress, voluntary organizations and the press that this issue, if not dealt with soon, could become a significant public and political problem."[17] The administration did not deal with this simply as a public relations problem, however, and its response revealed its connection to and confidence in the Movement's sources and positions. In response to letters written by private citizens upset by Lavin's visit, administration officials reiterated that the president was "watching events in Chile very closely" and would continue to "represent the concern of many U.S. citizens about reports of abuse of internationally recognized human rights in Chile."[18] These were more than empty assurances—the administration pursued information about these charges well after Lavin had left the United States, seeking out affidavits, canvassing the embassy, and meeting several times with Amnesty International to discuss its reporting and sources.[19] Moreover, the State Department stood behind Amnesty International's evidence internally, when disputes arose about the handling of the case with the U.S. ambassador to Chile, David Popper, a Nixon appointee. Popper criticized the administration's decision to act so decisively on unsubstantiated charges. Bill Luers at the Latin America desk countered that the evidence provided by Amnesty International was compelling. Luers continued, "Moreover, a persuasive factor, which frankly should have been considered before Lavin was even proposed for this travel grant was his association with the air war college during the time when it was by many valid reports the worst torture location in Chile. This is not simply guilt by association.

Given the infamous nature of that institution during a period when he was involved in its activities, the possibility of his knowledge, if not direct acquiescence in torture should have raised questions."[20] This logic reflected the broader changes in thinking about human rights taking place under the new administration, even as it revealed residual bureaucratic trends from the Ford years.

The administration moved to take symbolic actions beyond the Lavin affair. It signaled its disapproval of human rights violations in Chile by delaying for almost two months the formal interview to give credentials to Chile's newly appointed ambassador, Jorge Cauas. When Carter did meet with the ambassador at the end of March to accept his credentials, the short meeting focused almost entirely on the human rights situation in Chile and its negative impact on relations between the two countries. Carter also praised moderate improvements in recent months, telling the ambassador that he would publicize additional measures and assuring him that "the United States is prepared to go more than halfway over the next few months to see improved relations" if the Chilean government addressed its human rights problems.[21]

A proposed visit by former Chilean president and moderate opposition leader Eduardo Frei to the White House in May highlighted the significance of Chile to the administration's signature foreign policy initiative and the challenges it faced.[22] The visit, initiated by WOLA, became a forum for the administration to discuss and develop its policy vis-à-vis Chile as a whole.[23] In a memo to Brzezinski in anticipation for Frei's visit, Pastor cautioned, "The policy which we set towards Chile in the months ahead will also have very serious and lasting implications for our policy on human rights." With Chile as a harbinger of U.S. policy, Pastor saw two different approaches the administration could take to the Pinochet regime, each with their own challenges. The first was to "draw the line of 'gross violators' around Chile, declare it a pariah, and seek support for such a policy among other democratic countries." This would mean extending U.S. prohibition on loans to Chile to international bodies and financial institutions, supporting sanctions in the United Nations, holding high-profile meetings with opposition leaders, and "essentially keep[ing] a distant and cool posture." This strategy assumed that such pressures would ultimately lead to the emergence of a Chilean replacement for Pinochet. The second policy strategy would be "to try to bargain with Pinochet, seeking specific and concrete signs of moderation and minimal respect for human rights." Although Pastor did not recommend one strategy over the other, he noted that Carter's decision on whether to meet with Frei would essentially signal which of these two paths the administration intended to take.[24]

Frei's proposed visit highlighted the difficulty of creating pressure without swerving into the counterproductive interventionist or paternalistic role that its human rights policy sought to remedy. The administration assumed that the Pinochet regime would interpret Carter's meeting with Frei as "interference in internal affairs or perhaps even an effort to overthrow the present regime." This might lead to the cessation of any incremental progress on human rights in Chile that U.S. pressure had prompted thus far. That said, the core question remained: was U.S. policy pressure "at all effective? Or does the U.S. have anything to lose and perhaps something to gain by alienating the Pinochet government and declaring it a pariah?"[25] Could the administration improve human rights through bilateral initiatives without implicitly legitimizing Pinochet's government? In a memo to the vice president, Brzezinski succinctly outlined the dilemma the administration faced regarding Frei's visit. "If we refused to meet with [Frei], Pinochet would see it as an endorsement of his regime, and human rights groups in the US would say that our policy was only aimed at the Soviet Union." However, Pinochet was likely to regard a White House meeting with Frei as "a sign that the US is crowning his opposition, and he may accelerate the current wave of repression."[26] Complicating the politics of Frei's potential meeting was the simultaneous visit of another member of the Chilean opposition. Clodomiro Almeyda—foreign minister under Allende and leader of the leftist Unidad Popular party—had arranged an unpublicized meeting with Assistant Secretary of State Warren Christopher for the same week as Frei. The reception of two high-profile opponents of the regime in such close proximity reinforced the optics of interference in Chilean political life. Indeed, the U.S. embassy in Chile cautioned that "the reception of Cardinal Silva, Frei, and Almeyda in quick succession by White House officials . . . will cause unrestrained fury in Chile." In the margins of the report, Brzezinski replied, "Tough!"[27]

Still, the administration had been cautious about the specter of interventionism, particularly sensitive in Chile given the recent shared history of the two countries. In response to a PRM draft on Latin America in March, the State Department reported, "US intervention in the internal affairs of other countries . . . cast a pall" over regional relations, citing the U.S. intervention in Chile.[28] A May policy brief similarly cautioned, "Many in Latin American ruling circles regard our actions and words [on human rights] as intervention in their domestic affairs."[29] Even if this criticism was strategically deployed by the regimes targeted by new policies, it nevertheless had salience with a Latin American audience given the long history of U.S. regional hegemony. The Latin America Bureau queried, "Given our past history and current interests and programs, how do we deal with the continuing charge that we are interventionist in Latin America?"[30]

Seeking to limit damage to bilateral relations and minimize charges of intervention, the administration decided that Frei should meet with Brzezinski and Vice President Mondale instead of President Carter due to "scheduling difficulties." It also chose to keep the meeting an "informal discussion" with little press coverage and no official statement afterward. In an effort to maintain channels of influence and communication with Santiago, Luers met with the Chilean ambassador the day before Frei's visit. Luers stressed "that the Chilean government should not interpret this visit in any negative way." He continued, "Despite [U.S.] concerns over human rights questions, the U.S. government has no intention whatsoever to undermine or overthrow the present Chilean government"; the meetings were simply an opportunity for the Carter administration to hear from a wide range of voices. The Chilean ambassador, unmoved by this line of reasoning, observed that the Carter administration's "receiving two of the major opponents to his government at nearly the same time will be extremely difficult for his government to comprehend, and the resulting harmful effects on U.S.-Chilean relations cannot be 'minimized.' "[31]

The administration was concerned that Pinochet would rally a credible defense domestically by recasting pressures on human rights as another case of U.S. intervention in their internal affairs.[32] Still, the administration's own assessment was that its early pressures on human rights had been welcomed by popular opposition in Chile. A May report on the impact of Carter's human rights policy in Latin America noted that "many democratic opposition parties and groups like the Christian Democrats in Chile have hailed the new U.S. message and have been less reluctant to protest political repression."[33] This was reinforced by meeting with Movement activists, who reported that Chileans were "refreshed" by the administration's early policies, and encouraged the administration to keep the pressure on. WOLA, who orchestrated Frei's visit, believed that the United States had more leverage it could deploy before hitting the point of intransigence with the regime. In a meeting with Pastor ahead of Frei's visit, Eldridge encouraged the administration to keep pressure on the regime, arguing that the "Chilean government would be forced to accommodate itself to the United States because of economic conditions and particularly the copper industry."[34]

The administration's decision to welcome Frei to the White House despite concerns about angering Pinochet demonstrated a new approach to human rights policy—one that embraced symbolism to bolster the Movement's agenda and went beyond mere rhetoric to put new pressure on the regime. Moreover, it offered a unique opportunity to get a Chilean insider's view of the political currents and potentials. One of the central issues was Pinochet's capacity for reform. Indeed, Vice President Mondale opened the meeting by asking whether Frei "saw any possibilities of the present government evolving toward a more democratic one." Frei described Chile as being at a "crossroads, and that the armed forces was faced with a decision on whether it should turn towards democracy or towards increased repression." He asserted that the United States' position was "key to the future of Chile," but he cautioned that opponents of the current regime in Chile did not "seek American intervention or want the American government to be linked to any single party. But the U.S. can create conditions—by words, policies, and meetings—that will have great influence on the developments in Chile." He reiterated this point a moment later, saying, "At no time had he advocated the U.S. should either break diplomatic relations with Chile or use the U.S. Embassy for intervention. If democracy were to be imposed on Chile, it would be a failure." Brzezinski reassured him that the United States had no intention of directly intervening in Chilean internal affairs. He stressed that the Carter administration's human rights stance "is not cynical: it is sincere, but it is also not a crusade." He informed Frei that the administration sought to "identify" with human rights groups and democratic movements and create a "moral framework" for change to work within, but "effective implementation of this overall policy depends on the internal situation in individual governments." Mondale, who had remained quiet for most of the meeting, interjected at the end: "We are for human rights not because we are against Communism, but because we believe in human rights. In the past . . . we have gotten these two objectives—anti-communism and human rights—confused, and we often intervened in a clumsy way; a good example of this is Chile. . . . What we did in Chile in the last decade imposes on us a special responsibility to deal with the situation in Chile with good sense and respect for our own values as well as Chile's."[35]

Brzezinski and Mondale's meeting with Frei reflected the administration's concern for both the symbolism and effectiveness of its policies. The discussion revealed a desire for human rights policy that did not simply seek to score easy political points against the Soviet Union or orchestrate the overthrow of problematic leaders. Instead, it sought ways to support real change in human rights conditions and in the tone and content of U.S. foreign policy. The legacy of U.S. intervention was alive in the minds of the military regime, its opponents, and Carter administration officials, who would have to chart a careful path in order to be effective and remain credible on human rights. With Chile, this meant that the Carter administration would take a distant and critical posture from the Pinochet regime, without completely ostracizing or isolating it.

In an effort to mitigate charges of intervention and advance human rights issues more broadly, the administration increasingly bolstered the efforts of multilateral bodies. In addition to support for ongoing efforts by the United Nations, the Carter administration turned to the OAS as a key forum for its new human rights policy.[36] At the OAS General Assembly in April, Carter laid out his new approach to regional relations, rooted in the principles of nonintervention, ideological diversity, and human rights. As the OAS gathered in Grenada in June, the administration again used the meeting to showcase its commitment to human rights and rejection of Cold War interests that had previously underpinned its regional alliances with military regimes. The Chilean government, smarting from ongoing criticism and international censure, returned to a classic Cold War rationale to explain the Chilean government's ongoing denial of various rights. In a closed-door session, Chilean foreign minister Patricio Carvajal asserted that "the real cause of supposed repression of human rights is not poverty or economic hardship but subversion and terrorism sponsored by the Soviet Union. The problems of human rights and terrorism must be dealt with as one." Addressing the assembly, Vance offered a rousing rebuttal, arguing, "A state's efforts to protect itself and secure its society cannot be exercised by denying the dignity of its individual citizens or suppressing political dissent." In a clear rejoinder to Carvajal, Vance asserted that "respect for the rule of law will promote justice and remove the seeds of subversion." He continued, "Abandoning such respect, governments descend into the netherworld of the terrorists and lose their strongest weapon, their moral authority." He was particularly critical of Chile, mentioning Letelier's death specifically as he lamented recent instances of political violence in the hemisphere.[37]

This dismissal of Cold War rationales carried over into Vance's private meeting with Foreign Minister Carvajal. Although the administration sought to work with the Chilean government and was committed to nonintervention, Vance stressed that improved relations between the two countries depended on "marked progress" in observance of human rights by the Chilean regime. Vance identified three key areas where improvements were most urgent: the return to due process, including habeas corpus; the ongoing state of siege; and the conduct of DINA, particularly related to disappearances. Carvajal tried to garner support, or at least sympathy, by invoking Cold War concerns as the root cause of Chile's problems, blaming terrorism on Soviet subversion, not "hunger, social injustice or indifferent government." Carvajal continued, "If one really wanted to defend human rights, protecting people from terrorists was the first step." Vance rejected this rationale forcefully, responding, "Counter-terrorism was an unacceptable response to terrorism."[38]

Frei's visit and Vance's position at the OAS affirmed the administration's initial approach to Chile—prioritizing dissociation from its repressive Cold War ally and visible engagement with human rights proponents and democratic opposition. This was not only an issue of pressuring Chile on human rights but also a clear signal of the broader strategic calculus that underlay the administration's new regional policy. This strategy had relevance beyond the Chilean context. As Pastor concluded in a memo to Brzezinski following the Frei meeting, "US policy to Chile in the 1960s and 1970s have made or broken our policy to Latin America, and it could happen again. The decision we make in the next few months will not only have a great impact on what happens in Chile, but it will have important implications for our policy on human rights and our policy to Latin America." Pastor and others were skeptical that any U.S. effort would result in the immediate reform or replacement of Pinochet, but he hoped that moderated pressures from the United States would "lead to the return of civilian rule. Not immediately but in the medium turn."[39] The U.S. policy would focus not on orchestrating the removal of Pinochet from power but rather curtailing repressive practices under his leadership and reforms that would prevent future abuses. This approach rejected both U.S. interventionism and the Cold War alliances that underlay the current repression. Pinochet's vacillations between promising gestures and renewed crackdowns in the second half of 1977 reinforced deep skepticism of the Movement for Pinochet's capacity for real reform and challenged the administration's strategy and credibility on human rights.

Cooling Relations, Maintaining Influence

Human rights pressures from the Carter administration had provoked resentment from the Chilean government, yet there was also evidence the regime was responding. In June 1977 U.S. intelligence indicated that the Chilean

Foreign Ministry was pressing the military government to work with the United States on human rights issues and make concessions on its powers under the state of siege.[40] At the same time a CIA intelligence report at the end of May concluded, "The Pinochet government is reverting to the practices that have jeopardized its international standing since the 1973 coup," including torture, illegal detentions, and disappearances.[41] Although the first half of 1977 was especially notable for its absence of reported disappearances and killings between January and May, by June reports of gross violations were on the rise again.[42] Throughout 1977 the Pinochet government alternated between liberalizing measures to improve foreign perceptions and repressive tactics to squelch opposition and retain control domestically. This vacillation challenged the Carter administration to encourage positive developments without ignoring fundamental stasis in repressive institutions, a crucial balance for enticing greater concessions from the regime in Santiago without losing credibility with the Movement at home.

The Chilean government was facing pressure not only from the new administration in Washington but also from within. Carter's election coincided with an upsurge of activism within Chile. The issue of disappeared prisoners, in particular, plagued the regime's efforts to recast itself as moderate. In June 1977 a group of Chileans—mostly women and relatives of the disappeared—launched a hunger strike in Santiago to call attention to their plight and, more generally, human rights problems in Chile. The strike, coinciding with the OAS meeting in Grenada, focused international attention once more on Chile. A letter to the United Nations declaring the strike highlighted the failure of the Chilean courts and government to respond to petitions and requests for information. The strike's organizers concluded, "We cannot continue waiting; we cannot lose hope. That is why we think the time has come to say 'Enough!' "[43] The protest ended nine days later on June 23 with an agreement negotiated by UN Secretary-General Waldheim that the Chilean military government would investigate the whereabouts of thirty-six relatives of the strikers; the strike also renewed international attention and pressure on the regime to address its human rights record.

The Carter administration did not make a formal public statement of support for the hunger strike but leveraged the protestors' demands privately to raise the profile of human rights issues with the regime, and it encouraged "institutional changes needed to contribute to the situation that human rights violations, including disappearances, will permanently cease."[44] Thomas Boyatt, the minister-counselor at the U.S. embassy in Santiago, met with high-level Chilean officials to urge them to resolve the issues at the core of the strikers' demands, particularly the investigation into the disappeared.[45] In a meeting with Boyatt, Pinochet raged at Waldheim's message as "insolent and an interference in Chilean affairs," and he argued that recent U.S. "'demands' with respect to how Chileans ran Chile amounted to a gross intervention in Chile's internal affairs. Chile was not a US colony," he declared. Boyatt reminded him that the negative publicity from the hunger strike was not in "Chile's interest nor in the interest of U.S.-Chile relations." Moreover, the recent issues raised by Vance at the OAS—due process, state of siege, and the operation of DINA—"were neither demands nor intervention on our part, but a frank exposition of USG [U.S. government] concerns in the human rights area." The United States was "fully committed to its human rights policy" and sought to improve U.S.-Chilean relations through an "open and frank dialogue." In his report to the secretary of state on the meeting, Boyatt noted that Pinochet was "in high dudgeon" and that his stance on the hunger strikers "is very hard indeed." However, there may be some "give in Pinochet's position" on broader reforms. "After some blustering," Boyatt concluded, "we may see some progress on due process, state of emergency, and/or DINA."[46]

On July 9, two weeks after the hunger strike ended, Pinochet announced his Chacarillas Plan, charting a course for national elections in 1985 to establish a legislative body. The regime framed this decision as an indication that the country had weathered the worst of its insurgency and instability, and it could therefore lift emergency measures. A new, albeit modified, democracy would return the country to stability and greater prosperity. In doing so, the junta simultaneously sought to rationalize its past excesses as regrettable but necessary, and to move to a new phase of legitimacy and stability.[47]

The Movement met Pinochet's initiatives with open derision. One solidarity newsletter openly ridiculed the "authoritarian democracy" that Pinochet proposed, arguing that "the entire system is devised so that the Body to be elected in 1985 will make Pinochet President of the Republic." An open letter sent by three hundred "young Chileans" rejected Pinochet's proposal as "the same autocratic regime with a new façade." In place of Pinochet's proposal, the letter demanded a return to full constitutional rule within Chile and an end to the state of siege. Similarly, 852 trade union leaders published an open letter rejecting Pinochet's plan for a "protected" democracy.[48]

Pinochet's announced reforms reignited a long-simmering debate within the Carter administration over how to balance positive and negative inducements. As early as March 1977, Todman had argued that the administration should acknowledge small improvements in human rights conditions and concessions to human rights pressures. In discussions around the PRM on Latin America, Todman had consistently raised concerns that new human rights initiatives evoked fears of intervention for many Latin Americans, especially in Chile.[49] Given the fraught history of U.S. interference in Chile's internal affairs, the Latin America bureau advocated a strategy of warming relations with Chile in exchange for moderate improvements in human rights conditions.

Although Todman's approach came out of a concern for the history of intervention, it created rifts with the rest of the administration. Pastor stridently disagreed with Todman's approach, noting that it was "at odds with the rest of the administration on Chile and human rights in general." Pastor observed that the State Department faced two very different policy approaches to Chile. The Latin America bureau advocated opening dialogue with Pinochet, exchanging public support for "even the slightest diminishing repression. . . . The problem with this strategy," according to Pastor, was that "it would risk Presidential association either directly or indirectly with the most regressing government in the hemisphere for 'a pittance'" while ignoring the symbolic importance of Chile in U.S. politics. The State Department's Human Rights Bureau, by contrast, recommended disassociation from the regime in Santiago. The inconsistency in the administration's approach to Chile resulting from these two positions, Pastor concluded, "is not the result of the bureaucratic pushing-and-pulling . . . but rather the USG is presently pursuing these two options simultaneously."[50]

These tensions between encouragement and dissociation—and friction between each strategy's supporters—was evident in the administration's response to Pinochet's Chacarillas Plan. The Carter administration as a whole shared the Movement's skepticism, wary that the plan's changes were merely superficial. Pastor concluded that although Pinochet's proposal "does represent a departure from an earlier statement stating his intention to remain in power indefinitely, it is not a clear positive step."[51] At the same time, the administration did not want to discount the positive direction this could portend if followed by additional measures; two days after the announcement, a State Department spokesman called Pinochet's Chacarillas Plan "a positive step," trying to recognize it as a move in the right direction. Two weeks later, the State Department rejected "suggestions that it had eased its opposition to Chile's military junta," but it reported the following day that "the situation in Chile had improved this year," even as it noted that the administration "had made a number of recommendations on human rights areas of continuing American concern."[52]

The administration's tentative efforts to move away from a purely puni-tive policy, balancing diplomatic pressure with moderate praise for improve-ments, created confusion around the administration's stance and commit-ment to its signature policy. This seesawing in its public position reflected internal debates about how to balance the recognition of positive develop-ment in the hopes of encouraging further improvements in the face of on-going abuses and problems. Moreover, it reinforced public perceptions of inconsistency and insincerity on human rights. Pastor reported to Brzezinski that the Chilean government and other leaders facing criticism "won't have much trouble," making the case that the U.S. government had been "grossly inconsistent in its human rights policy." To make its pressures on human rights effective, the administration had to develop responses that distin-guished between "an announcement of intention and the implementation of a policy, and between real and cosmetic changes."[53]

Todman's visit to the region in August offered a crucial opportunity for the administration to "send a clear and uniform message" about its human rights policy to both the general public and the targeted governments. In his meetings with Chilean leaders, Todman was diligent in advancing the administration's agenda, which focused overwhelmingly on human rights issues. Todman reinforced Vance's message at the OAS, stressing the desire for better relations but making clear that it was contingent on improve-ments in human rights conditions. Todman also rejected Chilean efforts to reestablish a Cold War basis for relations by invoking fears of communist subversion. In a daily report to the State Department, Todman caustically described Foreign Minister Carvajal as launching "into his set piece on the international communist conspiracy and the distorted view of Chile it has fed to the world." Todman responded that "the US had taken the brunt of the Cold War but had reached the conclusion that anti-communism was not a sufficient banner to mobilize support around the world." Todman similarly turned aside Pinochet's complaints about an international com-munist conspiracy and stressed that the U.S. government was "not interested in overthrowing any government or intervening in the political life of any nation." Human rights, however, were the "centerpiece of the Carter admin-istration's foreign policy." He encouraged Pinochet to consider further steps toward normalizing conditions in Chile. Todman reported that Pinochet responded to his suggestions with "an amused smile," stating that he "had been considering reducing the state of siege but that ambassador Todman's visit had made it impossible since to do so would appear to be knuckling to international pressure."[54]

Pinochet's protestations about "knuckling to international pressure" were particularly pointed as earlier that same day he had announced his intention to abolish DINA, the Chilean secret police, replacing it with the new Centro Nacional de Información or National Information Center (CNI). DINA had been one of the three key areas for action on human rights raised by Vance and other Carter administration officials in recent months. The timing of the announcement, just before Todman's meeting with Pinochet, "left the clear impression that the measure is directly related to the Todman visit."[55] The junta had its own motivations to dissolve DINA, beyond courting U.S. opinion. Disbanding the organization was part of the junta's overall move toward normalizing domestic control, believing it had largely taken care of its internal threat. Moreover, the negative human rights image of DINA had become an embarrassment to the military government, particularly Pinochet, as DINA and its director, Manuel Contreras, had been directly under his command. By disbanding DINA, the Chilean government wanted to signal to the international community, particularly the United States, that it was trying to improve its human rights image—and subsequently, its international standing—even as it replaced DINA with CNI, an organization almost identical in function, if not reputation.[56]

Pinochet's announcement during Todman's visit was a substantial concession to human rights concerns expressed by the Carter administration. Despite internal concerns that the CNI would become "the functional equivalent of DINA," the Carter administration decided it should be "cautiously up-beat" about the announcement, wanting to temper enthusiasm given ongoing human rights problems.[57] Todman's press conference at the end of his visit, however, was more upbeat than cautious, offering an overwhelmingly optimistic view of the regime's recent human rights efforts. Todman praised the regime's recent progress on human rights and called the disbanding of DINA "very positive."[58] Todman stated that "he formed a 'better impression than I would have thought possible in such a short time,'" and he observed that Chile's image abroad did not match "the reality one finds on a visit."[59] Todman's statements reflected the Latin America bureau's preference for positive engagement. His seemingly unhesitant praise, however, muddled perceptions of the administration's position and cast it as unsympathetic to the vast ongoing human rights problems.

Although the Carter administration issued a rare retraction and correction of Todman's statement, it was widely interpreted as an easing of pressure by the administration and unleashed a hailstorm of criticism. A newsletter sponsored by the IPS stated that "the importance of Todman's trip and his perception of Chilean 'reality' lies in the Carter administration's apparent intention to tie improved relations with the Chilean junta to progress in human rights." The report concluded, "Unfortunately, Todman seems willing to accept official junta pronouncements as evidence of 'progress' and 'reality' without waiting for results or asking that long-standing human rights questions—such as the status of the disappeared or repression of labor union activity—be clarified."[60]

In a long letter to Pastor, Eugene Valesco—a prominent and well-respected human rights advocate in Chile—laid out a detailed criticism of U.S. assertions that Pinochet had improved human rights conditions or made serious steps toward democracy. "The most unfortunate and negative fact is that the State Department has rushed into congratulating the Pinochet Government. . . . Pinochet's proposal is a joke and does not mean a return to democracy. In this situation, the posture of the State Department means a solid backing for Pinochet's project and, therefore, a stimulus for its continuation. In other words, the United States has weakened all of its previous efforts and has placed in jeopardy a good deal of the progress that has been achieved." Moreover, Valesco continued, U.S. support for Pinochet's proposals ran counter to the position of the majority of Chileans, who had rejected the Chacarillas Plan. "It seems clear," he concluded, "that with these kinds of contradictions Pinochet will be in a position to prolong his tyranny rather than to cut it short."[61]

Another prominent Chilean human rights advocate, José Zalaquett, echoed Valesco's criticism publically. In a *New York Times* editorial, the former lawyer for the Vicaría lamented that the Carter administration "seems to lack criteria for appraising human rights violations and advances." Todman's statements, he wrote, overlook the many ongoing aspects of government repression in Chile, including union rights, censorship, attacks on the church, and the unresolved issue of the disappeared. "The cumulative effect of continued repression and the increased perfection of the state machinery for control and intimidation," he argued, "now allow the Chilean junta to turn gradually to less resounding forms of repression. To applaud this as progress is to praise a dictatorship for accomplishing its own goals." Zalaquett argued that the administration should look to the "citizenry's effective recovery of freedom" as its marker for progress, or else "it may find itself applauding success in its human rights policy where they do not exist, and thus, even unwillingly, endorsing an unrelenting dictatorship."[62] Pinochet's visit to Washington for the signing of the Panama Canal Treaty shortly after Todman's trip further confused and dismayed human rights advocates, who viewed the administration as retreating from its commitment to human rights.

Despite its public inconsistencies, the administration remained committed to pressuring the Chilean regime throughout 1977. Concluding that no "significant changes" in human rights conditions could be expected in the short term, the State Department recommended in November that cooperation with Chile "should be *kept to a minimum and that our relations should be cool.*"[63] This position reflected the administration's desire to change the U.S. government's association with these repressive Cold War allies and symbolized its new approach to the region. Moreover, a cool and correct posture would also signal to Congress, the Movement, and the international community that the administration was committed to its human rights agenda, that quiet diplomacy was not code for inaction.

To have a policy that not only distanced the United States from the Chilean government but also improved human rights conditions in Chile, however, the administration needed to guard against the impression that it was irrevocably hostile to the current Chilean government. A September report emphasized Pinochet's ongoing sensitivity to foreign criticism and "interference," noting that he "took a swipe at 'impatient' Chileans who seek foreign support for their aspirations." These comments reflected "Pinochet's stubborn determination to avoid the appearance of caving in to foreign pressures."[64] In response to a vote condemning Chile's human rights practices at the UN, another intelligence report noted the Chilean government's growing agitation with the Carter administration and warned that this frustration was likely to lessen U.S. influence on human rights conditions in the region. The report cautioned that "there is some danger of a resurgence of the siege mentality that characterized the Chilean Government during 1975 and 1976. Should the government become convinced that US and world opinion will be against it regardless of the measures it takes, slower progress in human rights, and perhaps even some recidivism, can be expected."[65] The administration needed to communicate to the Chilean government that a real improvement in human rights conditions would have tangible results in its relations with the United States. Yet Todman's efforts to do just that set off a wave of recrimination within the Movement and an internal debate within the administration regarding its strategy.

A State Department evaluation of regional relations after the administration's first year concluded that "our energetic human rights stance has gone a long way to undoing, in a remarkably short period of time, US identification with the Pinochet regime." It observed, however, that Pinochet "may have gone as far as he felt is consistent with his regime's security," and the challenge that faced the administration going forward was how to continue pressure "without jeopardizing the major points we've gained in domestic and international opinion?"[66] In 1978 dissent within Chile challenged the regime's legitimacy and image of moderation, while escalating tensions from the Letelier investigations stretched the Carter administration's influence to its limits.

Springtime of Dissent and the Disappeared

The year 1978 was a precarious one for the Chilean junta's domestic control and the Carter administration's human rights policy. Despite some seemingly conflicting messages from the Carter administration, it was clear that the 1976 U.S. presidential elections had fundamentally changed the junta's relations with the White House, previously its strongest supporter in the international community. Further, the Chilean government's democratizing plan and disbanding of DINA in 1977 had not precipitated the goodwill it anticipated, with neither its domestic constituency nor the international community. Pinochet in particular, as the face of the junta and its worst excesses, confronted escalating criticism and pressure from both domestic and international sources. In January 1978 WOLA described the country as "still dreary after all these years," even while noting that the human rights situation in Chile was "not comparable with the years immediately following the coup d'état." It labeled most of the regime's changes in the past year as "cosmetic," reporting, for example, that CNI had participated in the latest political arrests of fifty Chileans in November. WOLA anticipated that without further changes, the international ostracism of the regime would continue.[67]

Ongoing human rights pressures and a desire to consolidate political power domestically pushed Pinochet toward further liberalizing measures in early 1978. In March and April Pinochet lifted the state of siege, including the curfew that had been imposed since the coup. He permitted Jaime Castillo, a Christian Democratic leader exiled in 1976 for writing a letter to the OAS denouncing human rights abuses, to return to the country. Pinochet also moved to incorporate civilians into the government and lifted the censorship decree on printed matter. Manuel Contreras—increasingly linked to the Letelier assassination by the United States' investigation—resigned from the army to avoid further embarrassment and damage to the regime, especially to Pinochet, who was his direct superior at the time of the assassination.[68]

Perhaps the most significant and controversial measure came on April 19, 1978, when the Chilean junta issued blanket amnesty to anyone who had committed a criminal act in Chile between September 11, 1973, and March 10, 1978.[69] The regime cast the decree as a gesture of goodwill and reconciliation, indicating that the new government "does not harbor grudges and knows that pardon and forgetting [olvido] must open new paths to the reunified fatherland."[70] Intelligence reports, however, indicated that Pinochet implemented these actions in order to "end Chile's isolated international position" and ameliorate criticism of its human rights conditions.[71] The Vicaría reported that the amnesty law "basically reflected the government's decision to regard the phase of civil war and subversion as a phase that had now been left behind." It observed that the military government "presented the amnesty as a gesture of reconciliation" because it extended to any crimes committed by Allende officials.[72] Human rights activists were quick to point out that, although political prisoners benefited from the amnesty, so too did DINA officers and other government agents who had perpetrated the worst crimes against the civilian population.[73]

The junta's liberalizing measures, instead of diminishing pressure on the regime, amplified domestic and international criticism. The end of the state of siege in Chile, in conjunction with the earlier reorganization of DINA, provided an opening for domestic dissent.[74] The Vicaría noted, "This opening . . . made it possible for society as a whole to begin to react in a more coherent and effective manner to the violations of human rights and more generally to the military regime's actions. An incipient but clear opposition began to manifest itself in the realm of politics, labor, schools, and so forth." Human rights groups and family members were able to speak out publicly about ongoing repression. Cardinal Raúl Silva Henríquez, backed by the Catholic Church's Vicaría de Solidaridad, declared 1978 as "The Year of Human Rights in Chile." The Chilean press likewise took advantage of the less restricted environment, and the Vicaría reported that "even media that were not regarded as part of the opposition occasionally published information on human rights violations."[75]

Escalating criticism in Chile was echoed by the Movement in the United States. In a special report, "Chile: Justice in the Balance," WOLA cast these reforms as "a series of governmental machinations designed to protect itself from future judicial proceedings and to disguise new repressive measures in a cloak of legal rhetoric." The report continued, "While on the surface such measures seem to be praiseworthy, a detailed analysis reveals they are nothing more than deceptive maneuvers to improve the Junta's image, and more significantly absolve government personnel from possible criminal charges."[76] A solidarity newsletter similarly reported that "the essential element of the amnesty is that it is a self-amnesty for the junta, the DINA, and all those who have been responsible for crimes against the Chilean people." It continued, "The implications are even more ominous for the families of the disappeared political prisoners," arguing that the law prevented DINA agents for being prosecuted, even with evidence of their complicity in kidnappings.[77]

The problem of disappeared prisoners was a particularly bothersome one for the junta as it tried to establish a sense of normalcy and move beyond the excesses of the past. As the U.S. embassy in Santiago noted, "For the Chilean military the 'disappearance' phenomenon has continued so long, and involved so many people that even to seek scapegoats and publicly resolve a few cases may be an unfeasible option—it would only raise more unanswerable questions." Throughout 1977 the junta faced challenges in the courts and on the streets over the issue of the disappeared. In addition to the hunger strikes initiated in June 1977, the families of the disappeared continued their protest through legal mechanisms, filing writs of habeas corpus, and the Vicaría sued in Chilean courts to force the government to investigate disappearances. Although Amnesty International acknowledged that these efforts had proved "totally ineffective" at locating the missing Chileans, the legal measures offered one of the only ways to maintain pressure on the government and keep domestic and international attention focused on the issue. The U.S. embassy in Santiago reported that the group had "no illusions that the court will force the issue with the government," but it hoped that pressure on this issue would prevent further disappearances and curtailment of other abuses.[78]

Advocates thus reacted in dismay to the amnesty decree, which threatened to close their primary channel of dissent and pressure on the regime. Indeed, as soon as a week after the decree, the Chilean courts closed investigations into a number of disappearances, citing the new amnesty law. A U.S. embassy brief observed, "The courts have never been enthusiastic about involving themselves in situations making them look particularly powerless. Investigation into disappearances certainly gave that impression," and now the amnesty gave courts a chance to extract themselves from the situation.[79]

By the end of April, even as the regime sought to put the coup and its violent aftermath behind it as an unfortunate but necessary epoch, family members of disappeared prisoners and human rights advocates resumed highly publicized public vigils and hunger strikes demanding: *"Dónde están?"*

"Where are they?" In the week following the amnesty decree, relatives of the disappeared marched across downtown Santiago, ending at the secretary of the minister's office to deliver a letter, which suggested that the Pinochet regime was attempting to "sweep the disappeared issue under the rug" with the new amnesty law. The letter argued that "the wounds of the past cannot be healed until the GOC [government of Chile] gives an accounting for the fate of the 600 plus disappeared." A month later, sixty advocates, again mostly female relatives of the disappeared, escalated their protest with another hunger strike at the local UNICEF office and three churches in Santiago. The strikers denounced the amnesty law, which the courts were using to dismiss their cases, and chastised the government for failing to provide any substantial information regarding their relatives in the year since their last strike.[80]

These protests garnered widespread international attention, sparking solidarity strikes in Europe, Latin America, and the United States, with Senator Kennedy even visiting a demonstration in Geneva, Switzerland.[81] WOLA, Amnesty International, the Chile Committee for Human Rights, and other human rights groups utilized the personal testimonies coming out of Chile to raise awareness at the government and grassroots levels of the ongoing human rights problems in the country. In Chile three women entered the U.S. embassy for a twenty-four-hour strike, and embassy staff "arranged for them to be made comfortable."[82] On June 8, almost three weeks after the strikes began, the families and strikers decided to suspend the strikes at the urging and mediation of the Chilean bishops, with a promise from the Chilean Ministry of the Interior that answers would be forthcoming.

When the strikes had resumed in 1978, the Carter administration continued to affirm its support for the strikers in response to letters to Congress and solidarity groups. Despite concerns that the strike was being "exploited" for political purposes by communist groups, administration officials offered only affirmations of support for the strikers' goal of true accounting for the disappeared and institutional reforms to prevent future repression.[83] In early June, Community Action of Latin America (CALA) sent a cable to the White House expressing concern for the strikers and urging the U.S. government to support their cause. The State Department responded, "On numerous occasions we have expressed our concern to the Chilean Government at the highest levels and will continue to do so. We have also been in contact with the representatives of the families of those who have disappeared to discuss their problems with them." The letter also noted, however, the significant reduction in the number of arrests of political dissidents. The letter closed

by asserting that "we will do all we can to assure a more thorough accounting of those who have disappeared."[84] The administration had indeed been
working behind the scenes, making private overtures to the Chilean government and "expressing concern that the problem of the missing relatives cannot be simply swept away."[85]

The disappearances remained as thorny reminders of ongoing human
rights problems, yet the administration also acknowledged that there had
been a tangible improvement in human rights conditions in the past year.
An overview of human rights in Chile, sent from the U.S. embassy in Santiago at the end of May, stressed that "more has happened during this four-
month period than during any comparable period since 1974." It continued,
"At this time, it is fair to say that systematic, institutionalized, widespread,
gross violations of the rights of the person no longer exist in Chile." This did
not mean that the country did not still have problems with political and civil
rights or that the military government had ceded all its emergency powers
and authority, but "as fears of physical repression diminish, more dissenters
are willing to challenge the GOC." The question, as always, was how much
to praise these improvements when there remained gaping holes in accounting for past violations, as well as ongoing curtailment of less urgent but still
crucial rights. The report concluded that "the first third of 1978 has seen a
number of dramatic GOC changes to improve its human rights image. . . .
Overall the ambiance has changed for the better. Recidivism remains a possibility." The Latin America bureau concluded that "if these improvements
hold up, . . . we should soon begin to adjust our policies accordingly."[86] This
recommendation, however, was at odds with the political demands of key
members of both Congress and the Movement.

The upsurge in activism around the disappeared created new pressures
on the Carter administration's policy for visible, aggressive action on human
rights in Chile. The Movement saw the Carter administration's response to
Pinochet's inconsistent efforts as essential to human rights in Chile and revealing about its broader commitment to its human rights agenda. As one
WOLA newsletter observed in April 1978, "The future US position remains a
major factor in the puzzle. Will the US continue to commend Chile's military
government, as they have done twice in the past two weeks? Or, if the US
senses the ripening of conditions for an alternative to Pinochet, will it back
off from making references to Pinochet's 'positive contributions to improvement'?"[87] In many ways the administration had been asking itself the same
question since taking office: How much should it support incremental and
cosmetic changes in human rights conditions in Chile as positive progress?

How much pressure could it exert on human rights without provoking back-lash at U.S. interference?

Closing Loopholes

As the administration debated the appropriate balance between praise and pressure, the Movement was restless for more concrete measures. Given the administration's inconsistent public positions—reminiscent of the Nixon-Ford years—advocates sought action beyond symbolism to shore up a commitment to human rights in U.S. relations with Chile. Looking to hold the administration accountable for its rhetoric, the Movement returned to binding legislative mechanisms for IFIs, pointing to the ongoing government aid and private loans to Santiago despite existing restrictions. A WOLA report at the beginning of 1978 denounced the "continuing flow of military goods to one of the hemisphere's most brutal dictatorships." The administration, by not terminating "pipeline contracts" and labeling equipment not explicitly prohibited by the ban as "civilian," had supplied more than $57 million in arms to the Chilean government in the face of "what Congress intended to be an all-inclusive ban on military sales to Chile." Based on this ongoing material support, the report concluded, "Apparently, the administration places greater emphasis on maintaining close relations with the Chilean military than it does carrying out any of its promises to disassociate the United States from human rights violators abroad." The report called for greater pressure on the Carter administration to "enforce existing sanctions on Chile" and also advocated that Congress take further legislative action to close existing loopholes.[88]

The spring of 1978 saw a new push by Congress to codify human rights policy through legislation, not only "closing loopholes" but also extending human rights guidance into new areas. Rep. Donald Fraser offered amendments that made 502B language binding for security assistance and extended "gross violator" prohibitions to International Military Education and Training (IMET) programs and police equipment, arguing it provided "too close an identification between our government and governments guilty of gross violations." Similarly, a new House resolution sought to apply binding restrictions on gross violators to EXIM Bank loans. In a letter to members of Congress on behalf of the ADA, Bruce Cameron noted that EXIM received many more applications for loans than it could grant. It was logical, then, that such support not go to governments that consistently violated human rights. And yet, in the years since the coup and in spite of other sanctions, EXIM had supplied $194 million in bank loans and guarantees, insurance for exporters to the country—$2.3 million in 1978 alone. *"The Export-Import bank is not politically neutral—it is an economic institution which in its financing provides economic support for other governments."*[89]

These new legislative efforts reflected in part the perception that the administration was "inconsistent" with its application of human rights criteria to IFIs and multilateral institutions. The use of "voice and vote" to support human rights in these institutions was not widely shared among other member nations. Thus, although the administration had consistently voted against or abstained in cases involving Chile, it had been more cautious in most other cases, only voting against ten and abstaining in another seventeen out of the more than five hundred loans it had considered since coming to office. The administration recognized the symbolic importance of these votes, particularly to "disassociate ourselves from the inhumane excesses of a particular regime" or because of "past identification with a major human rights violator (e.g., Chile)." As debates over Chile had illustrated, however, the administration was also concerned that its espoused preference for "positive actions" was increasingly overshadowed by public expectations for punitive sanctions. Further, the administration was also receiving pressure from conservative senators for being "overly rigid" in its application of human rights criteria to IFI decisions.[90]

As Congress contemplated new legislation, the administration voted to approve a relatively small Commodity Credit Corporation (CCC) case of $38 million to Chilean farmers. In announcing the decision, the State Department stressed that the funds went to the farmers, not the government, and would primarily benefit U.S. agriculture. The statement also cited "encouraging political developments" within Chile but denied any deviation in the administration's emphasis on human rights. Despite these demurrals, the Movement seized on this as a harbinger of a new, more supportive approach to the Chilean regime. A CALA newsletter in May cautioned that the CCC loan indicated that the administration may look more favorably on a $40 million World Bank loan to Chile, up for a vote in the summer. In a speech on the Senate floor, Ted Kennedy railed against current policies of "back door" economic and military support for the Chilean government, and the supposed "liberalization" and "concessions" of the regime. "While encouraged by some recent events in Chile, we cannot afford to close our eyes to the serious human rights problems which remain," Kennedy warned.[91]

Kennedy's frustration about "back door" military aid was not only directed at the administration. Private bank lending to Chile had risen sharply since Congress had placed its ceiling on government aid in 1976. In early April the Chilean Central Bank had signed a deal acquiring $210 million in credit from private banks, including Morgan Guaranty, Chase Manhattan, and Citicorp, among others. A statement by the Chilean Bank on the arrangement called the credit the "most important and largest conceded to Chile in the last decade."[92] The Movement had consistently criticized private bank loans for bolstering the repressive regime in Santiago, enabling it to continue buying arms and stabilize its economic program despite the cutoff of official U.S. aid. Mark Hertsgaard, research fellow at the IPS, challenged the notion that the economic stability fostered by private bank loans had enabled political liberalization. In an April op-ed Hertsgaard decried the supposed improvement in Chile's human rights conditions. These changes, he wrote, are "no more than tactics designed specifically to help Pinochet ride out the crisis. The repressive apparatus that has straitjacketed Chilean society since the junta came to power remains in place." While the junta's recent concessions on political prisoners and the state of siege gave the facade of moderation, it hid the regime's ongoing violation of economic rights. "Many Chileans, especially those of poor and working classes, are without work, adequate nutrition, housing, clothing, and health care; conditions directly attributable to the economic policies of the military junta." Moreover, this economic deprivation required political repression to sustain it. "Only a government which banned political expression can safely inflict such a degree of human suffering on its people." Referring to the $1.5 million in private bank loans received by the junta, he argued that "this 'manna from heaven' allowed the junta to thumb its nose at international criticism. Indeed, Chilean repression could continue only because the Chilean government did not need to depend upon U.S. government or international lending agencies, with their ties to human rights groups, for economic assistance."[93]

Key members of Congress shared Hertsgaard's criticism. Sen. Henry Reuss, chairman of the House Banking Committee, sent telegrams to six major banks, arguing that loans to Chile "appear inconsistent" with guidance designed to prevent financial institutions from undermining the public interest. Citing a recently published IPS study, Reuss informed the banks that the $560 million in loans their institutions had offered to the Chilean government were "not helpful" in advancing U.S. human rights policy.[94] Senator Kennedy went further, advocating new legislation to monitor private bank activity. He argued that "U.S. private banks are undermining U.S.

government policy toward Chile." HR 12568 required that "domestic banks semi-annually report to the Secretary of treasury the amount of each loan to and investment in a foreign country, which is found to engage in a consistent pattern" of gross violations of internationally recognized human rights. Although the proposed legislation would not prohibit these loans, Kennedy and the Movement hoped to created public pressure that would deter banks from involving themselves with these regimes.[95] A solidarity newsletter championed the measure as "an essential FIRST STEP toward a Congressional cut-off of private bank loans to Chile." Summarizing these legislative developments, the newsletter concluded, "The current spate of activity in Congress right now with regards to the human rights situation in Chile provides us with an opportunity to let our voices be heard once again. The above-mentioned legislation can give us the lever to once and for all cut the junta's lifeline—economic aid from transnational corporations and private banks."[96]

New legislative proposals in the spring of 1978 seemed to move the administration further in the direction of sanctions as it scrambled for ways to acknowledge and encourage moderate improvements without losing credibility with key domestic constituencies. As with earlier legislation, the administration was concerned about maintaining its flexibility of options and protecting its prerogatives to determine the course of its foreign policy. Although the administration had voted overwhelmingly against support for Chile in IFIs, its desire to recognize the limited improvements in key areas created pressure within the administration to reassess these negative votes.[97]

Despite ongoing concerns about maintaining its flexibility for "extraordinary circumstances" and avoiding new legislative restrictions in general, the administration chose not to "spill blood" opposing them. In principle and practice, the administration already supported the premises of the legislation. Opposing the bills, which were likely to pass, would put the administration in an "awkward position."[98] Moreover, the administration shared the Movement's assessment that political repression was inherently tied with the regime's economic program. The U.S. embassy reported in July, "Chile's economic model, whatever its inherent merits, is dependent on and inextricably linked with a repressive political machine. To the extent that foreign lending props up the economic model so it maintains the political system." The report concluded, "In effect lending and investment decisions of the private sector have dissipated the impact of USG actions linking economic assistance to human rights." Private bank activities thus "conflict with and undermine USG policy goals and methods of implementation" in Chile.[99]

In mid-July the administration decided to maintain its present policy to vote against IFI proposals for Chile in deference to the developments of the Letelier case and the "sensitivity of our relations with Chile at the moment." It anticipated that, despite a desire to encourage positive trends, "any change in our present policy of opposition would be misinterpreted by the Chilean government and by important Administration, Congressional, and public currents of opinion here."[100] The administration, as it had before, prioritized demands for improvement over recognition of change. "Chile is an emotional issue and our attitude toward it is, rightly or wrongly, a symbol to many of our human rights commitment," Anthony Lake of the Policy Planning Staff wrote to Warren Christopher in August. At the same time, he urged, "we need to do more about the *positive promotion of human rights*," arguing that "the human rights policy, and American interests in general, ultimately will benefit if we do not seem to be using economic pressure to bring down a particular government. Repressive governments will be more likely to improve their performance if they believe something short of suicide will bring a lifting of economic sanctions."[101] Chile's symbolism to the administration's entire human rights agenda made it politically untenable to respond positively to recent limited improvements. Even as Chile's concessions in key areas merited some response, the looming Letelier case made even slight warming of relations politically untenable.

The Chilean Watergate

The U.S. government investigation into the assassinations of Orlando Letelier and Ronnie Moffitt retained a low profile within the administration's foreign policy until spring 1978. Indeed, the investigation had kept such a low profile that it was apparently necessary for Robert Lipshutz, counsel to the president, to reassure Isabel Letelier and Michael Moffitt that "the Carter administration has not let the investigation die."[102] The case suddenly gained new stature when Chile finally conceded to the extradition of an American citizen and former DINA agent, Michael Townley. Townley's subsequent testimony to U.S. officials, which would become the linchpin of the investigation, and his confession led to a U.S. indictment of three high-level Chilean intelligence officers—former head of DINA Manuel Contreras, his deputy Pedro Espinoza, and Armando Fernández Larios.[103] In April 1978 the U.S. government officially requested the extradition of the three DINA officers.

The information coming out of the Letelier investigation had far-reaching repercussions for U.S.-Chilean relations, not just as a human rights issue but also as an act of terrorism committed by a foreign government on U.S. soil. In April 1978 Pastor warned Brzezinski that "the investigation has reached the point where it is not only having a very large impact on our current relationship with Chile, but it may have an even greater impact in the months ahead."[104] The Chilean government's pretense of cooperation in the investigation had given way to stonewalling and charges of U.S. interference in its internal affairs. Pinochet knew that the United States would not be satisfied with anything short of extradition for the three men indicted by the U.S. courts in the assassination of Letelier and Moffitt, including Manuel Contreras. Pinochet also knew, however, that handing over Contreras would be taken as an admission of guilt and would critically weaken his position with key sectors of Chilean society and even within his own government. By the beginning of May a CIA assessment characterized the Letelier investigation as the "Chilean Watergate," with the "possibility that the crime will be linked to the highest levels of the Chilean government." If Contreras was found guilty, it would be hard for Pinochet to avoid also being linked with the assassination. In a significant shift in public opinion, most "educated Chileans had been forced to come to grips with the existence and activities of DINA," whereas a few months earlier they would have denied any government involvement in the assassination.[105]

Carter administration officials speculated that the condemnation Pinochet faced both domestically and internationally in 1978 could make him more receptive to democratic reforms, reasoning that "so long as Pinochet wants to hold onto power and so long as he remains vulnerable, he has shown himself responsive to pressure to accelerate the transition process and swallow other bitter pills." Pinochet's problems were a potential asset for the United States as it attempted to move Chile toward a more open and humane political system, but only if the administration was subtle in its efforts. According to U.S. ambassador to Chile George Landau, "The issue for [U.S.] policy, with or without Pinochet, remains as before: the application of pressures modulated so as to avoid backlash. Outside pressures on Chile have hastened internal reform; but the locally prevalent belief that the [U.S. government] wants Pinochet out and is using the Letelier case to that end, could be used to slow the transition by Pinochet or a new junta."[106] The Letelier case could be an important point of leverage for the United States on human rights issues as long as the administration avoided riling nationalist sentiment with overt intervention into Chile's internal political processes.

In June 1978 Landau predicted that they were "approaching the end of the road in U.S.-Chilean relations and it is only a matter of time before the Army leadership realized that the only way Chile will improve its relations with the rest of the world is by replacing Pinochet." Landau concluded, "The Letelier investigation is the catalyst which will finally galvanize the Chilean Generals to take the inevitable step." His assertion was based on the fact that although Chile had made progress on human rights in the last year, it received less credit for these changes than it might have due to Pinochet's presence.[107] The Letelier investigation and the more than six hundred disappeared persons, both linked to Pinochet, continued to dominate world opinion of Chile.

Pinochet, however, had begun to use the international coverage of the assassination for his own benefit. In May 1978 Pinochet launched a public campaign against "alleged U.S. interference in Chilean affairs," accusing the Carter administration of utilizing the Letelier investigation as a means to unseat Pinochet and destabilize the military government.[108] These themes of U.S. interference in domestic affairs and Chile's judicial system began to emerge in progovernment labor unions, newspapers, and youth groups. At the same time, Pinochet declined to take a position on the investigation and refused to extradite Contreras and the others, arguing that these were legal, not political matters that should be left up to the "independent" Chilean judiciary.[109]

By June this tactic appeared to be working. Although Pinochet still faced domestic pressures on human rights problems, reports from Chile noted that the " 'shock' impact of the evidence [in the Letelier investigation] has largely been dissipated by the manner in which it has dribbled out. Pinochet now has a strong, nationalistic defense going for him." The report noted, "It is easy for Pinochet's supporters (a majority of the populace) to believe all this is a carefully orchestrated plot by the CIA to topple Pinochet." Moreover, Pinochet's stonewalling tactics, particularly on Contreras's extradition, helped him shore up support from military leaders; they had been dissatisfied with Pinochet's liberalizing measures earlier that year, which appeared to be bending to foreign pressure and reinforced "the impression of a failing President."[110] Although the Letelier case was still potentially damaging for Pinochet by linking him, through Contreras, to an act of terrorism in the U.S. capital, an overly aggressive pursuit of the case by the United States could also strengthen Pinochet's position within Chile. An intelligence report in August noted, "Whichever way the Chilean court rules, international clamor for extradition would probably assist the regime to maintain and even increase its support at home because this would give Pinochet a nationalistic issue to use against his opponents. The President could argue that the international community was asking his government to overturn a ruling of Chile's highest court—in effect, calling on him to break the law of the land."[111]

Even before the Chilean court ruled on the U.S. extradition request, Pinochet managed to diffuse pressure domestically. The combination of his liberalizing measures in spring of 1978 and his careful play on national sentiment in the Letelier investigation solidified his support with the military and a significant percentage of the Chilean population. Pinochet's domestic support was further bolstered by significant economic growth in the late 1970s. Moreover, while the previous June Pinochet had talked openly, if perhaps disingenuously, about his possible removal, six months later "most Chileans see no alternative to the present regime."[112]

By early 1979 Pinochet seemed to have weathered the worst of the challenges to his authority, yet human rights remained the Achilles heel of the regime. The discovery of fifteen bodies in a lime kiln at Lonquén in November 1978 and the ongoing Letelier investigation both reinforced human rights efforts within Chile and with their supporters abroad, challenging Pinochet's popular support at home and international position. Pinochet's strength, then, hinged on how he responded to ongoing human rights issues, especially the Letelier case. Indeed, in the past two years, Pinochet had shown himself to be willing to take modest measure to improve human rights conditions and hence Chile's international standing, but only insofar as they did not threaten control domestically. To support U.S. requests to extradite the DINA officials would be to concede the military government's complicity in Letelier's death and could undermine his authority. Indeed, his intransigence in the face of U.S. demands—framed as defying yet another case of Yankee interventionism—had stirred up nationalistic support within Chile. Moreover, Pinochet had very little left to lose internationally: the UN continued to pass resolutions against his government, U.S. foreign aid had almost completely dried up, and international censure continued, yet he was still in power.[113]

On May 13, 1979, the Chilean supreme court, backed by the military government, rejected the U.S. petition to extradite any of the three Chilean officials the U.S. government believed to be responsible for the assassinations. The court rejected evidence linking the DINA agents, including former DINA head Miguel Contreras, to the assassination. They made this decision on the basis that Michael Townley's testimony was part of a plea bargain, or what they termed a "paid accusation." As such, all evidence derived from it was inadmissible in Chilean court.[114] Although the court would automatically review the decision, the ruling gave little indication that any change would result.

The Carter administration and human rights community were deeply dismayed, if unsurprised, by the ruling. Pastor reported to Brzezinski, "That decision was much worse than any one of us had anticipated."[115] The Carter administration immediately announced it was "gravely disappointed" in the court's decision and that it planned to appeal the decision and recall Ambassador Landau for consultation.[116] The day after the court's announcement, several members of the U.S. Congress called on the Carter administration to implement strong punitive measures. In a letter to the president on May 14, 1979, Senators Edward Kennedy and Frank Church urged him to recall Ambassador George Landau from Chile immediately and outlined other actions "appropriate in light of the Pinochet regime's continued denial of human and democratic rights." These actions included the suspension of all economic and military assistance and credits, including those already in progress; denial of all bilateral aid in accordance with the Foreign Assistance Act prohibiting "such aid to countries harboring international terrorists"; recall of all military personnel from Chile; and a review of U.S.-Chilean relations as a whole.[117]

Despite its genuine outrage at the ruling, the Movement had already mobilized in anticipation of just such a decision. In March, two months before the Chilean supreme court handed down its verdict, the National Coordinating Center in Solidarity with Chile urged members of Congress to demand that the administration use "its limited means" to press for extradition. It took particular aim at private bank loans to Chile. The group argued that "the economic stability which these loans are providing Pinochet allow him to thumb his nose at the U.S. government's request for extradition and at the Chilean people's demands for the full restoration of their human and democratic rights, including the right to know the whereabouts of more than 2,500 'disappeared' political prisoners."[118] By the beginning of April 1979, solidarity networks were mobilizing a letter campaign to Congress and the State Department "in the face of the expected refusal of the Chilean Supreme Court to extradict [sic]" the Chilean officials. The campaign supported the "full application of official pressure to achieve the extradition," detailing measures consistent with the forthcoming Kennedy-Church letter. Congressman Harkin, a solidarity newsletter reported, "is prepared to express the official outrage of the U.S. Congress," introducing a resolution at the appropriate time.[119]

In September the Movement took out an ad in the *Washington Post* to lobby the administration for a strong response to Chile's continued refusal to extradite the three Chilean officials. In an open letter to the president, both members of Congress and nongovernment advocates argued, "Nothing short of extradition can promote U.S. moral and national security issues. . . . Anything short of extradition means moral vacillation, shows political weakness and encourages terrorists to believe that they can get away with murder in the capital of the United States." It asserted that the U.S. government was "morally bound" to take the measures recommended by Senators Kennedy and Church in May. Two weeks later the House of Representatives passed a resolution condemning the killings and the Chilean government's continued refusal to extradite those believed to be responsible.[120] It called on President Carter to take the measures proposed by Kennedy and Church, and to "demand that the Pinochet regime restore fully to the people of Chile the rights they had traditionally enjoyed before the military coup, including the right of the more than fifty thousand Chilean exiles to return to their country and

Figure 9. IPS fellows Isabel Letelier and Michael Moffitt—the spouses of Orlando Letelier and Ronnie Moffitt—with Sen. Ted Kennedy (D-MA) at an IPS-sponsored human rights event. Courtesy of Wisconsin Historical Society, WHS-144521.

the right of the families of more than 650 disappeared political prisoners to be informed of their whereabouts."[121] The assassination had clearly become a vehicle to address a multitude of grievances against Chile, and the Carter administration's response would be taken as a measure of its commitment to human rights issues.

As these demands grew louder in public forums, the administration was confronting the very real limits of its influence on this case. The National Security Council identified the Letelier case as the "most serious" human rights issue with Chile, and the administration clearly had to take a stand if its human rights policy was to remain credible. Yet human rights considerations had already drastically limited economic and military aid to Chile, a fact that Pinochet was well aware of. With U.S. sponsorship, the UN had passed resolutions censuring Chile's human rights record; statements of moral outrage would do little to further the Letelier case. The administration's response to Chile's refusal to extradite needed to indicate the severity of its displeasure, but it had already employed the primary levers of influence without the desired outcome. Moreover, the administration did not want to harm its long-term human rights objectives or influence there. The administration—cognizant of the problematic history of U.S. intervention—clearly worried about provoking a stronger, counterproductive backlash within Chile with overt interference in its judiciary. A State Department memo weighing possible actions observed that Pinochet's government was still "somewhat responsive" to U.S. pressure on rights issues. More importantly, "the populace as a whole probably appreciates it so long as we do not intervene too egregiously in Chilean affairs. The latter caveat is important. *Our objective should be to maintain this delicate balance through the Letelier case, with the hope of improving it thereafter.*"[122] A moderate approach, however, would almost certainly alienate the strongest proponents of Carter's human rights policy within the United States.

On September 11, 1979, six years after the junta seized power in Chile, Viron Vaky, assistant secretary of state for inter-American affairs, outlined possible responses to the Letelier case. Even in the worst scenario, the bureau did not recommend the termination of private bank loans or the complete withdrawal of the U.S. ambassador from Chile, arguing that "doing so would have no positive effect on the Letelier case and would have a negative effect on our pursuit of our other interests in Chile." Such action would instead imply that the United States did not need a representative for the duration of Pinochet's rule, which he speculated could last five or six more years. "We could thus reduce our ability to exert influence over Chile and various important Southern Cone issues in that period."[123]

Private bank loans and IFIs—a sore spot and cleavage between the administration and Congress since its first months in office—once again became a critical point of contention. Vaky cautioned that trying to limit private institution lending could be "ineffectual or even counterproductive" if other foreign banks moved to replace them.[124] Moreover, it was in no way certain that private banks would be responsive to the government's request. Even before the ruling, groups such as CALA had approached private lenders, pleading with them to end financial support to the regime. One institution had responded by noting that although they were sympathetic to human rights concerns, they did not believe that private finance was an appropriate mechanism. After noting that it had been one of only three lenders to Chile during the Allende years, it continued,

> If the flow of international finance is choked off from any country, there is an inevitably negative impact on the economy of that country. Some suggest that this is positive because it would bring about positive social change; but it also suggests that the international banking community would shun its traditional role as an apolitical lender and attempt to interfere with the internal political and social processes of a country. Our experience suggests that economic dislocation is no guarantee for positive social reforms. Further, I must seriously question the right to make arbitrary decisions affecting the self-determination of people in another country.[125]

Chilean newspapers quoted the president of the Republic National Bank of New York as saying that "the United States government could only impede U.S. bank lending to Chile through legislative action" and pointed out that there was no precedent for such action, implying it would not be in the interests of the banks, or the financial interests of either the United States or Chile.[126]

This is not to say that the private sector was indifferent to the rise of human rights concerns. Robert Kemper, vice board chairman of Wells Fargo, had informed the administration the previous June, "If President Carter wishes to terminate lending by private US banks to Chile, he has only to say so." Although gaining support from private businesses for restrictions was unlikely to be so simple, banks had signaled an increasing sensitivity to public concern about human rights, particularly in Chile. Bank of America, for example, had expressed its support for the UN General Assembly's censure of human rights conditions in Chile, even as it continued to conduct business with the Chilean government. The administration also noted that Citicorp "without public announcement is going slow on new lending to Chile." On the whole, public engagement with human rights and the "political ramifications of the Letelier/Moffitt investigation has breached the social conscience of the banks."[127]

Still, it was unclear to the administration that sanctions on private banks would be supported by Congress or by the institutions themselves. U.S. ambassador Landau cautioned that "to impose these sanctions would be counter to stated U.S. policy, [and] would be more costly to the U.S. than to Chile." It also noted that "it would be difficult to obtain the necessary Congressional legislation [and] business/community participation." He argued that "while it may be necessary to risk damage, or even to do harm to our economic interests for the sake of a higher goal (justice, anti-terrorism), we should do so only if confident that our actions will have force and effect. That is, that they will either punish Chile in order that an example be set and/or that they will cause the GOC to alter its behavior and bring the murderers to fair trial." To propose such sanctions and be subsequently challenged by the business community and Congress would only further undercut the strength of the administration. "We must know that we have the votes before we announce our intentions," the memo warned. "Not to be able to deliver our threats would leave the U.S. appearing weak and embarrassed and by comparison Pinochet would be strengthened, even further lessening the chance that justice would be done, and also doing nothing to hasten the return of democratic institutions." Landau warned that, in determining an appropriate response to the court's ruling, "it would be a mistake to assume that we are going to cause the GOC grave difficulties." Moreover, "whatever we do probably will not result either in the punishment of the three officers for murder or a change in Chile's political leadership, we should be careful not to institute measures which, for domestic or foreign policy reasons, we will have to repeal unilaterally after a short period. Such actions would be worse than none."[128]

Although Landau noted that the Chilean government was concerned that the United States would reduce the flow of investment and lending in Chile, he cautioned that this concern "should not be overstated." Landau predicted that European and Japanese companies would likely take advantage of any void left by the United States in this situation, lessening the impact of such restrictions on private banking. Landau further pointed out that although the Chilean government feared that the United States would increase its support for opposition elements in Chile, this point of leverage had its limits as well. Landau cautioned that "less moderate leaders" would manipulate overt

U.S. support for opposition elements in Chilean society, and such actions would help reinforce rather than weaken the current government.[129] Given the U.S. history of intervention in Chile, direct and forceful U.S. policy could create an effect opposite to the one intended.

Regardless of the pitfalls of limiting private bank loans, the administration had to act to remain credible at home and to respond to an egregious violation of the United States' own sovereignty. Moreover, symbolic actions had paid moderate dividends with Pinochet in the past. Landau argued that, despite the obstacles to implementing significant punitive measures against Chile, "it is not in the U.S. interest to appear as a paper tiger on the Letelier/Moffitt issue. . . . It is important that we take some action. And, although not now a good bet, even symbolic gestures may prove to have substantial impact." Landau outlined the following possible actions: the termination of EXIM loans, program and personnel reductions including the removal of military advisors, annulment of the extradition treaty, and "obstruction and harassments," such as limiting access for Chile's national airlines to U.S. airspace and restricting the number of visas issued to Chileans.[130] These actions would counter the perception of an impassive Carter administration in the face of this defiance by the Chilean government and may have some future impact.

Secretary of State Vance agreed with Landau's assessment and ultimately recommended a path that implemented punitive symbolic actions that it could control. Vance, like Landau, noted that the court's decision made it highly improbable that the accused Chileans would be tried in Chile or held accountable for the assassinations. "It is likely," Vance concluded, "that this act of terrorism, committed on the streets of our nation's capital, will go unpunished." Chile, Vance argued, "bears a two-fold responsibility for these crimes." First, it was culpable in the planning and execution of the attacks. Second, it was remiss in its failure to investigate and bring to justice those responsible. "By its actions—and its inactions—the government of Chile has, in effect, condoned this act of international terrorism within the United States. We believe that it is essential that we make clear, both to Chile and to others throughout the world, that such actions cannot be tolerated."[131]

Vance, however, dismissed the "extreme measures" being suggested by some members of Congress, among others, "including enacting legislation to limit private bank lending to Chile, withdrawing our Ambassador, or even breaking relations altogether. I have considered these options, and while I share the outrage of those who have suggested them, I believe steps of this sort would not serve our interests in Chile or elsewhere." Vance instead offered several measures designed to signal the administration's extreme disapproval without damaging other interests, including ongoing human rights efforts. First, he recommended withdrawing Ambassador Landau for consultation and reducing the size of the staff in Chile. He stated that "no further diplomatic steps are possible at this time, short of recalling Ambassador Landau permanently or breaking relations, neither of which I recommend." Second, Vance advised terminating all projects currently in the FMS pipeline. Although there was only a small amount of equipment in question, due to restrictions in place since 1976, Vance advised that all remaining projects be terminated as quickly as possible, even if it entailed some termination costs. Third, although he suggested that the three defense attachés remain in Santiago, Vance recommended that Carter withdraw the military group (Milgroup). Fourth, Vance urged the president to enact the Chafee Amendment to the Export-Import Bank Act to block any further government financing to Chile, arguing that "Chile's actions in the Letelier case justify the invocation of this extraordinary remedy. While Congress intended that this sanction should be used only sparingly, it would be difficult to conceive of a more appropriate case than the present one—where high officials of a foreign government have been directly implicated in murders committed on United States territory, and where that government has effectively frustrated all attempts to bring the accused perpetrators of these crimes to justice." Along with this, Vance encouraged the president to deny export licenses for materials to the Chilean armed forces and deny the Overseas Private Investment Corporation (OPIC) guarantees. Finally, Vance stated that "in conjunction with the actions described above, I believe that we should issue a statement reiterating our grave concern and deep disappointment at the Chilean Government's actions, including in particular its failure to investigate this crime."[132]

On November 30, closely following Vance's recommendations, Carter announced the measures that the U.S. government would take in response to Chile's unwillingness to cooperate further in investigating the assassinations of Letelier and Moffitt. The administration would reduce U.S. personnel in Chile and terminate all foreign military sales, including those already in the "pipeline." The military advisory group would be phased out by 1980, and the EXIM Bank would end its "limited remaining financial operations in Chile" and no longer provide export insurance. OPIC would similarly end activities in Chile and would no longer guarantee investments. The U.S. government did not, however, recall Ambassador Landau permanently or move to block private loans and investment in the country.

The Carter administration implemented most of the measures recommended by congressional leaders, including invoking the Chafee Amendment, but its announced course of action drew strong criticism from the Movement. Many of the strongest human rights proponents in Congress expressed disappointment and disapproval that the administration would not permanently withdraw the ambassador or move to block private loans. Senator Kennedy continued to call for the permanent withdrawal of the U.S. ambassador and staff from Chile and stated that without the termination of private loans and investment, "Carter's response was weak and ineffective."[133] The IPS agreed with Kennedy, charging that the "measures amounted to 'little more than a wrist slap.'"[134] Peter Weiss, chair of the IPS board of trustees, had an opportunity to confront Robert Pastor about the Carter administration's handling of the case in 1980. The exchange quickly turned sour, as each reiterated the arguments about private finance and leverage that had been exchanged in the fall of 1979. Weiss reported to the IPS leadership, "I was told pretty bluntly that the U.S. had done all it was going to do in this case." Weiss in turn "suggested to Mr. Pastor that the Carter administration had let Pinochet, a petty military dictator, pull the wool over its eyes." Weiss concluded from this encounter that the "Carter administration doesn't feel the assassination was of sufficient importance to warrant any further steps than the one they have taken. . . . They think they did a strong job of demonstrating their dissatisfaction." The IPS obviously disagreed and voiced the dissatisfaction of many in the human rights community.[135]

The Letelier assassination had become one of the most visible markers of the administration's commitment to hold the Pinochet regime accountable on human rights issues; hence, it became a gauge to measure the administration's dedication to redirecting U.S. policies in the region away from its previous support of the dictator and interventionism in the name of stability, security, and anticommunism. The administration's options were bounded not only by past regional relations but also by Chilean realities and U.S. domestic politics. The Pinochet regime was susceptible to pressure on human rights, but only insofar as it solidified rather than threatened its control domestically.

In Chile the Carter administration sought a path that balanced between distancing the U.S. government from the dictatorship, maintaining pressure on the military leadership to improve human rights, and avoiding overt interference in internal affairs that would prompt a nationalist backlash. The Carter government did not coddle Pinochet, overlooking human rights abuses in the name of anticommunism, as past administrations had done. In response to human rights concerns, the administration reduced economic and military aid, utilized international bodies to press for improvement, and tried to create and support openings for change and dissent within Chile. Although it hoped for a democratic transition in the long run, the administration's policy objective was not to impose new leadership on Chile from without but to work with the government on specific measures guided by Chilean needs articulated by advocate networks.

The administration's approach to Chile manifested its attempt to rethink Cold War polarities and find a more nuanced way to engage the world as it existed, while remaining true to its core values. Although the administration failed to bring Letelier's assassins to justice, Carter's policies sought to address U.S. behaviors that had eroded human rights in the past and moved the United States toward a greater respect for sovereignty and ideological diversity in the Western Hemisphere. This policy, he believed, would better reflect the nation's values and bolster U.S. influence and interests in the region, even as its influence with particular governments diminished temporarily.

The Carter administration's policies would not have been as aggressive or successful at curbing abuses had there not been an active human rights movement within Chile to build on, and partners within Congress and the advocate community in Washington supplying information and mobilizing public opinion in support of its policies. Its successes were a product of its ability to leverage and amplify the grassroots work of a passionate and well-organized advocate community. The Movement had shifted the terms of debate before Carter even came to office, and it created pressure that kept human rights at the forefront of U.S.-Chilean relations. At the same time, Chile's overwhelming symbolic importance to a particular vision of human rights limited the administration's ability to nuance its policies and created tensions among allied actors.

Chapter 4

Weighing the Costs

Human Rights and U.S.-Argentine Relations

In September 1979 a delegation from the Organization of American States' Inter-American Commission on Human Rights (IACHR) visited Argentina to investigate human rights violations alleged to have taken place since the March 1976 coup. During the two-week visit, members of the commission spoke with human rights groups and government officials, visited prisons, and investigated alleged secret detention centers. Their report, released seven months later, established that the military government—not renegade paramilitary groups or rogue terrorists—was largely responsible for the violence and disappearances of the past three years.[1] The Argentine junta's invitation for the IACHR to visit was a turning point for human rights violations in Argentina and the culmination of a nearly two-year effort by the Carter administration to secure significant human rights concessions from the Videla government.

Argentina was the site of some of the most vigorous and comprehensive human rights diplomacy of the Carter administration.[2] Argentina's coup, coinciding with the 1976 presidential election, placed the country at the center of U.S. debates about human rights and relations with Cold War allies. Indeed, for the Movement, Argentina became a new front for strategies honed in Chile in the previous three years. Criticism of the Ford administration's country reports in January 1977 signaled that Argentina would be a key test-ing ground for the incoming Carter administration's linkage of human rights performance and foreign aid, and its commitment to dissociate the U.S. from repressive Cold War allies.[3] Unlike Chile, where Congress had significantly curtailed foreign aid before Carter took office, the new administration had a full array of instruments and options before it. Yet the administration's human rights diplomacy in Argentina rarely prompted the kind of reform and change in foreign conditions that advocates had hoped for. Robust hu-man rights initiatives and legislative mechanisms did disassociate the United States from abuses of its formerly close ally but were less effective at curtail-ing gross violations by the military regime. The administration's pressure on specific prisoners' cases yielded results, but the junta was much more resistant to dismantling the system of state terror and repression that per-petuated abuses.

Carter's Argentina policy—which a retrospective assessment labeled "one of the most difficult and vexing cases"—highlighted tensions between the dual objectives distancing the United States from dictatorships and bargaining with repressive regimes to improve specific human rights prob-lems.[4] The Movement advocated for dissociation and executive fidelity to congressional mandates as the best path to pressure the military regime to change repressive practices and return to civilian rule. Through cooling dip-lomatic relations and adhering to legislative instruments, the White House signaled its commitment to human rights and a reformed foreign policy. Both the Carter administration and many Argentine advocates, however, initially believed that the most likely path forward in Argentina was work-ing through "moderates" in the military regime. Moreover, the Carter ad-ministration had to avoid charges of U.S. intervention that could strengthen hardliners within the junta and generate a nationalist backlash to human rights pressures.

The Carter administration had built its foreign policy around the premise that the promotion of human rights would serve long-term national inter-ests by building the United States' stature and influence in the international system. In Argentina, however, its human rights initiatives increasingly con-flicted with other short-term interests, particularly economic growth and as-cendant security concerns. With a struggling economy at home and the loss of trade due to human rights legislation curtailing international investment, some Americans began to question how this policy served the national inter-est. Human rights might improve the country's standing in the long run, but its implementation was having an immediate and tangible negative effect.

This cost was made all the less palatable because the causal relationship between economic aid and human rights abuses was less direct than that of military assistance. The use of IFIs, designed to promote development and foster economic growth, also raised questions about the relative priority given to political rights at the expense of economic rights championed by much of the developing world.

By summer 1978 the Carter administration faced increasingly restrictive human rights legislation passed by pro–human rights contingents in Congress on one side and pressure about the "costs" of human rights policy for business and security interest on the other. Looking for a way to break the stalemate in its relations with Argentina and reduce these competing domestic demands, the administration ultimately secured a guarantee from the Argentine government for the IACHR visit in exchange for lifting its block on EXIM Bank financing for several projects, including a hydroelectric dam on the Yacyretá River. The visit by the IACHR was one of the primary objectives of the administration's human rights policy, and it provided a crucial platform for further human rights improvements but came at a cost to the administration's credibility with the Movement. Rising tensions with the Soviet Union and desire for Argentine cooperation on a grain embargo further reinforced the perception of the administration's "retreat" on human rights and undercut its standing with U.S. advocates. As it pursued a more complex array of issues in its bilateral relations with Argentina, the administration debated internally the most effective means of implementing its concern for human rights in bilateral relations. Yet the debate was always about *how* to advance human rights; the administration never reverted to a simplistic Cold War framework of excusing abuses in the name of anticommunism, nor did it simply jettison human rights in favor of competing security or economic interests.

The Dirty War and Double Messages

In July 1974 Argentine president Juan Perón died, leaving what one historian describes as a "howling political vacuum."[5] The country spiraled deeper into chaos as his wife, Isabel Perón, succeeded him as president, her term marked by political instability, economic inflation, strikes, and protests. In November the government imposed a state of siege and detained more than three thousand Argentines suspected of subversive activities. Bombings were frequent in Buenos Aires and other cities throughout Argentina. As the country faced

severe economic problems and deepening political instability, antistate violence increased from both new leftist guerrilla forces and right-wing paramilitary organizations.[6] By October 1975 Governmental Decree 2772 allowed
the military to assist in police actions throughout the country and gave the
military enormous latitude to act against anyone it deemed subversive.

Argentina was clearly in the throes of violence and repression by the
time the military took power in March 1976, and many Argentine citizens,
exhausted and scared after years of upheaval, welcomed the new military
government, hoping it would put an end to political unrest and economic instability in the country. The country was no stranger to military intervention
in its political process.[7] And when the military did seize power, it was nothing
like the dramatic Chilean coup three years earlier—no jets fired on the presidential palace, and no tanks filled the streets of Buenos Aires. In their address
to the nation the day after the coup, the heads of the three military branches,
Generals Videla, Massera, and Agosti, stressed national rebirth and duty as
the prime motivators behind the coup.[8] The new government proclaimed
that their primary objective was to rebuild the country, allowing Argentina
to realize its political and economic potential, become stronger and more
integrated, and end once and for all the cycle of violence that had marred its
development for decades.

In the name of stability, the military government undertook a complete
restructuring of the nation's institutions. The Proceso de Reorganización
Nacional (the Process of National Reorganization or Proceso) defined the
military government's rule and sought both the elimination of subversion
and the drastic reform of civic, economic, and political institutions that had
propagated instability and could be exploited by those seeking to weaken the
state.[9] To this end, the military severely limited all political activity, dissolved
the parliament, pursued drastic adjustments to the economic system, and
suspended emigration rights. It also prohibited the activities of many labor
and professional groups, including the right to strike and other forms of
work stoppage. It purged the universities and courts and required those remaining to pledge loyalty to the Proceso. It banned the press from publishing
anything with the effect of "disrupting, prejudicing, or lessening the prestige
of the activities of the Armed Forces."[10] Although these actions were severe,
many Argentines accepted them as a temporary necessity to reestablish law
and order.

The national reorganization not only curtailed civil and political rights; it
also inaugurated a new era of unprecedented state-sponsored violence. On
seizing power, military leaders warned that they would assume "the rigorous

task of eradicating, once and for all, the vices which afflict the nation." They prosecuted a "Dirty War" against unorthodox enemies who had to be eliminated if Argentina was to survive and prosper. It was a battle of good versus evil, civilization versus depravity, Christianity versus godlessness. Further, this Dirty War was part of the larger global struggle against communism.[11] The government used the labels "subversion," "enemy," and "terrorist" loosely, often including anyone who questioned military leadership. The linkage of internal subversives with a larger international communist threat justified unorthodox tactics and civilian casualties as an unfortunate but necessary cost in a national struggle for survival. Under the state of siege, legal guarantees evaporated and formal arrests soon became obsolete. More than eight thousand people were arrested as political prisoners, many of whom were tortured for several days before they were officially registered.[12]

The regime would become most notorious for its tactic of "disappearing" its victims. Individuals targeted by the regime were kidnapped from their homes, places of work, or public transportation, or they were simply abducted on the street by plain-clothed officers. They were usually taken to one of the 340 secret detention centers throughout the country, where they were tortured for weeks or months and later executed. The bodies were cremated, buried in mass graves, or dumped into the Río de la Plata or the Atlantic Ocean. Sometimes the victims were dropped, still alive and often heavily drugged, out of military helicopters into the ocean. When bodies started to wash up on the beaches, pilots simply flew farther out before disposing of their human cargo. The 1984 report of the Comisión Nacional sobre la Desaparición de Personas (National Commission on Disappeared People or CONADEP) reported almost nine thousand cases of such disappearances—3,830 in 1976 and another 2,966 in 1977—but has since revised the estimate to around thirty thousand.[13]

The phenomenon of the disappeared, which would become synonymous with the regime's excesses, initially had distinct advantages for the military government in Buenos Aires, which had learned from the growing international criticism of its counterpart in Santiago. In Argentina there would be no massive arrests or military in the streets to invite foreign criticism. Instead, the Argentine junta maintained a facade of normalcy while relying on the threat of simply being "disappeared." This strategy allowed the government to eliminate broadly defined "enemies of the nation" while denying any role in violations of human rights.

The Ford administration had also learned from the Chilean experience. While continuing to rely on regional strongmen sympathetic to U.S. Cold

War security interests, the Ford administration became more discreet in its support and sought to mitigate public relations problems stemming from the human rights abuses of its allies. Ford and Kissinger welcomed the Argentine junta, attempting to portray it publicly as moderate and restrained, and urging it to take care of its dirty business quietly and quickly.[14] Indeed, both the State Department and the Argentine government actively sought to minimize conflict with the U.S. Congress and the public over human rights issues arising from the new military government. Even as some in the State Department—responding to congressional mandates—pressed the regime on human rights, the message from Kissinger was clear: the Ford administration would not cause the regime any "unnecessary difficulties." In an October meeting Kissinger famously told Guzzetti to do what needed to be done, but do it quickly: "Look, our basic attitude is that we would like you to succeed. I have an old-fashioned view that friends ought to be supported. What is not understood in the United States is that you have a civil war. We read about human rights problems but not the context. The quicker you succeed the better."[15] At the same time, Kissinger cautioned that human rights abuses posed a public image problem and should be dealt with as such to alleviate growing pressure from the U.S. Congress and the international community.[16] Mitigating this "image problem," however, would become increasingly difficult with the Movement turning its attentions to problems within Argentina, and a new administration in Washington that was much more attentive to its concerns.

A Concern Both Legitimate and Germane

Congressional pressure and Movement activism made Argentina a necessary focus of the Carter administration's human rights policy from its first days in office. The Chilean coup had attenuated the international community to abuses of power by military governments, and activist networks were in place and responded quickly in the wake of the Argentine coup. Reaching out to existing groups in Argentina—especially the Asamblea Permanente por los Derechos Humanos (Permanent Assembly for Human Rights or Asamblea) and La Liga Argentina por los Derechos del Hombre (the Argentine League for the Rights of Man or La Liga)—solidarity networks and human rights organizations quickly began to publicize abuses perpetrated by the regime.[17] Coinciding with Carter's election in November, Amnesty International sent a high-profile delegation to Argentina to evaluate conditions and discuss human rights violations with government officials. The Argentine Mission Report resulting from this visit, released on March 1, 1977, detailed torture, political prisoners held without charges in "punitive conditions," and the complicity of the military government and police in the disappearances of civilians as well as widespread repression of civil and political rights.[18]

The Amnesty International report, released in the first months of the Carter administration, buttressed calls to terminate military aid to Argentina and helped ensure that human rights problems there would receive top billing by U.S. advocates and government officials alike. Drawing on findings from Amnesty's mission, the Movement targeted inaccuracies in the Ford administration's country report on Argentina in January 1977. Indeed, with aid to Chile already terminated, Argentina took on a significant symbolic role as a barometer of the new administration's commitment to congressional guidance on human rights.

The Movement's early emphasis on abuses by the Argentine junta influenced the Carter administration's human rights policy from the outset. Even before Carter's inauguration, administration officials sought out contacts and information from human rights and opposition groups in Argentina. During the transition period, Fred Rondon of the State Department's Latin America bureau wrote the U.S. embassy in Buenos Aires asking for detailed information about Argentine human rights groups and their contacts with the United States. Rondon also stressed that the embassy's human rights reports were "read avidly throughout our building. I guarantee you that Embassy Buenos Aires has a wide readership."[19] In a letter to the embassy a month later, praising their reporting on human rights, Rondon touted having "adopted an open-door approach to my job and made myself available to anyone interested in Argentina." Rondon took activists' information seriously, checking specific names in government lists of political prisoners with Movement contacts, concluding that the "GOA [government of Argentina] release lists are highly misleading."[20]

One of the first people to take advantage of Rondon's open door was Emilio Mignone, an internationally renowned lawyer and human rights advocate affiliated with the Asamblea, whose daughter Monica had been disappeared shortly after the coup. In a meeting with Rondon in January, Mignone emphasized the "all out nature of the conflict" and stressed the military's lack of concern about "innocent casualties." Mignone urged the Carter administration to talk directly and "frankly" to the Argentine junta to stress the centrality of human rights to relations between the two countries. This message had to come from all levels of government, especially the military.

"You must talk to the Argentine military through the Pentagon," Mignone explained, and for this reason, he recommended reducing rather than terminating military assistance, a course the administration ultimately took, reducing the slated Foreign Military Sales (FMS) budget for Argentina by half.[21]

Early contacts with Argentine advocates, along with Movement reports, underscored the massive violence taking place, making human rights the primary concern for bilateral relations. In an overview from the embassy during the administration's first days in office, Ambassador Robert Hill characterized relations between the two countries as "excellent" but noted that the junta's antisubversion campaign had produced "unwanted dividends" in its disregard for the rule of law and human rights. Hill, a Nixon appointee who had welcomed the coup the previous March, had become increasingly uneasy that violence perpetrated by the governing junta went beyond an unfortunate and temporary necessity to root out terrorism. He cast human rights as the most serious problem in relations between the two countries. "U.S. concern for human rights is in keeping with our long range objectives," he wrote. "If a healthy stable Argentine society is our primary objective, we can hardly applaud or condone practices which contribute to its antithesis. Our concern for human rights is both legitimate and germane."[22]

The Carter administration sought to avoid any ambiguity or double message about the emphasis it accorded to human rights. In a meeting with Argentine embassy officials in early February, Rondon underscored that the issue was not the "preoccupation of a few in Congress, but represent basic political forces at work in the United States," and one in which the new Carter administration placed "tremendous importance." While acknowledging the "terribly difficult problem" of terrorism, he warned that the U.S. "cannot accept that people with different views are persecuted, tortured, and murdered." The Argentine representative asked whether the U.S. embassy in Buenos Aires had conveyed a similar message, stressing, "It is essential for your same message to come from all channels. This did not happen in [the] past." Rondon assured him that "all levels" of the new administration would be advancing the same message. In separate meetings with military leadership, the U.S. embassy also "firmly disabused" them of the notion that human rights was a fringe concern. In a March meeting with Argentine counselor Juan Carlos Arlía, Derian empathized with the problems faced by the Argentine government, but she made clear that human rights was a central concern of both Congress and the new president, "not a device nor a political maneuver." In short, there would be no "double message" from this White House or dismissal of human rights as a minority view held by some overly vocal members of Congress and the U.S. public.[23] It was a message repeated at every level throughout the administration's first half year.

As with Chile, the administration's early robust advocacy for human rights in Argentina was tempered by concerns about interventionism. This concern was reinforced by Argentine contacts across the political spectrum. Mignone, for example, had cautioned in January against actions on behalf of human rights that would "put Argentina in a corner or isolate them."[24] The announced FMS cuts in February had "shaken" the military government, and Ambassador Hill reported that a "siege mentality" prevailed among the military leadership, making it unlikely that they would offer any changes beyond a "cosmetic toning down of abuses in order to assuage international criticism." The military was joined by the business community in its condemnation of the FMS cuts. Hill wrote that both American and Argentine businessmen "see our human rights policy as having evolved in a vacuum filled by impractical people with strange political ideas." They feared their businesses would suffer as a result and believed that the Carter administration had insufficiently considered U.S. interests before implementing these punitive measures on human rights grounds.[25]

More unsettling was criticism from those who condemned the government's repression but also suspected the United States of "acting for egocentric reasons." Notable among these individuals was Robert Cox, a U.S. citizen and editor of the English language *Buenos Aires Herald*. Cox was an outspoken advocate of human rights, but he believed the United States was "pursuing the right policy for the wrong reasons" and cast the administration's policy as a "latter-day version of our traditional imperialistic impulse, i.e. just another empty headed attempt to project our problems onto the world scene and impose our value systems on other people without due regard or much attention to their problems." He "bitterly opposed" the sanctions as "ineffective" and "counterproductive."[26]

Widespread concerns that aggressive policies on human rights would weaken Videla's "moderates" against hard-liners within the junta compounded the difficulties of balancing human rights pressures and respecting sovereignty. In his first report to the new administration, for example, Ambassador Hill had presented Videla as a moderate who "prefers conciliation to confrontation" and who had a tenuous control at best over the various security forces. "Worse," Hill continued, "there appears to be no better alternative. . . . The chances are that if Videla were replaced it would be by a hardline general who would exacerbate, not alleviate, the situation—and certainly so with respect to human rights."[27] This line of argumentation—often advanced by Videla himself—had been used during the Ford administration to avoid pressuring the Argentine junta on human rights issues, yet it was also reiterated by many of the Argentine opposition that the administration engaged in the early months.

In her "unofficial" visit to Argentina at the end of March, Derian heard time and again from diverse groups that Carter's human rights policies were the right idea with the wrong implementation because they weakened Videla and his moderate faction, thereby strengthening the hand of more strident members of the military leadership. Jacobo Korvadlov, the American Jewish Committee representative in Buenos Aires, feared that if "hardline generals" replaced "the moderate Videla" the country would move toward "totalitarianism and an official policy of anti-Semitism, which historically had been an off-shoot of totalitarianism." He therefore opposed the recent FMS "sanctions" against Argentina because they "would strengthen the hand of the totalitarian hardliners in the military."[28] José Luis de Imaz, a professor deeply concerned with Argentine human rights violations, found Carter's early initiatives "disturbing," stating that the United States was "pursuing the right ends with the wrong tactics." He warned Derian that current policies risked provoking a nationalist backlash to "intervention in the nation's internal affairs." If Videla was more of a "political animal," he explained, "he would have exploited the cut in military credits to whip up a nationalistic support for his government."[29] Former president Arturo Illia called Carter an "inspiration" and applauded his human rights policies as a move toward strengthening democracy in the hemisphere. Still, he stated that "as far as the Argentines were concerned, the return to civilian democratic government and respect for human rights were essentially questions which the Argentines would have to resolve for themselves."[30]

The perception of Videla's moderation was grounded in part in the widely shared belief that the political violence preceding the coup made the military takeover regrettable but necessary. The papal nuncio, Pio Laghi, stressed the background of political violence in understanding the current repression and argued that "groups of rightists not under the control of higher officers of the government" had perpetrated the most serious abuses. Still, he did not deny that the military leadership bore some responsibility. "They knew they have committed evil in human rights matters," he told Derian, "and do not need to be told of their guilt by visitors. This would be 'rubbing salt into the wounds.' "[31] Bishop Carlos T. Gattinoni, the head of the Evangelical Methodist Church and member of the Asamblea, also opined that "even longtime liberals such as himself . . . realized the coup was necessary and the country would have to go through a period of a conservative and firm re-ordering." Gattinoni attributed many of the current problems to the divide between Videla's moderate policies and the "hardline" forces in the navy and air force, which allowed "para-military" forces to operate beyond the control of the government.[32] Jacobo Timerman, editor of *La Opinión*, also stressed the unusual nature of the Argentine case and the violence that had preceded the coup, arguing that "the civilian government was guilty of extensive human rights violations and the military government is doing no more than its civilian predecessor in this field." Still, he approved of Carter's policy overall, saying it "has broken the mold that has characterized East-West relations (the cold war syndrome) since World War II." Unlike most of the other Argentines Derian met with, Timerman approved of the cut to FMS credits because, in his opinion, "it had finally stiffened the moderates and given them the courage to face up to the hard liners." Further, he believed it had energized the business community to back a moderate course in order to preempt further U.S. actions in the economic arena.[33]

Most of Derian's contacts, sympathetic to the regime or not, painted the picture of a moderate core to the military regime, somewhat justified in its excesses when placed in the context of the violence that had preceded the coup. Derian's meeting with the Asamblea Permanente, however, challenged any image of a moderate and restrained junta with horrific accounts of torture, describing the human rights situation as "barbaric." Rondon later recounted the meeting as "undoubtedly the most passionate exposition of the human rights picture which we experienced."[34] Thus, as the administration sought to be responsive to concerns about intervention weakening the elements in the junta most likely to be receptive to human rights concerns, the Asamblea's detailed accounts of abuses underscored the gross violations taking place that had to be addressed by the administration's own policy rationale and legislative mandates.

Information about gross violations by the Argentine regime also prompted Congress and the Movement to seek more aggressive measures from the administration. WOLA's newsletter noted, "Although there seems to be fairly wide agreement on 'a consistent pattern of gross violations of internationally recognized human rights,' in Argentina at present, there is a great shortage as to what might constructively be done."[35] WOLA asserted, "It would be much more sensible to make the tough political choices now, while the new administration has its options open and can demonstrate its commitment to a new morality in foreign policy." It pointed to the termination of security assistance as one material step the administration could take. This would "have an important symbolic effect" by signaling that the U.S. government "was not fully backing the military junta, as is generally assumed to be the case at present." This had the potential to push the military government to make concessions on human rights issues. Further, it would distance the U.S. government from the repressive regime, giving its human rights policy credibility in the short term and strengthening its position in Argentina in the long term.[36] In contrast to Mignone and other Argentine advocates, WOLA dismissed the value of maintaining military contacts as a means to advancing human rights and targeted ongoing military aid and training as a next step for disassociating the U.S. government from its Cold War ally, as well as ending material support for repression.[37]

Congress, similarly eager for bold policies commensurate with the human rights crisis in Argentina, also targeted military aid to the regime. In a letter to Secretary of State Vance in late February, Senator Kennedy praised the president's early statements on human rights and the preliminary cuts to the military assistance program, but he urged the administration to take further action. To underscore the urgency of the situation in Argentina, Kennedy attached a letter from a U.S. citizen and member of the Argentine Commission for Human Rights, Olga Talamante, detailing her torture and imprisonment after the coup. Kennedy suggested that, given the dire human rights conditions in Argentina, the military sales assistance slated for FY77 be withheld in its entirety. Alluding to the Ford administration's maneuvers to overcome congressional human rights restrictions on foreign aid, Kennedy concluded by warning, "I would hope that an effort would be made to insure that the object of reducing our military support of Argentina will not be undercut by any sudden spurt of commercial arms sales, which require license approval."[38] Rep. Robert Drinan (D-MA), who had participated in Amnesty International's mission to Argentina in November, also pressed the administration to do more. Rejecting charges that U.S. human rights pressures constituted "intrusion into Argentina's domestic affairs," Drinan instead argued that such actions represented "the simple and unassailable decision of our Government not to provide the tools of violence and repression to a military dictatorship which denies its citizens their most basic rights." He urged the Carter administration to terminate IMET programs slated for Argentina, averring that "$700,000 is a small sum but its symbolic significance is considerable." He noted that since his visit in November, violations by the regime had increased rather than decreased. "It is time for the United States to disassociate itself unequivocally from this repressive regime. To cease providing it with arms and weapons, and to terminate the training of its military officers—training which includes internal security programs."[39]

In a review of Carter's first one hundred days in office, the ADA expressed its hope that "the genuine concern expressed by this administration in human rights will finally end those supports to governments which permit them to oppress their own people." It called on the president to "spell out the extraordinary circumstances justifying continuing military assistance to Ethiopia, and Argentina, or terminate all military assistance."[40] The Movement and congressional proponents of human rights believed in legislative mechanisms as the best way to ensure a robust human rights policy that would elicit improvements from foreign governments and prevent their own government from being complicit in allies' abuses. The termination of these funds would thus have an important symbolic effect but would also underscore the costs to the junta of ongoing repression.

In the Hands of the Argentine Military

The administration was sympathetic to calls to action from Congress and the Movement but also wary of pushing too hard and alienating "moderate" military partners it believed it had to work with for improvements, which dovetailed with more pervasive concerns about intervention. Increasingly, however, Videla's supposed moderation was called into question by the magnitude of the ongoing violence and the junta's unwillingness to move beyond superficial restraints on state terror. A State Department summary of relations in early June noted that a year after the coup—even with security largely restored—the junta was not moving to normalize legal and political procedures. "On the contrary, they are polarizing society," failing to acknowledge the thousands of disappeared people and political prisoners. "Torture, disappearances, prolonged periods of incommunication, summary executions, intimidation of lawyers, journalists, and foreign refugees are undeniable." During its first six months in office, the Carter administration had "progressively" pressured the junta on human rights through reduction of military aid, routine denial of commercial arms purchases, votes against loans in IFIs, and numerous bilateral meetings, "unfortunately with little to show in return."[41]

Despite the lack of substantive improvements, the Argentine leadership did show increasing sensitivity to human rights and U.S. policy positions, even while sustaining the pretense of facing a dangerous guerrilla war.[42] In the lead-up to a June vote in the World Bank for more than $100 million in credits, Argentine officials asked the State Department "if it is too late for Argentine developments to influence [the U.S.] vote." Economy Minister José Alfredo Martínez de Hoz informed the U.S. embassy in Buenos Aires that, as a "gesture in response" to human rights concerns of U.S. officials, the Argentine government planned to announce the banning of a magazine that had recently published anti-Semitic materials, a release of some two hundred political prisoners, and a plan to "study the possible reinstatement" of the right for prisoners to leave the country in place of incarceration (or "right of option"). De Hoz asserted that "facts would show that there is a reassuring trend toward normalization and the rule of law in Argentina." These overtures signaled the junta's concern with its international image and eagerness to gain the Carter administration's good opinion. An article in the pro-junta *La Opinión* reported that the Argentine officials "flatly stated that the Government's recent actions were 'significant measures to counteract accusations from abroad and improve the country's image overseas.' "[43]

Many in the administration hoped that these efforts might be a signal of Videla's growing strength within the Argentine leadership and receptivity to further human rights initiatives. A recent State Department report on human rights conditions concluded that Videla "has demonstrated some success in curbing the hardline zeal for a right-wing take over." Moreover, human rights problems were being "aired more openly" in Argentina, including a public denunciation of torture by the Bishop's Conference and court criticism of the junta's "unsatisfactory responses to habeas corpus inquiries and judicial orders."[44] Although improvements were mostly cosmetic, they were a change from the intransigence of early months. In assessing these developments, the U.S. embassy concluded that "while the announcements in themselves show little by way of certifiable substantive change in government human rights practices, the government's decision to compile examples of human rights improvements demonstrates its rising sensitivity to the seriousness of the US human rights position."[45]

This tension between conciliatory rhetoric and limited improvements in conditions created competing pressures on the U.S. human rights policy. The administration's desire to avoid a purely punitive policy, together with Videla's supposed vulnerability, made it desirable to recognize and praise positive developments, however tenuous. A State Department human rights summary in mid-June concluded, "The Videla government continues to appear to have moderating influence on internal political and security matters and remains probably the most acceptable and only alternative to a more repressive regime espoused by military hardliners."[46] Max Chaplain, chargé at the U.S. embassy in Buenos Aires, was "impressed with the degree to which Martínez de Hoz has been able to elicit apparently positive GOA responses in sensitive human rights areas (albeit in order to elicit a favorable US vote)." The embassy urged that the administration "react favorably to this conscious step by the GOA to address [the] human rights situation."[47] Carter himself had been inclined to praise the Argentine government's June announcements and expressed his desire to make it "a matter of policy to acknowledge and express gratification for improvements in human rights once it has been determined that these improvements are real rather than cosmetic."[48]

The question of "real" versus "cosmetic" change, of course, was the crux of the issue. Ongoing gross violations made praising a mere declaration of intended reforms politically untenable. Coincident with the World Bank vote, Congress had passed new legislation, terminating all military aid to Argentina on September 30, 1978, if human rights conditions did not measurably improve. This legislation clearly signaled Congress's ongoing dissatisfaction with relations between the two countries. Despite concerns that anything but a "yes" vote would weaken Videla vis-à-vis hard-liners— thereby undermining human rights efforts—the administration chose to abstain from the World Bank vote. Vance explained the decision to Argentine foreign minister Montes the next day at the OAS meeting in Grenada, noting that recent actions by the regime had allowed the administration to abstain rather than vote against the loan. Vance assured them that the administration would "watch for further progress to see if we could soon vote in favor of loans." In response to Carter's desire to praise improvements, Vance warned the president that the Argentine announcements should be "viewed cautiously," given ongoing problems and lack of follow-through on previous promises.[49]

Vance's caution was prescient. More than a month after the World Bank vote, little had been done by the Argentine leadership and human rights conditions in Argentina remained "ominous," with disappearances, summary executions, and torture systematically deployed by the regime.[50] The administration, influenced by its Argentine contacts, clearly hoped that the violence that had marked the junta's first year in power was a regrettable response to security threats that had now been neutralized. By midsummer, however, these hopes faded. Although Videla presented himself as responsive to human rights issues, Washington continued to hear accounts that painted a very different picture of his leadership.

In June, Christopher, Derian, and Todman each met with former Argentine senator Hipolito Solari Yrigoyen, in a visit arranged by WOLA through Senator Kennedy's office. Yrigoyen had been arrested by the regime after the coup and tortured at a clandestine military location, an experience he recounted for Derian in their meeting. He rejected the notion that Videla was a moderate, holding the line against worse brutalities. Saying Videla "was not the worst of all leaders" would be "akin to saying there might have been someone worse than Hitler or Mussolini so everyone should be thankful." Videla, he said, was worse than Pinochet, "who at least openly declares his preference for authoritarian rule. Videla speaks of 'democracy,' 'due process' and human rights but he is lying when insisting that the situation in Argentina is improving." Yrigoyen attributed his own release to international efforts, and he noted that "specific foreign government measures may be disregarded publicly by leaders but cause uneasiness within 'the system.'" Although he warned the administration to act cautiously so as to avoid charges of intervention, he asserted that military did not want to be "isolated" from the United States and that this gave the Carter administration leverage for change.[51]

Yrigoyen told Christopher that Carter's human rights policies encouraged him. "We see this new policy reaching our people over the government," he said, "and the people know intuitively that this helps them." After the meeting he shared with Pastor that "the people of Latin America now feel that the United States is on the side of democracy rather than military dictatorships."[52] Yrigoyen's own reception by high-level U.S. officials underscored this very point. One solidarity newsletter reported that Yrigoyen's visit "added a new dimension to the emerging U.S. policy toward Latin America, which now appears to be willing to consider support for democratic alternatives in countries currently ruled by repressive military regimes." Reports of this visit in the international press, the article continued, "further exposed the hopes and expectations of domestic forces inside and out of Argentina." WOLA also praised the meeting in its newsletter, wondering, "Together with the Mondale-Frei and Christopher-Almeida meeting, is this an emerging trend to recognize democratic leaders and not just the defacto dictators we say we abhor?"[53]

The U.S. embassy's own reporting increasingly reinforced Yrigoyen's challenge to Videla's moderate image. In the summer of 1977 foreign service officer Francis Allen "Tex" Harris joined the embassy staff and threw an enormous amount of personal energy into his mandate to collect data on human rights violations.[54] Harris built extensive personal networks with advocates and government officials alike, seeking out established groups, particularly the Asamblea and Emilio Mignone, who in turn sent people to see him. Harris also made early connections with a group of women who had coalesced in April to protest the disappearance of their children in the Plaza de Mayo, a square in central Buenos Aires across from the Casa Rosada, the location of Argentina's executive branch. Though not obvious at the time, these women, joined by hundreds of others on the same mission, would in time become the face of human rights in Argentina, known both within their country and around the world as Las Madres de Plaza de Mayo (the Mothers of the Plaza de Mayo or Las Madres).[55] Harris attended the Madres' church services and visited them regularly at the Plaza de Mayo. He printed up thousands of business cards and passed them out at the Plaza de Mayo, asking people to come talk to him and explain to him what was going on. "The Mothers [of the Plaza de Mayo] were very suspicious at first," he remembered, "and then one came. It's really a word of mouth kind of thing," because the embassy was soon full of Argentines wanting to share information every day.

Indeed, Harris had made the unprecedented request that he be allowed to have regular hours in which Argentines could come into the embassy and report human rights violations, particularly the disappearance of family members. So from 2:00 to 4:00 p.m. every day, Harris and a secretary would see people in a small space, "like a bad dentist's office," and record their account on 5 × 8 cards. Given the type of sensitive information he was collecting and the U.S. government's previously warm relations with the junta, it is in some way surprising that Harris had any visitors at all. In a testament to his efforts to build trust and credibility with Argentines, the office was flooded and eventually became "almost unmanageable."[56]

Shortly after Harris's posting to Buenos Aires, the State Department began receiving extensive missives detailing human rights conditions in Argentina. Harris had begun to compile the information gathered through these interviews and meetings in tables and charts, "kind of a temperature chart," plotting disappearances week by week. The scope and scale of the violence startled him and other U.S. officials. His reporting belied the government line that this was just "military and police crazies against Montonero crazies." Instead, "we began to see the hand of the organization and the structure." Although other human rights groups in Argentina had come to similar conclusions and compiled similar reports, Harris's reporting went straight to Washington, providing a direct link between ordinary citizens in Argentina and the U.S. government. Moreover, Harris became a source the international press felt comfortable with. "I had no better or worse information than the *Liga* or the *Asamblea*," Harris noted, but his position as a U.S. government official gave the information extra weight and credibility. Harris had frequent off-the-record meetings with reporters in which he would share his charts and numbers, thereby raising the international profile of the advocate community's information and work.[57]

Harris and the embassy became a channel for the Carter administration to hear from the people of Argentina, not just its government. Harris described himself as a *"mediocampista.* I was the midfielder." Harris avowed that he was not "involved in the policy." The information he gathered, however, became a linchpin in the administration's implementation of legislative guidelines and informed high-level démarches to the Argentine government and the Carter administration's overall strategy. His officer evaluation report in April 1978 affirmed that "the materials he has prepared on the subject of human rights violations in Argentina have had a direct and continuous bearing on the policy the United States adopts toward this country."[58]

The embassy reports—creating an irrefutable picture of the violence perpetrated by the regime—were essential to the administration's deliberations in the summer of 1977. The embassy's data clearly indicated that no paramilitary forces were "operating out of control of the authorities" and that disappearances "appear attributable directly to security forces." The junta, however, was firmly entrenched politically, and therefore "the question of human rights will be clearly in the hands of the Argentine military" for the foreseeable future. Thus, even as it questioned Videla's moderation, the administration believed it had to work with, not around, the military regime.[59]

There Are No Moderates

After half a year in office, Argentina had become a critical test for the Carter administration's human rights policy. The administration had avoided the "double message" of the Ford years, but it had made little demonstrable impact on human rights conditions. The Carter administration, sensitive to charges of intervention, sought to deploy diplomatic overtures that would underscore its commitment to human rights but also signal a willingness to work with the military government. Yet working with moderates looked like a return to the "quiet" diplomacy of the Ford administration, amplifying criticism within the United States from those who wanted further disassociation from the regime. In August the administration dispatched both Todman and Derian to Argentina to try to move human rights issues forward and create a basis for more productive relations between the two countries.

Argentine advocates told the U.S. delegations that they saw no significant improvements in their government's human rights performance since the advent of the Carter administration. Indeed, repression had "intensified" with several high-profile arrests, including human rights advocate Adolfo Perez Esquivel and Jacobo Timerman. Emilio Mignone darkly observed that "like the sorcerer's apprentice, the government has set a security apparatus into motion and it could not now control it." Still, the group maintained that the Carter administration's best option was working through Videla and the "moderate group," targeting their policy to coax improvements on human rights issues without strengthening the hand of hard-liners. Even as they expressed appreciation for the U.S. government's efforts, some advocates cautioned the administration to use measures that targeted the military regime, not the general public. "No one cares about arms but economic steps could lead to a growth of anti-Americanism," one advocate warned. Another, however, disagreed, arguing that the United States was "enjoying greater popularity today in Argentina than it has for many years and U.S. actions designed to promote human rights, including negative action in the international banks, is seen in a positive light." The group focused on the right of option—a "great escape valve"—and the publication of lists of detainees as two measures that Derian could advocate for in her meetings. In addition to a return to the rule of law, these measures would give them instruments to advance their own advocacy internally.[60]

The advocates' suggestions were prominent in Derian's meetings with the military leadership the following day. She urged President Videla and Economy Minister Martínez de Hoz to "show its strength" by restoring due process and rule of law and appealing to its population for support. She acknowledged the difficulties the regime had faced since taking power, but she asserted that now was the time for the military to demonstrate its dedication to the Western values it professed and show the world the progress it had made in restoring those values in Argentina. This would not only help it address international criticism but also build "the good will of the people" of Argentina.[61]

Derian's tone was less cordial with Interior Minister Harguindeguy and Foreign Minister Massera. She noted the discrepancy between the Argentine government's talk of a defeat of terrorism and return to normalcy on the one hand, and the reports of ongoing repression and disappearances on the other, relying heavily on information from the embassy and advocate groups. Harguindeguy responded that her "preoccupation for the rights of the person are no less than the responsibility the GOA has for internal security." Derian pushed back, observing that the Argentine government's response to terrorism with more violence did not protect ordinary Argentines but rather made them "victims of the state," and she referred to the weekly vigils for missing family members held in the Plaza de Mayo. Derian similarly confronted Foreign Minister Massera on allegations of torture taking place at the Navy Mechanical School, a charge he flatly denied. Massera assured Derian that Argentina was "in the process" of returning to normalcy, and that the "end was in sight." Derian expressed her hope that this was the case, pointing to the Humphrey-Kennedy Amendment, which would limit military aid and cooperation between the two countries by October 1978 if human rights conditions did not improve. International opinion, she observed, was becoming increasingly hostile toward Argentina, stating that "it would be devastating if Argentina became the next Chile in the eyes of the international community." Derian pushed for real changes, warning against a "public relations approach," which would be met with skepticism and disbelief.[62]

Figure 10. Patricia Derian (center) with President Carter (right) and National Security Advisor Zbigniew Brzezinski (left), December 6, 1978. Courtesy of the Jimmy Carter Presidential Library.

Todman, arriving just days after Derian's visit, took a similar line in his meetings, asserting that "progress can be made more rapidly" on human rights and stressing the centrality of the issue to U.S. foreign policy. Todman told Videla that he had received "many reports" of human rights violations resulting from antiterrorist campaigns and that both the Carter administration and Congress "were strongly motivated to take a stand against any such abuse." Todman acknowledged the difficulties faced by the Argentine military, but now that its war on terrorism was winding down, "it would now be seen as a demonstration of strength if the GOA took measures with prisoners and other detained persons that reflected that strength," suggesting publication of a list of prisoners, reinstating the right of option, and returning to the rule of law. Argentina, Todman advised, "cannot expect international respect and support until internationally recognized rules of behavior are observed." Todman's and Derian's private overtures to the government were remarkably consistent and represented the administration's unapologetic promotion of human rights in the face of ongoing repression by the regime. As Todman concluded to Videla, continued human rights violations would "undermine any effort to strengthen relations between our countries." The junta's behavior put it firmly in the "gross violator category," making it the most important issue in U.S. relations with Argentina.[63]

By exerting pressure privately, the administration had sought to temper the appearance of intervention. Yet even these visits to engage the regime irritated nationalist sentiment. One Argentine newspaper defiantly asked, "And what if we investigated human rights in the U.S.?" Argentines were ready to "engage in dialogue as equals," but were not "accustomed to giving in to anyone's . . . scrutiny for no particular reason."[64] In an interview with an Argentine weekly periodical between the two visits, Foreign Minister Montes stated bluntly that the emphasis on human rights by the Carter administration did not fundamentally alter the junta's basic perceptions of national interest or hemispheric relations. "U.S. policy is very clear in this respect and I also believe that Argentina's position is very clear after the meeting of the Organization of American States in Grenada."[65]

Despite its public protestations, the administration's internal assessments indicated that the recent visits had impressed on the Argentine government the importance of these issues and "heartened public groups and political factions who seek correction of these abuses." During his visit to Washington to sign the Panama Canal Treaty in early September, Videla asserted publicly his "own heightened concern and intention to make his concern felt" in human rights, promising improvements by the end of the year.

The State Department was optimistic that Videla's trip to Washington and meetings with senior members of the administration for the Panama Canal Treaty signing would "strengthen his hand—as well as his resolve" to make improvements and rein in hard-line elements. Moreover, the administration noted an enlivened advocacy for human rights within Argentina following the visit. Derian's and Todman's human rights message, along with Harris's ongoing work in the embassy, clearly reached the Argentine public, as evidenced by an "outpouring of petitions"—almost 326 separate cases—asking them directly for help locating disappeared individuals.[66]

The Movement, by contrast, was less optimistic about both the Argentine government's promises and the administration's policies. Noting the complete absence of follow-through by Videla on any of the announced measures, U.S. advocates sought to further disassociate the United States from the Argentine regime. Its gross violator status could not be papered over with diplomatic niceties and vague declarations of intent, and the administration's evident desire to find positive developments only further undermined the credibility of its policies. As with Chile, Todman's statements following his visit belied his vigorous advocacy on behalf of human rights. His blithe assertion that the human rights situation was improving in Argentina was intended to signal to Videla and others that the United States was not irrevocably hostile to it and that "any human rights improvements would be recognized."[67] Yet when contrasted with Deputy Assistant Secretary of State for Human Rights Mark Schneider's more frank assessment of conditions before the House Subcommittee on International Relations some weeks later, Todman appeared to reflect a serious rift within the administration.[68]

This divide in the administration's public position raised the specter of Washington yet again transmitting the infamous "double message," and prompted speculation that the administration's human rights policy was "slipping from center stage."[69] In a letter to President Carter, the U.S.-based Argentine Commission for Human Rights denounced Todman's claims that "violations of human rights have been decreased" and that improvements were evident in all areas. "Amnesty International, and the International Commission of Jurists as well as the United States' Department of State and the United States Embassy in Buenos Aires are well aware of the long list of human rights violations which have taken place in Argentina *in the period immediately preceding Mr. Todman's visit to that country*," the letter noted.[70] WOLA lamented the apparent determination to use "carrots" in the face of ongoing problems, and observed that a key question "for both

Administration and Administration-watchers has become: What constitutes 'improvement' in human rights?"[71]

The Panama Canal Treaty celebrations similarly alienated human rights advocates in Washington. WOLA was critical of the administration's recent "insensitivity to the power of symbolic action," pointing to the recent "tete-a-tete meetings between Latin America's most notorious violators and President Carter in Washington."[72] At a Movement rally during the Panama Canal Treaty meetings, Congressman Tom Harkin shared his "outrage" that Videla, Pinochet, and others were going to be "honored" by the U.S. government at a state gala. Harkin announced that if Carter wanted the American people to believe his administration "stands unequivocally for human rights in Latin America, then President Carter ought to be meeting with such people as Cardinal Silva and Isabel Letelier and Ernesto Cardenal, Senator Hipolito Solari [Yrigoyen], who speak out for human rights and are laying down their lives for human rights in Latin America." He rejected the assurances by the Latin American leaders that human rights conditions were improving. "Anyone who believes them may as well believe in the tooth fairy. And the crucial question is, does our President believe them?"[73]

The administration did not, in fact, believe them. Despite encouraging assurances from the regime following each visit, human rights conditions remained dire. The military government had announced the resumption of the right of option, but no prisoners had yet been released under its auspices, and disappearances continued apace. By Vance's own visit to Buenos Aires in November, the military leadership had made few significant improvements, and the Carter administration's effort to find cooperative basis for relations had yielded little reduction of state violence. In their meeting with Vance, Derian, and Todman, members of the Asamblea reported that Videla's statements during his trip to Washington in September had raised their hopes, but "expectations of improvement have not been filled." Gattinoni stressed that "silence is the major problem in Argentina today"; the Asamblea and other Argentine human rights groups had difficulty getting any traction when the government refused to answer any of their inquiries into missing and detained people. Mignone observed, "Either the government knows and refuses to say what is going on, or the government does not know and therefore cannot say what is going on." He commented that he was uncertain which of these two options was worse.[74]

Vance's meetings with President Videla and Foreign Minister Massera in mid-November repeated the same message as Derian and Todman had received, and in return, the same promises—yet unmet—from the military leadership. Vance took the open yet cool tone of earlier visits, warning "in the event that tangible, visible progress in the human rights field failed to materialize in a way that could be reported to the world," the administration would have no choice but to vote against Argentine loans in IFIs. Moreover, legislative mandates would result in the termination of military aid and co-operation in less than a year if human rights conditions continued as they were now. The foreign minister said he understood the U.S. position but felt like a "mattress" being pushed from both sides, with the United States on one hand and the navy, which "saw the American position from a less enlightened viewpoint," on the other. Vance presented a list of some 7,500 names of disappeared people or people believed to be held under executive power, compiled by the U.S. embassy and State Department in cooperation with advocacy groups and family members.[75] Reflecting the many petitions he received from human rights groups and families in advance of his visit, Vance urged the government once again to make their own list of prisoners public and respond to inquiries on disappeared people, regularize detention procedures, and restore the right of option and rule of law.[76]

The month after Vance's visit saw some improvements, including the "Christmas Amnesty" and release of some 389 prisoners from executive detention and granting ten right-of-option petitions. The regime also announced that it had compiled a list of 3,607 individuals being held under executive power, which it would make public "at an opportune time." These positive signals were counteracted by a December raid on a meeting of Las Madres and the subsequent disappearance of eleven of its Argentine members and two French nuns. The regime made a clumsy attempt to alternatively blame it on "subversive nihilism," the Montoneros, or rival branches of the military, with the army and navy both implying the other was responsible in some way. In short, after a year of intensive effort by the administration, the regime gave greater lip service to human rights concerns, but the mechanisms of state violence—disappearances, torture, detention without charges—churned on, even as the threat of terrorist violence had been virtually eliminated. By the beginning of 1978 the administration had largely concluded that "there are no moderates" in the Argentine regime.[77]

Despite stagnation of U.S.-Argentine relations and human rights conditions, the administration believed that its human rights efforts were having a positive impact, both in Argentina and as part of a broader policy. Jessica Tuchman reported in January, "Virtually all world leaders are concerned with human rights. They know that now their human rights image is a significant factor in their standing in the international community—as well as in their relations in the US."[78] A State Department assessment of the administration's first year of human rights initiatives noted, "No authoritarian regime has fundamentally altered its political system, nor are the hardcore dictatorships likely to take action which they would perceive (in some cases rightly) as political suicide." Still, there were signs of improvement in many areas, and the report was optimistic that "a trend seems to have begun which could gather momentum and which already is improving the plight of individuals—including those under some still-authoritarian regimes. And since individuals are what the human rights policy is primarily about, even the scattered and partial successes registered to date are important. Moreover, even marginal reductions in repression offer more latitude to dissidents, which in turn contributes to an internal dynamic that may produce further change."[79] Christopher reported to the president in early January 1978, "One of the important effects of our human rights policy has been to give greater importance to private organizations dedicated to advancing the cause of human rights."[80] The administration's efforts had also begun to influence institutions that previously had no clear human rights mandate. In IFIs, after initial resistance, other countries were accounting for human rights conditions in their deliberations, with an increasing number joining with the United States to oppose loans to gross violators.[81]

In Argentina specifically, the report noted that although the regime was unhappy with human rights pressures, it had not yet damaged other U.S. interests, including nuclear nonproliferation. The report concluded, "We cannot know what price we might one day pay for the deterioration in our once close military relationships with Brazil and Argentina. That obviously depends in part on the political evolution of the countries themselves—an evolution to which the human rights policy, if successful, could contribute positively."[82] WOLA's first newsletter of 1978 went even further, reporting that "despite this stagnant situation, Carter's human rights stance has had a strong impact in Argentina." The newsletter pointed to the use of human rights rhetoric by the different branches of the military government in spats with one another. "Unequivocal evidence of the impact of Carter's human rights policy is that Admiral Massera . . . is pushing President Videla to produce lists of political prisoners." Although WOLA had no illusions about the military leadership's sincerity on human rights, the use of the issue in internal politics "is bringing the issue into public debate . . . and putting pressure on Videla to respond to human rights concerns."[83] Yet even as it saw its efforts begin to bear fruit in bilateral relations and international standards at the beginning of 1978, the administration faced new domestic pressures over the economic "costs" of its human rights mechanisms.

Treading a Middle Course

Growing concerns about the cost of human rights policies merged with familiar conservative charges that human rights priorities weakened traditional Cold War allies. In January 1978 a congressional delegation from the House Committee on Banking, Finance and Urban Affairs visited Argentina as part of a four-country tour to examine the actions of multilateral lending agencies the United States participated in, particularly the Inter-American Development Bank. The group returned from their trip troubled by the repercussions of the new human rights statutes in the operation of these institutions. The delegation, chaired by Rep. William Moorhead (D-PA), wrote to President Carter, stating that they all agreed that the U.S. government should continue to pursue its "human rights philosophy" through "Presidential proclamations and other official statements." However, they concluded from their visit that human rights mandates had been "too rigidly applied," leading to economic sanctions that were "not effective" and "counterproductive." Moreover, they claimed, this view was shared with "the people" of the countries they visited, who "seem to believe that moral suasion and the power of world opinion were more effective in achieving progress toward human rights than economic sanctions." In Argentina, for example, the delegation had met with three human rights groups, including Las Madres, and "the repeated refrain was 'don't use economic sanctions against our country.'" The delegation affirmed its support for "policy statements on human rights" and conceded that Congress "may have overreacted in attempting to put these statements in legislative form," but they also charged the State Department had "overreacted to expressions from the President and the Congress in a way that is not only detrimental to the U.S. but also to the people about whose human rights we are concerned."[84] In a follow-up meeting with the president, Congressman Moorhead charged that the "young zealots" on the Christopher Committee were hurting the United States' "good friends Chile and Argentina."[85]

The administration bristled at being chastised as "overly rigid" in incorporating human rights into economic aid and IFI decisions. In a memo to the president, Vance and Christopher noted that the administration preferred to use positive actions rather than "sanctions" in applying its human rights policy. "However," they wrote, "in addition to the general thrust of our human rights policy, we are explicitly required by a wide array of federal statutes to oppose grants or loans to human rights violators." They believed that the administration had "acted with moderation" in applying these statutes. Out of the hundreds of loans it had considered, human rights considerations had only resulted in votes against nine loans to five countries—Argentina, Chile, Paraguay, South Yemen, and Uruguay—and abstentions on fourteen more. In these cases there could be no doubt that the governments engaged in the "consistent pattern of gross violations" referred to by the legislation. Moreover, the administration had used the "needy people exception" generously, to the point that it undermined congressional confidence in the administration's human rights diplomacy. Brzezinski had reported in December 1977 that relations with congressional human rights proponents were "at a very low ebb," sharing with the president that "most human rights advocates in Congress believe that were it not for their continuing pressure and vigilance, the administration would renege on its commitment to human rights."[86] In short, members of Congress were criticizing the administration for complying with legislative mandates that the administration had sought to avoid for precisely these reasons.

In a response letter to the committee, Carter reaffirmed his administration's commitment to using "positive actions" and "normal diplomatic channels" to advance its human rights policies, rather than punitive measures. The letter pointed out, however, that although it had attempted to be flexible in its pursuit of its human rights objective, many of these "so-called 'sanctions'" resulted from compliance with federal statutes passed by Congress. It further highlighted efforts to channel bilateral economic assistance and IFI lending to countries that demonstrated a respect for human rights, countering the notion that its policy was all sanctions. The president's letter closed with a plea for cooperation between Congress and his administration to preserve the flexibility needed for an effective human rights policy.[87]

The Carter administration would continue to face this double bind of increasingly restrictive legislation and simultaneous criticism of its overzealous implementation throughout 1978, as Congress proposed new human rights measures for the EXIM Bank and OPIC.[88] At the same time, the administration confronted mounting domestic pressure to end unpopular limits on economic aid and foreign financing that affected U.S. exports and businesses.[89] In a May meeting with Pastor at the NSC, the U.S. Chamber of Commerce expressed "general fears about the damaging effects of our human rights policy," although when pressed by Pastor on specific issues of concern, they "agreed that we were successful treading a middle course in Argentina."[90] U.S. ambassador to Argentina Raul Castro similarly expressed his concerns about the mounting business costs and diminishing returns of human rights pressures, estimating that the hold on EXIM Bank financing to Argentina cost $750 million in U.S. trade. Given that European competitors were eager to replace U.S. investments, it had few long-term costs to the Argentines but denied "a very significant market to American Industry." Castro concluded that to deny EXIM Bank backing on human rights grounds was a "futile gesture, of no value to the cause of human rights in Argentina."[91] Argentine human rights abuses and legislative guidelines, however, gave the administration little choice. Some small improvements, such as the Christmas amnesty and publication of prisoner lists, had led the administration to modify its vote from "no" to an abstention on some international loans, but an affirmative vote was politically untenable with the current level of abuses.[92] Moreover, unless the Carter administration could present clear evidence of a cessation of the worst violations in Argentina, congressional legislation would terminate all military aid to the country on September 30. Amnesty International also launched a campaign to focus global attention on Argentina's ongoing human rights violations, including disappeared peoples, political prisoners held indefinitely, and secret detention camps.[93]

Facing competing pressures domestically and frustrated by the persistent gross abuses by the Argentine leadership, Secretary of State Vance and Secretary of Defense Brown proposed a high-level political visit to Buenos Aires in early summer 1978, tapping Undersecretary of State for Political Affairs David Newsom to head up the delegation. Arriving in Buenos Aires in late May, Newsom sought to induce some concessions from the regime that would alleviate domestic pressure on the administration and allow for a potential turnaround in relations between the two governments. To underscore that the human rights message came from not only the Department of State and Congress but also President Carter and Secretary of Defense Brown, two military officers joined Newsom's delegation.[94]

In his meetings with the military leadership, Newsom repeatedly emphasized three specific issues that, if addressed substantively, could help return relations between the two countries to a more cooperative basis: information about the disappeared; plans for normalizing arrest procedures and trials for those held without charges; and an invitation to the IACHR to visit. Newsom prompted them to give him dates, plans, and "hopes for normalization" to demonstrate the junta's willingness to address human rights problems. Unmoved, Videla responded that these were matters of internal affairs, and the country would return to democracy "when its house is in order," adding that "he would not be sincere if he were to give dates and numbers in order to save Mr. Newsom's visit." Although Agosti noted that the state of siege could be lifted "without any effect on the junta's ability to rule," he did not indicate that the junta was giving this any consideration. When Ambassador Castro, who was attending meetings with Newsom, asked about the 1,200 detainees who were being held without trial, explaining this was a difficult issue to defend within the United States, Agosti simply replied that all prisoners would eventually be judged, given the right of option, or released, without offering any further details about how and when that might happen. In short, the junta stonewalled Newsom and his efforts to find any positive indicators that would merit a reconsideration of U.S. policy positions.[95]

Newsom's meeting with several human rights groups—including the Asamblea, Moviemiento Ecuménico por los Derechos Humanos (MEDH), and Las Madres—only highlighted the continuing human rights problems. Unlike Derian's meetings with advocate groups the year before, there was less emphasis on "moderates" and "hard-liners." Emilio Mignone rejected the notion that the violence and disappearances were taking place beyond the control of the military regime. It was ridiculous, he argued, "to think that in a well-controlled dictatorship such as Argentina that 10,000 to 20,000 persons could disappear without a trace," or that a dictatorship that had been in power for two years could not control its own troops. Moreover, these groups asserted that the government had taken no significant measures to address these problems. The Asamblea had received a list of forty disappearances that month alone. Las Madres stressed that it was still impossible to receive any information about the disappeared, and MEDH presented information about the deplorable prison conditions of political prisoners, most of whom were being held without charges or prospect of a trial.[96]

The advocates were also less ambivalent about the Carter administration's multivalent pressures on the regime than they had been during Derian's visit. Newsom probed the advocates for their input on whether the Carter administration's policy was "effective," explaining that the U.S. government had halted aid and loans to Argentina in response to violations. Mignone asserted that human rights organizations "firmly supported the U.S. policy," adding that "aid to 'such an inhumane government' should be denied all together." Father Enzo Giustozzi stressed that ultimately, the "solutions to the human rights problems here must come internally," but he added that outside pressure could help facilitate that, especially as Argentine human rights groups continued to organize. He hoped that Carter's human rights policy would work "better than the previous policy of 'real politique.'" Rabbi Graetz added that external pressure was particularly helpful "as the Argentine human rights organizations mobilized more." Mignone suggested that a visit from the IACHR could have an important effect.[97]

Despite his evident desire to find some signs of progress to take back to domestic critics, Newsom received no evidence of any substantial progress on human rights problems. In closing his meeting with the advocate groups, Newsom acknowledged the "tragedy which exists here," but he enjoined them that "if there are demonstrated areas of progress these should be recognized." He confessed that he had "not yet identified any such areas."[98] The advocate groups had little to add. On his departure, Newsom stated publicly, "Argentina has a long way to go before [the] U.S. can consider improving relations." Unsurprisingly, the military government took offense at the statement. The visit, rather than reducing tensions, revealed the growing rift between Washington and Buenos Aires, with the military junta becoming more publicly defensive. It declared that although it may want good relations with Washington, it did not need the United States' military or economic aid, and it asserted that its battle against leftist subversion would be vindicated. It criticized the United States for "using Argentina as an ideological battleground between opposing forces in the United States government." Despite its seeming intransigence, the embassy reported that the regime was "strongly desirous of restoring its political prestige and economic importance in the world" and "seriously concerned not to become—or continue as—the next 'Chile' in international eyes."[99] Argentina's clear desire to be accepted by the international community and avoid becoming a pariah state gave the Carter administration some influence, but this was tempered by sensitivity "intervention" in its internal affairs and political dynamics within the military leadership.

Calculating the Costs

Relations between the two countries continued their downward slide throughout the summer of 1978. Toward the end of his May meeting with Newsom, Videla had offered to "place a positive weight on the Under Secretary's scale," and he shared that at the upcoming OAS General Assembly in June, the Argentines would extend an invitation to the IACHR to visit Argentina.[100] He asked Newsom to keep this news confidential until the General Assembly, and given the junta's penchant for broken promises, Newsom did not put much stock in the disclosure. At the OAS meeting in June, Argentina did invite IACHR as promised, but with so many restrictions on the delegation that it rendered the invitation moot.[101] Carter, in a clear rebuke to Argentine's ongoing intransigence, praised the work of the IACHR in his address to the OAS General Assembly, stating, "We consider this not an intrusion into the internal affairs of countries, but a mechanism by which those countries that stand condemned, perhaps erroneously, by the rest of the world, might clear their good name and prove to us and to the rest of the world that human rights indeed are not being violated." He also stressed, "Where basic human rights are concerned, all of our governments must be accountable not only to our own citizens but to the conscience of the world."[102] With no breakthrough on even an invitation to the IACHR, the administration denied EXIM financing for $250 million worth of hydroelectric equipment from Allis-Chalmers for a project at Yacyretá in the summer of 1978.[103] Less than a month later, Derian testified before Congress, reporting on the Argentine regime's use of "systematic torture and summary executions."[104]

The U.S. vote on the EXIM Bank loan, combined with the administration's increasingly blunt public assessments of the junta's human rights abuses, enflamed Argentine resentment and provoked charges of U.S. intervention and hegemony. The government "mouthpiece," La Opinión, called Carter's OAS speech "paternalistic" and "closer to Theodore Roosevelt's 'big stick doctrine' than the 'good neighbor policy.'" Foreign Minister Montes's own speech at the OAS asserted that his government "energetically rejects the attitude of those members of the continental community who assume prerogatives over the problems of others," and he later lamented "the regrettable power abuse exercised by some powerful nations who use human rights as their single and restricted topic of dialog with other countries, usually those in the developing world."[105] It was an obvious deflection but a shrewd defense, seeking to mobilize anti-interventionist sentiment and hint that human rights was one more way the United States asserted hegemonic control over the region. The military leadership increasingly espoused the belief that the real intention of U.S. human rights pressures was to unseat the military government. Pointing to events in Chile, the Argentine leadership "read the Letelier case as a US effort baldly to overthrow the Pinochet regime, i.e., a resurgence of traditional Yankee Imperialism in the hemisphere under the benign guise of promoting universal human rights."[106]

These themes of "Yankee Imperialism" were echoed by the Argentine press. A fiery article in Clarín rejected Derian's assessment of a dire human rights situation in the country, charging that her statements were "a clear case of intervention in the internal affairs of other states." Noting the Carter administration's stated intention to move the country away from its past alignment with dictatorships, the article observed, "In reviewing the past, the U.S. government could have corrected the old misperceptions and moved to a cooperative attitude aimed at overcoming the structural problems of its continental neighbors." It instead developed a "simplistic formula" that did not address past excesses or account for current subversion that endangered the very rights it purported to defend. "The idea that 'something must be done and fast,' leads to aggressive acts, such as vetoing credit for a hydro-electric dam." This project, it argued, would have "improved the quality of life of many Argentines, an issue with which Ms. Derian was so concerned." The anger of the Argentine leadership was a "natural and immediate reaction in defense of sovereignty." *La Nación* similarly charged that the issue was not about a disavowal of human rights, because "no Argentine who loves freedom and justice can disagree with the essence of a policy statement of human rights."[107]

Popular anti-American sentiment, which the military government stoked, was clearly evident throughout Argentina during the summer of 1978. A state-sponsored radio station ran hourly segments for more than a month after the EXIM decision, declaring, "Mr. Carter: Keep your money or use it for negroes in your country who are dying of hunger. We do not need your money to build Yacyretá any how." The U.S. embassy reported a "flare-up" of "patriotic public avowals from professional organizations and the citizenry at large." The embassy received more than two hundred postcards praising the military government's success in ending the domestic war, representing a "rash of letter-writing from ordinary citizens expressing nationalist indignation over the campaign to defame Argentina from abroad." At the same time, these public statements were not all negative. Hidden within their patriotic denouncements of foreign interference were tentative calls for an end to the state of siege and a return to normal legal order from the public. It was, the U.S. embassy noted, "the first timid signs of public pronouncements against the 'dirty war.'"[108]

Anti-Americanism in Argentina heightened growing domestic criticism of the Carter administration's human rights policies, particularly its use of IFIs. David Rothstein, an American businessman operating an Argentine finance corporation in the United States, pointed to the futility of export restrictions, arguing that several other countries could easily provide the equipment in question. In a letter to Pastor, he asserted that "the only real victims in this lamentable affair are the American corporations who would have received the orders and the workers who would have produced the goods." Rothstein labeled the Argentine policy "unrealistic and grossly unfair," pointing out that Iran, South Korea, and Algeria all received authorization for their EXIM credits. Arguing that Argentina was just now emerging from an exceptional period of terrorism and chaos, he concluded that "friendship and understanding . . . will improve the situation far more than bravura actions which do nothing but fan anti-Americanism throughout every sector of the Argentine population."[109] A letter from Harry Gray at United Technologies similarly opined the loss of jobs and exports to restrictive human rights clauses on EXIM loans and licenses. He reported that human rights restrictions were holding up 25 percent of the estimated annual gross sales for the corporation's New York plant, a plant that had already laid off 123 of its 693 workers in the past year. His dismay at being unable to obtain a license for export was only heightened by the fact that the products in question had no connection to human rights violations or security issues. "Certainly I have no argument with the principles of human rights espoused by our government," he wrote. "I must question, however, restraint of trade as a tool to achieve improvements in foreign governments' human rights because it damages the U.S. economy through lost jobs and long-range loss of markets, and its effectiveness is practically undetectable."[110]

Gray's letter revealed an important aspect of linking economic aid and commercial financing to human rights performance: while the linkage between military aid and human rights abuses was fairly self-evident, the relationship between exports and business financing and human rights behaviors was more abstract. Even Argentine advocates themselves, while applauding the symbolic meaning behind these decisions, had often cautioned against using economic "sanctions" that potentially affected the broader population more than the regime. For U.S. advocates in Congress and the Movement, however, votes in the IFIs were a clear signal of their government's support for repressive regimes, reminiscent of the Ford administration's use of these instruments to get around congressional restrictions on direct military aid. Moreover, the Movement argued that bringing human rights criteria to bear on IFI's decisions was not simply punitive—it was also about allocating limited resources to those governments that had made positive changes and supported human rights advances, rather than those who continued to perpetrate violence.

The Argentine response to the EXIM decision and Derian's testimony amplified the administration's concerns about stoking anti-American backlash in Argentina. Pastor lamented the recent EXIM Bank decision, although he acknowledged that the law gave the administration little choice.[111] He reported to Brzezinski that he was "absolutely astounded by the sheer quantity of the trade we have, in effect, embargoed against Argentina," reporting internal estimates that human rights concerns had held up approximately $1.25 billion in nonmilitary exports to Argentina alone.[112] Pastor warned that "one of the problems with our relationship [with Argentina] right now is the sheer weight of our instruments."[113] John Renner at the NSC opined that if denial of U.S. trade was likely to improve human rights conditions, these costs would be justified, but with European businesses ready to step in, it was likely to be a "minor inconvenience" for the Argentine government. "We get the worst of both worlds," Renner concluded. "U.S. exports are reduced by a large amount and our human rights objectives are not furthered. Good policy avoids these no-win situations."[114]

By August the NSC increasingly cautioned that the administration's current policy in Argentina opened it to criticism that human rights was not conducive to other interests, and was perhaps even counterproductive. Secretary of Defense Brown, skeptical of the emphasis on human rights, expressed concern that deteriorating relations with Argentina endangered a wide range of interests at stake in the region: "While our human rights policy is very important, we need also to take into account that Argentina is a key nation with respect to our non-proliferation policy." He warned that a "go-it-alone Argentina" could be counter to U.S. interests on any number of security considerations. Brown called for the administration to take some "positive steps" to reverse the growing antagonisms between Washington and Buenos Aires—suggesting this might also actually help human rights issues as well.[115]

Even U.S. ambassador to the United Nations Andrew Young, a staunch proponent of the administration's human rights initiatives, was worried that the administration "may be inadvertently undercutting our attempts to integrate human rights, economic and social development and basic human needs by using financial pressure to promote one kind of human rights at the expense of another." Blocking projects such as the hydroelectric dam at Yacyretá may both limit development in target countries and cost U.S. jobs and weaken the domestic economy. Further, "such a policy reduces our leverage to the zero point," with limited payoff on human rights concerns because other governments stood ready to step in and provide the goods in question. Young recommended the administration reconsider its decision on the Yacyretá project, presenting it to Congress and the Argentine government as support for economic rights, even while the administration remained seriously concerned about civil and political rights in Argentina.[116]

Yet even as some in the administration questioned the utility of IFIs for a viable human rights policy, the commitment to the policy as a whole remained. In an expansive review of bilateral relations for Brzezinski, Pastor reaffirmed that Argentina was one of the most problematic human rights violators in the world, an important symbol for the administration's commitment to its human rights policy. He noted that Amnesty International's newly launched "Argentina campaign" was helping make the country "this year's Chile." Despite the current stalemate and his own reticence about the use of IFIs, Pastor rejected the idea that the administration had "gone too far" and "pushed our policy beyond its effectiveness." He granted that the administration may have "overloaded the circuits," but given the legislative mandates, it was hard to argue with the internal logic of the administration's approach. "Anything less, or a step backwards from the place we currently find ourselves," Pastor argued, "would be judged as a Presidential retreat," undermining its credibility on the issue as a whole with crucial domestic constituencies.[117]

Looking beyond the immediate Argentine stalemate, Pastor argued that the human rights policy had succeeded in helping the U.S. recapture the ideological initiative in the hemisphere, appealing to the imagination and sensibilities of the younger generation. "Carter is clearly viewed as a man of great moral stature in Latin America, and that inspires the young and the democratic and embarrasses, and unfortunately, sometimes infuriates some of the conservatives and the military. Carter's stature has translated into real influence unlike anything the U.S. has had since we turned in our gunboats, and at the same time, it has given the U.S. *a future* in Latin America, which we had almost lost." Pastor cited the Argentines' eagerness to improve relations, despite antagonisms, as evidence of the administration's ideological upper hand, noting that the regime was using any channel available—including Henry Kissinger—to try to regain U.S. support and approval. He acknowledged that the administration was in a precarious position but concluded that it would "be a mistake and an injustice if we turned our policy around at this time." Two weeks later, as if to underscore his final point, Pastor forwarded to Brzezinski a fourteen-page account from the U.S. embassy of a conversation with Alfredo Bravo, copresident of the Asamblea. Bravo had recently been released by the military government, in part due to U.S. lobbying on his behalf. Bravo shared in great detail his experience of being "disappeared" and tortured at the hands of the military government, stating that he hoped this information would reinforce "what you are fighting for." Pastor, obviously moved by the account, told Brzezinski simply, "I believe his story is important as we begin to lay the groundwork for a new strategy to Argentina."[118]

The administration focused on the invitation to the IACHR as an achievable first step to walk relations back from the brink without giving up on crucial human rights issues.[119] At the very end of August, the Argentine embassy proposed a meeting between Videla and Vice President Mondale in Rome while both attended the funeral for Pope Paul VI. "I think that this is the opportunity we have been waiting for," Pastor wrote Brzezinski.[120] Indeed, the September 4 meeting broke the impasse between the two governments. Mondale reassured Videla that the United States wanted good relations between their two countries, but "human rights are a central concern." Mondale was quite direct, offering support for EXIM financing in exchange for an invitation to the IACHR. "We would not link your actions to our own," Mondale explained, but if Argentina could get human rights conditions "turned around"—perhaps by inviting the IACHR— "then we could move ahead, for example, on Allis-Chalmers."[121] Videla repeatedly affirmed that his government shared the administration's concern about human rights, but he complained frequently about U.S. public criticism of the regime, casting it as "intervention." Videla claimed that, more than once, Argentina had been about to issue an invitation to IACHR but had to postpone the announcement because of "U.S. criticisms projecting intervention."[122] Mondale reassured him that the Carter administration had "no desire to interfere in the affairs of your country. We have enough domestic problems of our own. If we can get on the road to progress in human rights, this whole other vista will open."[123] After the meeting, General Viola told Ambassador Castro that "he now believed that the U.S. does value its relations with Argentina" and reassured him that the United States would "definitely see changes and improvements in the human rights field soon."[124]

Indeed, by the end of the month the embassy reported "certain attitudinal changes" that "give us hope for basic revisions in the system of repression," noting a decrease in reported abuses.[125] The administration released its hold on $270 million in EXIM credits, and on October 17 the Argentine government announced publicly that it had "responded favorably" to a request by the IACHR for a site visit.[126] By leveraging legislative restrictions to create a sense of urgency and simultaneously offering positive inducements for cooperation, the administration finally broke the impasse in relations, walking itself back "from the brink without appearing as if it is we who blinked first."[127]

After the Breakthrough

The Mondale-Videla meeting was a breakthrough for bilateral relations and resulted in the realization of one of the administration's primary human rights objectives in Argentina. The official invitation to the IACHR by the Argentine government was an accomplishment in and of itself, breaking the previously "monolithic" opposition of the Southern Cone countries to the commission. Moreover, it created an environment for greater improvements of human rights within the country, and it empowered Argentines to push for changes on their own terms, as well as establishing a sense of account-ability for past abuses. The "breakthrough" brought with it little respite from mounting debates within the United States about the relative balance of "carrots" and "sticks" to advance Carter's human rights agenda. New pressures over the policy's "costs" compounded ongoing charges of backsliding and inconsistency by the policy's staunchest advocates.[128]

Within the administration, divides were growing over how to implement the commitment to human rights. The summer crisis in U.S.-Argentine relations amplified frustration within the Department of Defense and National Security Council with the State Department's unilateral implementation of legislative mandates and démarches to Argentina. At the end of August, Pastor groused to Brzezinski that the State Department was making decisions in a "haphazard, uncoordinated manner," without a coherent framework that was "publicly defensible." The NSC was increasingly concerned that an ad hoc approach would be "misinterpreted in the U.S. as a retreat from the President's human rights policy" and would open the administration "to charges of inconsistency."[129]

The NSC's concerns about the lack of consultation and appearance of inconsistency were heightened by the State Department's decision to ap-prove an extra IMET agreement just days before the congressional block on military assistance went into effect. The State Department had made the decision at the urging of the Department of Defense, presenting it as a good-will gesture to the Argentine leadership for its IACHR agreement. "I see the need to send some positive signals but haven't we already done that?" Jessica Tuchman Mathews wondered in a policy assessment for Brzezinski. After the EXIM decision and release of spare parts and safety-related munitions,

"IMET seems just too much." The appearance of executive retreat on human rights priorities was "hardly conducive to good congressional relations."[130]

Going forward Mathews recommended that the administration focus on long-term trends rather than respond to every small movement—positive or negative—from Buenos Aires. Despite the recent success in linking EXIM credits to the IACHR visit, she argued that "in reacting to short term changes we inevitably condemn ourselves to follow a jerky and inconsistent policy, for change that is lasting and meaningful on a societal scale seldom occurs in less than a year's time."[131] A quid pro quo strategy inevitably forced the administration to backtrack when the Argentines failed to uphold their promises, reinforcing the appearance of inconsistency on its human rights approaches.

Despite some optimism that the invitation to the IACHR heralded a clear turning point, human rights conditions in Argentina remained dire at the beginning of 1979, returning the administration to familiar debates over strategy. In January the Human Rights Bureau pushed for additional measures "to underscore our concerns and bring pressure to bear on the Junta," recommending voting against all IFI loans except those that met basic human needs requirements, denying all commercial licenses of military-related equipment, and denying, or at least delaying, all EXIM financing for new projects in Argentina. Derian hoped that the preparations for the IACHR would bring about some improvements, but she asserted that "we should not rely exclusively on this event."[132] Vaky and the Latin America bureau, on the other hand, argued that January marked "an important turning point," noting the absence of reported disappearances in February and March. "I realize we have had assurances before," he acknowledged, but the administration should take seriously the diverse indicators of improvement. "It would be tragic and ironic," he argued, "if we were to adopt a more restrictive policy toward Argentina just at the moment when the leadership has begun to move and respond to our concerns." A hostile or indifferent reaction to the improvements would "wither these favorable trends and surely weaken the position of Videla and Viola, frustrating their efforts to effect improvements." Contrary to Derian's recommendation, he advised that "a tougher position now may be exactly the wrong thing to do at the wrong time."[133]

Internal divides over the strategy complicated the administration's efforts to balance competing pressures from the U.S. public, the Argentine regime, and Congress. Following its decision to resume EXIM financing in September, the administration was "whip-sawed from both left and right" over U.S. policy on Argentina. Pastor recounted to Brzezinski pressure from

Rep. Gus Yatron's (D-PA) staff to authorize the sale of more spare parts for military equipment, while the president of the Argentine-American Banking Association recommended "trying to back off and give Videla a little breathing room." On the same day, he faced complaints that Congress had not been adequately consulted on the approval of the Allis-Chalmers deal. Congressional proponents of current legislation charged that the administration's recent actions were "outrageous" and "violated the spirt of the Kennedy-Humphrey Amendment," questioning whether the president had considered the "implications" of this decision for his broader human rights agenda.[134]

For the Movement and its congressional allies, the administration's concessions on EXIM funding were unwarranted in the face of ongoing abuses, regardless of the IACHR invitation. WOLA argued that "Videla, the 'least bad' of the military, is not a worthy object of U.S. support" and reiterated its intention to pressure the administration to fully implement legislation that would deny bilateral economic and military aid to Argentina.[135] There could be no basis for cooperative relations without measurable actions from the junta, such as an earnest accounting for the disappeared or a timeline for a return to civilian rule. Congressional proponents of the human rights policy such as Senator Kennedy charged the administration with "getting soft" on Argentina.[136] In a letter to the EXIM Bank president, Rep. Les Aspin (D-WI) expressed his concern about the decision to finance the Argentine project and stressed that it was "important that government agencies and businesses alike communicate the U.S. concern of human rights to countries flagrantly violating the same."[137] Harkin, facing the failure of legislation to extend new human rights standards to the IMF and EXIM Bank, lamented that "the day of 'linkage' amendments tying aid, both direct and indirect, to human rights standards for right-wing governments is over."[138]

Forces working against the Movement's human rights agenda had become increasingly influential in domestic politics, as evidenced by the defeat of Harkin's new legislative proposals. The delay of EXIM funding by the State Department had riled up the business community, and many now partnered with members of Congress resistant to the administration's human rights policies. Conservative members of Congress became increasingly vocal in questioning the policy's costs—in regard to economic and security interests. Sen. Ernest Hollings (D-SC), for example, sent a letter to President Carter supporting the resumption of military training with Argentina. Referencing the domestic terrorism the Videla government faced, Hollings argued that human rights "is a two way street" and stated that he was "convinced that President Videla wants to do the right thing but there are real limitations on his ability to maneuver." Hollings's letter implicitly argued that the United States should not weaken anticommunist "friends," pointing to Videla's military training in the United States, which "undoubtedly fortified" his "good basic instincts." The recently approved military training would not only assist Videla in bringing peace and stability to Argentina; it was also in the United States' own best interest.[139] The midterm elections reinforced conservative resistance to the administration's human rights agenda. Just as 1974 had brought in a new reform-minded class that helped establish human rights concerns in foreign policy, the 1978 midterm elections saw the defeat of some of human rights' staunchest supporters, such as Donald Fraser and James Abourezk.[140] In their place was a new, more conservative Congress, one less amenable to human rights and the Carter administration.[141]

New business and Cold War security pressures from the right were clearly evident in the administration's deliberations over its position on Argentina in multilateral development banks (MDBs) in early 1979. Writing to Vance in March, Brzezinski conceded that the human rights situation in Argentina "may just be the worst in the hemisphere," but he asked Vance to consider "what is the most effective approach to Argentina to encourage them to respect human rights. What approach will permit us to sustain in the U.S. our overall human rights policy?" Brzezinski cautioned that although the United States clearly had the ability to influence events in Argentina, U.S. policy's impact on human rights conditions is "never as direct or as much as we want." Brzezinski warned that punitive actions, such as negative votes in MDBs, "not only enrage the right-wing ideologues, we also arouse the business sector and the media in the U.S." Just as Movement advocates had created pressures that had to be calculated into policy decisions, ascended right-wing security and business concerns now framed the viability of policies. Brzezinski did not disavow human rights objectives or even the use of "voice and vote" in IFIs, but he did caution that given the new domestic political realities the administration had to "move carefully and explain our position—in the U.S. and elsewhere—before taking any steps lest we jeopardize our overall human rights policy." Brzezinski recommended a "cool and correct" posture that avoided "punitive" measures such as no votes but also sought to keep up pressure through bilateral and multilateral approaches until human rights conditions improved and the regime moved toward democratization.[142]

Throughout the summer of 1979 the administration found itself attacked from both the Left and the Right. While a new, more conservative Congress and agitated business community continued to question the costs of human rights for the nation's security and prosperity, the Movement and its congressional partners challenged the administration's commitment to human rights. In May, Christopher defended the administration's policy in front of the House Subcommittee on International Relations, chaired by Don Bonkers (D-WA) after Fraser's departure. Responding to questions about the administration's "inconsistencies" in applying the policy, Christopher retorted—quoting Freud—"Maturity is the ability to live with ambiguity." Less glibly, Christopher explained that the administration sought to recognize "trends," not just "overall performance," in making decisions about military and economic support. Moreover, he asserted that "even when we went ahead with military and/or economic support to a government, we could make clear our continuing concern over violations."[143] Current legislative mandates, however, did not account for trends, putting the administration's approach at odds with congressional guidance and reinforcing the notion of executive indifference to the core principles of human rights legislation. A diverse array of advocate groups, meeting with staff from Human Rights Bureau in May, shared that while they were "strongly supportive" of the administration's policy, they were also "deeply disturbed" by its "uneven application." In the past year they perceived a "clear backing away from strong human rights advocacy" by the administration, pointing to recent approaches to Argentina.[144]

In testimony before Bonkers's subcommittee, Jo Marie Griesgraber of WOLA gave a detailed view of the Movement's ambivalent assessment of the administration's policy, calling it "flawed" but "a quantum leap forward" from previous administrations. Griesgraber praised the administration's commitment to raising the profile of the issue, asserting that the policy "has earned the United States innumerable friends among all those people in Latin America who espouse democracy." At the same time, Griesgraber pointed to problems with inconsistency, citing recent decisions in the EXIM bank and IMF, as well as the administration's inclusion of Videla, Pinochet, and other "repressive regimes" in the celebrations for the Panama Canal Treaty signing in September 1977. These "ambiguities," Griesgraber argued, underscored the necessity of binding legislative mandates to "institutionalize" human rights policy. "If there are some problems from a sympathetic president, what can one expect from an unsympathetic president?!" she wondered. "The Nixon years have taught the American people that, imperfect though they may be, laws are a more secure protection than presidential discretion." She urged the administration to not relax its "non-interventionist human rights policy until governments permitting popular participation and rule by law are restored to Latin America." She closed her testimony by arguing that, despite this criticism, WOLA was on record as "staunch supporters of the human rights policy." Calling attention to the "mounting pressure from many sectors on the Administration and the Congress to back away from the human rights policy because of what are perceived as heavy economic costs," she argued that a sustained commitment to human rights "will bear a lasting fruit that far outweighs any possible short term economic sacrifices."[145]

Even as it remained committed to its human rights policy, the administration found the "costs" hard to ignore. Tense bilateral relations and subsequent restrictions made their impact felt in numerous industries. In August 1979 leather workers in New Hampshire faced the loss of six hundred jobs due to the lack of Argentine hides. Accusing the administration of responding inadequately, the workers planned a "large scale" protest, warning, "Mr. President no hides means no jobs for us which means no votes for you."[146] Assessing the administration's policy in August, Vaky summarized that the administration's goal was to "find ways to deal with (and hopefully improve) the human rights situation, without at the same time cutting ourselves off from a large and important country whose role and weight can affect our global policies."[147]

Despite its difficulties garnering public support and internal consensus for its policies, by September it was clear that the announcement of the IACHR visit had initiated a decisive turning point for human rights conditions in the country. Videla and Viola were both forthcoming with Vaky about their intentions, saying that the IACHR visit was "the precise catalyst they needed to push in the direction of improvement." Videla's faction within the regime was further strengthened when it arranged for papal mediation of the Beagle Channel dispute with Chile. This, along with the promotion of moderates in military positions previously held by hard-liners who challenged Videla's authority, all served to strengthen Videla's control over the security apparatus in the country and his leadership over the government in the beginning of 1979. By April, representatives from the International Red Cross verified that prison conditions had "clearly improved" and reported that they expected further progress in the lead-up to the IACHR visit. Beginning in 1979 the number of disappearances dropped dramatically, with only twenty-two reported in the first six months, contrasted with an average of fifty per month in 1978. The Argentine courts also demonstrated an increasing willingness to press the government over habeas corpus petitions and the disappeared. Moreover, the government had given up the pretense that it had no control over disappearances. Although the Argentine government maintained that it had no knowledge of the fate of the disappeared, many of the so-called moderates stated repeatedly that "disappearances would be held at a minimum and preferably down to zero."[148]

The country still had significant human rights problems. Ambassador Castro called the right of option proceedings a "fiasco"; moreover, the government had taken no action to account for the disappeared, and emergency measures still curtailed broad political and civil rights.[149] In August 1979 police raided the offices of the Asamblea and other human rights groups, charging they had inflated numbers and manufactured data for the habeas corpus petitions.[150] Still, 1979 saw some of the most significant improvements in human rights conditions to date in the country, which could be attributed in part to the IACHR visit. Although the military leadership had resigned itself in some ways to an "unfavorable" report, it also hoped to use the visit to "shut the door on the past and start over again with a clean slate." By relegating human rights violations to a messy but necessary past, Videla hoped to consolidate his control domestically.[151]

The IACHR visit in September unleashed a media barrage, which made it impossible for any Argentine to ignore human rights questions but also enflamed a nationalist backlash from certain quarters. Visuals of family members of the disappeared waiting in large numbers to present their cases to the delegates were juxtaposed with "pro-Argentine" protests against the violation of Argentine sovereignty. As the embassy reported, although the visit "may have made human rights an issue for many hitherto unconcerned or uncaring Argentines, it is less certain it changed very many minds."[152]

Despite polarized reactions, the visit clearly codified the human rights issue in public debate and emerging political discussions. The *Buenos Aires Herald* argued that regardless of the report, political parties "have, inevitably, begun to incorporate the abuses of basic human rights that have taken place in the last few years into their list of charges against the government." Although this concern for human rights could be positive, the politicization of the issue could "drive a wedge" between the military and the public, resulting in an emotional backlash and a return to chaos and instability. The article thus concluded, "It is in the government's own best interest to defuse the explosive problem of human rights as quickly as possible."[153]

Thus, going into 1980 Argentina awaited two reports that would solidify its image in the international community, determine U.S. policy, and shape political dynamics within Argentina—the IACHR report and, perhaps more significantly, the State Department's annual country report on human rights conditions. In December the Argentine ambassador expressed his concern about the State Department report, stating that his government "attached great importance to the report and its contents; for the GOA, it would be the most important document presented to the U.S. Congress in 1980."[154] Even before either report was issued, however, new global strategic concerns eclipsed human rights as the primary issue of contention in the U.S.-Argentine relationship.

A Question of Balance

By 1980 the Soviet invasion of Afghanistan, the revolution and hostage crisis in Iran, the upheaval in Central America, and domestic economic problems pushed the Carter administration into a state of crisis management.[155] In this environment, short-term problems eclipsed long-term objectives. With its energies and attentions focused on these unfolding crises, the administration gave its human rights policy, particularly in Latin America, considerably less public attention. Behind the scenes, however, the administration continued to factor human rights into its decisions, even as ascendant security concerns and East-West tensions garnered increased attention.

In high-profile cases such as Argentina, the administration now faced the question of how to integrate new East-West considerations into its ongoing policy objectives, including human rights. Tensions with the Soviet Union following its December 1979 invasion of Afghanistan, and the Carter administration's decision to respond with a grain embargo, put new demands on relations with Argentina. As one of the largest global exporters of grain, Argentina's participation in the embargo was critical to its success, yet the regime's human rights record complicated cooperation between the two governments.[156] Although human rights conditions had improved dramatically in the past year, serious problems remained, particularly the junta's ongoing silence about the fates of thousands of "disappeared" people.[157] The State Department country report reflected the administration's efforts to balance recognition of recent improvements and the still-dire state of human rights. The administration chose to approve the Human Rights Bureau's more detailed and negative version of the report, despite concerns expressed by the Latin America bureau and resistance from Brzezinski. The report was personally cleared by Vance, signaling the significance of Argentina to the administration's broader human rights agenda.[158]

Seeking to improve cooperation between the two governments in the face of complex issues in bilateral relations at the end of January, the administration dispatched Gen. Andrew J. Goodpaster as special emissary. The focus of the Goodpaster mission was to secure Argentine support for the grain embargo, yet even here, human rights was a necessary part of the conversation. Goodpaster, reflecting the Department of Defense's stance, took a softer line on abuses by the military government, but he made it clear that the United States could only go as far as supporting Argentina in some positions at the UN. The administration offered to "coordinate agendas" for the upcoming UN General Assembly, promising to support "moderate approaches" but also insisted the United States would "maintain the integrity" of the commission's work.[159] The administration thus held out the opportunity for greater cooperation and closer relations, easing from its "cool and correct" posture of recent years, but this was highly circumscribed. Indeed, just weeks after Goodpaster's visit, the U.S. delegation at the UN supported the creation of a five-member commission to examine the issue of the "disappeared," clearly focusing on the Argentine case.[160]

Even as it remained committed to its bilateral approaches on human rights, the Carter administration's public emphasis on more traditional security concerns in the Middle East and Soviet Union, and its evident desire to work more closely with Argentina on these objectives, cast doubt on its continued commitment to a foreign policy that transcended Cold War rivalries. WOLA's newsletter in January 1980 reported, "Official U.S. perception of the world seems to have shifted rather substantially." WOLA lamented that the "golden years" of human rights now appeared over, and East-West relations seemed to trump human rights. WOLA speculated that the Goodpaster delegation "must have been given something to offer as reciprocity for Argentine cooperation" on the grain embargo, presuming that that "something" was an easing of pressure on human rights. WOLA feared that as the Carter administration sought to "line up countries behind immediate anti-Soviet moves," its human rights policy would be the casualty.[161] Still, WOLA expressed its hope that after his reelection, Carter would drop the new "Cold War focus and return to his earlier more mature perspective of viewing Third World developments in their own terms."[162]

The Movement's growing unease with the Carter administration was evident in their tepid support for Carter's reelection campaign, especially in contrast to the enthusiasm for Ted Kennedy's bid for the Democratic Party's nomination. The ADA had launched a "Draft Kennedy" campaign the past July—even before Kennedy had declared his candidacy—lamenting

Figure 11. "Human Rights Hot Air Balloon" by Oliver Harrington ca. 1980. Courtesy of Dr. Helma Harrington.

the "absence of leadership" on progressive liberal issues under Carter.[163] Although their support was largely articulated in terms of domestic policy, Kennedy's clear record on human rights in Latin America and Carter's apparent elevation of more traditional security concerns reinforced the necessity of challenging a sitting president for the party's nomination.[164] While never formally weighing in on the Democratic primary, WOLA championed Kennedy's seventeen years of action for social justice in Latin America and long-standing commitment to human rights "long before it became politically fashionable."[165] Even as the ADA endorsed Carter in the general election, the endorsement was halfhearted at best, with damning dissent from core members such as Arthur Schlesinger, Jr.[166]

Vance's resignation in April 1980—widely seen as a repudiation of more hard-line interventionist attitudes within the administration—along with the proposed military aid budget signaled to the Movement that the Carter administration was turning to a more traditional Cold War approach to Latin America. WOLA interpreted Edmund Muskie's appointment to replace Vance as secretary of state as a move to shore up centrist domestic support at the expense of its human rights policy. "Even moderates," WOLA cautioned, "have not found themselves immune to the argument that U.S. allies are being undermined by symbolic acts with human rights content." Derian reported to Christopher at the end of April that the "human rights community and public increasingly think the policy has been downgraded if not discarded." She cautioned that "over identification" with repressive regimes was harming the administration's credibility, and she expressed her own worry that new policy concerns would "dilute our human rights principles and policy," pointing particularly to the recent evolution of U.S.-Argentine relations.[167]

The grain embargo—and the administration's willingness to move away from its position of disassociation from Argentina to secure it—represented the rising importance of East-West issues in Carter's foreign policy in the last year. Even so, the administration never abandoned human rights as a central issue of its policy or returned to a traditional Cold War calculus in its regional relations. The administration was clearly troubled by Soviet overtures to Argentina, as well as Brazil, but these did not overshadow the policy and strategies it had developed over the past three years. The administration saw Argentina as "key" to the grain embargo's success; without Argentina's participation, it would be difficult to convince other nations to hold the line.[168] The administration was not concerned, however, about a lasting alignment of Argentina with the Soviet Union, creating a beachhead for communism in the hemisphere or even aiding in Central American revolutions. The administration saw Argentina playing a "short term game in the grain, trade, and perhaps nuclear arena," distinguishing between political ties and economic cooperation.[169] Argentina's cooperation with U.S. initiatives such as the grain embargo—which it refused to endorse publicly, even though it had agreed to certain limits privately—was crucial to the administration's global policy, but bilateral relations were not subsumed completely by this objective.

A May Policy Review Committee (PRC) identified three major interests in relations with Argentina: East-West relations, nuclear nonproliferation, and human rights. The issue paper laid out the administration's basic approach as managing relations "in a way that strengthens Argentina's sense of identification with the West, to pursue interests in a balanced fashion that takes into account Argentine deep-seated nationalism, and to achieve these goals without compromising our human rights objectives by diminishing or appearing to have diminished our interest in human rights conditions." The critical question was, "what is the appropriate human rights stance for the U.S. in this period in light of Argentine performance and our other interests?" This question fed internal debates over strategy, but with the exception of DOD, the administration took it for granted that its human rights position would remain a central component of bilateral relations and a hallmark of the administration's foreign policy. In the face of new strategic concerns, the administration settled on the middle path, a course it had charted since the IACHR visit. Christopher argued that it was a matter of "tone" and that the administration should acknowledge the progress that had been made, even as David Aaron noted there "was no reason to improve relations dramatically . . . directly after they have stuck their finger in our eye on the grain issue."[170] If improvement continued, the administration could reconsider some military cooperation and other public signals of a warmer relationship in 1981 after Viola had replaced Videla as president.[171]

One of the key points of contention in the administration's discussion of its human rights policy was how to address the question of the thousands of "disappeared" people, whose fate was still unknown. The disappeared remained a loaded issue for both the regime seeking to move itself toward moderation and Carter's human rights policy. In March the U.S. embassy had questioned whether "an accounting of the fate of thousands of disappearances is a realistic objective at this time." It recommended that while the issue should remain on the administration's agenda "on humanitarian grounds," it should not make "our relations with Argentina hostage to this issue."[172] The Human Rights Bureau had strongly rejected the embassy's recommendation, arguing, "If we turn our backs on this issue we will be condoning state terrorism and mass slaughter on a scale hitherto unknown in South America in peacetime."[173] For the human rights community in Argentina and the United States, this was the core issue and the predominant symbol of repression by the military regime. Despite the overwhelming significance of the disappeared to human rights in Argentina, the administration was not optimistic that further pressure from the United States would move the military government toward any substantial effort to resolve this issue. As with the Letelier case in Chile, the administration was reaching the limits of its influence. As one State memo summarized: "We cannot drop the issue from its hitherto prominent place in our diplomatic dialogue because this would signal we have turned our back on the atrocities. At the same time, we can make clear that the issue of 'accounting' in our policy means something other than bringing the guilty to account." Christopher concluded that while the "fate of the disappeared should not be a central requirement for improvement of our relations, it should remain an important US objective."[174]

The decision to offer limited opportunities for cooperation in the face of new strategic interests reflected the political cost of moving against established human rights mechanisms. Indeed, the very day of the PRC meeting, Christopher received a letter from Kathryn Sikkink at WOLA, urging the administration to stay firm on its commitment to human rights. Calling Argentina a "test case for U.S. human rights policy," she urged the administration to not lose sight of the long-term interests supported by human rights policies in the face of short-term strategic demands. "What the U.S. would gain from a policy shift on U.S. human rights policy towards Argentina at this point is doubtful. What we would lose in terms of credibility, prestige and a long-term contribution to stability and justice in the Southern Cone is both serious and immediate." Christopher's office responded, reassuring WOLA that "no change in U.S. human rights policy is contemplated," and affirming the administration's commitment to encouraging improvements in human rights conditions in Argentina. The letter acknowledged that the United States had other interests in bilateral relations, such as the Soviet grain embargo and the Olympic boycott. "We believe," he wrote, "it is in the U.S. interest to seek Argentine cooperation in such areas, without compromising our human rights concerns." Still, he reiterated, even though the situation had improved, "our concern has not diminished, and normal relations with Argentina will not be achieved while the human rights situation in Argentina remains a problem."[175]

Indeed, Movement pressures reinforced the administration's decision to hold off further warming of relations. The administration's concern with Movement restiveness about its Argentine policy was evident throughout the summer. In June Brzezinski's staff warned in a draft evening report for the president, American NGOs "are increasingly registering with us their concern that a new US policy toward Argentina will have the effect of drastically downgrading, if not scuttling, your human rights policy." Lincoln Bloomfield, who had taken over for Jessica Tuchman Mathews on human rights at the NSC, advised that "we should consider ways and timing of publicly clarifying the revised policy, both to scotch erroneous and harmful rumors, and also to reinforce at home (and in Argentina) the sense of undiminished U.S. human rights concerns which have been such a vital and successful element of your Latin American policies."[176] Five days later, when Brzezinski had not forwarded the item to the president, Bloomfield and Thomas Thorton reiterated, "We find increasing distress among American private groups about a changed policy they know only through rumors, leaks, and speculation. We are getting a good deal of pressure from people who think they know what the new policy is and are very concerned that we will simply lose interest in the noxious human right violations practiced in the past by the Argentine Government." They recommended that the State Department clarify its policy approach to Argentina to quell "harmful rumors at home."[177]

Public concerns moved the administration to clarify policy guidance internally to ensure that directives to upgrade relations with Argentina were not "overzealously interpreted in ways that would undermine your human rights policy."[178] Indeed, Christopher reported to the president that NSC staff was working to ensure that human rights "remains a central objective and that there is no intention to downgrade this objective" in light of new security interests. Forwarding the memo to Carter, Brzezinski added his own recommendation that "as we proceed to develop closer relationships, DOD/ JCS and other agencies involved with Argentina would continually reaffirm the importance which the Carter Administration attaches to human rights and democratization."[179]

The year 1980 did not mark a dramatic warming of relations with either the Videla or Pinochet regimes, as the Movement had feared. Argentine involvement in Bolivia's military coup in July further stalled efforts for a modest warming in relations between Washington and Buenos Aires.[180] Thus, even as human rights received less public emphasis in Carter's final year in office, it remained at the core of the administration's conceptualization of national interests and foreign policy. By late summer the Movement had become more restrained in their own criticism of the administration in light of the impending presidential election. In its last newsletter before the 1980 U.S. presidential election, WOLA called Carter's policy in Latin America a "sea-change" in regional relations. Even as the administration "clearly distanced itself" from the most repressive regimes, its emphasis on working with "moderates" rather than pressing for a rapid return to civilian rule limited the reach of its policy. In the Southern Cone, WOLA opined, "a bolder U.S. position would at least have increased the likelihood that a more rapid and genuine democratization might be underway." It lamented the renewal of "traditional 'security' threats," viewing it as a "serious and fundamental threat" to human rights, pointing to warming relations with Argentina as evidence. Despite competing pressures, however, "human rights was given sufficient place in policy toward Latin America as to alter its character." The group hoped that Carter's reelection would usher in a return to the "golden days" of human rights, but they feared that the "genie of militarism and a reactionary nationalism are out of the bottle."[181]

Two weeks after his failed bid for reelection, Jimmy Carter stood before the General Assembly of the OAS and reflected on his administration's contribution to regional affairs over the past four years. He recalled his first visit to the organization in April 1977, where he had envisioned state relationships based on self-determination, pluralism, and human rights. "As all of you know," he said, "the cause that has been closest to my own heart is the cause of human rights." Although he placed a greater emphasis on left-wing violence and "terrorism" than he had in his first address, Carter still advocated a broad spectrum of rights, including food, health care, and education as well as bodily integrity and personal liberty. Moreover, this commitment was now broadly engrained in regional relations. "Today no government in this hemisphere can expect silent assent from its neighbors if it tramples on the rights of its own citizens. The costs of repression have increased, but so have the benefits of respecting human rights. I pray that this progress will continue, although I know from experience that progress is not always easy as we defend human rights." In celebrating this elevation of human rights in regional relations, Carter acknowledged that his administration's policies were embedded in a broader effort. "Hemispheric support for human rights is a historic movement," he asserted. "I take pride in being part of that movement." Carter concluded his address by affirming that "the future lies with those who cherish [human rights] and those who are willing to defend them." He dismissed the idea that the "agenda will change when I leave my office."[182] Human rights would indeed remain a central issue in U.S. relations with Latin America in the coming years, but the incoming Reagan administration would radically alter the shape and meaning of the debate.

Chapter 5

The Reagan Reinvention

A Cold War Human Rights Vision

During the 1976 presidential campaign, Carter had positioned himself as an outsider who would reform government with a return to morality, decency, and basic American values. By 1980 many voters saw him as part of a broken system in Washington and wanted change again. Reagan offered a different course forward, one that identified the system itself as fundamentally flawed.[1] Reagan's sunny optimism, and his catchy admonishment that government could not fix the problem, government *was* the problem, appealed to a beleaguered nation fatigued by economic stagnation and international crises. Reagan's successful campaign built on a coalition that embodied the complex threads of a conservatism ascendant but in flux. There were significant differences among the factions in Reagan's conservative coalition, but there was virtual unanimity that Carter's foreign policy was naive and dangerous in its underestimation of the Soviet threat to U.S. national and security interests.[2]

Human rights diplomacy was not a dominant issue of the 1980 presidential campaign, but it reinforced a number of themes that shaped the contours of the election and the respective visions of the candidates. For Carter, human rights represented his administration's successes, a symbol of a renewed commitment to openness with the American people about their government's international activities, and a self-critical policy that advanced U.S. influence and long-term interests in a complex, multilateral world. Time and again, Carter championed his administration's human rights diplomacy as a central element of a reconfigured foreign policy marrying principle and power.[3] For the Reagan campaign, Carter's human rights policy was another symbol of the Carter administration's weakness, inconsistency, and overall inability to deal with the core priorities of the nation—strength vis-à-vis the Soviet Union and economic recovery. Reagan took up the drumbeat of conservative criticism—most prominently displayed in Jeane Kirkpatrick's 1979 article for *Commentary*, "Dictators and Double Standards"—that cast Carter's human rights agenda as hopelessly biased and wrongheaded in its attacks on stalwart anticommunist allies, particularly in Latin America.[4] Reagan's constant inquiry, "Are you better off?" although not targeting human rights specifically, raised the issue of the policy's costs, as did his emphasis that both security and the economy had been damaged by human rights policies that restrict exports and international loans, linking domestic issues to conduct of foreign policy. Carter's primary challenge from Ted Kennedy similarly contended that American jobs and the economy were "being held hostage" by Carter's inability to resolve foreign crises.[5] Despite being grounded in liberal critiques of the president, Kennedy's arguments echoed those increasingly made by Republicans: the Carter administration's foreign policy—whether checking Soviet aggression or advancing human rights in Argentina—was weak, incompetent, and a distraction from critical domestic issues.

Reagan's successful bid for president initiated not the end of human rights diplomacy but a fundamental reconceptualization of its meaning and relationship to national security, particularly in the Western Hemisphere.[6] The Reagan administration approached human rights within a reinvigorated Cold War framework, where communism was the preeminent threat to human rights globally. This construction, championing a limited range of civil and political rights, downplayed the human rights violations of pro-American governments in the face of the much greater moral flaws and violations of communist regimes. The Cold War framing of human rights under Reagan empowered a pairing of military power and moral values, leading the United States to not only *not* limit arms sales to repressive right-wing governments but also to conceptualize military aid as a critical aspect of both hemispheric defense against communism and the advancement of human rights. As it recast the causative relationship between U.S. military aid and repression, it also reassigned the fundamental causes of human rights violations in the region; abuses stemmed not from overzealous governments but communist subversion, with military governments defending their populations from foreign terrorists. This notion, promoted by military governments themselves, drew the United States and military regimes closer once again, as partners in arms for human freedom. As with Carter, Latin America was the crucible to test the boundaries of the Reagan administration's new instruments and reorientation of human rights policy. The administration's efforts to bring "balance" to human rights initiatives by emphasizing violations in the Soviet Bloc reinforced, rather than diminished, the importance of Latin America in framing U.S. human rights policy. Reagan's emphasis on military aid and traditional allies bolstered the central position of Chile and Argentina as potent symbols of the battle over human rights in U.S. policies.

Even as Reagan brought a new Cold War sensibility to U.S.–Latin American policy that focused on Cuban threats and Central American conflicts, advocates in Congress and the Movement defended their existing formulation of human rights policy—one that stressed the dissociation of the United States from repressive regimes, regardless of their anticommunist credentials. Despite declining fortunes of the Left in electoral politics in 1980, the Movement's human rights agenda did not end with Carter's defeat. Advocates utilized strategies that had evolved under Ford and Carter to advance their agenda and protect its legislative instruments in the face of an openly antagonistic administration with a competing paradigm grounded in Cold War logic.

During the Reagan administration the Movement continued to use human rights as a check on executive power over foreign policy. Congress and advocates challenged the logic and efficacy of Reagan's approach. The markedly warmer relations between Washington and military governments in Chile and Argentina raised pointed questions about the Reagan administration's own evenhandedness and double standards, and undermined its message on communist abuses. The Movement's approach to Latin America was central to defining public perceptions of Reagan's human rights policy as ineffective and inconsistent—the very criticisms he had lodged against the Carter administration. The Movement forced the new administration to articulate a more broadly conceived understanding of human rights even as the administration worked to develop alternative policies and languages that reflected a return to Cold War verities.

By 1982 the Movement and the administration had reached a stalemate. Throughout Reagan's first year in office, congressional and public pressure pushed the administration into a clearer affirmation of human rights in principle and articulation of its policy instruments and objectives. Yet the agenda that emerged by the end of 1981 represented an almost total reinvention of 1970s human rights discourse by recasting it around the defense of freedom and the "free world," thereby shifting it from the self-critical, anti-interventionist policies of the 1970s to one that embraced military force and Cold War allies as a central aspect of advancing human rights globally. Movement and congressional resistance to the reorientation of Carter-era policies led Reagan to soften his overt focus on communist abuses, but the Reagan administration retained its broader vision of arming allies as part of advancing rights. Advocates thus succeeded in keeping the issue at the forefront of public debates over the administration's policy, but they could not prevent the fundamental transformation of the meaning and purpose of human rights diplomacy. Reagan's first year in office thus highlights the uniquely self-critical construction of human rights that defined the 1970s, as well as the enduring dynamics of human rights as a mechanism for democratic oversight of executive power in foreign policy.

The End of Confrontation Politics

Reagan offered a starkly different vision from Carter not only for the role of government at home but also for an unapologetic return to a Cold War framing of America's place in international affairs. In a 1980 campaign speech Reagan asserted, "The Soviet Union underlies all the unrest that is going on. If they weren't engaged in this game of dominos, there wouldn't be any hot spots in the world."[7] Reagan's anticommunism shaped his view of human rights. In early campaign material, Reagan affirmed that human rights "should be an important factor in any U.S. foreign policy equation" but must be weighed against other interests. Carter's "quixotic" and "inconsistent" policies, he charged, prioritized human rights at the expense of broader foreign policy objectives, hurting both bilateral relationships and global U.S. interests. Drawing on prevalent neoconservative critiques, Reagan developed an increasingly pointed criticism of the Carter administration's human rights policy for failing to meet U.S. security objectives and national interests of containing communism. Reagan called the policy "hypocritical" and championed the notion of a "double standard" made famous by Jeane Kirkpatrick.[8] Reagan argued that the Carter administration "legitimized abusers" in East Germany, China, and Cuba, who failed to live up to international agreements and human rights standards, while in Chile and Argentina it unfairly targeted anticommunist regimes making moderate improvements. Indeed, he praised both Chile and Argentina for improving their economic positions and fostering stability necessary for security and economic growth. Reagan similarly blamed human rights restrictions on exports and international loans for exacerbating U.S. economic problems.[9]

From his first days in office, Reagan's approach to human rights and U.S.–Latin American relations reflected the influence of his administration's Cold War priorities. On February 20 Secretary of State Alexander Haig announced the administration's intention to lift restrictions for EXIM loans to Chile and invite the Chilean navy to participate in UNITAS naval exercises. In a policy memo to the president, Haig argued that "these are the two most annoying aspects of current policy under Executive Branch control." He noted, "Among friendly countries looking to the United States for leadership, our relations with Chile are uniquely encumbered by congressional and executive sanctions." He observed that despite recent improvements in Chilean human rights conditions, U.S. policies had become more rigid. Moreover, he argued that these sanctions unfairly disadvantaged U.S. exporters and damaged U.S. security interests in the hemisphere given Chile's "strategic location and naval tradition." National Security Advisor Richard Allen strongly supported the move to lift restrictions, stating that these measures were "precisely the actions to be taken now to improve relations with that country."[10]

The administration similarly sought to normalize relations with Argentina. Just days after announcing its plans to lift restrictions on Chile, an Interagency Group on Argentina recommended that the administration seek to repeal or revise restrictive legislation, particularly the Humphrey-Kennedy Amendment. The group argued that, like restrictions on Chile, this legislation was detrimental to U.S. economic and security interest. Moreover, the Argentine government viewed the statute as "the core of hostile U.S. policy toward Argentina." The group recommended against asking Argentina for any specific commitments on human rights issues in exchange for repealing the act. Instead, the administration should develop an approach to U.S.-Argentine relations, in which human rights was a factor, but secondary to other security and economic interests.[11]

The administration emphasized its desire to reestablish traditional alliances with the Southern Cone and prioritize Cold War security concerns in the region by sending Special Emissary General Vernon Walters to visit Chile and Argentina at the end of February. In Chile, Walters met separately with both Pinochet and Foreign Minister Rojas to convey that President Reagan was "anxious to improve relations." Walters did not press the Chilean leadership directly on human rights, although he made oblique references that the Chilean government "must help" to improve relations by avoiding incidents that could be utilized by "hostile media." Walters held similar meetings with the Argentine leadership, where the heads of the Argentine armed services briefed him on the "external communist intervention in Salvador." Walters assured them that the Reagan administration was "determined to put a stop to extraneous intervention in [the] American Hemisphere." Walters reported that the meetings were "extremely friendly and candid." No mention was made of human rights.[12]

The early flurry of activities to reestablish relations with the Southern Cone culminated in a "private" visit to the United States by Argentina's president-elect, Roberto Viola, including a meeting with President Reagan and Secretary of State Haig in the Oval Office on March 17. Reagan welcomed Viola, stating that he wanted better relations, asserting that the "proper relationship" between the two nations was "one of open communications." He lamented the "strain" in bilateral relations in recent years, adding his belief that "the factors that caused it could be easily eliminated and will be in his administration." Viola replied that he "shared these views totally," and he affirmed that the two countries "belonged to the same group of nations who shared a love of freedom." Viola explained that he "did not oppose human rights," noting it was an idea consistent with Argentina's national values and history, but he objected to past policies that were "discriminatory" and "not global in reach." He continued promising Argentina would be a willing partner in efforts to "contain Communism and promote freedom."[13]

The meeting underscored the White House message that human rights would not impede relations with friendly, anticommunist regimes. The Reagan administration's emphasis on communist subversion in the region both redefined past excesses by the military governments and provided the basis for renewed relations, deemphasizing human rights violations. Both Reagan and Haig responded sympathetically to Viola's depiction of violations resulting from a "real war" fought in Argentina against terrorists, effectively framing the dirty war and abuses by the Argentine military as necessary to protect human rights and curb violence.[14] Haig reassured Viola that there would be "no finger pointing" on human rights and the administration would address any problems "quietly and confidentially." Reagan added that "there would be no public scolding or lectures." When Viola quipped that he "hoped there would be no private scoldings either," Reagan responded that "anything we ask for will be with a *por favor*." In a separate meeting, Viola assured Secretary Haig that the Reagan administration "could count on Argentine support and collaboration" against Soviet influence in the region, but he also asserted that the Humphrey-Kennedy Amendment was an "impediment" to renewed bilateral military relations. Haig responded by assuring him that the administration intended to "change" the amendment and put more funds into military training. Haig did mention that "human rights is an issue in the Congress," but he raised no other concerns or qualms on the topic. Indeed, he concluded the meeting by reassuring Viola again that "there would be no more lectures on human rights."[15]

Viola's visit provided an object lesson in how the Carter and Reagan administrations would deal with repressive regimes in different ways. Although both administrations believed that U.S. policy had to work through "moderates" in the military leadership, the Carter administration had used bilateral meetings, such as those for the Panama Canal Treaties, to encourage and reinforce movement toward better human rights progress through candid and sometimes uncomfortable conversations about violations. The Reagan administration's prioritization of East-West issues and willingness to seek repeal of restrictive legislation without any human rights concessions undermined its credibility on human rights. The absence of any pressure on human rights in its early approaches to Chile and Argentina echoed the "silent diplomacy" of the Ford-Kissinger years. Indeed, Allen went so far as to add a caveat to Haig's summary memorandum on Viola's visit for the president to underscore that human rights problems should be addressed only in private. "While continued progress on human rights is necessary," Allen stated, "we need to say this privately avoiding *altogether* the public criticism so often employed by the previous administration."[16] The Carter administration had also preferred to address sensitive issues privately first, but by preempting the option to press an avowedly friendly regime publicly, the Reagan administration lost crucial leverage for quiet diplomacy.

The Reagan administration's early overtures to the military governments in Chile and Argentina fit an emerging pattern in its human rights approach. In a televised interview with Walter Cronkite two weeks before Viola's visit, Reagan maintained that his past criticism of human rights diplomacy was a product of the policy's selectivity, not its fundamental values. The Soviet Union, he charged, was the "greatest violator today of human rights in all the world." Given this, Carter's policy of pressuring allies seemed imprudent if they could help curtail Soviet-Cuban expansion, which inherently threatened human rights. When asked if the need for "military allies and bases should take precedence over human rights considerations," Reagan responded, "No." He elaborated, "We have an alliance with a country that, as I say, does not meet all of [our human rights standards], we should look at it that we're in a better position remaining friends, to persuade them of the rightness of our view on human rights than to suddenly . . . pull the rug out from under them and then let a completely totalitarian takeover that denies what human rights the people had [*sic*]." When Cronkite pressed him, asking, "Doesn't that put us in the position rather of abetting the suppression of human rights for our own selfish ends?" Reagan replied, "Well, what has the choice turned out to be? The choice has turned out to be they lose all human rights because there's a totalitarian takeover."[17] Reagan's first months in office presented a stark choice on human rights: back anticommunist allies regardless of their human rights practices or enable a totalitarian takeover that would ultimately lead to even more severe repression.

Reagan's conflation of human rights and anticommunism was evident in the administration's early efforts to rethink U.S. policy in Latin America. An April policy draft for hemispheric relations almost diametrically opposed the Carter administration's construction of human rights as a challenge to Cold War security interests. Replacing Carter's emphasis on multilateralism and ideological pluralism, the new policy focused on the strategic threat posed by Cuba, and by extension the Soviet Union. The administration did not ignore the question of human rights but left the issue largely implicit, emphasizing that its approach would be "*balanced and realistic*," and asserted that "we will not allow any single issue to dominate our relationships with the hemisphere," with human rights listed as the first example of past failures to do so. The draft memo manifested the administration's emerging position that human rights could and should be pursued as something that derived from other policy goals, rather than a distinct objective. "The assurances of basic human liberties will not be achieved by alienating friendly governments which incompletely satisfy abstract standards in this regard. An ideologically motivated and selectively applied policy of human rights is detrimental to the achievement of practical progress in the human rights area. . . . This means that policy on human rights must be integrated into the totality of our foreign policy, not pursued as if it were somehow insulated from it." This notion rested on the presupposition that an anticommunist foreign policy inherently advanced human rights. Thus, the administration could assert that "promotion of the rights of man is a high priority of this administration," despite the issue's absence from sections detailing U.S. interests in the region.[18]

Perhaps the most revealing aspect of the administration's engagement with human rights in the region was its casting of "terrorism in any form as a violation of the most basic of human rights, the right to life." Asserting that "security relationships will receive a higher priority," this linkage of "terrorism"—almost always meaning communist subversion—with human rights violations recast traditional security relationships as an asset for advancing human rights in the region. This allowed the administration to argue that the resumption of military aid was not only good for U.S. security interests and bilateral relations but also a pragmatic aspect of promoting human rights. Similarly, economic assistance that aided the development of markets and liberal economies was conducive to U.S. security and economic interests, and it provided a bulwark against communist influence that would erode human rights in the long run. The policy memo argued that the real obstacle to U.S. interests in the region was the "decline of economic and security assistance as policy tools," rather than the political repression it had targeted. Citing Argentina as an example, it asserted that denial of arms transfers "is a good example of a policy that has not worked," as target countries had simply responded by turning to the Soviet Union and others to supply arms.[19]

Reagan's emphasis on developing free markets and private enterprise, a reflection of his domestic economic program, necessarily foreclosed the acceptance of what Carter called "diverse models of development," a central component of reassessing Cold War frameworks that had led to U.S. intervention in the past. Although the policy affirmed that "security, development, and freedom are indivisible and proper goals requiring cooperation among governments," it returned to a narrower model of what it accepted as "legitimate" economic development, once again casting collective and socialist programs as dangerous products of outside influence and interference.[20]

The administration's early approach to its Latin America policy revealed the way Cold War security concerns fundamentally reframed all major policy instruments. If communist-sponsored terrorism was the primary security threat and cause of human rights violations in the region, military aid, international financial institutions, and promotion of free-market economics all supported a liberal, Western-oriented political climate that would ultimately advance human rights. A speech drafted in May for a forthcoming visit to Argentina, for example, eschewed the notion of an inherent conflict between human rights and the nation's interests in the region; the administration's focus on combating terrorism "does not contradict support for human rights but [is an] essential precondition for it." It continued, "Opposing Soviet imperialism and its surrogates [is an] equally integral part of a human rights policy, as the expansion of Soviet power and Communist political systems is the most fundamental threat to human rights in the contemporary world." This logic had critical implications for existing human rights mechanisms. "Preservation of the independence and identity of peoples and nations is [the] first task of any genuine human rights policy, and this requires maintaining military strength sufficient to deter threats to this."[21] Resumption of military aid thus served to advance, not undermine, human rights interests.

Addressing the conservative, business-oriented Council of the Americas at the beginning of June, Assistant Secretary of State for Inter-America Affairs Thomas Enders set out the administration's new Cold War construction of regional relations. Enders presented a bipolar struggle between communist subversion advanced by Cuba and embattled governments who looked to the United States for support. Enders promised to "focus on the source of the problem" by targeting Cuba, which "has declared covert war on its neighbors—our neighbors. The United States will join with them to bring the costs of that war back to Havana." This threat required a reassertion of U.S. military power as a key component of regional policy, helping embattled countries "defend themselves." Enders contended that "once insurgents take arms with outside support, there is no alternative to an armed response," pointing to U.S. military assistance to El Salvador as a model. Military assistance would be accompanied by U.S. efforts to expand "self-determination: political and social progress," through "legitimate elections, or the carrying out of appropriate land reforms, or containment of violence from whatever quarter." In this depiction, the primary threat and cause of regional instability was not structural inequality or state-sponsored repression but external subversion; arming governments, regardless of their record, would ultimately advance U.S. interests and bring "freedom" to Latin America.[22]

The overwhelming focus on the communist threat in the Caribbean and Central America also recast U.S. relations with the Southern Cone. Enders legitimized the notion that the military governments' repression was a justified response to external subversion and "deadly challenges from urban terrorists of extreme violence." He credited the military regimes—not the Carter administration's policies or international human rights activism—for recent improvements in human rights conditions, arguing that "the broad trend is unmistakably toward liberalization, the end of abuses and the substitution of elected for emergency rule." As a result, the United States should offer its "friendship" to these countries to encourage progress toward open democracies and open economies. Enders rejected the "confrontation politics" practiced by the previous administration in the region, criticizing them for "campaigning against our friends where it suits us, yet demanding their help where it meets our interest."[23] The policy framework, by casting anticommunist regimes as inherent "friends" of the United States, failed to question the cost of allying with repressive governments or differentiate between leaders and the broader population.

In order to implement its vision of regional relations, which rested on military alliances, the administration had to grapple with existing legislation mandates explicitly designed to obstruct close relationships with repressive regimes. The administration had made no secret of the fact that it desired to repeal or at least limit restrictive legislation tying foreign aid to human rights performance. The administration also opposed country-specific legislation on the principle that it "reduces the flexibility of the President to conduct foreign relations." The administration argued that these kinds of "blanket restrictions" were counter to hemispheric security interests, especially as the conflict in Central America elevated the importance of Chile and Argentina for U.S. national security strategy. In meetings with officials from both Argentina and Chile, the administration professed its desire to normalize relations "as quickly as possible" and cited country-specific legislation as a "major impediment" in both cases.[24]

The Reagan administration largely viewed existing human rights legislation and the principle of "linkage" as counterproductive. In its effort to diminish these restrictions, the administration found considerable latitude in the interpretation of the statutes, particularly on international loans, noting that there was no "legislative or executive definition of what constitutes a 'consistent pattern of gross violations.'"[25] Anticipating that Congress would scrutinize any vote on high-profile cases such as Chile and Argentina for broader signals on regional and human rights policy, the State Department's Human Rights Bureau and Policy Planning Staff advocated abstaining on votes for Chile and Argentina in June. The Latin America bureau, by contrast, favored a positive vote on loans for Chile and Argentina, arguing that neither country presently met criteria for being a "gross violator" and that an affirmative vote would be consistent with the high-level reassurances given to both governments that the Reagan administration sought to improve relations. Abstention, the Latin America bureau feared, would "be viewed as a weakening of that commitment, extending beyond the MDB issue."[26] The Latin America bureau carried the day, and on July 1 the Treasury Department sent a letter to Congress announcing the administration's determination that the current human rights conditions in Chile, Argentina, Uruguay, and Paraguay "[do] not require U.S. opposition to MDB loans in these countries." A week later administration officials voted in favor of two international development bank loans to Chile totaling $161 million, the first affirmative U.S. votes for the country in four years.[27]

The IFI vote capped six months of evolving human rights policy in Latin America that had implications well beyond the region. The Reagan administration's approach to Latin America reflected a narrowed rights agenda that more easily fit within the administration's revival of Cold War assumptions. Human rights was not absent from regional relations, but a new emphasis on security, alliances, and military aid necessarily rejected the premise of dissociation tied to 1970s legislative efforts. Instead, the emphasis on communist subversion as the preeminent threat to both rights and regional stability meant that human rights policy could be advanced through the pursuit of national security objectives by means of arms transfers and military assistance. The administration's early policies left human rights as an implicit objective, holistically advanced by the broader Cold War strategy, rather than treating it as a discrete objective. In dismissing dissociation as ineffective for advancing human rights, the administration opened itself to charges of hypocrisy and double standards. Moreover, dissociation was a marker of executive commitment, one that targeted reform of both foreign behaviors and the U.S. government's own exercise of power.

Defending Dissociation

Reagan's repudiation of the Movement's agenda was widely seen as a repudiation of human rights itself. For a skeptical advocate community and Congress, the Reagan administration's early efforts to lift restrictions on U.S. aid and MDB funds and its moves to revive relations with Chile and Argentina underscored his administration's apparent indifference, if not outright hostility, toward human rights. The Movement viewed the administration's restoration of Cold War axioms as the basis of regional relations as inherently antagonistic to the human rights agenda they'd crafted since the Chilean coup. Even before Reagan had been sworn in, WOLA had anticipated that the new administration, "portraying Latin America as an ideological battleground between the forces of communism and democracy[,] will obscure the real economic, political and social problems facing the hemisphere."[28] In response to the administration's early actions warming relations with the Southern Cone, the Movement mobilized to defend dissociation and promote a vision of U.S. interests that transcended Cold War imperatives. In doing so, resistance to Reagan's reinvention of human rights exposed the issue's utility as a check on presidential power and exercise of democratic oversight of foreign policy.

The State Department's February 20 announcement that it intended to lift EXIM restrictions on Chile and invite the Chilean navy to participate in UNITAS exercises was swiftly and loudly denounced by the Movement. The Letelier-Moffitt Fund sent out a newsletter condemning the move, as a "symbolic gesture to warm up to the Chilean dictatorship [that] could be the first step to an eventual full restoration of economic and military aid." It urged readers to speak out "to let the administration know that such action will be met with swift condemnation on the part of the general public and Congress as well." Tom Harkin issued a press release, circulated by WOLA, stating that he was "appalled by the cynicism and hypocrisy of the decision." Kennedy issued a similar statement criticizing the administration's actions and charging it with a double standard in its fight against international terrorism, by "associating with a military regime which has not only engaged in the repression of its own citizens, but which is responsible for the terrorist assassinations" of Letelier and Moffitt. An IPS press release argued that the decision "offends both human rights concerns and rational statecraft," warning that the administration had "ignored the basic lesson of the last decades: that no Administration can gain support for a foreign policy which spurns the values of America."[29]

Human rights groups similarly attacked the warming of U.S. relations with the Argentine military regime. As the administration made arrangements for Viola's visit, the Movement kept up a steady drumbeat of criticism on ongoing human rights violations in Argentina, challenging the Reagan administration's assertions that repression had abated. In March WOLA circulated reports of raids on the Buenos Aires offices of human rights organizations and the arrest of six prominent Argentine human rights leaders, followed by the detention of sixty-eight relatives of the disappeared, all members of Las Madres.[30] In its newsletter WOLA situated these arrests in a broader trend of increased repression in the lead-up to Viola's Washington visit. "This upsurge in human rights violations in Argentina," WOLA reported, "was followed by a request by the Reagan administration for lifting a ban on military sales to Argentina." The same WOLA newsletter analyzed the State Department country reports for 1980. In Argentina new disappearances had decreased significantly, but ongoing government obstructionism prevented any accounting for the thousands of people still missing in the dirty war.[31]

The administration's nomination of Ernest Lefever for assistant secretary of state for human rights—announced on the same day the State Department stated its intention to lift restrictions on EXIM financing to Chile—became the primary outlet for debates over the meaning and implementation of U.S. human rights policy. Lefever, the founder and president of the neoconservative Ethics and Public Policy Center, had been a vociferous critic of the Carter administration's human rights policy. Lefever was part of the rising neoconservative critique of Carter's foreign policy and human rights, articulated in his widely circulated 1978 article, "The Trivialization of Human Rights." In the article Lefever charged that the Carter administration's application of human rights was "misguided," "counterproductive," and "capricious," and would have "catastrophic consequences for the security of the United States and the cause of freedom in the world."[32] Comparing policies and statements in Chile and Argentina to Cuba and Cambodia, Lefever charged that the Carter administration was "preoccupied with minor abridgement of certain rights in authoritarian states" while it "often overlooks the massive threat to the liberty of millions" in communist countries. Relations with Chile, Argentina, and South Korea all evidenced the way that "a consistent and single-minded invocation of a human rights standard . . . would subordinate, blur, or distort other essential considerations." In short, the Carter administration's application of human rights missed the critical moral battle of its time—the fight against communism.[33]

His criticisms of Carter's approach, hinging on traditional Cold War conceptions of national security and the authoritarian-totalitarian distinction, led him to argue against the current legislative mechanisms linking military and foreign aid to human rights performance. He instead asserted that the best way for the U.S. government to advance human rights was by arming and defending anticommunist allies "who are threatened by totalitarian aggression. This requires security guarantees, military assistance, and in some cases, the presence of U.S. troops on foreign soil." Moreover, Lefever argued that the United States lacked a "moral mandate" to reconfigure foreign societies. Thus, "beyond serving as a good example and maintain[ing] our security commitments, there is little the U.S. government can or should do to advance human rights, other than using quiet diplomatic channels at appropriate times and places."[34]

Given Lefever's well-publicized rejection of the major mechanisms and fundamental assumptions of the existing human rights policy, it is unsurprising that his appointment was met with almost instant condemnation from the Movement. For the advocates who had built these policies over the past decade, Lefever's stance was almost a caricature of a conservative vision of human rights. They targeted Lefever's narrow view of human rights, which appeared to address only communist regimes while excusing anticommunist allies that implicated the United States in gross abuses. A scathing editorial in the *Nation* argued, "Even in the long procession of Reagan appointees professing their antagonism to the objectives of the agencies they have been chosen to lead, Lefever stands out." It continued, "If the choice of a man to fill this post were delegated to a search committee consisting of President Chun of South Korea, Prime Minister Botha of South Africa and President Pinochet of Chile, Lefever is the man one would expect them to appoint."[35] Even more inflammatory were Lefever's statements that seemed to dismiss the very premise of the Human Rights Bureau he had been tapped to lead.[36] As the battle over his nomination heated up, criticism widened to include charges of bias in his center's research in favor of large corporate donors.[37] Lefever's personal travels to South Africa and Guatemala also called into question his seemingly untroubled relationship with governments that had massive human rights problems.

By the time of his confirmation hearings on May 21, 1981, Lefever's nomination was embattled. In the lead-up to his testimony, Lefever charged that the opposition to his appointment was "communist inspired." This charge appeared not only paranoid but also ridiculous given that among those slated to testify against his appointment were groups devoted to human rights violations in the Soviet sphere, such as Helsinki Watch and the Committee for Soviet Jewry. Lefever subsequently denied having used the phrase "communist inspired," only to be immediately rebutted by two congressmen. From there, the hearings devolved, with Lefever struggling to answer questions about the financing of his center and concerns about bias in its studies. Lefever walked back earlier statements calling for the repeal of all human rights laws, stating he had "goofed." He maintained, however, that U.S. human rights policy should focus primarily on "aggressive acts by a country beyond its borders," clearly implying that international communism should be the primary target of U.S. policies. Relying on the authoritarian-totalitarian distinction, Lefever argued for "quiet diplomacy" with friendly, anticommunist regimes.[38]

At the close of the hearings, the *New York Times* reported that Lefever was "self-destructive" and had been an "extraordinarily evasive witness, unresponsive, disingenuous, so much so that he annoyed Senators of both parties."[39] The day after the hearings, Senators Cranston, Tsongas, and Dodd called for Lefever to withdraw his name from consideration for the post, citing his "misleading and evasive testimony" and the troubling allegations of unethical behavior at the center.[40] Even sympathetic press, such as the *Washington Star*, reported following the hearings that Lefever was in for some "tough times," noting, "He has only one major enemy. His mouth."[41] Despite a last-ditch effort to salvage his candidacy, Lefever withdrew his name from consideration on June 5, following a 13–4 vote against his appointment by the Senate Foreign Relations Committee.

Despite being a remarkably ineffective witness, Lefever's conceptualization of human rights policy was not out of step with the Reagan administration's vision for transforming the fundamental scope and application of the policy. As the *Wall Street Journal* argued, "The current criticisms of the Administration policy are in the end not especially powerful, but it is sure that if not answered more skillfully they are going to succeed in discrediting a good thing."[42] Indeed, Lefever's positions were very much in keeping with Reagan's emerging vision of a new human rights policy that fit more neatly within a Cold War worldview. This approach resonated with many, as evidenced by the letters of support Lefever's nomination elicited, drawn primarily from ethnic affinity groups from communist countries in Eastern Europe, as well as from Vietnam. These groups decried the perceived bias and "double-standard" in Carter's human rights diplomacy that seemed to them to ignore the glaring problem of communist human rights abuses. They also expressed concern for traditional Cold War security issues. These groups applauded Lefever's position as a corrective to the Carter years, and they called for a more "balanced" human rights agenda.[43]

Lefever and the approach he advocated represented an attack on the foundations of the policy the Movement had built, but it was not a dismissal of the issue as a whole by the administration. A *Washington Post* editorial summarized that Reagan needed "someone who conveys unequivocally that a hard anti-Soviet policy pointed at the large issue of freedom is not inconsistent with a human rights policy designed to enlarge the sphere of individual rights and liberties—everywhere. Mr. Lefever . . . has failed utterly to convey the idea. . . . Far from adding something of value to the Reagan foreign policy, he denies the President the one valid contribution he could be expected to make." The editorial concluded that "Mr. Lefever's rigidity and narrowness are a parody of what a productive conservative human rights approach could be."[44] Even as Lefever's candidacy faltered, the logic behind his position continued to take shape within the administration.

The bumbling of Lefever's confirmation hid the Reagan administration's increasingly coherent vision of human rights policy. Erratic behavior and questionable practices at his think tank undid his nomination more than framing of human rights as anticommunist practice. In the face of the Reagan administration's effort to dismantle or disregard the basic frameworks they had built, the Movement and their partners in Congress escalated their efforts to use human rights as a means to check presidential power and defend their agenda of anti-interventionism and dissociation.[45] In July Don Bonkers, chair of the Congressional Subcommittee on Human Rights and International Organizations opened hearings on the administration's early policy actions, stressing the centrality of Congress—not the executive—in laying the foundations for existing human rights policy. Bonkers cited "disturbing trends" in the administration's actions that seemed to deliberately undermine congressionally mandated human rights provisions. Bonkers stressed that existing legislation manifested an intent by Congress and the American people to aid in the advancement of human rights globally, but it also represented a "determination to disassociate and distance themselves from governments that perpetuate consistent and gross violations of universally-recognized human rights. This underlies the historical concern of the Congress and the American people" for human rights.[46]

The question of executive compliance became a center point for evaluating the administration's intention on human rights as a whole. The lack of congressional consultation by the State Department only seemed to underscore the administration's indifference to legislative intent.[47] During the hearings Harkin questioned the absence of human rights from the administration's criteria for evaluating arm sales. Walter Stoessel, undersecretary of state for political affairs, represented the administration, responding, "Our position is that human rights certainly will continue to be one of the criteria in determining the appropriateness of arms sales, but it will not be the only one." It would not be "singled out" but "interwoven in all our considerations." Harkin was clearly not satisfied with this response. "I do not wish to be argumentative," he responded, "but if you have seven factors and you don't list human rights, it is conspicuous in its absence." Bonkers sharply questioned the administration's assertion that the governments in Chile and Argentina, among others, were not "clear and consistent violators," and he noted that the law did not provide for "improvement" as a metric for evaluating human rights conditions.[48]

Committee members also rejected the administration's premise that arms sales could advance human rights as fundamentally at odds with the legislation's logic of dissociation. In his opening statement Stoessel had avowed, "We believe that enhancing a security relationship can sometimes also enhance our ability to persuade other countries to improve their human rights situations." Stoessel defended the administration's early approach as "effective," asserting that "to pillory these countries, particularly when there has been progress, would be counterproductive and would be resented." Rejecting the premise of dissociation, he claimed, "Our influence on human rights can extend only as far as our reputation for reliability to friends and allies and the respect we generate from our adversaries."[49] Drinan noted that the primary purpose of 502B "was to disassociate the US from governments which violate human rights, which violate the integrity of the person through detainment, torture or killing, etc. In other words, the law was meant to end U.S. association and/or complicity in the repressive practices of a foreign government. . . . Security assistance, in our judgement, whether aid or sales, is never neutral." Offering military aid to improve rights, he warned, "certainly violates the spirit of the law in most cases, the letter of the law in a smaller number. The tyrants of repressive regimes are likely to consider the fact of military aid more seriously than human rights rhetoric and infer that they have U.S. sanctions for their acts." Rep. Jim Leach (D-IA) acknowledged there was "validity [in] the notion that terrorism may be the greatest human rights violation. I do not necessarily think it follows however, that counterterrorism is the antidote to terrorism. Our arms sales unfortunately tend to enhance and sometimes partake in the occurrence of counterterrorism whereas other antidotes might be found in the economic or social arena, or even involve more action in the arena of arms control itself." For Leach, the administration's formulation of human rights in regional relations missed the critical link between U.S. military power and intervention, and human rights abuses in the hemisphere. Bonkers concluded the July 14 hearing by stating, "I have to tell you that I am concerned by what I see as a pattern, the aim of which is to dismantle our human rights policy."[50]

The disproportionate emphasis on the Soviet Union slighted one of the defining features of the 1970s framework—that of self-reflection and accountability for the United States' own actions. Rep. Dante Fascell (D-FL) elaborated, "The way in which we behave internationally has a very real effect not only on how we are perceived, but on who we *are*. . . . The human rights policy, in that sense, functions as a compass to ensure we stay on course. So, I think it can be seen that our human rights policy is not just for others. It's for us, too." The Reagan administration's overwhelming focus on communist behaviors subverted this dimension of existing policies and the element of accountability they provided for the United States' own actions.[51]

Lefever's failed nomination and the vigorous defense of existing human rights mandates in Congress can be seen as a success for the liberal vision of human rights, but that success proved incomplete as new challenges arose in the coming months.[52] Congressional hearings showcased the resistance to the administration's early approach to human rights mandates but also highlighted the struggle for control of foreign policy between the executive and Congress at the heart of human rights initiatives, with Latin America occupying a central symbolic position. Indeed, the human rights policies of the 1970s had been about the behavior of foreign governments but also sought to reform the practices of U.S. policy making and exercise greater restraint over executive privilege in foreign affairs.

Challenging Double Standards

One of the distinctions between past and present policy that had troubled congressional leaders and the Movement during the fight over Lefever's nomination and the July congressional hearings was the Reagan administration's almost exclusive focus on the Soviet Union and communist violations, which opened the administration to charges of its own double standard. Stoessel presented the Reagan administration's approach as a corrective to the past administration's inconsistencies, asserting, "Ours is not a policy of selective indignation, rather it is one of balanced and evenhanded condemnation of human rights violations wherever they occur." Rep. Jonathan Bingham (D-NY) countered that the Reagan administration seemed to have little hesitation publicly disclaiming the records of communist countries, even as it championed "quiet diplomacy" with anticommunist allies. "It does seem to me that this administration has made a record of backing away from applications of our human rights policies from the past administration, particularly in Latin America in such a way as to create a perception that we are not as interested in pressing for human rights as we were. . . . I have in mind the loosening up of our attitudes toward Argentina, toward Chile." Fascell similarly argued against the communist focus as counterproductive. "That's just an anti-Soviet policy. I don't see such a policy attracting much international support. The fact is, our human rights policy up till now has attracted very substantial international support." Fascell noted that human rights didn't always have to be the top consideration, but "if the policy is constantly subordinated, or if a pattern of selective application emerges, we invite condemnation for hypocrisy and call our own international intentions into question."[53]

During the July hearings, John Shestack, president of the International League for Human Rights, charged, "The administration is selective, inconsistent, and disappointing. It fails to condemn vigorously the vicious human rights violations in Argentina or continued abuses in Uruguay and Chile." Shestack was particularly disheartened by the most recent meeting of the UN Commission on Human Rights. He depicted the 1980 session as "the most productive" in the commission's history, and he contrasted that with the "loss of that leadership" during the most recent meeting, the first during Reagan's tenure. The administration's efforts to "accommodate" Argentina, for example, undermined the delegation's support of a "strong resolution on disappearances." He concluded, "The whole climate was one that questioned the U.S. commitment to human rights. Instead of the United States being a leader and a champion of human rights, it was regarded with suspicion and as hostile to the concept."[54]

Indeed, during the summer of 1981 the contrast between the Reagan administration's condemnation of communist violations and its approach to Chile, Argentina, and other right-wing regimes opened it to charges of double standards and seemed to negatively impact the entire human rights enterprise. The Reagan administration's break with the Carter era policies that dissociated the United States from repressive military regimes in the region was perhaps most visible in Chile. In July the U.S. delegation to the UN reversed the long-standing U.S. position on the special rapporteur to Chile, voting against its continuation. In doing so, the administration argued that it was not abandoning "the traditional U.S. emphasis on human rights" but rather rejected a "double standard" that had unfairly penalized countries such as Chile and represented the Reagan administration's "unique sense of strategy and tactics."[55]

The Reagan administration's warming relations with Chile and Argentina and its diplomatic silence on government abuses contrasted sharply with its aggressive and unapologetic promotion of human rights through the Conference on Security and Cooperation in Europe (CSCE) established by the Helsinki Final Act. Reagan, like many other conservatives, had initially rejected the Helsinki Accords as appeasing the Soviets, urging President Ford not to sign them in 1975. During most of his presidential campaign, Reagan remained skeptical of the Helsinki process, famously questioning it in a *Time* magazine interview in June. "I have an uneasy feeling that going to Madrid [for the follow-up conference] is negating what we thought we could accomplish by boycotting the Olympics. If the athletes can't go, why should the diplomats go?"[56] Yet in October 1980, as his presidential campaign entered the final stretch, Reagan issued a public statement unequivocally backing the upcoming conference at Madrid and calling for a "militant advocacy posture on human rights by the U.S."[57] This reversal created significant uncertainty about the incoming administration's approach to the conference, but from the outset of his tenure, Reagan backed a "vigorous" human rights policy at Madrid as the vanguard of his approach to the issue in Eastern Europe.[58]

Under the leadership of Max Kampelman, human rights received the "highest priority" at the Madrid conference.[59] Carter appointed Kampelman as chairman of the U.S. Delegation to the CSCE Review Conference in Madrid in 1980. In a "most unusual decision," Reagan asked him to remain, giving remarkable and unexpected continuity to U.S. strategy there from Carter to Reagan.[60] The U.S. delegation deployed a strategy of "non-stop documentation" and frank public criticism of Soviet abuses. Kampelman recounted that the U.S. approach to human rights abuses at Madrid was a "hard-nosed cataloguing of specific human rights abuses. Facts were laid bare, names were named, crimes cited," influenced by his predecessor at Belgrade, Arthur Goldberg.[61] The U.S. delegation's focus on specific communist abuses increasingly received support and attention from Western European allies.[62] Kampelman paired his robust public diplomacy with frequent bilateral meetings with the Soviet delegation, where he also frankly and frequently raised human rights concerns. Kampelman "implemented and innovated" the U.S. approach at Madrid that amplified human rights to an unprecedented degree, yet he also had strong White House support for his efforts. Testifying before the Helsinki Commission in early 1982, Undersecretary of State Lawrence Eagleburger asserted that the CSCE was "terribly valuable to the whole process of American foreign policy." Eagleburger particularly stressed its importance to human rights, noting that "Helsinki gives us a forum that the Soviets simply cannot ignore, nor can the people of the world ignore, to remind the world of their failures to meet their commitments under the Helsinki Final Act."[63]

Kampelman's direct, specific overtures to the Soviets on human rights reflected Reagan's own approach in communications with Leonid Brezhnev in the first year. Reagan unapologetically raised issues of Soviet compliance with the Helsinki Accord's human rights mandates and particular prisoners' cases, linking improved relations to Soviet action on these issues. But Reagan also made clear his desire to work through and beyond these issues. In a meeting with Andrei Gromyko in September, Haig pressed the Soviet foreign minister for progress on human rights issues at the Madrid conference, citing the "political reality in the U.S." He explained, "Should there not be at least some progress on this score, the climate for improving relations between us would be complicated." He asked Gromyko to give "important consideration" to the case of Anatoliy Shcharanskiy, a Jewish dissident and jailed Helsinki monitor who had become one of the Reagan administration's target cases. When Gromyko dismissed Shcharanskiy as "a little criminal" and a "nobody," Haig cautioned that his case and others "were of very great significance to the President as a manifestation of an improved dialogue. On top of that, this was a matter of great interest to a number of Congressmen and Senators."[64]

At the Madrid Conference, the Reagan administration rejected allied concerns that too much public pressure on human rights might "ostracize" the Soviets and lead to a breakdown of relations and the entire Helsinki process.[65] Pairing public diplomacy with private overtures, the administration made clear to the Soviet leadership that human rights was a priority and a prerequisite for cooperation on Soviet priorities, particularly disarmament. In a personal letter to Brezhnev in November 1981, Reagan again urged the Soviets to address the Helsinki guarantees of family reunification and the release of specific political prisoners, saying they would "have a favorable effect on deliberations in Madrid, and on relations between our two countries. . . . I am personally concerned with the particular cases under discussion between Secretary Haig and your representatives," he stressed.[66]

The Reagan administration had little hope for sustained Soviet reform but saw these negotiations as "an opportunity to try to get some people out of the USSR." Moreover, a breakthrough on a high-profile case such as Shcharanskiy's would also ease some domestic pressure on human rights and "would demonstrate that the Administration's approach to human rights produces more results than rhetoric." The Reagan administration sought to achieve "balance" between human rights demands and security objectives, a strategy that revealed the potential of pairing frank human rights discussion with serious bilateral engagement.[67]

The administration's vigorous promotion of human rights violations at Madrid made its silence on violations by anticommunist allies all the more deafening. In early August, U.S. ambassador to the United Nations Jeane Kirkpatrick made a high-profile visit to six Southern Cone nations—including Chile and Argentina—signaling the administration's priority of elevating security interests and improving relations with the governments of the region. Kirkpatrick "took full advantage" of her visit to "convey the message that the Reagan administration intends to treat Chile and other friendly Latin American states as full partners in our effort to reassert Western interests and values." Kirkpatrick met privately with government leaders, including Pinochet, signaling that the military regimes were no longer estranged from Washington. Even more telling than the high-profile meetings with Pinochet and his cabinet was the lack of parallel meetings with prominent human rights groups and opposition leaders. Kirkpatrick had a "carefully orchestrated reception" with several democratic opposition leaders and spoke to members of the American Chamber of Commerce. However, she relegated leaders of the human rights community to meetings with her support staff. This, combined with Kirkpatrick's statements that the administration sought to "normalize completely its relations" with Chile and did not view the Letelier case as an "impediment" to this goal, led many in the human rights community to conclude that "quiet diplomacy" was the complete abandonment of human rights objectives there.[68]

The day after Kirkpatrick's visit, the Chilean government expelled four prominent human rights advocates—including Jaime Castillo, president of the Chilean Commission on Human Rights and lawyer for the Letelier family in Chile—raising pointed questions about the efficacy and sincerity of the Reagan administration's human rights policy. Castillo had met with Kirkpatrick's staff during the trip, stressing that contrary to the current administration's assertions, Carter's policies "had in fact been effective in Chile in curbing violations of human rights." He and others in the human rights community were thus troubled by Reagan's rejection and criticism of these policies. The current approach, he claimed, had resulted in a "hardening" of the Chilean government's position. He pointed specifically to the problems of internal exiles, lack of accounting for disappeared persons, and attacks on lawyers, expressing he was "surprised and concerned" by U.S. government statements claiming that human rights in Chile had been "much improved" in the past year.[69]

Castillo's expulsion days after his meeting with U.S. officials placed the Reagan administration on the defensive and underscored the public perception that it lacked a substantial human rights policy beyond easy Cold War criticism of its communist adversary. The administration had already publicly defended Kirkpatrick's decision to not meet with opposition leaders because of a tight schedule, asserting that a staff meeting shouldn't be seen as "less significant." At his press conference the day after the expulsion, Secretary of State Haig asserted that "this administration supports the right of peaceful political dissent in Chile as elsewhere in the world. It is particularly unfortunate that one of the persons [expelled by the GOC] was founder and President of the Chilean Human Rights Commission." When pressed by reporters, "Kirkpatrick was just there. Do we consider it in anyway connected with her visit?" Haig responded with a terse, "No."[70]

Despite public disavowals of any connection between Kirkpatrick's visit and U.S. policy with the expulsion, the administration's frustration with the Chilean government's action was clearly evident in Ambassador Landau's meeting with Chilean foreign minister Rojas shortly after the incident. Rojas acknowledged that the "timing of the move was very bad" but argued that it was "necessary," warning that "the Marxists had many helpers, including people with good intentions who let themselves be used for Marxist purposes." The only way to prevent terrorism or a return to the chaos of the Allende years was to remain firm, "even when anti-communist figures like Jaime Castillo had to pay the price when they let themselves be used by others." Rojas thus cloaked himself in the anticommunist security rationales that the administration itself had used to justify the revitalized relationship. Landau responded that the Chilean government had done a disservice to both U.S. and Chilean governments "by taking steps which serve largely to reinforce a negative image and thus give ammunition to Chile's enemies." He continued that "such actions on the heels of the Kirkpatrick visit were particularly thoughtless because as he could see from the question raised in the department press briefing, the press was looking for a connection with the visit."[71]

Indeed, the Movement seized on the expulsion as indicative of broader policy failings. In an interview with the *Washington Post*, Claudio Orrego, a former member of the Chilean parliament, charged that "the visit of Ambassador Kirkpatrick was received by the government as meaning the enthusiastic and unconditional support of the Reagan administration for the Chilean government and as the explicit derogation of the United States' human rights policy." He continued by stating that the visit was a "tragedy for the democratic opposition of Chile."[72] The Chile Committee for Human Rights issued an urgent action alert, charging that "Kirkpatrick's visit merely reiterated the Reagan administration's position on the continued human rights violations in Chile by giving the illegitimate dictatorship the green light to continue with these illegal practices of torture, arbitrary detention, mass arrests, internal exile, expulsion, and the denial of the right to live in one's homeland." A Council on Hemispheric Relations press released stated, "Reagan Administration's myopic Chilean policy ignores heightening levels of repression," charging that the expulsion highlighted the failure of the administration's "quiet diplomacy."[73] In a letter to Pinochet, WOLA cast the action as "only the most recent example of your regime's continual attempts to stifle all political opposition and repress legitimate discussion of government policy, both inside and outside your borders." It argued that the "great majority of the American public," along with members of Congress and private organizations, "repudiated this action" and the broader repression it symbolized. The letter concluded, "It portends further isolation for the Chilean regime in the world context and a more rapid isolation of President Reagan from the great majority of concerned citizens of this country."[74]

Kirkpatrick, who had been "too busy" to meet with Castillo in Santiago, made time to meet him a month later in Washington. In the meeting Kirkpatrick conceded that "nobody believes that Chile is a democracy or that opposition is allowed free rein." She concluded, however, "While we would greatly prefer that all governments were democratic and observed human rights, there are severe limitations in terms of our power as to what we can do. The administration has a human rights policy and believes it morally correct. Its intention is not to create a perfect world but to leave a freer world than it found." She affirmed her willingness to take up the issue of exile that Castillo had raised, a promise she kept the following week in her meeting with the Chilean representative to the UN, Manuel Trucco.[75]

Kirkpatrick's meeting with Castillo was emblematic of the administration's broader logic on military alliances and rights. Her willingness to engage on the individual issue had little impact on the overall thrust of the administration's policy, particularly its determination to normalize relations with both Chile and Argentina, regardless of human rights conditions. In a September meeting, Stoessel again reassured the Chilean ambassador that the administration "will move as quickly as possible to repeal or modify the Kennedy Amendment" as part of its broader effort to normalize relations. Stoessel did advise Chilean ambassador Valenzuela that the Castillo incident was counterproductive to the administration's efforts, but he couched this in terms of a public relations concern rather than any moral or principled objection to the action. For Congress and segments of the American public, "passions still run high concerning Chile," and the administration worried that actions such as the expulsion of Castillo "[provided] ammunition to those who do not want U.S./Chile relations to improve." Throughout the fall, the administration continued to stress that its policy on Chile recognized "progress" on human rights in recent years, especially as the Letelier-Moffitt case seemed to be at a legal dead end.[76]

The human rights community disagreed vigorously with the administration's depiction of an improved regime, arguing instead that the Reagan administration's permissive attitude toward violations by allies had contributed to the deterioration of conditions within Chile. A Chilean report distributed through the American Friends Service Committee, for example, documented an increase in Chilean human rights violations, attributing them in large part to the changes in U.S. government attitudes since the outset of the Reagan administration. The September report stated, "The international isolation that has plagued the [Chilean] government ever since its bloody takeover in 1973 is now less acutely felt." It continued, asserting that Pinochet was empowered by the "dramatic turnabout in relations with the United States," citing Jeane Kirkpatrick's visit and Castillo's subsequent expulsion. The report concluded that the Pinochet regime's "political stability (backed by increasingly severe repression) has never been greater," resulting in a more aggressive foreign policy, particularly in Central America.[77] U.S. advocates depicted the administration's efforts to improve relations with Santiago—particularly its efforts to repeal legislation limiting military aid and training to the country—as an example of its hypocrisy on human rights. A WOLA news brief in September argued, "Before rewarding Chile with the benefits of full relations, the Chilean government must produce concrete results to establish that there has been definite improvement in human rights and thereby demonstrate their consideration for the U.S. government and its policies. The U.S. cannot reward it for nothing, and especially at a time of increased rights violations."[78]

A core critique of the administration's policies was the growing hypocrisy engendered by its Cold War emphasis. In testimony before the Congressional Subcommittee on Human Rights and International Organizations in September, Orville H. Schell from the Lawyers Committee for International Human Rights claimed, "It is the policy of the Reagan administration to make strong rhetorical statements in favor of human rights as an integral part of our foreign policy and then, with the other hand, in instance after instance, to relegate human rights to a subsidiary position overridden by various military, cold war, and commercial considerations." He continued, "In practice, the administration has systematically de-emphasized human rights both in our bilateral and multilateral decision making." Schell lamented, "While certain countries, notably the Soviet Union, have been singled out for virulent criticism of their domestic practices. Other countries, notably those in the Southern Cone of South America, which are notorious for their gross violations of human rights, have been showered with our largesse." This "double standard of treatment," he argued, "utterly destroys the credibility of the U.S. position" well beyond Latin America. At the Madrid conference implementing the Helsinki process, for example, Max Kampelman's efforts had been "greatly hampered by the authoritarian-totalitarian doctrine which Mrs. Kirkpatrick has been espousing." Schell contrasted Madrid with the U.S. delegation to the UN's Commission on Human Rights, where "so much time was spent on checking out how matters had been handled vis-à-vis Argentina, Chile, and other South American countries that little attention was paid to other countries with the result that there was disillusionment on the part of our allies." Schell, who had attended the UN proceedings in Geneva, noted "a distinct feeling, air of lack of enthusiasm for human rights in general."[79]

Indeed, human rights proponents from well beyond the Movement's base cautioned that the administration's silence on authoritarian allies critically weakened its ability to promote human rights in the Soviet sphere at Madrid and beyond. Warren Eisenberg of B'nai B'rith stated that the "concern and commitment" to human rights evidenced at Madrid must "be applied to Latin America." Eisenberg cautioned, "Just as human rights is indivisible, so too must a common standard be applied in exposing and judging human rights violations and abridgements. . . . Selective morality subverts the very standards of human rights. For our leadership in the human rights field to be credible and effective, it must have an across-the-board, universal character."[80]

Perhaps most damning was Aryeh Neier of Helsinki Watch, who expressed his frustration that U.S. initiatives at Madrid "may be undermined by the failures of the United States elsewhere." He continued, "Inevitably, US policy toward Latin America is going to loom large in the discussions by European government leaders. They will talk about the failure of the United States to promote human rights in Latin America." Neier stated that the administration's invocation of the authoritarian-totalitarian distinction and the resulting double standard in its policy approach was the major impetus for the formation of the new Americas Watch Committee, an offshoot of Helsinki Watch. He explained that although Helsinki Watch's efforts focused on the Soviet sphere in Europe, to be effective the group had to advocate for human rights everywhere. "It became incumbent upon us to swim against the Reagan administration tide and deal with the friendly authoritarian countries of Latin America which engage in systematic abuses of human rights." Neier concluded, "Except for the continuing strong advocacy of human rights at the Helsinki review conference at Madrid, the Reagan administration's human rights record is a disaster."[81]

The overwhelming conclusion of the hearing's participants was that the administration's approach perpetuated a "double standard" that was in violation of both the letter and the spirit of the laws that Congress had constructed over the past decade. Reagan's disregard for the congressional intent to avoid U.S. identification with repressive regimes was particularly galling and at odds with the new vision of national interests constructed through human rights in the past decade. David Carlinger of the International Human Rights Law Group explained, "The human rights laws . . . ensure that the U.S. is not associated with human rights atrocities around the world. They put teeth in a human rights policy which is commensurate with our international obligations and our own values and traditions." Many in Congress shared the Movement's conviction that the administration was increasingly and deliberately subverting human rights objectives, especially in Latin America. In opening comments before the Subcommittee on Human Rights and International Organizations, Bonkers observed that "this administration is less than enthusiastic in its support of those provisions in the Foreign Assistance Act and other provisions of the law," warning that Congress "fully intends for the law to be implemented."[82]

By early fall, nine months of administrative action impressed on concerned audiences in Congress and the human rights community that human rights foreign policy was reserved exclusively for bludgeoning communist adversaries. The prevailing opinion was that "quiet diplomacy" with high-profile cases in Latin America was really "silent diplomacy," where Washington once again condoned government abuses as long as they were framed as anticommunist initiatives. Moreover, the administration's consistent effort to revise or repeal legislation showed a contempt for congressional intent and democratic oversight of foreign policy making. An October newsletter by the Coalition for a New Foreign and Military Policy warned of the Reagan administration's "disappearance" of the nation's human rights policy. The administration's approach in its first nine months in office evoked the "haunting spectre of a return to policies which support repression, rely on military solutions and repeat the policy mistakes of the past three decades."[83]

The group focused on the resumption of military aid to repressive regimes and attacked the core logic that offering security assistance to repressive regimes could advance human rights. This logic, they argued, went against the clear congressional intent of the legislation: "to remove the U.S. from complicity or direct involvement in human rights violations committed by other nations." The group concluded that the Reagan administration "does not believe a human rights policy serves the national interest; indeed it is seen as an obstacle to achieving Reagan's foreign policy goals." This belief, they wrote, put the administration at odds with the human rights community, which viewed human rights both as a way to "support and increase the influence of the voices of democracy and reform throughout the world" and advance U.S. strategic interests and national values. Criticizing the administration's tendency to evaluate "all policy through the prism of East-West conflicts," the article denounced Reagan's failure to acknowledge the "limits or consequence of military action in today's world." Further, "What the administration also fails to recognize is that the absence of a strong even-handed human rights policy is self-defeating to its own stated objective of providing a model to the third world distinct from that of the Soviet Union. It turns human rights into a cheap propaganda tool easily disregarded by the Soviets and increases the vulnerability of human rights advocates living in the USSR and Eastern Europe."[84] The Reagan administration's human rights double standard, in short, undermined its efficacy abroad and eroded its credibility at home. Moreover, this criticism was not just grounded in the administration's failure to live up to a particular vision of human rights policy or an expression of doubts over the current approach's efficacy. It also reflected the way the human rights agenda had merged with congressional checks on Cold War presidential powers and the public's right to shape a foreign policy that represented its values and its interests.

A True Human Rights Policy

The lack of institutional structure and policy frame for human rights was damaging administration efforts to implement a wide swath of policy objectives, including a new direction in human rights and reorientation of U.S.–Latin American relations. Responding to unrelenting pressure from Congress and the Movement, in late fall the administration offered a clear articulation of human rights, developing it as an explicit policy objective and naming Elliott Abrams as assistant secretary of state for human rights.[85] In doing so the administration sought to temper criticism about its double standard by distancing itself, at least rhetorically, from the Kirkpatrick distinction and conceding that gross violators of all stripes had to be condemned. Yet even in this move to more clearly embrace an "evenhanded" approach and explicit support for human rights, the policy framework offered a fundamentally different vision of human rights and U.S. power and interests than the past decade. The new policy framework codified nascent strands of a conservative Cold War human rights policy that had driven the administration's approach since its first days in office. This approach, while elevating human rights to an explicit policy objective, was not a "turnaround" but a co-opting of the popular language for new policy ends, evident in the reorientation of U.S.–Latin American relations the past spring.

On October 2 Eagleburger and Paul Wolfowitz wrote to Haig, cautioning that although the administration had "established a new direction" for human rights foreign policy, there was "an urgent need" to create a more coherent policy framework. Clearly responding to the recent hearings, they warned that "Congressional belief that we may not have a consistent policy threatens to disrupt important foreign policy initiatives" and that "human rights has been one of the main directions of domestic attack on this Administration's foreign policy." They emphasized the need for a clearly articulated approach to human rights to get out ahead of these attacks and do more than respond to legislative mandates. "Such a policy," they wrote, "is intrinsically defensive; it allows our critics to define the issues."[86] Moreover, congressional backlash to the administration's human rights initiatives was not just a liability for domestic public opinion; it was also creating resistance to key policy initiatives in areas such as Central America, as evidenced by new reporting requirements attached to assistance for El Salvador.[87]

On November 5 the *New York Times* published a lengthy excerpt of a State Department policy memo, leaked by the administration, asserting that human rights "is at the core of our foreign policy because it is central to what America is and stands for." The administration, in making its commitment to human rights explicit, clearly sought to deploy human rights within a Cold War framework. "Human rights," the memo stated, "conveys what is ultimately at issue in our contest with the Soviet bloc. The fundamental distinction is our respective attitudes toward freedom. Our ability to resist the Soviets around the world depends in part on our ability to draw this distinction and to persuade others of it." Rejecting the liberal vision of the previous administration and its self-reflective elements, the memo decried "neutralism" and "relativism" of past human rights policies: "Why arm, and why fight, if the two superpowers are morally equal?" Human rights policy would be "at the center of our response" to communism, conveying to domestic and international audiences the "central distinction in international politics between free nations and those that are not free." It was a bipolar world once more, and human rights were not only the crucial marker between the two sides but an important instrument in that battle.[88]

In addition to its Cold War focus, the administration also articulated both explicitly and implicitly a narrowing of the spectrum of rights the administration intended to pursue with its policy. Perhaps most telling was the aside at the beginning of the memo's second paragraph, which read: "'human rights,'—meaning political rights and civil liberties."[89] Although the administration should not try to change the name of the Bureau of Human Rights and Humanitarian Affairs, anticipating that such a move would create counterproductive resistance and "needless controversy," it would start to use different language to distinguish its goals from those of the previous administrations and highlight the central distinction noted above. "We should move away from 'human rights' as a term and begin to speak of 'individual rights,' 'political rights,' and 'civil liberties.'"[90]

The changes proposed in the memorandum were not merely rhetorical. They had significant implications for the application of human rights in foreign policy that would fundamentally change the shape and scope of U.S. human rights diplomacy, as seen in its initial approach to Latin America. By casting the Soviet Union and communism writ large as the ultimate threat to human rights, the administration minimized the conflicts between security interests and its human rights policy. "Friendly" governments with problematic human rights records could now join the battle for human rights, and the United States must maintain its "reputation as a reliable partner for our friends so as to maximize the influence of our quiet diplomacy."[91] It was a critical transformation that converted abusers into protectors of rights, fundamentally challenging the original logic behind legislative linkage of military and economic aid to human rights performance.

Rather than an alternative to militarism, the Reagan administration harnessed human rights more explicitly into the larger moral and strategic battle against communism. It returned to a confident vision of American power, where human rights could be promoted and realized through the muscular support of "friendly" anticommunist allies. Unlike the Carter administration, where human rights explicitly sought to restrain military force as an instrument of U.S. influence and power in the international system, the return to a Cold War framing relegitimized elements of overt intervention, military aid, and regime change that the Carter framework had eschewed.

Nonetheless, responding to the relentless charges of hypocrisy by Congress and advocates, the administration's new policy also tempered its association with the "Kirkpatrick distinction" that had been so roundly criticized by the Movement and Congress. The administration must be "prepared to pay a price," elevating human rights over other concerns for national security and economic interests at times. "A human rights policy means trouble, for it means hard choices which may adversely affect certain bilateral relations. At the very least, we will have to speak honestly about our friends' human rights violations and justify any decision wherein other considerations (economic, military etc.) are determinative. There is no escaping this without destroying the credibility of our policy. . . . *Despite the costs of such a real human rights policy, it is worth doing and indeed it is essential.*"[92]

Despite these caveats, the memo was rife with contradictions, similar to those that had plagued the Carter administration. It advocated that its human rights policy avoid prescribed responses, balancing a number of factors such as economic and security interests, as well as the "pressures a regime faces." It continued, however, by stating that the policy must be applied "evenhandedly. If a nation, friendly or not, abridges freedom, we should acknowledge it, stating that we regret or oppose it." Public condemnation without tangible material consequences would likely be viewed by both domestic and international audiences as hypocritical and cynical. The contradictions of a "balanced" yet context-specific approach were apparent in its examples of how to properly vote on MDBs. The memo recommended that the administration's policy should abstain from or vote against loans to friendly countries that abused rights. In the next sentence, however, it asserted that it should "motivate improvement in human rights" by supporting loans to acknowledge substantial progress. Yet in cases such as Chile and Argentina, both conditions—ongoing serious human rights abuses and progress—existed concurrently. Moreover, as the congressional hearings in July had made clear, congressional mandates had no language that acknowledged "progress" as a metric for foreign aid decisions; the criteria was "gross and consistent violators."[93]

During the summer, Congress and human rights advocates of all persuasions had been almost universal in their criticism of the administration's failure to appoint a new head of the Human Rights Bureau following Lefever's failed nomination. On October 30, just days before the memo was published, the administration named Elliott Abrams to lead the bureau. Abrams had previously served as assistant secretary of state for international organizations, and perhaps more importantly he had strong credentials with core members of Congress who shared a new conservative framing of human rights, having worked for both Senators Scoop Jackson and Patrick Moynihan (D-NY).[94]

Congress reacted enthusiastically to Abrams's appointment. Charles Percy (R-IL), the chair of the Senate Committee on Foreign Relations, opened Abrams's confirmation hearing by stating that the appointment "signals a real commitment by the administration to take the high road when it comes to human rights." He declared, "I am strongly encouraged by the selection of Elliott Abrams for this sensitive post and confident that his nomination will serve as a loud and clear signal to the rest of the world that the United States places human rights at the top of its foreign policy agenda." Percy was joined by his fellow committee members in his unstinting praise for Abrams. Moynihan, for whom Abrams had worked, noted, "He has impressed us all with his loyalty and his fidelity to principle and his large concern to see American Government succeed. I am sure he will carry those same principles into his new assignment." Sen. Claiborne Pell (D-RI) stated, "The President's and the Secretary's belief in human rights is shown by the fact that they are going to appoint an activist secretary in the job. And I look forward to working with Mr. Abrams. I am sure he will do an excellent job. I am delighted both that the job is being filled and that you are the man who is filling it."[95]

The enthusiasm expressed by congressional committee members for Abrams's appointment was more than a simple response to having the post filled or even their confidence in Abrams. Coinciding with the release of the State Department memo detailing the administration's human rights approach, Congress viewed Abrams's appointment as signaling a move away from the double standard innate to the "Kirkpatrick distinction." Percy remarked that the administration's choice of Abrams for the post "reflects the view that many of us in the Senate repeatedly have expressed, namely it is a terribly flawed policy only to speak out against human rights in Communist

Figure 12. Elliott Abrams (center) with President Reagan, pictured here in 1986. Image courtesy of the Ronald Reagan Presidential Library.

countries and nations with which we do not have friendly relations." Abrams himself affirmed this sentiment in the hearing, stating that he supported the policy detailed in the memorandum. He continued, "I am an absolutist in the sense that we need to be concerned with all human rights abuses."[96]

During his confirmation hearing, Abrams presented a vision of U.S. foreign policy that would be guided by two rules—"tell the truth" about human rights conditions, regardless of competing interests and governmental ideologies, and "try to be effective," by implementing context-specific measures.[97] He stated that in some cases, public denunciations would be advisable while in others, private diplomatic pressures would be the first course of action. Regardless, the "choice of tactics should be made with a practical goal in mind." Abrams's two rules suggested an evenhanded approach, driven by pragmatic calculations rather than ideological commitments. Yet Abrams maintained the administration's emphasis on Soviet and communist abuses of human rights and subtly criticized the past emphasis on "friendly" anticommunist regimes. "At the UN human rights commission, one sometimes has the impression that human rights in the world are in great shape, just absolutely wonderful shape, except for Latin America; that is the only place on the face of the Earth where there is not full recognition of all human rights. There is an element of surrealism in that." Abrams was even more forceful when questioned on El Salvador. "Should the United States renounce its efforts in El Salvador, it seems to me the result would be the takeover by a Marxist-Leninist regime," he observed. "I think we have enough experience to know what that means for the human rights of the people of El Salvador."[98]

Despite the rhetoric of a consistent application of principles, Abrams's testimony on the administration's relations with Chile and Argentina evidenced that the Kirkpatrick distinction, while subdued, was still very much present in the administration's policy framework. Abrams stated that, in general, he was in favor of the recent decision to support MDB loans to these countries. "In each of those cases, I would think that we can do more by trying to work with the government and pressure it as strongly as we can to continue any favorable trends, than by this kind of public denunciation." When questioned by Sen. Larry Pressler (R-SD) about Argentina specifically, Abrams acknowledged that the situation there "was terrible and harrowing," but he concluded, "It would be very foolish of us not to take account of the great improvements that have taken place in the human rights situation in Argentina. It was for that reason that the administration decided to change the U.S. voting pattern in international banks." Abrams expressed his desire that U.S. policy should help Argentina "continue to evolve" as it addressed contentious issues such as the "disappeared."[99]

Like the policy memorandum, Abrams's testimony evidenced a significant slippage in the use of "liberty," "democracy," and "freedom" in place of human rights. Abrams defended the tacit narrowing of human rights in the administration's memorandum and supported the exclusion of economic rights. Percy questioned whether the memo deployed "too narrow a definition of rights," asking, "Should economic rights be considered as well?" Abrams acknowledged the importance of defining rights and stated, "I feel rather strongly that we have to be very, very careful about using the term 'economic and social rights.'" He cautioned that these "so-called" rights were "impossible to realize in most countries." Rather than "rights," they should be considered "aspirations." To label them as fundamental rights, on par with political rights and civil liberties, would create "intellectual confusion" that might create the impression that all rights were aspirational. Abrams's vision fits with the Cold War, liberal capitalist vision of the administration, where rights were something that individuals possess against the state, not something acquired by state action.[100]

Despite these differences with congressional leaders on human rights, Abrams's confirmation hearing stood in stark contrast to Lefever's six months earlier. Abrams seemed to convey a deep commitment to the principle of human rights, even as he presented a policy with fundamental differences in both application and logic from those of the past decade. In one of the most revealing exchanges, Sen. Charles Mathias (R-MD), alluding to Lefever, asked if Abrams had any "personal reservations about any of the statutes that relate to human rights." Abrams assured the committee that he had none. Rather than stopping there, however, he continued in a surprisingly forthcoming summation of the political dynamics between Congress and the executive contained in the human rights legislation:

I think to be completely frank, I want to go beyond that answer though. I think that [the human rights statutes] represent a period, in the 1960s and 1970s . . . when the Congress came to lose any sense of confidence that the executive branch was carrying out foreign policy in the way it wanted in many areas, not just the area of human rights, and there came to be a much greater activism on the part of Congress in a number of areas, including human rights. In that sense, the thing that disturbs me about the statutes is not what they do, because I would hope that we would do that anyway, but what they represent. What they represent is a feeling on the part of the Congress that the administration, any administration, will not have a firm human rights policy unless Congress pushes very, very hard. My hope would be that someday—and I am talking about 10 or 15 years from now, I think realistically—the Congress would come to see these statutes as not particularly useful because it would be so clear that every administration was following these policies anyway. . . . In that sense, the only way to create this climate of confidence and to make you sure that this is being done is to have these statutes on the books, and so they belong there.[101]

With this bald acknowledgment of the congressional-executive power struggle over this legislation, Abrams sought to reassure Congress that human rights statutes would be interpreted, but not avoided or subverted.

The Movement did not share congressional enthusiasm for Abrams or optimism that his appointment marked a new commitment to human rights by the administration. WOLA's November newsletter cautioned that neither Abrams's appointment "nor the memo are likely to bring a significant change in U.S. policy" pursued by the Reagan administration in Latin America. The group was skeptical of Abrams, "clearly a neo-conservative with an ideological perspective similar to that of U.N. Ambassador Jeane Kirkpatrick," and assumed his approach would be congruent with the administration's flawed approach to human rights on display at the United Nations. Although the group expected that Abrams would "probably restore some of the Bureau's influence in the policy making process," it also noted that the Human Rights Bureau was only "marginally involved" in developing the new policy memorandum, which did not bode well for its position in the State Department bureaucracy. Indeed, the only optimism WOLA expressed regarding the administration's actions in recent weeks was that "even this administration cannot jettison human rights as an element in U.S. foreign policy. . . . While its perspective on human rights is often one-sided, the Administration recognizes that public opinion, both in the U.S. and abroad, requires that it retain human rights as a concern of U.S. foreign policy."[102]

Two days after Abrams's confirmation hearing, former congressman Father Robert Drinan, now president of ADA, spoke in front of a group of law students, comparing the "moral revolution" of the Carter years with the uncertainty and narrowing of human rights policy under the current administration. "Will the period of 1974 to 1980 be seen as the Golden Age of human rights," he wondered, "or will it be regarded as a noble experiment which faded away?" He conceded that the Reagan administration had demonstrated a commitment to the Helsinki Accords, but beyond that he questioned its fidelity to the legislative backbone of human rights policy. Like WOLA, Drinan did not expect Abrams's appointment to bring a substantial change in the administration's core approach to human rights, particularly its Cold War emphasis. He anticipated that Abrams would "continue to stress, as all administration official have done, the alleged distinction between authoritarian and totalitarian regimes."[103]

For Drinan, an effective, earnest human rights policy could not coexist with outdated Cold War notions of a bipolar world struggle. If containing communism remained the principal objective of U.S. foreign policy, there was likely to be "little emphasis on the violation of human rights in authoritarian nations since we are most anxious to cultivate these countries in order that they will form with us an alliance against the communist bloc."[104] In a speech the following day, he cast these policies as counterproductive and short-sided, rejecting the "magic of the Marketplace" as a cure-all. Drinan characterized the administration's Cold War emphasis and lack of concern for economic and social rights as an expression of "disdain for the Third World." This contempt, he argued, manifested in its narrow and hypocritical application of human rights policy, would "only breed and bring trouble." American interests and American values demanded a rejection of the administration's "perniciously over-simplified rhetoric" that typified its approach to the developing world and human rights more broadly.[105]

The ongoing skepticism and resistance of the human rights community following Abrams's confirmation was perhaps unsurprising given the combative nature of relations between advocates and the Movement in the first year. Abrams's confirmation hearing was a rare moment of goodwill and bipartisanship with Congress in Reagan's first year of human rights efforts.[106] Even as the administration had rolled out Abrams's nomination and the policy memorandum, it had pressed ahead with lifting restrictions on military aid to Argentina and Chile, underscoring the fundamental disconnect between the administration's agenda and that of the Movement. Abrams did not offer a new direction for the administration's approach to human rights. Rather, it was a softening of key points of disagreement and clarification of deeper philosophical underpinnings driving the decisions. Indeed, in conjunction with the State Department policy memo, the administration moved from an implicit human rights agenda innately advanced by Cold War security interests to an explicit policy objective. This gave rise to a more rigorous, coherent policy, but one still fundamentally at odds with the 1970s agenda the Movement had built.

An Extremely Broad Consensus

Abrams was sworn in on Human Rights Day, December 10, 1981. Speeches marking the day reflected the ongoing divides between the administration's policy and the broader human rights community that would dominate relations in the coming months. Reagan had issued a proclamation five days prior, marking the beginning of Human Rights Week and Bill of Rights Day. The proclamation, light on substance, reaffirmed the country's deep-rooted commitment to human rights, codified by the Constitution. Reagan's rhetoric was an easy fit with his broader agenda of small government and individual rights, arguing, "Mankind's best defense against tyranny and want is limited government—a government that empowers its people, not itself." Reiterating the narrowed definition laid out in the October policy memorandum, he continued, "Above all, human rights are rights of individuals: rights of conscience, rights of choice, rights of association, rights of emigration, rights of self-directed action, and the right to own property."[107] Reagan promised to continue to advance these rights and principles both at home and abroad. Thus, in his address, Reagan both omitted any commitment to the full spectrum of rights embodied in the UN declaration—which the day purported to celebrate—and reduced human rights to a derivation of American principles rather than a broader universal ethic to which the United States belonged and contributed.

Despite the seeming goodwill and optimism of Abrams's confirmation hearing just three weeks earlier, Congress was not going to scale back its pressure on or criticism of the administration's approach to human rights. In their own observance of Human Rights Day, members of Congress commemorated their own role in creating a modern human rights mandate for the U.S. government, recognized the work of advocacy groups, and called the administration to action on a number of pressing human rights issues. Rep. Bonkers opened the session, recalling the work of Congress in creating legislative instruments for a "true human rights policy." Bonkers lamented the "deterioration of this country's commitment" to human rights in the last year, citing the administration's efforts to resume military aid to Argentina and reversal of MDB restrictions on both Chile and Argentina as evidence of its indifference to congressional mandates. Further, even pressure on the Soviet Union, he charged, had been half-hearted and subsumed by other interests. Congressman Harkin compared Reagan's first year unfavorably with the Carter administration's efforts. "We all acknowledged that the Carter policy has flaws, but in comparison with what we have seen in the past 11 months, it is a model of sobriety and effectiveness." Since Reagan's inauguration, "the new administration has launched a full-scale attack on the policy of human rights."[108]

Congress also challenged the administration's separation of authoritarian and totalitarian regimes, not only the basis of hypocrisy but also national interests. Relating the lesson that had driven much of the past decade's human rights policy, Rep. Hall (D-TX) warned, "Cozy relations with repressive foreign governments can ultimately hurt more than help. Recent experience demonstrates that victims of repressive governments are not quick to forget US identification with their former leaders." Moreover, he argued that a credible human rights policy was critical for the nation's international influence, particularly "in the keen competition for the allegiance of the world's unaligned nations." Rep. Ottinger (D-NY) similarly decried the administration's " 'diplomacy of complicity' with the world's worst offenders of human rights." He argued, "The administration's weak human rights policies contradict our moral and strategic interests and thwart the President's stated goal of halting Soviet expansionism. . . . We simply hand the cause of freedom and liberty to the Soviets and their proxies by siding with repressive regimes in South Africa, Latin America, South Korea, and elsewhere." He summed up the overall sentiment of the day's proceedings, stating, "I remain greatly concerned about the administration's commitment to maintaining human rights as a fundamental component of our foreign policy."[109]

Harkin expressed some hope that Abrams would usher in a new phase of human rights for the administration, observing, "He seems to be a man of intelligence and good faith and we wish him well. He can, if he chooses, help end the hypocrisy and callousness that has characterized the administration's nonpolicy on human rights." Harkin offered a nine-point agenda for Abrams to implement, clearly informed by the debates over the policy's application in Latin America. Harkin's first five points all targeted the implementation of existing congressional mandates: upholding prohibitions on military sales to countries such as Guatemala, voting against MDB loans for countries such as Chile, and preventing OPIC from granting loans to countries with troubled human rights records. Harkin also urged Abrams to help implement a policy that would utilize established diplomatic channels to advance a robust human rights agenda. This included linkage of trade to human rights actions and unilateral diplomatic actions, "even in countries where we lack influence." Finally, he should help develop symbolic actions that "underscore, reiterate, and dramatize the depth of the American belief that human rights are a prerequisite to a just and safe world," including meeting with "human rights advocates, opposition leaders, clergy, and ordinary citizens involved in human rights cases."[110]

Indeed, one of the critical tasks for Abrams and the Human Rights Bureau was reestablishing a productive working relationship with the human rights community and demonstrating to them a clear commitment to human rights. In Abrams's first months in office, Lister tirelessly organized meetings and events for Abrams and the advocate community. In preparation for one representative meeting with the International Commission of Jurists (ICJ) and Helsinki Watch, Lister wrote to Abrams, "I am sure you know two main questions in the Movement at this time are: 1) does this Administration have a human rights policy; and, 2) do we intend to keep silent on human rights violations by friendly right-wing governments."[111] Lister was optimistic that Abrams could bring the Movement around with open dialogue and a clear explanation of the administration's policy plans.

In an off-the-record meeting with Amnesty International at the end of January, Abrams conceded that the administration "had got off to a bad start" on human rights. The "ugliness" of the Lefever hearing resulted in a "period of silence on human rights due to the angry and bitter feelings at the way Lefever had been treated on the Hill and in the media more generally." Despite the rocky start, Abrams assured them that he believed there was "an extremely broad consensus on human rights policy: that [it] should be a strong element in U.S. foreign policy and that it cannot be the only element in foreign policy." Abrams's remarks on the shape of the administration's policy followed the broad contours laid out in the October memo and his confirmation hearings, namely, that the administration would have one standard but different tactics for friendly and antagonistic governments. Abrams also acknowledged that there arose a "credibility problem when one pursues implementation of the human rights policy through quiet diplomacy as opposed to public rhetoric." He was optimistic, however, that public education and visible actions, such as votes in international forums, would build support and legitimacy for the policy. Moreover, he noted that an "'enormous ruckus' is rightfully raised by non-governmental organizations and Congress people, but roles should not be confused." The "fundamental goal" of his office was to "continue the institutionalization of the human rights factor in U.S. foreign policy." He asserted that the good faith and effort would be evident in the forthcoming country reports, in which "there is a level of continuity" with previous reports.[112]

Despite the positive tone of Abrams's comments, clear divides still emerged on familiar points. Abrams faced resistance on his statements that "quiet diplomacy" was the desired path for "friendly" regimes and that the United States should not push for human rights changes that would fundamentally weaken allied governments. He clarified that "in Argentina, to go for the resolution of the disappeared" would be foolish, for example, "because you can't ask these governments to do that which would be the equivalent of suicide." This point raised the hackles of many in the room. One member of the audience stated that he was "reassured by your presentation up until I heard you quoting the gospel of Jeane Kirkpatrick." Other subsequent questions and comments pointed out that this approach seemed to "undermine the position of non-governmental (dissident) groups." Abrams qualified his statements, arguing that the United States should support groups by meeting with them, such as the congressional delegation's meeting with Emilio Mignone on a recent trip to Argentina. Still, Abrams cautioned that some groups "have political goals beyond the promotion of human rights," and his role was to draw the distinction between the two.[113]

In a meeting with WOLA two weeks later, Abrams took the opportunity to underscore the administration's commitment to human rights, pointing to the Human Rights Bureau's increased staffing and influence. Abrams told the WOLA members that the bureau "had gotten itself back into the policy ballgame much quicker than had been expected." Abrams asserted that the secretary of state's recent note supporting the bureau's work "made it hard for the Bureau to be ignored." WOLA responded to Abrams with both optimism and concern. Joe Eldridge said he was "buoyed" by Abrams's recent statements on human rights, particularly his "statements questioning the duality of authoritarian vs. totalitarian regimes." He expressed concern, however, for ongoing administration policies in Chile, Argentina, and Central America. Afterward, Lister wrote gleefully to Abrams, "Frankly, the WOLA meeting was *excellent*. It will have wide and rapid repercussions in most of the Movement."[114]

Lister's optimism and Abrams's individual rapport with advocates did not translate into broader credibility for the administration's policies with the Movement and Congress. In hearings before the Subcommittee on Human Rights and International Organizations at the end of February 1978, the tone was markedly cooler than Abrams's confirmation hearings some three months prior. Members of the committee clearly remained dubious about the administration's broader policy. Although Abrams conceded there were differences from past administrations' decision-making processes, he forcefully defended the current approach, asserting, "I won't accept that my level of commitment is not higher or at the level of that of Patt Derian, nor that Secretary of State Haig and now National Security Advisor Clark lack commitment or interest in human rights." Bonkers responded by pointing to the rather lackluster performance regarding human rights at the United Nations, particularly the matter of the special rapporteur on Chile as a difference that went beyond strategy.[115]

Abrams and committee members again sparred over the definition of human rights. Congressman Leach pointed out the troubling implications of the administration's dismissal of economic rights from its stated human rights objectives. "It is one thing to point out that rights are open to differing interpretations," Leach observed, "but the fact is, it is a very profound matter when the U.S. indicates that these (economic and social rights) should not be considered rights," pointing to both the U.S. Declaration of Independence and the UN Universal Declaration of Human Rights as giving ample precedent for advancing a broad agenda of rights. "I fear," he concluded, "that you have become a bit too involved in sophistry in too great an effort to separate this Administration from the Carter Administration." Abrams welcomed the exchange but returned to his now familiar point that "when we mix 'goods' with 'inalienable rights' that go to the core of human existence, then we allow those goods to be used as an excuse for the disallowance of rights." It was an argument that was now familiar but unpersuasive for many on the committee who saw it as a departure from the core intent and scope of the original law.

The narrowed definition was germane to the debates over the deployment of military aid as an instrument of human rights. Leach returned to his earlier point regarding the flaws in the administration's narrow definition of rights, pointing to El Salvador. "Life is essential—food is essential. Intertwined with policy is that view because you send guns instead of butter. Poverty, and illiteracy, are the problems, not the East-West struggle. Certification of human rights and needs of that country should be based on the reality of the urgent need for more food, more books, not military hardware." Abrams argued that military aid in El Salvador played a critical role in promoting human rights and advancing democracy by allowing the government to defend itself against leftist violence. "To say that we must deal with the root problem is not to say we don't have to deal with security problems." Abrams maintained that "non-communist from communist is not the distinction" used in determining who received aid, "although that is the way it often works out in practice." When Rep. Mervyn Dymally (D-CA) pressed him by asking, "The good guys are those that are friendly to the U.S. without any concerns for their human rights situation?" Abrams curtly replied, "No."

Abrams also defended an affirmative role for military aid in advancing human rights. The question, he asserted, was not only about the practices of the policy and the impact if the United States went ahead with the assistance. "What if we stop?" he continued. "We would not be meeting those responsibilities [of the legislation] to take a security policy that would result in a Castroite form of government in El Salvador." Bonkers challenged him, asking, "Are you saying the ends justifies the means, that is, that to pursue the 'better situation—something of a political utopia'—justifies present violations?" Abrams replied that the government was making a clear effort at reform, but "to cut off aid under the guide of a human rights policy is madness." No matter how much he tried to nuance it, the debate inexorably returned to the fundamental divide between past policy and present.

Abrams's appointment marked a more systematic engagement with human rights, but he could not bridge the divide between the 1970s framework and the new administration's objectives. The reorientation of human rights as a Cold War project negated the fundamental premises and instruments of the past decade. This resulted in large part from the divergence from the 1970s framing and assumptions, particularly the question of definition and return to Cold War axioms about the relationship between security relationships and human rights abuses. For many in the Movement, the Reagan administration's emphasis on military power made it impossible to have a viable human rights policy in the way they had conceived of it in the 1970s, as a check on U.S. interventionism, which would move the United States toward a multilateralist position and embrace pluralism in the developing world.

During his confirmation hearing, Abrams rejected the impression that had arisen in the first nine months of the administration that human rights was a partisan issue or the exclusive purview of liberals. "One thing had become clear during the course of the debate, namely, that the left was laying claim to human rights and thereby claiming that a conservative administration could not have and could not be expected to have a human rights policy." He claimed that this belief, often shared by both left and right, must be rejected.[116] Despite its seeming rejection of the fundamentals of human rights policy, such as legislative prohibitions on military aid, during its first year in office the Reagan administration reformulated the very premises of U.S. human rights policies to make a conservative claim on the issue.

Resistance from the Movement pushed the Reagan administration to articulate a coherent vision and challenge the imbalances evident in a Cold War approach to human rights. Yet even as the administration recalibrated its approach after the first year, there was no "turnaround" but rather a move from implicit incorporation of human rights as a natural derivative of a Cold War foreign policy to an explicit objective and component of U.S. national interests. As the administration moved to a more comprehensive policy and softened its overt embrace of the Kirkpatrick distinction, its policy framework remained grounded in Cold War assumptions and reversed the policy logic of the past decade that emphasized dissociation and anti-interventionism. The replacement of Alexander Haig with George Schulz in spring of 1982 moved relations with the Movement into a stalemate. It lost some of the open hostility of early years, but basic discord in aims and emphasis remained.

Reagan's presidency shaped expectations for U.S. human rights policies and instruments in the years to come by shifting from an introspective examination of U.S. power and its consequences to one confident in the inherent goodness of American intentions and focused on the misdeeds of others. In doing so, it relegitimized elements of overt intervention, military aid, and regime change that the Carter framework had eschewed. "I've often wondered," Reagan mused, "about the shyness of some of us in the west to stand for these ideals that have done so much to ease the plight of man and the hardships of our imperfect world."[117] Rather than an alternative to militarism, Reagan harnessed human rights more explicitly into the larger moral and strategic battle against communism. It returned to a confident vision of American power, where human rights could be promoted and realized through the muscular support of "friendly" anticommunist allies, echoing the modernization theories of yesteryear and laying the groundwork for modern iterations of "nation-building."[118]

Conclusion

The Golden Years of Human Rights?

For Movement advocates, the human rights vision of the 1970s was intimately connected with a reckoning with the U.S. failures of Vietnam, Cold War national security strategy, and, of course, Chile. It was, as Robert Drinan had noted, a "noble experiment," and the period from 1974 to 1980 marked its "golden years."[1] The Movement and the Carter administration shared a vision of human rights as a way to improve not only the world but also the U.S. government and its policies. This is not to say the Movement's views were universally shared, or that human rights faded away after the 1970s. Rather, human rights continued to serve as an instrument of its time, a powerful idea and language, flexible and indelible. With the advent of the Reagan administration, U.S. human rights policy took on new forms, more closely tied to the traditions of American military strength and liberal internationalism that have marked the twentieth century. The very factors that made Reagan's human rights policy so frustrating for the 1970s Movement—its willingness to champion human rights as almost synonymous with anticommunism and American values, its pairing of military force with the expansion of freedom, and a narrowing of legitimate rights to those that could fit easily within a liberal capitalist democracy—also resonated with a broader American audience and residual Cold War understandings of national interest. Whereas

Carter-era human rights policy had questioned the inherent goodness of American hegemony, pursued more multilateral methods of advancing U.S. national interests, and sought to bring greater democratic accountability to the United States' own government, Reagan once again moved forward with a confident vision of American power, laying the groundwork for modern iterations of nation building and human rights as regime change. The Carter administration's human rights policy was far from perfect or consistent. It was, however, a uniquely self-reflective policy that restrained U.S. intervention and addressed abuses taking place in areas where the United States was most directly complicit in empowering violators.

A provisional National Security Council appraisal of the Carter administration's human rights policy in 1981 observed that, paradoxically, human rights "was at the same time one of the most widely praised transformations of the American self-image and its reflection abroad, and one of the most controversial and widely criticized."[2] Perhaps both the appeal and the undoing of the 1970s self-critical vision for human rights was its ability to encompass seemingly contradictory meanings and objectives. Human rights was about moral necessities and national interests; about bolstering U.S. power and restraining military interventionism; about challenging Cold War alliances and a bipolar worldview and regaining the ideological upper hand with the communist world; about engaging governments as they were without excusing behaviors that offended the most basic human sensibilities; about promoting policies consistent with U.S. values without trying to remake the world in the United States' image. It was about principles. And it was about power.

The Movement's advocacy and the Carter administration's policies reflected these tensions. As opposed to more traditional interests such as trade and security, the connection between human rights and national interests was not always obvious. Although Carter, like advocates before him, promoted human rights as a new form of power in the international system and a poll of attraction for the developing world in particular, there was no good mechanism to measure international goodwill and influence. Further, the connection between U.S. policy and human rights improvements in foreign countries was often tenuous at best. No autonomous government would credit changes in repressive behavior to foreign pressure.

The difficulty in evaluating and even defining success in human rights conditions and policies created fissures between otherwise allied forces. Quiet diplomacy, although often effective for targeting specific changes, only further obscured the connection between U.S. actions and foreign behaviors.

The administration emphasized a flexible policy that would make these decisions on a case-by-case basis, hinging on the local particularities and conditions of each case. Although this may have reflected a complex world, it
complicated efforts to communicate the policy's logic and goals to a broad
audience, raising charges of inconsistency and hypocrisy. Residual distrust
of the executive branch from the Nixon and Ford eras colored relations
between the administration and human rights proponents at home, compounded by the U.S. legacy of intervention that directed and restricted U.S.
policy options. The divides between Carter and the Movement over how to
pursue the administration's human rights policy demonstrate the limits on
the power of the president in the late Cold War, especially on human rights
issues. Reagan felt these restraints in the battle over Lefever's appointment.
Reagan's subsequent transformation on human rights reflected a lesson
Carter had come to learn all too well: the Cold War "imperial presidency"
was over. Advocates and Congress intended to sustain a much more active
role in foreign affairs and international security.

At the same time, Congress and the Movement pushed Carter to remain
committed to his human rights agenda in the face of constant competing
pressures and demands. The Movement's advocacy helped expand U.S. diplomacy beyond contacts with the governing elites and reach the general
population in the United States and abroad. Although the Movement often
criticized the administration for legitimizing repressive regimes through ongoing engagement, the administration also sought to legitimize dissenting
groups through similarly high-profile meetings and discussions, often facilitated by Movement actors in Washington. In countries such as Chile and
Argentina, the administration consistently sought out opinions and perspectives beyond traditional government channels, interacting with church and
family groups, opening up its embassies in an unprecedented way to the
citizens of the country. The administration's pairing of human rights with a
greater respect for national sovereignty and nonintervention in its approach
to regional affairs gave rise to a complex but uniquely sensitive approach to
regional relations informed by advocate networks across the hemisphere.
The Carter administration's Latin America policy tread a careful path that
did not condone government violence but also did not simply try to impose a solution from Washington. Its diplomacy sought to apply pressure
for changes that would open spaces for Latin Americans to shape their own
governments and control their own destinies.

In a 2007 interview, Chilean human rights leader José Zalaquett asserted,
"Jimmy Carter contributed to ameliorate the image of the 'ugly American,'

and to soften the 'Yankee Go Home' kind of approach of the '60s to a great extent. . . . People felt that he was reasonably serious about human rights, and therefore that the superpower would not really be complacent toward Pinochet. . . . With Carter, people (at least people in South America) felt that it was different."[3] Joe Eldridge of the Washington Office on Latin America concurred, reflecting in 2008, "A lot of his initiatives failed, but I know Carter saved a lot of lives. I just know that he had a tremendous impact. Certainly, on Latin America."[4] The legacy of the Carter administration's relationship with the Movement went beyond specific policy accomplishments and failures; it was a legacy that helped legitimize human rights in international relations and moved the U.S. government to embody those concerns in its policies and procedures.

Human rights and U.S.–Latin American relations in the 1970s offers fresh insight into the potentials and dilemmas of a foreign policy of human rights today. The Movement and the Carter administration framed human rights as part of the United States' broader strategic aims in the world. Vietnam had demonstrated that military power was woefully inadequate on its own to deal with the challenges the nation faced in an increasingly multipolar world. As the United States increasingly relies on foreign populations, not just governments, to operate in the world, it would be well served to think of an honest, self-reflective and context-specific human rights policy as its liaison to those populations, and an instrument for helping shape an international environment conducive to other national interests.

A credible human rights policy must also be self-reflective. One of the elements that distinguished the Movement's advocacy and Carter's policies from those that followed was the use of human rights to address the United States' own shortcomings and problematic behaviors. Part of the United States' continued struggle to develop a successful human rights policy is due in part to the fact that it continues to frame human rights as something that happens beyond the nation's boundaries, perpetrated by other governments; policy makers view it as a problem that the U.S. government needs to fix, rather than a product of local particularities interacting with an international system that the United States is part of and helps shape. Although its ability to remake foreign governments and societies is limited, the United States can control its own behavior and policies. Its instruments and approach to human rights should reflect this. Perhaps the most unique element of Carter's policy in Latin America was its anti-interventionist ethos. Many times the United States cannot fundamentally change the nature of foreign governments. It can, however, push for significant improvements on specific issues and change its own policies that enable—directly and indirectly—human rights abuses. Taking steps to remedy its own human rights problems will give strength and validity to its advocacy on behalf of egregious violations perpetrated by others.

In June 1984 members of the Movement gathered in Washington, D.C., to celebrate the Washington Office on Latin America's tenth anniversary. Diane LaVoy, WOLA's first director, sent a letter from Chile to be read to the group. LaVoy lamented that she was missing the festivities but observed, "I find it's appropriate to mention Chile and WOLA in the same sentence. WOLA's early history—the part I know well—was shaped by Chile." LaVoy recalled that a movement had been brewing before WOLA's establishment and before the coup in Chile, but that the 1973 coup had galvanized this intent into action. For LaVoy, the legacy of WOLA's first ten years was not only the ongoing campaigns to reform repressive government institutions in Chile or Argentina. It was also the effort to reform the very core of U.S. foreign policy, in Latin America and beyond. WOLA, she cheered, has "succeeded in making public criticism of U.S. government policy and actions more accurate and effective. I like to say WOLA is red-white-and-blue."[5]

WOLA's celebration of human rights as patriotic criticism suggests a different role for human rights in U.S. foreign policy than the externally focused, often interventionist paradigm that has followed. It is one that first examines the costs and casualties of American power, that eschewed military intervention, and opened state power to popular governance. In 1983 Father J. Bryan Hehir of the U.S. Catholic Conference received the Letelier-Moffitt Memorial Human Rights Award. Speaking to an audience of Movement advocates, Hehir reflected on their role in advancing human rights over the past decade. "What we try to do when we attempt to impose human rights criteria on other forms of power—political, economic, and military—in the foreign policy equation, is we seek to use the very fragile instrument of moral suasion, the fabric of moral sinew, to control and contain the power of the modern state." Hehir concluded by quoting Pope John Paul II: " 'Rulers must be supported and enlightened by public opinion that encourages them, or where necessary, expresses disapproval.' That's a vocation for all of us."[6] In a world transformed over the past four decades, it remains a vocation for all who are committed to human rights.

Acknowledgments

Writing a book is hard. I would have found it nearly impossible without the support and encouragement of so many people, and it is a great pleasure to have an opportunity to thank them here.

First of all, I would like to thank the people who allowed me to talk to them about their experiences for this project: Patricia Derian, Joe Eldridge, Tex Harris, Pedro Matta, John Salzberg, and José Zalaquett. They all shaped fundamentally my thinking about this topic and the questions I pursued. I have enormous respect for their work on behalf of human rights, and I hope they find that reflected in the following pages, even if they do not agree with my interpretations and conclusions. Joe and Tex were especially generous with their time, and I appreciate their willingness to not only share their experiences but also think abstractly with me about the role of human rights in U.S. foreign policy.

I would not be where I am today without the inspired teaching and mentoring of professors who are deeply invested in both their research and their students. This project, and indeed my career in history, can be traced to my first class with David Schmitz at Whitman College. David's exemplary teaching opened a new world to this erstwhile biology major, and my work as his research assistant sowed the seeds of intellectual curiosity for this topic and a love of archival research. I am grateful for his abiding support as a mentor and friend these many years. My profound thanks go to my graduate advisor, the indomitable Jeremi Suri. During my time at the University of Wisconsin, he was my toughest critic and strongest advocate, exactly what a graduate advisor should be. Working with Jeremi has made me a more creative, rigorous thinker, and pushed me to be a better writer. His unflagging positivity, enormous energy, and limitless curiosity never cease to amaze me, and his commitment to extending his scholarship to the classroom and beyond is an inspiration to me. I thank Bill Reese for his kindness and intellectual generosity throughout my time in graduate school. I am grateful that Steve Stern incorporated me into the Latin American cohort at Wisconsin. Steve was unstinting with his time and support; I have enormous respect for his ability to make the most complex ideas accessible without oversimplifying them, and for the conceptual creativity he puts into both his teaching and his writing. I was also fortunate to have the opportunity to study with Lynn Sharp and Julie Charlip at Whitman College, both of whom continue to shape my work in their own ways.

Graduate school would not have been nearly as rewarding, intellectually or personally, without the friends I made among my fellow students. I am grateful for the serendipity (or bureaucracy) that placed me in an office with Andrew Case, Holly McGee, and Heather Stur. Our time together in 5260 made grad school a whole lot more fun, and I am thankful for the friendships that have deepened well beyond the boundaries of Madison, Wisconsin. I also want to thank my good friend Jennifer M. Miller. She deserves special recognition for reading many very rough drafts of papers, chapters, presentations, and applications over the years. She has helped clarify and improve my writing and thinking countless times, and I appreciate that we can delve deeply into historiography, politics, and pedagogy, and then have an equally passionate conversation about Harry Potter and the Gilmore Girls. Debbie Sharnak has been indispensable in helping me refine this book. Her commitment to grounding studies of human rights movements in their real-world meanings and implications reminds me of what is at stake in our scholarship. Debbie, it's surely a mitzvah to provide thoughtful comments on a bloated manuscript draft while interviewing for jobs, facing a pile of end-of-the-semester grading, and caring for a child who refuses to nap.

Although it is impossible to name them all here, I would like to thank the many archivists and librarians that helped me during my research. So many of them went above and beyond to find obscure materials, point me toward collections I would have otherwise overlooked, and make suggestions that have fundamentally shaped this project. I'm also indebted to many scholars who have inspired and supported me at various points throughout my career: Elizabeth Borgwardt, Tim Borstelmann, Jason Colby, Frank Costigliola, Sheyda Jahanbani, Andy Johns, Patrick Kelly, Barbara Keys, Jana Lipman, Fred Logevall, Kyle Longley, Evan McCormick, Alan McPherson, Michael Schmidli, Brad Simpson, Sarah Snyder, Kathryn Statler, Jessica Stites Mor, Lauren Turek, Dustin Walcher, and many others in the SHAFR community.

I'm very proud to have this book included in the U.S. in the World Series with the writing of so many wonderful scholars, and working with Cornell University Press has been a real pleasure. I am truly grateful to Michael McGandy for his guidance and good humor over the years. His quiet support has meant more to me than he knows. I am indebted to Mark Bradley for bringing me into the series and for his early and sustained interest in my research, and his confidence in this project. I also want to thank David Engerman, Jennifer Savran Kelly, and Clare Jones for their work shepherding this project to its conclusion.

This project would not have been possible without financial support from the Robert Teeter Scholarship at the Gerald Ford Library, the Society for Historians of American Foreign Relations, the University of Virginia's Miller Center for Public Affairs, the George M. Mosse Fellowship Program, the Simon Dubnow-Institute in Leipzig, Germany, the Department of History and the Vilas Research Fund at the University of Wisconsin, and Amherst College. I am deeply grateful to Brian Balogh and the National Fellowship Program at University of Virginia's Miller Center for Public Affairs (now at the Jefferson Scholars Foundation), not only for the generous financial support I received but also for the commitment to helping scholarship, including mine, find a place in our national debates and policy making. I also want to thank John Tortorice and the George M. Mosse Fellowship Program for bringing so many wonderful opportunities and people my way.

Much of the work on this manuscript took place at the University of Cincinnati, and I am forever grateful for the hard work and generosity that made my position there possible. I could not have asked for better colleagues and friends than I found in my colleagues in the History Department. Steve Porter not only knows where to find the best tasting menus and bourbon distilleries—he is a model of collaboration and openness that I seek to emulate. His unguarded welcome and genuine enthusiasm for my appointment made all the difference. I also have to thank Willard Sunderland and Chris Phillips for going to bat for me with the administration more than once.

It is no small gift to be at a thriving liberal arts college in this moment in academia. I would say I am lucky to have found my professional home at

Amherst College, but I am increasingly aware that what we often call good luck is actually good people working hard to make things possible. And there are many, many good people at Amherst College who have made so many things possible for me and my family. I am grateful for the entire Amherst College History Department, which is full of individuals whose passion for their research and teaching inspire me, and whose generosity of spirit make them a delight to be around. Special thanks to Ellen Boucher, Frank Couvares, Alec Hickmott, and Mary Hicks for their thoughtful feedback and support. I'm also grateful for the community and support I've found among the amazing scholars beyond the History Department. Judy Frank and Yael Rice both have spent many hours writing in solidarity with me, particularly during the final push to bring this manuscript to completion. Special thanks go to my student research assistants Matthew Randolph, Soledad Slowing-Romero, Keenan Szulik, and Natalie De Rosa for their efforts tracking down obscure documents, translating illegible scribbles, and careful proofreading. I also want to thank Nick Zerbib and his family for supporting my work as they celebrate Gordie Levin's legacy at Amherst.

Finally, I want to express my enormous gratitude to my friends and family who have supported and sustained me throughout this long process. Thank you to Neil Kornze and Stacia George for both their friendship and their comfortable couches in Washington, D.C., during my impoverished graduate school years. Jessica Weitzel, Amanda Pischke Husk, Daryl Haggard, and Susan Kimball should receive a special prize for their good-natured forbearance of my nerdy historical references. They generously allowed me to complain about my work when I needed, and to escape from it when I wanted. To my family—the Walkers, the Gordons, the Miroedovas, and the Noys—thank you for all your support, especially your tolerance for family vacations and gatherings often being subordinated to chapter deadlines and research trips. To my parents, Big Rob and Paula, thank you for always believing in me and supporting me in every way imaginable, for never even suggesting I study something "practical," for encouraging me to follow my dreams, for being so excited about where I've landed (even though it is all the way across the country), and for always making it so wonderful to come home to Oregon. My gentle jokester Asher and my bold and effervescent Maya—you both bring me so much joy. When I think of why human rights matter, I think of you. And finally, this book is dedicated to Adi Gordon, with love, for all the sacrifices he's made over the years so we could be on this journey together. In the words of the great Tom Waits, "I'm gonna take it with me when I go."

Notes

Introduction

1. Zbigniew Brzezinski to Jimmy Carter, "Nineteen Bilaterals: The Significance of Treaty Signing for Inter-American Relations," n.d. [September 1977], *Foreign Relations of the United States* (hereafter *FRUS*), *1977–1980*, vol. 24: *South America; Latin America Region*, ed. Sara Berndt (Washington, D.C.: Government Printing Office, 2017), document 23.

2. Donnie Radcliffe, "Celebrating the Panama Pacts . . . and Courting the Senate," *Washington Post*, September 9, 1977, B11.

3. Paul W. Valentine and B. D. Colen, "District Put under Heavy Security," *Washington Post*, September 8, 1977, A19.

4. John M. Goshko and Joanne Omang, "President Briefs Torrijos on Plans for Pact Signing," *Washington Post*, September 7, 1977, A1.

5. James Abourezk to Jimmy Carter, August 29, 1977, White House Central Files (hereafter WHCF), box CO-15, CO 33 (Chile) Executive, Jimmy Carter Presidential Library and Archive, Atlanta, GA (hereafter JCL); Zbigniew Brzezinski to James Abourezk, September 21, 1977, WHCF, box CO-15, CO 33 (Chile) Executive, JCL; Donald Fraser to Jimmy Carter, August 31, 1977, WHCF, box CO-9, CO1–9, 1/20/77–1/20/81, JCL.

6. John Burton to Jody Powell, September 6, 1977, WHCF, box CO-15, CO 33 (Chile) Executive, JCL.

7. Remarks of the President on Pinochet's Visit, September 6, 1977, Backup Material, Daily Diary, JCL.

8. John M. Goshko, "Carter, Torrijos Sign Panama Canal Treaties," *Washington Post*, September 8, 1977, A1.

9. Ibid.

10. "67 Minutos Entre Carter y Pinochet," *El Mercurio*, September 7, 1977, Muñoz Files, Writing and Research, box 12, Pinochet Research, 1970–2000, Washington Office on Latin America Records, David M. Rubenstein Rare Book and Manuscript Library, Duke University, Durham, North Carolina (hereafter WOLA Duke Records).

11. See Greg Grandin, *Empire's Workshop: Latin America, the United States, and the Rise of the New Imperialism* (New York: Metropolitan Books, 2006); Stephen Rabe, *The Killing Zone: The United States Wages Cold War in Latin America* (New York: Oxford University Press, 2016); Kathryn Sikkink, *Mixed Signals: U.S. Human Rights Policy and Latin America* (Ithaca: Cornell University Press, 2004); David F. Schmitz, *The United States and Right-Wing Dictatorships* (Cambridge: Cambridge University Press, 2006).

12. Advocacy, in this analysis, is the public promotion and defense of a particular issue, not only in the pursuit of immediate solutions, such as the release of a particular political prisoner, but also with the objective of altering the normative behaviors and beliefs of government actors and the public. It is through this type of "frame" shift that activists can effect change on the most basic level. Thus, the primary objective of almost any advocate group is to change the frame of reference through which political and social agents view a problem. Political scientists Margaret Keck and Kathryn Sikkink argue that by changing norms, advocates "contribute to changing perceptions that both state and societal actors may have of their identities, interests, and preferences, to transforming their discursive positions, and ultimately to changing procedures, policies and behaviors." Margaret Keck and Kathryn Sikkink, *Activists beyond Borders: Advocacy Networks in International Politics* (Ithaca: Cornell University Press, 1998), 3.

13. This work joins a growing body of literature stressing the centrality of Latin America to the emergence of evolution of international human rights norms and practices. Patrick Kelly writes, "No single region of the world played a more pivotal role in these sweeping changes than the Americas, which were both the target of human rights advocacy and the site of a series of monumental developments for regional and global human rights politics." Mark Bradley notes, "The centrality of Latin America for U.S. understandings of human rights in the 1970s was also driven by the long history of U.S. imperialism in the region and by more recent Cold War–inspired overt and clandestine interventions by the U.S. government in support of the military regimes in the Southern Cone." Patrick William Kelly, *Sovereign Emergencies: Latin America and the Making of Global Human Rights Politics* (Cambridge: Cambridge University Press, 2018), 3; Mark Philip Bradley, *The World Reimagined: Americans and Human Rights in the Twentieth Century* (New York: Cambridge University Press, 2016), 181; see also James N. Green, *We Cannot Remain Silent: Opposition to the Brazilian Military Dictatorship in the United States* (Durham: Duke University Press, 2010), 16; Kathryn Sikkink, *Evidence for Hope: Making Human Rights Work in the 21st Century* (Princeton: Princeton University Press, 2017), 55–93.

14. In his 2005 essay in the *Journal of Policy History*, Robert McMahon argued that the history of U.S. foreign relations is, "intrinsically, a Janus-faced field, one that looks both outward and inward for the wellsprings of America's behavior in the global arena." He continues by noting that although new international and transnational approaches have reinvigorated the field of diplomatic history, they have often overshadowed this duality in recent literature. Robert McMahon, "Diplomatic History and Policy History: Finding Common Ground," *Journal of Policy History* 17, no. 1 (2005): 97.

15. Scholars have examined the importance of both human rights advocacy and diplomacy in the 1970s from a variety of angles, but until recently these two dimensions of the 1970s "human rights moment" have remained largely separate in the historical literature. The first wave of scholars explored the Carter presidency as either the high-water mark of human rights

commitments or, more often, as misguided and naive. Many of these works do not account for the significance of congressional and nongovernment precursors in shaping the formulation and implementation of Carter's human rights policies. See Gaddis Smith, *Morality, Reason, and Power: American Diplomacy in the Carter Years* (New York: Hill & Wang, 1986); Burton I. Kaufman and Scott Kaufman, *The Presidency of James Earl Carter, Jr.* (Lawrence: University Press of Kansas, 2006); Herbert D. Rosenbaum and Alexej Ugrinsky, eds., *Jimmy Carter: Foreign Policy and Post-Presidential Years* (Westport, CT: Greenwood, 1994); David Skidmore, *Reversing Course: Carter's Foreign Policy, Domestic Politics, and the Failure of Reform* (Nashville: Vanderbilt University Press, 1996). For a summary of the early historiography on Carter's human rights policy, see David F. Schmitz and Vanessa Walker, "Jimmy Carter and the Foreign Policy of Human Rights: The Development of a Post–Cold War Foreign Policy," *Diplomatic History* 28, no. 1 (January 2004): 113–17. Though there is a wide and thoughtful literature on human rights advocates that illuminates the motivations and strategies of these actors, these works often set up a simple narrative of resistance: advocates who care about human rights versus bureaucrats who worry about power, strategic interests, and image. This literature has added a richness of outside voices and nongovernment actors often missing from other issues and more traditional histories of U.S. foreign relations, but it has tended to privilege the views of advocates over policy makers. New works on the history of human rights have begun to integrate the work of advocates and high-level diplomacy. See, for example, Barbara Keys, *Reclaiming American Virtue: The Human Rights Revolution of the 1970s* (Cambridge, MA: Harvard University Press, 2014); William Michael Schmidli, *The Fate of Freedom Elsewhere: Human Rights and U.S. Cold War Policy toward Argentina* (Ithaca: Cornell University Press, 2013); Sarah B. Snyder, *Human Rights Activism and the End of the Cold War: A Transnational History of the Helsinki Network* (New York: Cambridge University Press, 2011); Sarah B. Snyder, *From Selma to Moscow: How Human Rights Activism Transformed U.S. Foreign Policy* (New York: Columbia University Press, 2018).

16. George Lister, the first human rights officer at the State Department's Latin America desk, often labeled "leftist-liberal" circles concerned with human rights in Latin America "the Movement" in internal State Department memos. Lister was one of the first State Department officers to give sustained attention to human rights. The first reference to "the Movement" I found appeared in a June 1975 memo from George Lister to Assistant Secretary of State William Rogers, forwarding an Amnesty International letter to Secretary of State Henry Kissinger. Lister wrote, "I told 'the movement' that it would be a good tactic to have some thank you letters go to HAK [Kissinger] for moving on Chilean detainees/refugees." George Lister to William Rogers, June 17, 1975, box 12, folder 10 W. D. Rogers, George Lister Papers, Nettie Lee Benson Latin American Collection, University of Texas at Austin (hereafter Lister Papers).

17. In *Reclaiming American Virtue* Barbara Keys argues that human rights "helped redefine America to Americans, for they were about American identity even more than they were about foreign policy." This work supports that assertion but also challenges the notion that human rights politics necessarily attempted to elide the "shame and guilt" of Cold War foreign policy as epitomized by the Vietnam War. Keys argues that for "moderate liberals who had come to see the war as immoral and a stain on the country's honor, promoting human rights in America's right-wing allies spotlighted evil abroad and offered a way to distance the United States from it, alleviating their sense of responsibility." She continues by saying that liberal visions of human rights "were in important ways much more about feeling good than about feeling guilty." She concludes, "Human rights had become a topic about *there*, even more than about here." This is undoubtedly true for many in the broader human rights movement, but for the influential subset of human rights actors focused on right-wing dictators in Latin America and beyond, abuses "over there" were very much a product of dysfunction "here." *Keys, Reclaiming American Virtue*, 3–4, 7.

18. Many scholars have discussed a "movement" of nongovernment human rights actors in the late 1960s and early 1970s, while varying on which organizations to include and how to define their agenda. See Bradley, *World Reimagined*, 201–7; Kenneth Cmiel, "The Emergence of Human Rights Politics in the United States," *Journal of American History* 86, no. 3 (December 1999): 1231–50; Kelly, *Sovereign Emergencies*, 167–207; Keys, *Reclaiming American Virtue*, 178–213; Schmidli, *Fate of Freedom Elsewhere*, 56–82; Snyder, *From Selma to Moscow*.

19. Lars Schoultz, *Human Rights and United States Policy toward Latin America* (Princeton: Princeton University Press, 1981), 75.

20. Keys, *Reclaiming American Virtue*, 181. For more on AI-USA, see Bradley, *World Reimagined*, 203–7; Cmiel, "Emergence of Human Rights Politics"; Keys, *Reclaiming American Virtue*, 183–213.

21. Keys notes, "The AI-ADA partnership gave Amnesty's US section a backdoor entry into lobbying work it was enjoined from doing openly, while the ADA gained access to research it did not have the capacity to obtain itself." Keys, *Reclaiming American Virtue*, 209.

22. The HRWG was coordinated by Bruce Cameron of the ADA and Jacqui Chagnon of Clergy and Laity Concerned (CALC). WOLA, the Friends Committee for National Legislation, the National Council of Churches, the U.S. Catholic Conference, Amnesty International's Washington Office, the Institute for Policy Studies, the Council on Hemisphere Affairs, Americans for Democratic Action, and many Latin American Solidarity networks—Argentine Commission for Human Rights, Chile Committee for Human Rights, Chile Legislative Center, Non-Intervention in Chile, among others—were active in the group. According to Lars Schoultz, more than seventy organizations participated in the working group, even while almost half of those chose not to join the CNFMP, choosing to maintain their autonomy or declining to formally commit to the avowedly leftist politics of the group. Still, by 1977 "virtually every Washington-based NGO concerned with promoting humane values in United States foreign policy had become a member of the Group." Schoultz, *Human Rights and United States Policy*, 75–77.

23. Congressman Donald Fraser, for example, was the president of the Americans for Democratic Action from 1974 to 1976. For more on Congress's role in early human rights efforts, see Keys, *Reclaiming American Virtue*; Schoultz, *Human Rights and United States Policy*; Sikkink, *Mixed Signals*, 51–76; Sarah B. Snyder, "'A Call for U.S. Leadership': Congressional Activism on Human Rights," *Diplomatic History* 37, no. 2 (April 2013): 372–97; Snyder, *From Selma to Moscow*, 148–67.

24. Kelly writes, "By the late 1970s, WOLA and AI-USA had established themselves as primary links in a chain of human rights activism that interlocked in Washington." Kelly notes the tensions that arose at times between radical and moderate factions within the human rights movement but argues that they were united by a "shared repudiation of U.S. Cold War policy and a genuine concern for Latin American victims of violence." Kelly, *Sovereign Emergencies*, 205–207.

25. See Mark Lawrence, "Containing Globalism: The United States and the Developing World in the 1970s," in *The Shock of the Global: The 1970s in Perspective*, ed. Niall Ferguson, Charles S. Maier, Erez Manela, and Daniel Sargent (Cambridge, MA: Belknap Press of Harvard University Press, 2010), 205–19; Daniel Sargent, *A Superpower Transformed: The Remaking of American Foreign Relations in the 1970s* (New York: Oxford University Press, 2015); Schmidli, *Fate of Freedom Elsewhere*; Schmitz, *United States and Right-Wing Dictatorships*; Schmitz and Walker, "Jimmy Carter," 113–17.

26. For more on the global impact of the Chilean coup on human rights in the 1970s, see Kelly, *Sovereign Emergencies*; Margaret Power, "The U.S. Movement in Solidarity with Chile in the 1970s," *Latin American Perspectives* 36, no. 6 (November 2009): 46–66.

27. The most extensive account of the Carter administration's human rights policy in Argentina is Schmidli, *Fate of Freedom Elsewhere*; see also Sikkink, *Mixed Signals*.

28. Jimmy Carter, "Inaugural Address of President Carter," *Department of State Bulletin* 76 (January–June 1977): 121.

29. See Carl Bon Tempo, "From the Center-Right: Freedom House and Human Rights in the 1970s and 1980s," in *The Human Rights Revolution: An International History*, ed. Akira Iriye, Petra Goedde, and William Hitchcock (New York: Oxford University Press, 2012), 223–44; Keys, *Reclaiming American Virtue*, 103–26.

30. Michael Ignatieff, *Human Rights as Politics and Idolatry* (Princeton: Princeton University Press, 2001), 19.

1. The Chilean Catalyst

1. Author interview with Joe Eldridge, Washington, D.C., October 7, 2009. There are a number of different media accounts of the visit that vary slightly in detail. I have based my narrative on Joe Eldridge's recounting in our October 2009 interview.

2. Press release from the Embassy of Chile, "Visit to Chile of Representatives Messrs. Moffett, Miller and Harkin," March 16, 1976, WOLA Papers, Geographic Files, Chile, Ahern, box 56, Flyers, Leaflets, WOLA Duke Records.

3. Quoted in Jack Anderson, "Iowan 'Crashes' Chile's Secret Villa," June 5, 1976, *St. Petersburg Times*, Private Institutional Records, Washington Office on Latin America, Washington, D.C. (hereafter WOLA Private Records).

4. The number of people detained at Villa Grimaldi quickly dropped off after 1976. Before the visit, more than 240 prisoners who passed through there simply disappeared. After the trip, the numbers dwindled, and only four disappeared after 1976. Villa Grimaldi, Corporación Parque por la Paz, "Lista de detenidos (as) desaparecidos (as) y ejecutados (as) politicos," http://villagrimaldi.cl/listado-de-detenidos-as-y-ejecutadosas-politicosas/, accessed February 9, 2020.

5. See Green, *We Cannot Remain Silent*; Keys, *Reclaiming American Virtue*, 98–102; Sikkink, *Mixed Signals*, 54–60.

6. See Lawrence, "Containing Globalism"; Lien-Hang T. Nguyen, "The Vietnam Decade: The Global Shock of the War," in Ferguson et al., *Shock of the Global*, 159–72; Sargent, *Superpower Transformed*.

7. Historian Edward Berkowitz notes that "the postwar perception of the president as a powerful, benevolent figure who acted in the nation's interests ended with the release of the [Nixon] tapes." Edward D. Berkowitz, *Something Happened: A Political and Cultural Overview of the Seventies* (New York: Columbia University Press, 2006), 28.

8. See Schmitz, *United States and Right-Wing Dictatorships*, 128–37; Peter Kornbluh, *The Pinochet File: A Declassified Dossier on Atrocity and Accountability* (New York: New Press, 2003); Julian Zelizer, *Arsenal of Democracy* (New York: Basic Books, 2010), 262–63.

9. Memo from Lister to Rogers, June 17, 1975, box 12, folder 10 W. D. Rogers, Lister Papers.

10. Barbara Keys argues that a liberal vision of human rights was "in important ways much more about feeling good than about feeling guilty." She argues, "Instead of seeking fundamental structural change in conditions that produce searing inequality and injustice, mainstream human rights campaigns in the 1970s conveyed the notion that the problem lay in individual evil perpetrated by small numbers of wrongdoers, rather than fundamental injustices in which Americans, too, were implicated." While this was certainly true for a certain subset of U.S. human rights proponents, the Movement viewed their advocacy to limit foreign aid as having substantial material consequences for repression as well as acting as an indicator of moral condemnation.

The act of distancing was not simply an emotional one, but one with tangible effects on the ability of foreign regimes to perpetrate abuses against their own citizens. Keys, *Reclaiming American Virtue*, 4, 8.

11. For more on the rise of human rights activism in the 1970s, see Bon Tempo, "From the Center-Right"; Cmiel, "Emergence of Human Rights Politics"; Akira Iriye, *Global Community: The Role of International Organizations in the Making of the Contemporary World* (Berkeley: University of California Press, 2002); Keck and Sikkink, *Advocates beyond Borders*; Kelly, *Sovereign Emergencies*; Samuel Moyn, *The Last Utopia: Human Rights in History* (Cambridge, MA: Belknap Press of Harvard University Press, 2010); Snyder, *From Selma to Moscow*. For particular emphasis on human rights abuses in the communist sphere, see Snyder, *Human Rights Activism*.

12. For a concise discussion of Chilean exceptionalism and its uses during the Allende period, see Steve J. Stern, *Battling for Hearts and Minds: Memory Struggles in Pinochet's Chile, 1973–1988* (Durham: Duke University Press, 2006), 29–32.

13. See Tanya Harmer, *Allende's Chile and the Inter-American Cold War* (Chapel Hill: University of North Carolina Press, 2011). For more on the wider regional importance of the Cuban Revolution, see Thomas C. Wright, *Latin America in the Era of the Cuban Revolution* (New York: Praeger, 1991). For an overview of Chilean political culture in the decade before the coup, see Arturo Valenzuela, *The Breakdown of Democratic Regimes: Chile* (Baltimore: Johns Hopkins University Press, 1978).

14. José Zalaquett, a young lawyer at the time, remembered feeling that "the winds of history were blowing in our direction and that our boat would reach safe harbor regardless of our crazy handling of the steering wheel. We were so inebriated with an idea that somehow, we felt that mistakes were of no relevance, that history would take care of it. And all of a sudden you wake up and there is a disaster. Made by them [the military junta] but paved by us." Author interview with José Zalaquett, Santiago, Chile, July 2, 2008.

15. Thomas C. Wright, *State Terrorism in Latin America: Chile, Argentina, and International Human Rights* (Lanham, MD: Rowman & Littlefield, 2007), 51–55.

16. Some estimate that the military detained as many as fifty thousand individuals throughout Chile. The Chilean foreign minister reported the number to be a much lower 10,900. Ibid., 52.

17. In contrast, in the same time period, only fifty-two soldiers, seventeen police, and twelve sailors had been killed in armed attacks. Pamela Constable and Arturo Valenzuela, *A Nation of Enemies: Chile under Pinochet* (New York: W. W. Norton, 1993), 20. For an official account of human rights abuses in the immediate aftermath of the coup, see *Report of the Chilean National Commission on Truth and Reconciliation*, trans. Phillip Berryman (Notre Dame: University of Notre Dame Press, 1993), 129–45.

18. In its "Chilean Declaration of Principles," the military leaders warned against the excesses and weaknesses of democracy, arguing that the exercise of debate and dissent needed limits for the protection of democracy itself. "Never again must a naïve democracy allow within its midst organized groups, acting under the guise of misunderstood pluralism, to foster guerrilla violence to attain power, or feigning respect for democracy, to further a doctrine or morality, whose objective is the construction of a totalitarian state. For this reason, Marxist parties and movements will no longer be admitted into our civic life." Quoted in Patricia Weiss Fagen, "Repression and State Security," in *Fear at the Edge: State Terror and Resistance in Latin America*, ed. Juan E. Corradi, Patricia Weiss Fagen, and Manuel A. Garretón (Berkeley: University of California Press, 1992), 44. The authors note that it was published in 1974 in glossy format for international as well as domestic consumption.

19. DINA's mandate was to "produce the intelligence necessary to formulate policies and planning, and to adopt measures to procure the safeguarding of National Security and

development of the country." *Report of the Chilean National Commission on Truth and Reconciliation*, 82, 474–75, 472.

20. The "positive meaning of liberation," as historian Steve Stern labels it, was the junta's intention to rebuild Chile, with a healthier, stronger Christian democracy and civil society that would usher in a new, more prosperous, and harmonious era for all Chileans. Stern, *Battling for Hearts and Minds*, 58. Pinochet embraced a missionary, almost messianic image for himself, asserting, "I am a man fighting for a just cause: the fight between Christianity and spiritualism on the one hand, and Marxism and materialism on the other." Quoted in Constable and Valenzuela, *Nation of Enemies*, 79.

21. The Chilean National Commission on Truth and Reconciliation noted that "the concerns of the new military authorities to maintain a structure or image of legality made them particularly cautious in dealing with members of the judiciary." Its Decree Law No. 1 stated that "the powers of the judicial branch [remain] fully in force." *Report of the Chilean National Commission on Truth and Reconciliation*, 117. Indeed, by the time it filed its mass habeas corpus petition in March 1974, the committee believed it was gathering information about approximately 80 percent of the detentions in Santiago. Pamela Lowden, *Moral Opposition to Authoritarian Rule in Chile, 1973–90* (New York: Macmillan, 1996), 34. For more on Chile's legal culture during the Pinochet years, see Lisa Hilbink, *Judges beyond Politics in Democracy and Dictatorship: Lessons from Chile* (New York: Cambridge University Press, 2007).

22. Immense pressure from the regime on the Catholic Church for its human rights activities precipitated the change from Comité Pro-Paz to the Vicaría. Rather than abandoning its efforts, as the junta had hoped, the Catholic hierarchy formally sanctioned and embraced these activities, thus providing greater institutional support and protection. See Lowden, *Moral Opposition*; Stern, *Battling for Hearts and Minds*, 111–15.

23. The AFDD, constituted primarily of women, had its roots in small family groups initiated under the Comité Pro-Paz as a way for victims' family members to support one another and aid the Comité in its legal efforts. With the closing of the Comité, the AFDD grew into a powerful organization in its own right, although it continued to be housed in the Vicaría's building. In its early years, the AFDD relied on the Vicaría to shelter and support it, yet it also developed its own patterns of resistance and protest against the regime. It supported the Vicaría's legal petitions, but as legal cases failed, the group decided on a more public path, holding public vigils and protests, and most famously, hunger strikes. FASIC formed from Protestant churches' response to the dissolution of the Comité Pro-Paz in the fall of 1975 that had led to the establishment of the Vicaría. Initially, FASIC took up where CONAR had left off, focusing on foreign citizens who were targeted by the regime, and retaining the support of the United Nations for its work. FASIC was not sheltered by the high-profile Catholic Church in the way the Vicaría was, and as such, it was generally less confrontational in its efforts. It focused its legal energies on finding foreign refuge for those seeking to flee the country, rather than challenging the regime directly. FASIC also did important relief work domestically and played a particularly critical and early role in attending to the mental health of individuals released from detention and torture centers. Comisión Chilena de Derechos Humanos, founded in 1978, used a more aggressive approach in its advocacy, publishing figures of abuse, detention, and disappearance much higher than those used by the Vicaría, as it culled through police reports and other sources. Mark Ensalaco, *Chile under Pinochet: Recovering the Truth* (Philadelphia: University of Pennsylvania Press, 2000), 62.

24. The government campaign against the Comité, for example, came to a head in September 1975, when Pinochet and Cardinal Silva met in person and Pinochet, citing evidence that the group was harboring terrorists, requested that the cardinal close the Comité or he would have to order him to do so. Silva reluctantly agreed and officially announced the closure of the

Comité Pro-Paz on November 14, 1975. Silva, however, took the opportunity to present a subtle warning in response to Pinochet's request, predicting that its closure "in all probability will incur—within and especially outside of Chile—appreciably greater damages than those which you claim to be avoiding." Ibid., 61.

25. Zalaquett interview.

26. One of its founding members reported that after these trips, representatives from the two groups talked almost daily via telephone, and the groups shared information about political prisoners, human rights abuses, legal cases, and new arrests. Ann Marie Clark, *Diplomacy of Conscience: Amnesty International and Changing Human Rights Norms* (Princeton: Princeton University Press, 2001), 52; Darren G. Hawkins, *International Human Rights and Authoritarian Rule in Chile* (Lincoln: University of Nebraska Press, 2002), 57.

27. For a model of this "boomerang" pattern, see Keck and Sikkink, *Activists beyond Borders*, 13.

28. Wright, *State Terrorism in Latin America*, 75.

29. For more in-depth explorations of the National Security Doctrine, see Corradi et al., *Fear at the Edge*; Margaret E. Crahan, "National Security Ideology and Human Rights," in *Human Rights and Basic Needs*, ed. Margaret E. Crahan (Washington, D.C.: Georgetown University Press, 1982), 100–127; Brian Loveman and Thomas M. Davies, eds., *The Politics of Antipolitics: The Military in Latin America* (Wilmington, DE: Scholarly Resources, 1997); Louis Roniger and Mario Sznajder, *The Legacy of Human-Rights Violations in the Southern Cone: Argentina, Chile, and Uruguay* (New York: Oxford University Press, 1999), especially chapter 1; Alain Rouquié, *The Military and the State in Latin America* (Berkeley: University of California Press, 1987).

30. For the longer trajectory of U.S. support for right-wing governments in Latin America, see David F. Schmitz, *Thank God They're on Our Side* (Chapel Hill: University of North Carolina Press, 1999); Schmitz, *United States and Right-Wing Dictatorships*; Walter LaFeber, *Inevitable Revolutions: The United States in Central America* (New York: W. W. Norton, 1993); Rabe, *Killing Zone*; Alan McPherson, *A Short History of U.S. Interventions in Latin America and the Caribbean* (Chichester, U.K.: Wiley-Blackwell, 2016).

31. Arthur Schlesinger, for example, envisioned a "middle class revolution where the processes of economic modernization carry the new urban middle class into power and produce, along with it, such necessities of modern technical society as constitutional government, honest public administration, a responsible party system, a rational land system, an efficient system of taxation, mass education, social mobility, etc." Arthur Schlesinger to John F. Kennedy, "Report to the President on Latin American Mission," March 10, 1961, *FRUS 1961–1963*, vol. 12: *American Republics*, ed. Edward C. Keefer, Harriet Dashiell Schwar, and W. Taylor Fain III (Washington, D.C.: Government Printing Office, 1996), document 7.

32. Examining the Dominican Republic, John F. Kennedy famously summed up the dilemma for policy makers; there were three possibilities "in descending order of preference: a decent democratic regime, a continuation of the Trujillo regime or a Castro regime. We ought to aim for the first, but we really can't renounce the second until we are sure that we can avoid the third." Quoted in Schmitz, *Thank God They're on Our Side*, 236. See also Stephen G. Rabe, *The Most Dangerous Area in the World: John F. Kennedy Confronts Communist Revolution in Latin America* (Chapel Hill: University of North Carolina Press, 1999), 34–40.

33. Military rulers throughout the hemisphere seized power from civilian politicians on the grounds that politics itself had become a liability, creating instability and blocking economic development. Louis Roniger and Mario Sznajder write, "Military command perceived democracy itself as corrupt, inefficient, and leading to greater suffering and eventually to a wider curtailment and even the annihilation of civil and political rights by the Communists and their allies, if the latter were allowed to take hold of the reigns of state." Roniger and Sznajder, *Legacy of Human-*

Rights Violations, 20. By 1975 the United States had trained more than seventy thousand Latin American soldiers at more than a hundred different institutions. The U.S. Army Southern Command's School of the Americas alone trained more than twenty thousand officers in the 1960s. These programs stressed the communist threat and techniques used by Marxist subversion in their counterinsurgency training, highlighting the connections between national security and political and economic order. As one Argentine army report from 1962 observes, these joint training programs "bring out clearly that the principle enemy of our civilization and way of life is to be found in the very heart of our national communities." It took very little for these lessons and techniques to be turned from external enemies to internal ones. Wright, *State Terrorism in Latin America*, 25.

34. Jeremi Suri notes that although Nixon first proposed the strategy as part of Asian policy, "for Kissinger this was a well-considered global strategy." Kissinger was reticent to make democracy a guide for policy making: "The third world, including China, did not figure as a space for the extension of democracy or the defense of vital interests. It was a 'grey area' where the United States had to project a powerful image and weaken potential enemies before they grew strong enough to challenge Washington where it really mattered." In this context, the democratic practices, or lack thereof, were of little import to larger U.S. concerns. Jeremi Suri, *Henry Kissinger and the American Century* (Cambridge, MA: Belknap Press of Harvard University Press, 2007), 236.

35. The 1969 Report of the U.S. Presidential Mission for the Western Hemisphere, or "Rockefeller Commission," provided the intellectual underpinnings for the Nixon administration's approach to Latin American relations and underscored the dangerous potentials of instability and communist subversion in the region. The report rejected the notion of restricting support for these pro-U.S. military governments on moral grounds, arguing that "the authoritarian and hierarchical tradition which has conditioned and formed the cultures of most of these societies does not lend itself to the particular kind of popular government we are used to. . . . For many of these societies, therefore, the question is less of one of democracy or a lack of it, than it is simply of orderly ways of getting along." Rockefeller reported, "Growing instability, extremism, and anti-U.S. nationalism," had brought regional relations to a crossroad. "This crossroad—this challenge to our system of democracy and to the very survival of our values and ourselves—is not rhetorical. It is factual. Either we meet this challenge, or the prospect is for revolutionary changes leading we know where not." U.S. Presidential Mission for the Western Hemisphere, "Rockefeller Report on Quality of Life in the Americas," *Department of State Bulletin* 61 (1969): 515, 507, 539. A National Security Council report later that same year noted that societies navigating the perilous passage to "modern" economic and social systems, radicalism, and "rising nationalism posed a significant threat to U.S. interests, particularly when taken in conjunction with a Soviet presence and a Soviet willingness to offer itself as an alternative to Latin dependence on the U.S." The report added, "Diplomatic relations are merely practical conveniences and not measures of moral judgment." National Security Council Interdepartmental Group for Inter-American Affairs, "A Study of U.S. Policy toward Latin America," NSSM 15, March 1969, National Security Council-Institutional Papers, NSSMs, box H-134, Richard Nixon Papers, National Archives II, College Park, Maryland (hereafter National Archives II).

36. "Rockefeller Report," 504–5.

37. Allende had been a boogeyman for U.S. officials, even before the Nixon administration; as early as 1964, the CIA wrote on Allende's presidential bid, reporting, "Of all the Latin American nations, Chile offers the Communists their best prospects for entering and potentially dominating a government through the electoral process." The U.S. government took these threats seriously, spending more than $3 million in aid programs and CIA covert actions to build Chilean support for Eduardo Frei, Allende's opponent, in 1964. In 1970 the Nixon administration also funded CIA

activities in an unsuccessful attempt to prevent Allende's election. U.S. Congress, *Covert Action in Chile, 1963–1973: Staff Report of the Select Committee to Study Governmental Operations with Respect to Intelligence Activities, United States Senate* (Washington, D.C.: Government Printing Office, 1975), 1–78.

38. "Memcon-NSC Meeting-Chile (NSSM 97)," November 6, 1970, National Security Archive, "Chile: 16,000 Secret Documents Declassified," November 13, 2000, http://www.gwu.edu/~nsarchiv/news/20001113/.

39. Quoted in Kornbluh, *Pinochet File*, 80.

40. Ibid., 114. For more on U.S. covert operations in Chile in the lead-up to the Chilean coup, see Kornbluh, *Pinochet File*, and U.S. Congress, *Covert Action in Chile*.

41. Department of State, "Chile Contingency Paper: Possible Chilean Military Intervention," September 8, 1973, box 2196, Record Group 59, U.S. Department of State Records, National Archives II.

42. Quoted in Kornbluh, *Pinochet File*, 113.

43. Only two months after the coup, U.S. aid had surged, securing debt relief for Chile, offering economic assistance, supporting and encouraging other international financial institutions to help. By 1974 U.S. aid had risen to $116 million in economic assistance and $16 million in military aid. The World Bank and Inter-American Development Bank offered Chile more than $111 million in loans that same year. U.S. Congress, *Covert Action in Chile*, 34; Schmitz, *United States and Right-Wing Dictatorships*, 103.

44. A CIA intelligence report, a little more than a month after the coup, estimated that about 1,600 civilians had been killed between September 11 and October 10, a number at variance with the junta's publicly reported statistic of approximately six hundred people. The report concluded that the military had more than twenty detention centers throughout the country, only a few of which the Chilean government acknowledged publicly. Aside from the statistics and political analysis, even intelligence officials could not help but note the brutality of the regime. One Defense intelligence report observed that the methods used by the Chilean military were "straight out of the Spanish Inquisition and often leave the person interrogated with visible bodily damage." CIA Intelligence Report, "Executions in Chile since the Coup," October 27, 1973, "Electronic Briefing Book No. 212: Pinochet: A Declassified Documentary Obit," National Security Archive, December 12, 2006, http://www.gwu.edu/~nsarchiv/NSAEBB/NSAEBB212/index.htm; Department of Defense Intelligence Report, February 5, 1974, Chile Declassification Project, Defense Intelligence Agency, box 1, National Archives II.

45. David Popper to Henry Kissinger, "FY75 76 CASP Chile," March 13, 1974, Chile Declassification Project, State Department Collections, U.S. Department of State FOIA Electronic Reading Room (hereafter Chile Declassification Project), available at https://foia.state.gov/Search/Search.aspx.

46. Scholars have argued over whether this 1970s moment was a new phenomenon or a continuation of earlier movements. Yet almost all acknowledge the dramatic rise of groups and political attention to the issue. See Kenneth Cmiel, "The Recent History of Human Rights," *American Historical Review* 109, no. 1 (2004): 117–35; Keck and Sikkink, *Advocates beyond Borders*; Moyn, *Last Utopia*.

47. Historians Margaret Power and Julie Charlip argue, "The story of U.S. solidarity with Latin America illustrates the nonofficial side of U.S. relations with Latin America and challenges the idea that only the U.S. government develops and implements foreign policy." Margaret Power and Julie Charlip, "Introduction: On Solidarity," *Latin American Perspectives* 36, no. 6 (November 2009): 7. See also Kelly, *Sovereign Emergencies*, 94–133.

48. Political scientist Lars Schoultz notes, "By 1977, the combined interest groups concerned with the repression of human rights in Latin America had become one of the largest, most active, and most visible foreign policy lobbying forces in Washington." Schoultz, *Human Rights and United States Policy*, 75.

49. Power, "U.S. Movement in Solidarity with Chile," 48.

50. Margaret Power and Julie Charlip write that solidarity is a difficult term to define, but it "reflected the creation of a bond between North Americans and Latin Americans, the sense that we had a common goal and similar values." Power and Charlip, "Introduction: On Solidarity," 4. See also Alison Bruey, "Transnational Concepts, Local Contexts: Solidarity at the Grassroots in Pinochet's Chile," in *Human Rights and Transnational Solidarity in Cold War Latin America*, ed. Jessica Stites Mor (Madison: University of Wisconsin Press, 2013), 120–42; Brenda Elsey, "As the World Is My Witness: Transnational Chilean Solidarity and Popular Culture," in Stites Mor, *Human Rights and Transnational Solidarity*, 177–208; Patrick William Kelly, "The 1973 Chilean Coup and the Origins of Transnational Human Rights Activism," *Journal of Global History* 8, no. 1 (March 2013): 165–86; Vania Markarian, *Left in Transformation: Uruguayan Exiles and the Latin American Human Rights Networks, 1967–1984* (New York: Routledge, 2005); Kelly, *Sovereign Emergencies*, 94–133; Power, "U.S. Movement in Solidarity with Chile."

51. James Green's work demonstrates that Brazilian advocates were critical precursors for the grassroots challenges to human rights abuses perpetrated by military dictatorships allied with the United States in the 1970s. See Green, *We Cannot Remain Silent*. For the broader impact of Latin American activists on the emergence of global human rights paradigms in the 1970s, see Kelly, *Sovereign Emergencies*.

52. Community Action on Latin America, "Statement on CALA's Theory and Practice," [1975?], M80–048, box 1, Chile Activities Sept 75–Jan 78, Community Action on Latin America, Records 1971–1991 (hereafter CALA Records), Wisconsin Historical Society, Madison (hereafter WHS). For more on CALA's history, see Kelly, *Sovereign Emergencies*, 172–84.

53. Orlando Letelier to Bruce C. Vandervort, December 6, 1971, mss 491, box 1, Crisis Conference on Chile-Correspondence, CALA Records.

54. CALA, "What's Happening in Chile," September 1973, Publications, mss 491, box 1, CALA Records.

55. *CALA Newsletter* 3, no. 3 (November 1973), Geographic Files, Chile, Ahern, box 56, CALA, 1972–73, WOLA Duke Records.

56. For early focus on torture, see Barbara Keys, "Anti-Torture Politics: Amnesty International, the Greek Junta, and the Origins of the Human Rights 'Boom' in the United States," in Iriye et al., *Human Rights Revolution*, 201–22; and Keys, *Reclaiming American Virtue*, 75–102.

57. As Judy Tzu-Chun Wu writes, "the global Third World played a significant role in inspiring the political imagination of American activists who connected domestic aspirations for social justice with global critiques of imperialism." Judy Tzu-Chun Wu, *Radicals on the Road: Internationalism, Orientalism, and Feminism during the Vietnam War* (Ithaca: Cornell University Press, 2013), 9.

58. Frank Teruggi to CALA, May 1, 1972, M80–048, box 1, Chile Correspondence-With Chile, CALA Records.

59. Marcial to CALA, September 6, 1972, M80–048, box 1, Chile Correspondence-With Chile, CALA Records.

60. An October 14 news summary, for example, reported on the formation of CONAR and the reports of several Catholic and international organizations detailing atrocities that they had witnessed or of which they had firsthand accounts. CALA, "News Summary," October 14, 1973, mss 491, box 1, Publications, CALA Records.

61. Newsletter, Non-Intervention in Chile, October 1973, mss 491, box 1, Publications, CALA Records.

62. The *Progressive*, for example, wrote to CALA shortly after the coup, thanking the group for the information it had sent the periodical about the situation in Chile. "We have read them with much appreciation," wrote the publisher, Morris H. Rubin. "Indeed, we have been able to rework part of our own presentation, which will be the lead article in the November issue, to include some helpful material in the collection you brought me." Morris H. Rubin to CALA, October 1, 1973, M80–048, box 1, Letters to Editor, CALA Records.

63. DC Chile Coalition Flier, [October 1974], box 12, folder 9 W. D. Rogers, Lister Papers.

64. "NICH Political Perspectives," [1975], M82–359, box 3, Chile, CALA Records.

65. Pamphlet, National Coordinating Center in Solidarity with Chile, "We Who Support the People of Chile," February 1974, Geographic Files, Chile, Ahern, box 56, Flyers and Leaflets, WOLA Duke Records.

66. Ibid.

67. CALA, "What's Happening in Chile," September 1973, mss 491, box 1, Publications, CALA Records.

68. Margaret Power has documented the impact of Chilean exiles not only on solidarity organizations but also more broadly, arguing that they had a "significant political and emotional impact on the North Americans with whom they came into contact." She continues, "As a result of their presence and their testimony, many North Americans learned directly what the U.S. government had done in Chile and the misery its actions had caused many Chileans." Power, "U.S. Movement in Solidarity with Chile," 56.

69. CALA, *Community Action on Latin America Newsletter* 3, no. 2 (October 1973), WOLA Papers, Geographic Files, Chile, Ahern, box 56, CALA 1972–73, WOLA Duke Records.

70. Wright, *State Terrorism in Latin America*, 68.

71. Thomas Wright and Rody Oñate note, "Having lost the battle at home, they sought to undermine Pinochet from the 'external front.' Upon arriving at their exile destinations, many reconstituted their parties" and became part of the budding international human rights network. For an overview of the Chilean exile community, see Thomas C. Wright and Rody Oñate, eds., *Flight from Chile: Voices of Exile* (Albuquerque: University of New Mexico Press, 1998), 69; Bradley, *World Reimagined*, 183.

72. Sikkink, *Mixed Signals*, 53–55; Green, *We Cannot Remain Silent*, 55–75.

73. Some of the earliest groups to promote human rights and lobby for these issues in Washington included Clergy and Laity Concerned, the U.S. Catholic Conference, the National Council of Churches, and the Friends Committee on National Legislation. For more on WOLA's formation and work, see Coletta Youngers, *Thirty Years of Advocacy for Human Rights, Democracy and Social Justice* (Washington, D.C.: Washington Office on Latin America, 2006).

74. Ibid., 6.

75. Eldridge had arrived in Chile shortly after Allende's election as part of a group of U.S. missionaries called the Project for Awareness and Action. He was there during the September 11 coup and in the following days, he witnessed the military's repression taking place around him. Further, security forces raided his group's offices and arrested two of the Maryknoll sisters taking part in the project, detaining them in Estadio Nacional before they were later released. Author interview with Eldridge, April 25, 2008. See also Kelly, *Sovereign Emergencies*, 184–90; Snyder, *From Selma to Moscow*, 120–21.

76. Eldridge interview.

77. Lars Schoultz notes that WOLA served as "an informal link between Latin American citizens and the Washington foreign policy bureaucracy." Schoultz, *Human Rights and United States Policy*, 77.

78. Schoultz argues that WOLA's newsletter, *Latin America Update*, quickly became "by far the most reliable source of information on humanitarian issues in Latin America" and "gained influence by providing the most reliable data available in the United States on repression of human rights in Latin America." Ibid., 79, 78.

79. See ibid., 80–82, 86–88.

80. See also Sikkink, *Mixed Signals*, 60–61.

81. For background on the Institute for Policy Studies, see Institute for Policy Studies, *First Harvest: The Institute for Policy Studies, 1963–1983* (New York: Grove Press, 1983); Vanessa Walker, "The Paradoxes of Human Rights Diplomacy: The Institute for Policy Studies and U.S.–Latin American Relations in the Carter Administration" (MA thesis, University of Wisconsin–Madison, 2004). See also Paul Adler, "'The Basis of a New Internationalism?' The Institute for Policy Studies and North-South Politics from the NIEO to Neoliberalism," *Diplomatic History* 41, no. 4 (September 2017): 665–93; Brian Scott Mueller, *Democracy's Think Tank* (Philadelphia: University of Pennsylvania Press, forthcoming).

82. In an influential article in 1976, Orlando Letelier drew explicit links between the violence against civilians in Chile and the economic system promoted by the military junta. "It would seem to be a common-sense sort of observation," Letelier argued, "that economic policies are conditioned by, and at the same time modify, the social and political situation where they are put into practice. Economic policies are introduced precisely in order to alter social structures." Orlando Letelier, *Chile: Economic "Freedom" and Political Repression* (London: Institute of Race Relations, 1976), 5.

83. Richard Barnett, Letter to the Editor, *New York Times*, January 2, 1976, box 20, Letters to the Editor, Institute for Policy Studies Records (hereafter IPS Records), WHS.

84. The memo noted, playfully, the group's disappointment at being excluded from John Dean's "list of political enemies of President Nixon." Although it was "tongue in cheek," it expressed sincere concern that "in the perception of the White House or the Washington scene in general, ADA is not considered a threat." Jon Blum to Congressman Donald M. Fraser, June 29, 1973, M97–135, box 4, folder 9, "F," Americans for Democratic Action Records (hereafter ADA Records), WHS.

85. Schoultz, *Human Rights and United States Policy*, 82.

86. Americans for Democratic Action Resolution, "The International Human Rights Crisis and the 1976 Presidential Campaign," June 1976, M2001–087, box 1, National Board Meeting, ADA Records.

87. Schoultz, *Human Rights and United States Policy*, 75.

88. Pamphlet, Coalition for a New Foreign and Military Policy, "$1.7 Billion for Dictators?" 1976, M94–371, box 5, Coalition for a New Foreign and Military Policy, CALA Records.

89. David P. Forsythe, *Human Rights and U.S. Foreign Policy: Congress Reconsidered* (Gainesville: University Presses of Florida, 1988), 2.

90. One senator, John Sherman Cooper (R-KY), noted in 1971 that U.S. involvement in Vietnam and Southeast Asia caused many in Congress to reconsider "the scope of the respective congressional powers and the President's powers" in foreign affairs. Quoted in Robert David Johnson, *Congress and the Cold War* (New York: Cambridge University Press, 2006), 190.

91. Although they did not necessarily have a unified agenda—a flaw that would undermine their effectiveness in the coming years—they did share some common traits. Rep. Tip O'Neill recalled, "These youthful, able, talented people—they didn't like the Establishment, they didn't like Washington. They didn't like the seniority system. They didn't like the closeness of it, and they came down here with new ideas." Berkowitz, *Something Happened*, 93. See also Keys, *Reclaiming American Virtue*, 75–102; Sikkink, *Mixed Signals*, 52–53.

92. Historian Robert David Johnson notes that "the final years of the Cold War also featured a profound shift in the internal balance of power within Congress, as for the first time, the House emerged as the more powerful branch on international questions." Johnson, *Congress and the Cold War*, xxii.

93. Next to Hersh's article on the front page of the September 8 *New York Times*, for example, was a column on Soviet Jewry and the efforts by Senators Jackson, Vanik, and Ribicoff to secure emigration guarantees for this community. Bernard Gwertzman, "U.S. Devises Plan for Rise in Flow of Soviet Jews," *New York Times*, September 8, 1974, 1.

94. Jackson's efforts were supported not only by traditional anticommunist forces within the United States but also by many in the Jewish community. Migration patterns in the early twentieth century had created family connections between the Soviet and North American Jewish communities. More generally, Soviet mistreatment of its Jewish and Christian minorities mobilized sympathy among United States coreligionists. The Jackson coalition thus brought together traditional anticommunist forces with religious and minority groups concerned with extended family and religious communities within the Soviet sphere, as well as those interested in broader considerations of human rights.

95. As Henry Kaufman, Jackson's biographer observed, Jackson "believed that the Cold War was a struggle with a terminal point, which would end with the breakup of the Soviet Union and the collapse of the totalitarian system." Robert G. Kaufman, *Henry M. Jackson: A Life in Politics* (Seattle: University of Washington Press, 2000), 248. See also Bon Tempo, "From the Center-Right"; Keys, *Reclaiming American Virtue*, 103–26.

96. See Keys, *Reclaiming American Virtue*, 156–58; Sikkink, *Mixed Signals*, 65–76; Snyder, "'Call for U.S. Leadership'" and *From Selma to Moscow*, 148–57.

97. U.S. Congress, *International Protection of Human Rights, Hearings before the Subcommittee on International Organizations and Movements of the House Committee on Foreign Affairs*, 93rd Congress, 1st Session, 1974 (Washington, D.C.: Government Printing Office, 1974), ix, 1.

98. Salzberg recalled that Fraser encouraged the witnesses to think out loud, to explore the moral and philosophical nature of the question at hand, as well as the practical policy applications. John P. Salzberg, "A View from the Hill: U.S. Legislation and Human Rights," in *The Diplomacy of Human Rights*, ed. David D. Newsom (Lanham, MD: University Press of America, 1986), 15–16.

99. Author interview with Eldridge, October 7, 2009.

100. Salzberg, "View from the Hill," 20.

101. The first witness to testify in the hearings, for example, was Niall MacDermot, the secretary-general of the International Commission of Jurists and prominent member of Amnesty International. Later witnesses included Martin Ennals, the secretary-general of Amnesty International, and Thomas Quigley of the U.S. Catholic Conference and a founder of WOLA. Fraser structured the hearings so that State Department officials could not only hear the other witnesses—sensitizing them to the concerns of nongovernment actors and congressional members on human rights—but also let them offer a response to others' testimonies by scheduling them as the last witness. Ibid., 16, 15. Sikkink argues that the Fraser committee hearings were unique in "the quality of the conversation between Fraser and many of his witnesses. Through his carefully crafted questions, the chair invited the witness to think aloud with him about the shape of a new policy." Sikkink, *Mixed Signals*, 68.

102. U.S. Congress, House Committee on Foreign Affairs, Subcommittee on International Organizations and Movements, *Human Rights in the World Community: A Call for U.S. Leadership; Report* (Washington, D.C.: Government Printing Office, 1974).

103. Quoted at https://www.govinfo.gov/content/pkg/USCODE-2010-title22/html/USCODE-2010-title22-chap32-subchapII.htm.

104. Salzberg notes that "the subcommittee also heard testimony from nationals of the country—lawyers, political opposition figures, church and other non-governmental representatives—who not only had firsthand knowledge but in some instances were themselves victims of repression. To provide balance, the subcommittee often had witnesses who defended the human rights record of the foreign government under scrutiny." Salzberg, "View from the Hill," 15.

105. For more on Ford's decision, see Gerald R. Ford, *A Time to Heal: The Autobiography of Gerald R. Ford* (New York: Harper & Row, 1979), 87.

106. Seymour M. Hersh, "CIA Chief Tells House of $8-Million Campaign against Allende in '70–'73," *New York Times*, September 8, 1974, 1.

107. Possibly the strongest indication of Ford's decision to stay the course on Nixon's foreign policy was his retention of Henry Kissinger as secretary of state. In a meeting with Latin American ambassadors just days after taking office, Ford stressed his full faith in Kissinger, explaining, "The Secretary's relationship with me is of the closest kind. I have the highest respect and regard for him. Our relationship has extended over fifteen years." Stephen Low to Henry Kissinger, "Memcon on Meeting with Latin American Ambassadors," August 10, 1974, National Security Advisor Files (hereafter NSA), Latin American Affairs Staff, Subject Files, box 11, Ford Briefings Aug–Sept 1974, Gerald Ford Library, Ann Arbor, Michigan (hereafter GFL).

108. Memo, Agency Briefing Papers on Major Foreign Policy Issues, August 17, 1974, NSA, Latin American Affairs Staff, Subject Files, box 11, Ford Briefings Aug–Sept 1974, GFL. The discussion in the following paragraphs comes from this document.

109. For more on the Church committee, see David F. Schmitz, "Senator Frank Church, the Ford Administration, and the Challenges of Post-Vietnam Foreign Policy," *Peace and Change* 21, no. 4 (October 1996): 438; Schmitz, *United States and Right-Wing Dictatorships*, 128–37.

110. U.S. Senate, *Final Report of the Select Committee to Study Governmental Operations with Respect to Intelligence Activities*, April 26, 1976 (Washington, D.C.: Government Printing Office, 1976).

111. Quoted in Kornbluh, *Pinochet File*, 223.

112. Senator Edward M. Kennedy to Ms. J. Ellenz, October 26, 1973, M80–048, box 1, Correspondence—Senators, Congressmen, Government Officials, CALA Records.

113. Memcon, State Department Regional Staff Meeting, December 5, 1974, document 5, "The Pinochet File," National Security Archive, http://www.gwu.edu/~nsarchiv/NSAEBB/NSAEBB110/index.htm#doc8, February 3, 2004.

114. At the staff meeting, Kissinger asked: "Also, I'd like to know whether the human rights problem in Chile is that much worse than in other countries in Latin America or whether their primary crime is to have replaced Allende and whether people are now getting penalized, having gotten rid of an anti-American government. Is it worse than in other Latin American countries?" Rogers simply answered, "Yes." Ibid.

115. Memcon, State Department Regional Staff Meeting, December 20, 1974, document 6, "Pinochet File," National Security Archive.

116. Memcon, Secretary of State's Regionals' and Principals' Staff Meeting, December 23, 1974, document 7, "Pinochet File," National Security Archive. The discussion in the following paragraphs comes from this document.

117. "If it happens in Chile now," Kissinger explained to his staff about the legislation, "then it will be Korea next year. There isn't going to be any end to it. And we are going to wind up in an unbelievable precarious position, in which no country can afford to tie up with us, unless it is a pure democracy, then we will find some other reasons."

118. For more on Kissinger's response to early congressional human rights efforts, see Barbara Keys, "Congress, Kissinger, and the Origins of Human Rights Diplomacy," *Diplomatic*

History 34, no. 5 (November 2010): 823–51, and *Reclaiming American Virtue*, 153–77; Schmidli, *Fate of Freedom Elsewhere*, 65–68; Snyder, *From Selma to Moscow*, 131–39.

119. Secretary of State to All Diplomatic Posts, January 17, 1975, James Wilson Papers, 1986 Accretion 9/75–12/75, box 6, GFL.

120. This post reported as a deputy secretary to the secretary of state and also took over preexisting responsibilities for refugees and migration, as well as POW/MIA issues. The organization would also be responsible for agency and department programs associated with human rights issues, such as disaster relief and food programs. Memo Organization of Humanitarian Affairs, March 18, 1975, James Wilson Papers, Human Rights, Subject Files, box 1, HR and HA Office Organization and Personnel Matters, GFL.

121. In a letter to the Senate Foreign Relations Committee in May 1975, Deputy Secretary of State Ingersoll noted that "this is a new position created in response to Congressional interest and the Department's recognition that efforts to address a variety of humanitarian concerns were uncoordinated and less than fully effective." Robert S. Ingersoll to Senator Javits, May 10, 1975, James Wilson Papers, Human Rights, Subject Files, box 1, HR and HA Office Organization and Personnel Matters, GFL.

122. A country analysis strategy plan (CASP) outlines specific goals and policy analysis for a country, which embassy officers and relevant officials use to guide programming and initiatives. AmEmbassy Santiago to Department of State, "FY1976–77 CASP for Chile," May 18, 1975, Chile Declassification Project.

123. The four dissenting officers were John B. Tipton, political officer; Robert S. Steven, political officer; Arthur B. Nixon, labor attaché; and Michael K. Lyons, political officer. AmEmbassy Santiago to Department of State, "FY1976–77 CASP for Chile," May 18, 1975, Chile Declassification Project.

124. Stephen Low to General Brent Scowcroft, "Disarray in Chile Policy," July 1, 1975, NSA, Presidential Country Files, Latin America, box 3, Chile (2), GFL.

125. A White House briefing memo in spring 1975 summarized relations between the two countries as good, despite the fact that the Chilean government "resents" the congressional limits on aid and had made no significant concessions on the human rights issue. Memo, "Presentation of Diplomatic Credentials Ceremony," April 29, 1975, WHCF, CO 33-Chile 8/9/74–9/30/75, box 12, GFL.

126. Memcon, Secretary's Meeting with Foreign Minister Carvajal, September 29, 1975, document 8, "Pinochet File," National Security Archive.

127. "Chile—Round 2," "New Dialogue—Old Rhetoric," *Legislative Update, Latin America* (April/May 1975), WOLA Private Records.

128. John C. Bayley, Letter to the Editor, May 29, 1975, M80–048, box 1, Correspondence-Senators, Congressmen, Government, CALA Records; Department of Treasury, Letter to John Bayley, June 13, 1975, Correspondence-Senators, Congressmen, Government, CALA Records.

129. Memo, Carlyle Maw to Henry Kissinger, "Response to Section 502 B—Security Assistance and Human Rights," May 3, 1975, James Wilson Papers, 1986 Accretion, 5/75–8/75, box 6, GFL.

130. Ibid.

131. The East Asia bureau made similar decisions in South Korea, where security concerns with the fall of Vietnam and Cambodia placed a heightened emphasis on its East Asian ally. The briefing memo noted that a reduction in foreign aid to FY75 levels would "indicate responsiveness to Congressional concern without inflicting serious damage to the ROK security position," even if reducing them below that level would pose too great a risk of destabilizing the Park government. Still, the East Asia bureau recommended that the secretary accept the current proposed level of

funding ($176.6 million) despite acknowledging that doing so was "likely to be considered a flat rejection of Congressman Fraser's express desire to dissociate the U.S. to some extent, from the Park Government" and risked provoking "a major reaction" from Congress that may result in even deeper cuts. The other five countries singled out for attention, with the exception of Spain and Uruguay, which had already been scheduled for a reduction in aid, followed a similar pattern. In Brazil the ARA recommended against cutting off any additional aid as "that reduction would not appear consistent with efforts to strengthen relations with Brazil." Ibid.

132. Thomas Quigley of the USCC and the HRWG, for example, testified before Congress in May 1975 on the impending Foreign Military Sales and Security Act, challenging the notion that it served U.S. security interests or the interests of Latin American populations. "Testimony of Thomas Quigley on Behalf of Division for Latin America, United States Catholic Conference before the Senate Foreign Relations Committee on S.1443 The Foreign Military Sales and Assistance Act," May 4, [1975], Geographic Files, Chile, Ahern, box 54, 1972–73, n.d., WOLA Duke Records.

133. "Foreign Military Sales," *Legislative Update, Latin America* (August 1975), WOLA Private Records.

134. Quoted in "Human Rights—Score One," *Legislative Update, Latin America* (September 1975), WOLA Private Records.

135. Memo from George Lister to William Rogers, "Harkin Amendment," September 16, 1975, box 12, folder 10 W. D. Rogers, Lister Papers.

136. *Chile Newsletter* 2, no. 3 (June 1975), Geographic Files, Chile, Ahern, box 57, Chile Newsletter, WOLA Duke Records.

137. "Human Rights—Score One," *Legislative Update, Latin America* (August/September 1975), WOLA Private Records.

138. Pamphlet, Coalition for a New Foreign and Military Policy, "Cracking the Priorities Dilemma," M94–371, box 5, Coalition for a New Foreign and Military Policy, CALA Records.

139. George Lister to William Rogers, "Harkin Amendment," September 16, 1975, box 12, folder 10 W. D. Rogers, Lister Papers.

140. Memo, "Issue Papers," September 17, 1975, NSA, Latin American Affairs Staff, Subject Files, box 10, Issues and Accomplishments in Latin America (2), GFL.

141. James Wilson to Robert Ingersoll, "D/HA Staffing Problems," October 2, 1975, James Wilson Papers, Subject Files-HU, box 1, HR and HA-Office Organization and Personnel Matters, GFL.

142. "Foreign Assistance Bill—Human Rights Amendment Review," *Legislative Update, Latin America* (October 1975), WOLA Private Records.

143. George Lister to William Rogers, "Bishop Helmut Frenz," March 4, 1975, box 1, Declassified Materials, Lister Papers; George Lister to William Rogers, "Tomic Lunch," August 12, 1975, box 1, Declassified Materials, Lister Papers; George Lister to William Rogers, "Chile Independence Day Rally," September 19, 1975, box 12, folder 10 W. D. Rogers, Lister Papers.

144. George Lister to William Rogers, "U.S. Religious Activists," August 5, 1975, box 12, folder 10 W. D. Rogers, Lister Papers.

145. Joe Eldridge to William Rogers, November 19, 1975, box 7, folder 3 Eldridge, Lister Papers; William Rogers to Joe Eldridge, November 28, 1975, box 12, folder 10 W. D. Rogers, Lister Papers.

146. Specific objectionable provisions included an amendment introduced by Kennedy to cut off MAP and FMS credits to Chile, country reporting demands, and congressional override of appropriations by concurrent resolution. Robert McClosky to Henry Kissinger, "Security Assistance," December 24, 1975, Loen and Leppert Files, box 10, Foreign Assistance (I), GFL.

147. "Christmas Latin America: Military Might for Military Men," *Legislative Update, Latin America* (November 1975), WOLA Private Records.

148. "Year-End Roundup: Human Rights in Latin America," *Legislative Update, Latin America* (December 1975), WOLA Private Records.

149. Americans for Democratic Action, "1976 ADA Platform: Public Policy Recommendations," M97–135, box 35, ADA Records.

150. "Year-End Roundup: Human Rights in Latin America."

151. Memo, "Summary of the Functions and Services Being Performed by the Chile Coordination Group," Mauer Files, IV.1, Chile Coordination Group 1975–6, Amnesty International of the USA, Inc: National Office Records, 1966–2003, Rare Book and Manuscript Library, Columbia University, New York (hereafter AIUSA Records).

152. Pamphlet, National Coordinating Committee for Solidarity with Chile, "Chile: No More Aid," [1976], M82–359, box 2, National Coordinating Committee for Solidarity with Chile, CALA Records.

153. Anthony Lewis, "For Which We Stand: II," *New York Times*, October 2, 1975, Geographic Files, Chile, Ahern, box 55, WOLA Duke Records.

154. A *Washington Post* article noted the bill was also supported by those desiring to cut the budget—particularly the arms budget. Laurence Stern, "Arms Sales Bill Opposed," *Washington Post*, February 1, 1976.

155. Cable CALA to Senator Gaylord Nelson, February 9, 1976, M80–048, box 1, Correspondence-Senators, Congressmen, Government, CALA Records.

156. "Chile—Congress Continues to Press," *Legislative Update, Latin America* (March/April 1976), WOLA Private Records.

157. Press Release, "U.S. Representatives Tom Harkin (D-Iowa), George Miller (D-Cal.), Toby Moffett (D-Conn.)," March 17, 1976, Geographic Files, Chile, Ahern, box 56, Flyers Leaflets, WOLA Duke Records.

158. A list of questions provided to Harkin by IPS focused attention on the state of relations with the United States and the "reaction to the U.S. Senate cut off of military shipments from U.S. to Chile." It also encouraged the delegation to seek out details on exiles, DINA, and nonrecognized prisoners and detention camps. Institute for Policy Studies, "Interview Questions," [March 1976], MSS 1075, box 47, Tom Harkin Chile Questions 1976, IPS Records.

159. Press Release, March 17, 1976, WOLA Duke Records.

160. In a congressional briefing following the trip, Toby Moffett corrected this statement, saying the trip had been partially funded by Methodists and Fund for New Priorities in New York City. The embassy continued by attacking Eldridge directly for his "support to the Allende government and opposition to the present Chilean government" and closed by noting that the trip was financed by the "National Council of Churches." Embassy of Chile Press Release, "Visit to Chile of Representatives Messrs. Moffett [*sic*], Miller, and Harkin," March 16, 1976, Geographic Files, Chile, Ahern, box 56, Flyers Leaflets, WOLA Duke Records.

161. Pamphlet, Coalition for a New Foreign and Military Policy, "$1.7 Billion for Dictators?" 1976, M94–371, box 5, Coalition for a New Foreign and Military Policy, CALA Records.

162. National Legislative Conference on Chile Materials, May 16–17, 1976, Geographic Files, Chile, Ahern, box 55, WOLA Duke Records.

163. Jim Cannon to President Ford, "S. 2662-International Security Assistance and Arms Export Control Act," May 1, 1976, White House Records Office, Legislation Case File, 5/76 S.2662 (1), GFL.

164. Bruce Cameron to Representatives, May 17, 1976, M97–135, box 21, legislative mailings 1973–1976, ADA Records.

165. Congressional Voting-Economic and Military Aid, May 28, 1976, M82–359, box 2, National Coordinating Center in Solidarity with Chile, CALA Records.

166. Coalition for a New Foreign and Military Policy, "Action Alert: Protect Human Rights Victories on House Floor," May 26, 1976, M82–359, box 1, Amnesty International, CALA Records.

167. Jim Cannon to President Ford, "H.R. 13689-International Security Assistance and Arms Export Control Act of 1976," June 30, 1976, White House Records Office, Legislation Case Files, GFL.

168. Telecon, Henry Kissinger and William Rogers, June 3, 1976, from "Kissinger State Department Telecons," National Security Archive, October 1, 2004, http://www.gwu.edu/~nsarchiv/NSAEBB/NSAEBB135/index.htm#chile.

169. Lars Schoultz argues that "there exists no parallel to this address in the first seven years of the Nixon-Ford Administration. The message to American diplomats was that the value of human rights in United States policy toward Latin America had increased considerably." Schoultz, *Human Rights and United States Policy*, 111–12. See also Snyder, *From Selma to Moscow*, 141–42.

170. "Statement by Secretary Kissinger, June 8, on Human Rights," *Department of State Bulletin*, July 5, 1976, 2.

171. Ibid.

172. "A Harsh Warning on Human Rights," *Time*, June 21, 1976, M82–359, box 3, CALA Records.

173. Kissinger stated, "An initial review [of the commission's work on human rights in Cuba] confirms our worst fears of Cuban behavior. We should commend the Commission for its efforts—in spite of the total lack of cooperation of the Cuban authorities—to unearth the truth that many Cuban political prisoners have been victims of inhuman treatment. We urge the Commission to continue its efforts to determine the truth about the state of human rights in Cuba." "Statement by Secretary Kissinger, June 8, on Human Rights," 3, 4.

174. Memcon Kissinger-Pinochet, June 8, 1976, National Security Council, Presidential Country Files, Latin America, box 3, Chile (3), GFL.

175. Brent Scowcroft to Gerald Ford on Kissinger at OAS, June 9, 1976, NSA, Trip Briefing Book and Cables for Kissinger, box 25, June 6–13, Latin America, HAK Messages for the President, GFL.

176. Brent Scowcroft to Gerald Ford on Kissinger at OAS, June 10, 1976, NSA, Trip Briefing Book and Cables for Kissinger, box 25, June 6–13, Latin America, HAK Messages for the President, GFL.

177. Henry Kissinger to Gerald Ford, "Significance of Santiago," July 8, 1976, NSA, Presidential Country Files, Latin America, box 3, Chile (3), GFL.

178. On March 24, 1976, the Argentine military overthrew the government of Isabel Peron, establishing a right-wing military government that would become one of the most notorious violators of human rights in the hemisphere. See chapter 4.

179. Meeting Memo, July 9, 1976, "Electronic Briefing Book No. 133: Kissinger to the Argentine Generals in 1976," National Security Archive, August 27, 2004, http://www.gwu.edu/~nsarchiv/NSAEBB/NSAEBB133/index.htm.

180. George Lister to Harry Shlaudeman, "Senate Democrats' Human Rights Attack," October 3, 1976, box 15, Correspondence, Shlaudeman, Lister Papers; George Lister to Harry Shlaudeman, "Tomorrow's Lunch," October 20, 1976, box 15, Correspondence, Shlaudeman, Lister Papers.

181. Ed Koch to Diane LaVoy, September 29, 1976, Administration Files, General Management, History, box 27, Early History, WOLA Duke Records.

2. Words Are Not Enough

1. Lloyd F. Bitzer, *Carter vs. Ford: The Counterfeit Debates of 1976* (Madison: University of Wisconsin Press, 1980), 295–96, 322.

2. Ford answered, "I don't believe, Mr. Frankel, that the Yugoslavians consider themselves dominated by the Soviet Union. I don't believe that the Rumanians consider themselves dominated

by the Soviet Union. I don't believe that the Poles consider themselves dominated by the Soviet Union. Each of those countries is independent, autonomous. It has its own territorial integrity. And the United States does not concede that those countries are under the domination of the Soviet Union." Ibid., 298.

3. Ibid., 296, 314, 322.

4. Eldridge interview, April 25, 2008. In her memoir Jeri Laber, a founder of Human Rights Watch, writes, "I still remember hearing Carter talk about human rights in one of his televised pre-election debates with Gerald Ford. *Is he talking about what we're doing?* I asked myself incredulously. Within a short time, the words 'human rights' seemed to be on everyone's lips." Jeri Laber, *The Courage of Strangers: Coming of Age with the Human Rights Movement* (New York: Public Affairs, 2002), 80.

5. Jimmy Carter, "Inaugural Address of President Carter," January 20, 1977, *Department of State Bulletin* 76 (January–June 1977): 121.

6. Quoted in "Editorial Note," December 12, 1974, *FRUS 1977–1980*, vol. 1: *Foundations of Foreign Policy*, ed. Kristin L. Ahlberg (Washington, D.C.: Government Printing Office, 2014), document 1.

7. Jimmy Carter, "New Approach to Foreign Policy," May 28, 1975, *FRUS 1977–1980*, vol. 1, document 2.

8. See Mark Mazower, "A Strange Triumph of Human Rights," *Historical Journal* 47, no. 2 (June 2004): 379–98; Kathryn Sikkink, "Reconceptualizing Sovereignty in the Americas: *Houston Journal of International Law* 19, no. 3 (1996–97): 705–24; Greg Grandin, "The Liberal Traditions in the Americas: Rights, Sovereignty, and the Origins of Liberal Multilateralism," *American Historical Review* 117, no. 1 (2012): 68–91.

9. Jimmy Carter, "Our Foreign Relations," March 15, 1976, *FRUS 1977–1980*, vol. 1, document 4.

10. Address by Jimmy Carter, "Relations between World's Democracies," June 23, 1976, *FRUS 1977–1980*, vol. 1, document 6.

11. Zbigniew Brzezinski, *Power and Principle: Memoirs of the National Security Advisor, 1977–1981* (New York: Farrar, Straus & Giroux, 1983), 7.

12. Carter, "Relations between World's Democracies."

13. The platform noted, "In the last eight years, our relations with Latin America have deteriorated amid high-level indifference, increased military domination of Latin American governments, and revelations of extensive American interference in the internal politics of Chile and other nations." "1976 Democratic Party Platform," July 12, 1976, American Presidency Project, https://www.presidency.ucsb.edu/node/273251.

14. Ibid. For more on the Democratic Party platform, see Keys, *Reclaiming American Virtue*, 234–35; Sikkink, *Mixed Signals*, 74.

15. "1976 Democratic Party Platform."

16. Ibid. For more on the wing of the party that embraced traditional Cold War security precepts, see Keys, *Reclaiming American Virtue*, 103–26; Snyder, *From Selma to Moscow*, 18–41. The Helsinki Final Act, also known as the Helsinki Accords, signed in 1975, was the final act of the Conference on Security and Cooperation in Europe. This act provided a framework for improved relations between communist and capitalist nations in Europe and the United States. The accords contained important guarantees to protect and improve human rights observance among the signatory nations, including the Soviet Union and its satellite states. These provided a tangible means for Western governments and advocates to pressure the Soviet Union on its human rights performance, and they became a crucial instrument for domestic actors to challenge the Soviet Union's ongoing abuses of basic human rights. For the definitive work on these accords and the impact of the human rights provisions, see Snyder, *Human Rights Activism*. For more on divides in the Democratic Party, see Thomas Borstelmann, *The 1970s: A New Global History from Civil*

Rights to Economic Inequality (Princeton: Princeton University Press, 2012), 37–62; Keys, *Reclaiming American Virtue*, 225–26, 239, 249–50; Schmidli, *Fate of Freedom Elsewhere*, 91–92; Mary E. Stuckey, *Jimmy Carter, Human Rights, and the National Agenda* (College Station: Texas A&M University Press, 2008), xxvi, 21–24; Zelizer, *Arsenal of Democracy*, 270–300.

17. Address by Jimmy Carter, "Addressing B'nai B'rith," September 8, 1976, *FRUS 1977–1980*, vol. 1, document 9. Keys argues that the speech "adroitly melded liberal and conservative priorities," and she identifies it as a "key step in the evolution of Carter's efforts to define a new foreign policy." Keys, *Reclaiming American Virtue*, 236–37.

18. Minutes of ADA National Board Meeting, March 20, 1976, M2001–087, box 1, ADA Records.

19. "El Salvador: Early Test of the New Morality," *Legislative Update, Latin America* (November/December 1976), box 5, folder 2, WOLA, Lister Papers.

20. The other issue the group identified was rising unemployment. "ADA's Laundry List for the New Administration," December 7, 1976, M97–135, box 4, folder 4, Carter, Pres. Jimmy, ADA Records; Americans for Democratic Action, "An Open Letter to President Carter," November 13 and 14 [1976], M2001–087, box 1, National Board Meeting, ADA Records.

21. "Human Rights and the Presidential Campaign," *Legislative Update, Latin America* (September/October 1976), box 5, folder 2, WOLA, Lister Papers; ADA, "Open Letter to President Carter."

22. Quoted in Cyrus R. Vance, *Hard Choices: Critical Years in America's Foreign Policy* (New York: Simon & Schuster, 1983), 30. Brzezinski came from the post-1945 academic circle of foreign policy specialists, as McGeorge Bundy and Henry Kissinger did; Vance represented the "Wall Street lawyer" who moved between public service and corporate practice in the tradition of Dean Acheson, John Foster Dulles, and Henry Stimson. Both Vance and Brzezinski had been members of that ultimate foreign policy establishment institution, the Council on Foreign Relations, as well as the Trilateral Commission. For more on Carter's selection of Vance and Brzezinski, see Betty Glad, *An Outsider in the White House: Jimmy Carter, His Advisors, and the Making of American Foreign Policy* (Ithaca: Cornell University Press, 2009), 18–28; Scott Kaufman, *Plans Unraveled: The Foreign Policy of the Carter Administration* (DeKalb: Northern Illinois University Press, 2008), 17–23.

23. U.S. Congress, Senate Committee on Foreign Relations, *Nomination of Hon. Cyrus R. Vance to Be Secretary of State: Hearing before the Committee on Foreign Relations*, 95th Congress, 1st session, January 11, 1977 (Washington, D.C.: Government Printing Office, 1977).

24. Ibid.

25. In response to questions by various committee members over how this executive-legislative partnership would work, Vance proposed to meet regularly with relevant congressional committees "to just come, sit with you, and discuss with you any questions which you may have on your mind and wish to raise." He additionally offered his personal office number as a signal of his commitment to openness and collaboration, and he promised to "seek out your views on many of those thorny issues which we face." Ibid.

26. Carter addressed this new international environment when he observed, "The world itself is now dominated by a new spirit. Peoples more numerous and more politically aware are craving and now demanding their place in the sun—not just for the benefit of their own physical condition, but for basic human rights." "Inaugural Address of President Carter," 121.

27. Pastor had been part of the Linowitz Commission on U.S.–Latin American relations and had a wide array of contacts among the individuals and organizations in and out of government concerned with Latin American issues. Brzezinski noted in his memoirs, "I intentionally recruited several individuals whose views were more 'liberal' than mine, but whose expertise on foreign affairs I very much respected." Brzezinski, *Power and Principle*, 75.

28. Derian had been a civil rights activist and one of the founders of the Mississippi Civil Liberties Union. She was also one of the organizers of the Mississippi Freedom Democratic Party, which had challenged the exclusion of blacks from the Mississippi Democratic Party delegation in 1964. Lars Schoultz wrote, "If President Carter wanted an assistant secretary who could present forcefully the case for human rights and who was not intimidated by established bureaucratic procedures, there could have been few better choices than Derian." Schoultz, *Human Rights and United States Policy*, 126. See also Keys, *Reclaiming American* Virtue, 259–61; Schmidli, *Fate of Freedom Elsewhere*, 85–88, Sikkink, *Mixed Signals*, 121–22.

29. Schneider, like Derian, had arrived at human rights through his involvement in the civil rights movement of the 1960s. As a student at Berkley, he worked with the ACLU on civil rights issues before volunteering for the Peace Corps in El Salvador. On returning from Central America, Schneider went to work for Sen. Edward Kennedy as an American Political Science Association fellow. See Schoultz, *Human Rights and United States Policy*, 126; Sikkink, *Mixed Signals*, 57–58.

30. Jessica Tuchman to Zbigniew Brzezinski, "Human Rights," January 24, 1977, *FRUS 1977–1980*, vol. 2: *Human Rights and Humanitarian Affairs*, ed. Kristin L. Ahlberg (Washington, D.C.: Government Printing Office, 2013), document 4.

31. Ibid.

32. On January 21 Andrei Sakharov sent a public letter to President Carter, decrying the human rights situation in the Soviet Union, detailing the Soviet government's abuses of human rights advocates, and urging Carter to assist in the release of Soviet political prisoners. A week later the State Department had released a statement declaring that "any attempts by the Soviet authorities to intimidate Mr. Sakharov will not silence legitimate criticism in the Soviet Union and will conflict with accepted international standards in the field of human rights." This was followed by an open letter to Sakharov by Carter, expressing his "appreciation to you for bringing your thoughts to my personal attention." Carter reassured him that "the American people and our government will continue our firm commitment to promote respect for human rights not only in our own country but also abroad," promising to "use our good offices to seek the release of prisoners of conscience." Both letters were published in the *New York Times*. "Text of Sakharov Letter to Carter on Human Rights," January 29, 1977, https://www.nytimes.com/1977/01/29/archives/text-of-sakharov-letter-to-carter-on-human-rights.html; Gates to Knoche, "Brzezinski Meeting on Human Rights," *FRUS 1977–1980*, vol. 2, document 7, n. 4; Christopher S. Wren, "Sakharov Receives Carter Letter Affirming Commitment on Rights," *New York Times*, February 18, 1977, https://www.nytimes.com/1977/02/18/archives/sakharov-receives-carter-letter-affirming-commitment-on-rights.html.

33. "Draft Outline for a Human Rights Strategy for the United States," February 2, 1977, Records of the Office of the National Security Advisor (hereafter NSA), Brzezinski Materials, Subject Files (tab 7), box 28, Human Rights 2–4/1977, Jimmy Carter Presidential Library, Atlanta (hereafter JCL).

34. Jessica Tuchman to Zbigniew Brzezinski, "Human Rights Proposal," February 18, 1977, *FRUS 1977–1980*, vol. 2, document 16.

35. Anthony Lake to Warren Christopher, "Attached Action Memorandum on Human Rights," March 25, 1977, *FRUS 1977–1980*, vol. 2, document 29.

36. Memorandum for the Record, "Human Rights PRM Meeting," February 28, 1977, *FRUS 1977–1980*, vol. 2, document 22; Lake to Christopher, "Attached Action Memorandum on Human Rights."

37. Tuchman to Brzezinski, "Human Rights Proposal."

38. Jimmy Carter, Address to the U.N. General Assembly, March 17, 1977, *Department of State Bulletin* 76 (1977): 329–33.

39. Lake to Christopher, "Attached Action Memorandum on Human Rights."

40. "Draft Outline for a Human Rights Strategy."

41. The IPS released its *Southern Connection* on February 28, 1977. Chaired by Sol Linowitz, an attorney and former U.S. ambassador to the OAS, the Linowitz Commission was a bipartisan effort, with twenty members drawn from government, academic, and business circles, and funded by the Ford Foundation. Human rights advocates included Rev. Theodore Hesburgh of the University of Notre Dame and Rita Hauser of Freedom House. Released on December 20, 1976, the report was addressed to the new president and Congress, as well as the people of the United States. Commission on United States–Latin American Relations, *The United States and Latin America, Next Steps: A Second Report* (New York: Center for Inter-American Relations, 1976), 1 (hereafter Linowitz Commission); Institute for Policy Studies, *The Southern Connection* (Washington, D.C.: Institute for Policy Studies, 1977); George Lister to Terrance Todman, "IPS Latin America Report," February 27, 1977, box 15, folder 12 Todman, Lister Papers.

42. The *Southern Connection* opened by asserting that "for too long, the United States has approached inter-American relations as if its own economic and military power implied an inherent right to determine unilaterally the character of U.S.–Latin American relations. While the policies of each historical period have been marked by different slogans and characteristics, they all emanated from an unquestioned presumption of U.S. superiority that was reflected in direct and indirect intervention in the internal affairs of nations throughout the hemisphere." *Southern Connection*, 1–2.

43. It urged that "the proposed bill applying the human rights principle to all arms sales be approved and enforced. This step would permit Congress to veto any U.S. weapons deals with countries that systematically violate human rights." Ibid., 20.

44. The report notes that "the Chilean military government, which took power in 1973 with a program of virulent anti-communism and of national development based on the free play of market forces[,] has proven itself one of the most oppressive in the history of Latin America." Ibid., 5.

45. The commission recommended: "In providing economic assistance, bilaterally or through multilateral organizations, the United States should try to avoid supporting regimes which systematically and grossly violate fundamental human rights." Linowitz Commission, 9.

46. Ibid., 1; *Southern Connection*, 2, 4.

47. *Southern Connection*, 6, 5.

48. Linowitz Commission, 9.

49. Robert Pastor was the chief staff person for Latin American Affairs at the National Security Council. Guy Erb, a specialist in "North-South" relations at the NSC, also participated in the drafting of the report. Pastor received his appointment before the *Southern Connection* was completed and hence was not a final signatory. Nonetheless, he clearly engaged in the ideas presented through his participation in the committee's work, even if he could not or would not formally endorse them.

50. "Commission on United States–Latin American Relations," December 20, 1976, box 29, folder 20, Lister Papers; Jimmy Carter to Sol Linowitz, February 3, 1977, WHCF, box CO-9, CO 1–9 1/20/77–1/20/81, JCL.

51. PRM/NSC-17 Review of U.S. Policy toward Latin America, January 26, 1977, NSA, Staff Materials, North/South Pastor (tab 24), box 65, JCL.

52. "Our concern over human rights, the nature of relations with military regimes, our past policies toward Cuba, the revelations of CIA activities, and some activities of multinational corporations affect the way we view ourselves and have significant implications for how others view us. The common thread linking these concerns is U.S. intervention in the internal affairs of

other countries. Covert intervention in Chile in 1970–73 led the United States to become identified with the military dictatorship that replaced Allende, and associated us to some extent with its subsequent abuses of human rights. U.S. actions designed to control Latin American behavior have ranged from economic sanctions to direct military intervention. They have cumulatively cast a pall over our motives and aroused suspicions that may take years to overcome." Presidential Review Memorandum NSC-17, "Review of United States Policy toward Latin America," March 12, 1977, NLC-17–26–1–1–3, JCL.

53. The study noted, "Our reaction to political change in Latin America is critical. Our major interventions of the post-war period . . . have probably had more impact on our relations than all our resource-transfers and business activities combined. They were motivated by a strong East-West bias." Noting the new multilateral power dynamics, the report argued, "In a world of increasing centers of power, the United States will continue to have a security interest in the region's stability and friendship—but our policy goals are increasingly economic and political." Ibid.

54. Ibid.

55. The PRM provoked significant discussion over the nature of the "special relationship" and whether a regional policy was inherently paternalistic and parochial. Many believed that Latin America policy should be reframed as part of a broader prioritization of North-South issues. However, the historical relationship and existing policy frameworks, as well as "collective consciousness in Latin America," all supported the continuation of a regionally targeted policy, even as they moved to embed this in a larger multilateral context of global issues. Robert Pastor noted, "The fact that the President chose Latin America as the one region to have an overall policy review, and the fact that he is being besieged to speak on Pan American Day and to give a major policy address on Latin America, and the fact that the President has repeatedly expressed a special interest in Latin America—all of these are indications that we cannot move from our current policy . . . to no policy in one step." "Minutes of a Policy Review Committee Meeting," March 24, 1977, *FRUS 1977–1980*, vol. 24, document 7; Robert Pastor to Zbigniew Brzezinski, "PRC Meeting on Latin America," March 14, 1977, *FRUS 1977–1980*, vol. 24, document 5.

56. Pastor to Brzezinski, "PRC Meeting on Latin America," italics in original.

57. "Minutes of a Policy Review Committee Meeting," italics in original.

58. Pastor argued, for example, that "human rights should enter into all U.S. decisions with regard to the developing world, but the U.S. should not adopt any automatic or fixed formula." Pastor to Brzezinski, "PRC Meeting on Latin America."

59. PRM NSC-17, "Review of U.S. Policy toward Latin America."

60. "Minutes of a Policy Review Committee Meeting."

61. One object of contention within the administration was how explicit to be in this goal. An early draft of the speech contained the passage "we know this is a pluralistic world with many diverse relationships; working together requires restraints in power. My country will respect and observe those restraints. We will not abuse intelligence and security systems or use methods of manipulation or intervention that we reject at home." This had been vigorously crossed out by one reader and had "good" written next to it by another. Ultimately, the passage was not included in the speech. State Department Memo for Zbigniew Brzezinski, "Presidential Speech on Latin America," March 30, 1977, NSA, Brzezinski Materials, Country Files (tab 6), box 58, OAS, JCL.

62. Jimmy Carter, "President Carter's Pan American Day Address," April 14, 1977, *Department of State Bulletin* 76 (January–June 1977): 454.

63. Lake to Christopher, "Attached Action Memorandum on Human Rights."

64. Ibid.

65. Zbigniew Brzezinski to Jimmy Carter, "Weekly National Security Report #3," March 5, 1977, *FRUS 1977–1980*, vol. 1, document 26.

66. Bob Barber, "Pressure Mounts to Cut Aid to Juntas," *Guardian*, February 9, 1977, Newspaper Clippings File, WOLA Private Records.

67. https://www.gpo.gov/fdsys/pkg/STATUTE-90/pdf/STATUTE-90-Pg729.pdf.

68. Amnesty International, Clergy and Laity Concerned, WOLA, the National Council of Churches, and the U.S. Catholic Conference all contributed to the reports. Members from AI met with Cameron to go over the final letter and the country reports, as well as deliver the letter to Richardson on August 31. There was "vocal opposition" to the need to include "left dictatorships." However, Bruce Cameron, supported by AI, argued that "neither staff nor Members of Congress with whom we were working would feel credible and therefore be willing to act unless these were included." Hence, Peru was added to the list of countries targeted. Bruce Cameron to Hubert Humphrey, August 30, 1976, M97–135, box 21, Legislative Mailings 1973–1976, ADA Records; Bruce Cameron to Paul, September 18, 1976, M97-135, box 22, CDFP, ADA Records; Amnesty International Washington Office to the Executive Board, "Office Activities since the October 15th Report," November 18, 1976, series II.1, box 5, folder 11, AIUSA Records.

69. Cameron to Humphrey, August 30, 1976.

70. Amnesty International Washington Office to the Executive Board, "Office Activities since the October 15th Report." The Movement had cultivated some sympathetic, but limited, partners within the Ford administration's State Department, with whom they had a good working relationship. Members of Amnesty International spoke directly and candidly with Ken Hill at the State Department, trying to find a compromise between the complete classification of the 1976 country reports and their public release. Hill seemed anxious to help and "dispel any notion that the Department was temporizing or trying to cover up embarrassing mistakes." Indeed, he offered to meet with Amnesty International members to talk about the situation in individual countries, and he noted that government sources were often less than candid "because the U.S. government was so often believed to be in league with the government on whom a report was being made." By November Amnesty International's Washington staff concluded that "the State Department intends to adhere to its position regarding classification of the reports. Any public challenge will mean a long and possibly acrimonious battle." Ric to Ginger, "502B Reports," October 30, 1976, series II.1, box 5, folder 11, AIUSA Records.

71. The countries included were Argentina, Haiti, Indonesia, Iran, and the Philippines. U.S. Department of State, *Human Rights and U.S. Policy: Argentina, Haiti, Indonesia, Iran, Peru, and the Philippines, Reports Submitted to the Committee on International Relations, U.S. House of Representatives by the Department of State, pursuant to Section 502B(c) of the International Security Assistance and Arms Export Act of 1976* (Washington, D.C.: Congressional Printing Office, 1976); Americans for Democratic Action, "Human Rights and U.S. and Foreign Policy," January 14, 1977, box 24, folder 14, Lister Papers. Emphasis added by HRWG to original language in the Congressional Presentation Document.

72. "Responsible reports from international legal and human rights groups alleging widespread and routine torture by police and army personnel with the sanction of government leaders are downgraded or disregarded entirely," the letter complained. Coalition for a New Foreign Military Policy to Jimmy Carter, January 17, 1977, M97–135, box 23, Subject Files 74–84, Human Rights, Legislative Program, ADA Records; "Argentina—Armies of the Night—Can It Continue?" *Legislative Update, Latin America* (January/February 1977), WOLA Private Records.

73. Coalition for a New Foreign Military Policy to President Carter, January 17, 1977; Coalition for a New Foreign and Military Policy, Press Release, January 17, 1977, box 29, Coalition for a New Foreign and Military Policy, Lister Papers.

74. Zbigniew Brzezinski to Jessica Tuchman, "Human Rights," January 17, 1977, *FRUS 1977–1980*, vol. 2, document 3; *FRUS 1977–1980*, vol. 2, document 4.

75. Tuchman to Brzezinski, "Human Rights," January 24, 1977; Jessica Tuchman to Zbigniew Brzezinski, "Budget—Security Assistance and Human Rights," February 3, 1977, WHCF, box HU-1, Executive 1/20/77–2/28/77, JCL. Italics in original.

76. Tuchman to Brzezinski, "Budget—Security Assistance and Human Rights," February 3, 1977; Jessica Tuchman to Zbigniew Brzezinski, "Evening Report," February 4, 1977, NLC-28-21–3–14–0, JCL.

77. Lake to Christopher, "Attached Action Memorandum on Human Rights."

78. Robert Pastor to Jessica Tuchman and Robert Kimmitt, "Security Assistance," February 11, 1977, NSA, Staff Materials, North/South Pastor (tab 24), box 1, Argentina, JCL.

79. Jessica Tuchman to Zbigniew Brzezinski, "Budget—Security Assistance and Human Rights," February 7, 1977, NSA, Brzezinski Materials, Subject Files (tab 7), box 28, Human Rights 2–4/1977, JCL.

80. "A Draft Outline for a Human Rights Strategy for the United States," February 2, 1977, NSA, Brzezinski Materials, Subject Files (tab 7), box 28, Human Rights 2–4/1977, JCL. In March, for example, Tuchman argued that legislation on military assistance was "ill-conceived and was causing more problems than it solved. She expressed the hope that on the basis of the Administration's performance in this field that Congress could be persuaded next year to remove this requirement." Memorandum for the Record, "Meeting with Ms. Tuchman and Mr. Kimmitt on Intelligence Support in the Human Rights Field," March 28, 1977, *FRUS 1977–1980*, vol. 2, document 30.

81. Memcon, "Human Rights and Security Assistance," February 8, 1977, *FRUS 1977–1980*, vol. 2, document 11.

82. Action Memorandum, Kempton Jenkins to Cyrus Vance, "Call to Congressional Human Rights Leaders," February 10, 1978, *FRUS 1977–1980*, vol. 2, document 13.

83. Memcon, "Human Rights and Security Assistance," February 8, 1977.

84. Bruce Cameron, "Human Rights and Security Assistance: A Proposal for Reform," February 14, 1977, M97–135, box 23, Legislative Program: Subject File 74–84, Human Rights, ADA Records.

85. "Testimony of Bruce Cameron Legislative Representative on Behalf of Americans for Democratic Action before the Senate Foreign Relations Subcommittee on Foreign Assistance," March 4, 1977, M97–135, box 23, Legislative Program: Subject File 74–84, Human Rights, ADA Records.

86. He observed, "Economic issues have assumed increasing political importance. . . . Equality of economic opportunity has become the paramount goal of diplomacy for 150 developing nations, just as it has been the goal of disadvantaged citizens and regions in American history." "Statement by Secretary of State Vance before the Senate Committee on Appropriations Subcommittee on Foreign Operations," February 24, 1977, *FRUS 1977–1980*, vol. 1, document 22.

87. Ibid.

88. Warren Christopher, "Human Rights: An Important Concern of U.S. Foreign Policy," March 7, 1977, *Department of State Bulletin* 76 (1977): 289–91.

89. As one internal memorandum noted, "We're for human rights, but they're [Republicans] for human rights too. This is not to say that there is no difference. We just haven't been articulating that difference very well." Jim Fallows to Jimmy Carter, "Jerry Doolittle on Notre Dame Speech Draft," May 20, 1977, Hertzberg Donated Materials, Speech Files, box 1, Notre Dame Speech, JCL.

90. "U.S. Military Assistance for Latin America—A Little New but a Lot of the Same," *Legislative Update, Latin America* (March/April 1977), Widener Library, Harvard University, Cambridge, Massachusetts (hereafter Widener Library).

91. An alternative amendment sponsored by Congressman Reuss and Senator Humphrey avoided binding language and instead called on U.S. officials to use their "voice and vote" to advance human rights in IFIs. Zbigniew Brzezinski to Jimmy Carter, "Proposed Administration Position on Human Rights Amendments to International Financial Institution Legislation," April 13, 1977, *FRUS 1977–1980*, vol. 2, document 33.

92. Bruce Cameron to U.S. Representatives, April 4, 1977, M97–135, box 21, Legislative Mailings 1977, ADA Records; Legislative Memo, Chile Legislative Center, "Human Rights and International Loans," April 12, 1977, M82–359, box 2, National Coordinating Committee for Solidarity with Chile, CALA Records.

93. Bruce Cameron to U.S. Representatives, April 4, 1977; Legislative Memo, Chile Legislative Center, "Human Rights and International Loans," April 12, 1977.

94. Brzezinski to Carter, "Proposed Administration Position on Human Rights Amendments to International Financial Institution Legislation."

95. Zbigniew Brzezinski to Jimmy Carter, March 5, 1977, Brzezinski Donated Materials, box 41, Weekly Reports, JCL.

96. Cyrus Vance to Jimmy Carter, "International Financial Institutions Authorization Bill," April 15, 1977, Staff Offices, Office of the Secretary (Handwriting File), box 16, JCL.

97. Ibid.; Jessica Tuchman to Jane Pisano and Zbigniew Brzezinski, "Proposed Administration Position on Human Rights Amendments to IFI Legislation," April 13, 1977, Staff Offices, Counsel (Lipshutz), box 19, Human Rights and IFI Legislation, JCL.

98. Jessica Tuchman to Zbigniew Brzezinski, "Human Rights," April 20, 1977, *FRUS 1977–1980*, vol. 2, document 38.

99. "State Department: Mixed Signals Secure Somoza Aid," *Update Latin America* (May/June 1977), Widener Library.

100. Cyrus Vance, "Human Rights and Foreign Policy," April 30, 1977, *Department of State Bulletin* 76 (1977): 505.

101. Ibid.

102. Vance, *Hard Choices*, 46.

103. "One Hundred Days of the Carter Administration," April 26, 1977, M97–135, box 4, folder 27, ADA Records; "Press Release: ADA Adopts 1977 Platform," May 5, 1977, M97–135, box 30, Press Releases 1977, ADA Records.

104. Tuchman argued, "Although we run the obvious risk of getting worthless mush out of it, I believe that it would be useful to force even the more philosophical issues onto paper. Otherwise, we will constantly be responding to the issues as they arise in an ad hoc manner and will probably continue to drift into the kind of mess we are now in on the IFIs." Tuchman to Brzezinski, "Human Rights," April 20, 1977.

105. Jane Pisano to David Aaron, "Interagency Group on Human Rights," May 6, 1977, *FRUS 1977–1980*, vol. 2, document 41.

106. Schneider proposed retracting the request for a PRM on human rights on the basis that that policy was being resolved and that "overall coordination will be hampered by interfering in process already set in motion by NSC April 1 memo." Mark Schneider to Patricia Derian, "PRM Meeting," May 23, 1977, *FRUS 1977–1980*, vol. 2, document 49.

107. Telegram from the Department of State to All Diplomatic and Consular Posts, "Secretary's Human Rights Speech. For Ambassador from Acting Secretary," April 30, 1977, *FRUS 1977–1980*, vol. 2, document 39.

108. Shortly before Vance gave his speech, Carter sent him a note stating, "The Law Day speech is very good. I'll do a much broader speech at Notre Dame. Good luck in Georgia. They'll like you & the speech." Address by Cyrus Vance, "Human Rights and Foreign Policy," April 30, 1977, *FRUS 1977–1980*, vol. 1, document 37.

109. Jimmy Carter, "University of Notre Dame: Address at Commencement Exercises at the University, May 22, 1977," *Public Papers of the President, Jimmy Carter, 1977* (Washington, D.C.: Government Printing Office, 1978), 957–58.

110. Vance also circulated Carter's speech to all U.S. ambassadors. "To ensure that the priority which the President and the Secretary place on human rights is fully reflected at your post, I request that you continue to give human rights matters your personal attention and you direct the Embassy's work on human rights." Telegram from the Department of State to All Diplomatic Posts, "Priority Attention to Human Rights," May 28, 1977, *FRUS 1977–1980*, vol. 2, document 51.

111. Memorandum for the Record, "Initial Meeting of Interagency Working Group for PRM—28 (Human Rights)," May 24, 1977, *FRUS 1977–1980*, vol. 2, document 50.

112. Warren Christopher to Charles William Maynes, "U.S. Policy on Human Rights: Actions to Be Taken," May 30, 1977, *FRUS 1977–1980*, vol. 2, document 52.

113. David Aaron to Zbigniew Brzezinski, "Human Rights," April 12, 1977, *FRUS 1977–1980*, vol. 2, document 32. For more on internal divides within the administration, see Scott Kaufman, *Plans Unraveled*, 30–32; Schmidli, *Fate of Freedom Elsewhere*, 97–98, 107–15; Tuchman to Brzezinski, "Human Rights," April 20, 1977.

114. PRM NSC-28: Human Rights, July 8, 1977 (hereafter PRM on Human Rights), Robert Lipshutz Files, box 19, JCL. The discussion in the succeeding paragraphs is taken from this document.

115. "Rosalynn Carter's Latin America Trip: Sea Legs for New Policy," *Update Latin America* (May/June 1977), Widener Library.

116. "OAS in Grenada: Obstacles to a Hemispheric Human Rights Policy," *Update Latin America* (May/June 1977), Widener Library.

117. Pastor to Brzezinski, "Evening Report," May 18, 1977, NLC-24-99-6-2-9, JCL.

118. Ginger McRae to Whitney Ellsworth, David Hawk, and Andrew Blane, "IPS Luncheon," June 29, 1977, series II.1, box 5, folder 11, AIUSA Records.

119. ADA to U.S. Senators, June 8, 1977, M97–135, box 21, Legislative Mailings 1977, ADA Records.

120. Minutes, Human Rights Working Group, July 12, 1977, M94–371, box 5, Coalition for a New Foreign and Military Policy, CALA Records.

121. "Human Rights: Scorecard of the 95th Congress," *Update Latin America* (July/August 1977), Widener Library. Italics in original.

122. Bruce Cameron to U.S. Representatives, September 9, 1977, M97–135, box 21, Legislative Mailings 1977, ADA Records. Italics in original.

123. In Chile, Todman called the abolishment of DINA "very positive," and after his visit to Argentina, Todman stated, "Everyone I talked with believes there has been an important improvement in all areas." "U.S. Official Has Talks in Argentina," *New York Times*, August 16, 1977, 6; see also "A U.S. Official Praises Chile's Action on Police," *New York Times*, August 14, 1977, 46; "Limited Rights Advances Are Reported by Todman," *New York Times*, August 26, 1977; "U.S. Rights Drive Asks Aid of Latin Military," *New York Times*, August 17, 1977, 7.

124. Horacio Lofredo, Argentine Commission for Human Rights to Jimmy Carter, August 31, 1977, NSA, Staff Materials, North/South Pastor (tab 24), box 1, Argentina, JCL. Italics in original. For more on Todman's meetings, see chapters 3 and 4.

125. The authors of the *Southern Connection* wrote, "We believe that a mutually satisfactory resolution of the status of the Panama Canal is a crucial step in rethinking the Southern Connection," the report stated. "The need for a new Treaty that clearly recognized Panama's sovereignty in the area is, significantly, an issue on which all Latin American and Caribbean nations agree." *Southern Connection*, 7.

126. Memo Brzezinski to Carter, "Nineteen Bilaterals: The Significance of Treaty Signing for Inter-American Relations," n.d. [September 1977], *FRUS 1977–1980*, vol. 24, document 23.

127. Lofredo, Argentine Commission for Human Rights, to Jimmy Carter, August 31, 1977.

128. "Dictators in Washington," *Chile Legislative Center Bulletin* (October 1977), M93–165, box 158, Chile—Culture and Education, IPS Records.

129. "An Open Letter to President Carter," *Washington Post*, September 7, 1977, A20.

130. James Abourezk to Jimmy Carter, August 29, 1977, WHCF, Executive, box CO-15, CO-33 Chile, JCL.

131. Zbigniew Brzezinski to James Abourezk, September 24, 1977, WHCF, Executive, box CO-15, CO-33 Chile, JCL; Jody Powell to John Burton, September 9, 1977, WHCF, Executive, box CO-15, CO-33 Chile, JCL.

132. When Carter raised the issue, Pinochet boldly affirmed the importance of human rights principles and asserted, "The military coup was designed precisely to preserve human rights." Pinochet's use of human rights rhetoric to legitimize brutalities, no matter how insincere or hypocritical, speaks to the degree to which human rights rhetoric had become entrenched in international diplomacy in recent years. In the meeting, Carter "noted that he had no inclination to disagree with Pinochet's assessment of the situation in Chile. Yet, in the eyes of the world, Chile still had a human rights problem. The President asked for Pinochet's suggestions on how the problem could be alleviated—how to improve the world perception and demonstrate that the progress was real. He asked if he, the UN or the OAS could help." Pinochet responded by suggesting that "everyone should come to Chile to see . . . that what is going on inside of Chile is not what they say." Carter, in response, "picked up on the latter point and asked Pinochet to what degree he would permit outside observers. He did not want to interfere but saw outside observation as a way of clearing up the allegations." Memcon, President Carter/President Pinochet Bilateral, September 6, 1977, Chile Declassification Project.

133. The fallout from the images could have been avoided, had Carter heeded the warnings of two different congressmen that such photos would damage his reputation with the advocate community. In a telegram to Carter, Congressman Fraser had suggested he avoid such photo ops. "In light of the fact that the U.S. policy with respect to these governments varies widely, and that sufficient evidence in the past has shown pictures taken with the President and certain leaders has been expressly misused and abused, I would urge that you avoid any potentially detrimental or compromising publicity with the respective leaders." Congressman Burton also urged that "no individual photos be permitted with the president and either General Pinochet or General Videla. Such photos, I feel, would appear as duplicitous to the American people, and would discourage those inside Chile and Argentina who work for the restoration of human rights and democratic government." The administration could have easily avoided at least individual photos with the most problematic leaders, thereby preventing the very scenario that both Fraser and Barton had warned of and raising doubts about his credibility with the advocate community. Donald Fraser to Jimmy Carter, August 31, 1977, WHCF, box CO-9, CO 1–9, 1/20/77–1/20/81, JCL; John Burton to Jody Powell, September 6, 1977, WHCF, Executive, box CO-15, CO-33 Chile, JCL.

134. "Latin America Policy: Where to Jimmy?" *Update Latin America* (September/October 1977), Widener Library.

135. Ibid.

136. Susanna McBee, "Fears That Carter Is Easing on Rights Expressed on Hill," *Washington Post*, October 25, 1977, Newspaper Clippings File, WOLA Private Records.

137. Ibid.

138. Presidential Directive, NSC-30, "Human Rights," February 17, 1978, Vertical Files, Presidential Directives, JCL.

139. Zbigniew Brzezinski to Jimmy Carter, "NSC Report for 1977: A Critical Self-Appraisal," January 12, 1978, NLC-128–9–13–5–1, JCL.

140. Ibid.

3. A Special Responsibility

1. Quoted in Mary McGrory, "A Murder's Buried under a Junta's Lies," *Chicago Tribune*, September 27, 1976, C4.

2. Chilean Decree 588 quoted by Orlando Letelier in an op-ed piece he wrote just days before his murder. It was published posthumously in the *New York Times*. Orlando Letelier, "A Testament," *New York Times*, September 27, 1976, 31.

3. Between September 1973 and May 1976, Sen. Edward Kennedy and Rep. Donald Fraser alone sponsored more than a dozen hearings on Chile. See chapter 1 for more on these hearings and Orlando Letelier.

4. As noted in chapter 2, Carter showcased human rights problems in Chile in his second presidential debate with Gerald Ford.

5. "Transcript of News Conference Held by President-Elect Carter in Georgia," *New York Times*, November 15, 1977, 32; "The Carter Administration," *National Coordinating Center in Solidarity with Chile Newsletter* (February / March 1977), M80–048, box 4, National Coordinating Center in Solidarity with Chile / National Chile Center (hereafter NCCSC), CALA Records.

6. Quoted in Vicaría de la Solidaridad, *Informe* [Internal Monthly Report of the Vicaría], November 1976, 27, Arzobispado de Santiago Fundación de Documentación y Archivo de la Vicaría de la Solidaridad, Santiago, Chile (hereafter Vicaría Archive). The report continued, however, by saying that Carter's statements on November 15, after the election, seemed to indicate that his campaign statements were not completely made without responsibility ["no eran tan 'sin responsabilidad'"] and that respect for human rights would be a "predominant" consideration for the United States.

7. "Fear and Loathing in Santiago," *Chile Committee for Human Rights Newsletter*, January 1977, Geographic Files, Chile, Ahern, box 60, Unsorted Serials, WOLA Duke Records.

8. "Fear and Loathing in Santiago"; *Informe*, October 1976, 6, Vicaría Archive. Darren Hawkins argues that "human rights pressures helped lead to limited yet important changes in discourse and behavior in Chile's authoritarian government from 1976 to 1977." Hawkins, *International Human Rights and Authoritarian Rule*, 102.

9. *Informe*, November 1976, 26, 27, Vicaría Archive; AmEmbassy Santiago to Secretary of State, "Release of Chilean Detainees: The Talk of the Town," November 26, 1976, Chile Declassification Project; Foreign Broadcast Information Service, "Foreign Media Reaction to Change in U.S. Administration," November 26, 1976, Chile Declassification Project.

10. "Foreign Media Reaction to Change in U.S. Administration," November 26, 1976, Chile Declassification Project.

11. Mary McGrory, "This 'Victory' Needs a Closer Look," *Washington Star*, November 22, 1976, M94–371, box 5, CNFMP, CALA Records.

12. "Editorial: Premature Euphoria," *Chile Committee for Human Rights Newsletter*, January 1977, Geographic Files, Chile, Ahern, box 60, Unsorted Serials, WOLA Duke Records.

13. Secretary Vance to President Carter, "Evening Report," January 24, 1977, NSA, Brzezinski Papers, Subject Files (tab 7), box 17, JCL. The invitation had been issued under the Ford administration during the postelection transition, and Lavin's visit overlapped with Carter's inauguration. The program operated under the jurisdiction of the Fulbright-Hays Act. Its purpose was "to enable current and potential opinion leaders and decision makers to gain through first-hand experience in the U.S. more accurate perception and deeper understanding" of the country. Secretary of State to AmEmbassy Santiago, "Press Guidance re Visit of Ltc. Lavin," January 25, 1977, Chile Declassification Project.

14. The National Coordinating Center in Solidarity with Chile reported that it had "contacted appropriate committees throughout the country and was joined by the National Council of Churches, Amnesty International, and other organizations in protesting the visit." "Junta Torturer Expelled from the U.S.," *National Coordinating Committee in Solidarity with Chile Newsletter* (February/March 1977), M80–048, box 4, NCCSC, CALA Records.

15. Jack Anderson, a reputable journalist sympathetic to the Movement's agenda, had been reporting on Chile since the coup. Secretary of State to AmEmbassy Santiago, "Allegations against Cmdt. Jamie Lavin," January 24, 1977, Chile Declassification Project.

16. Secretary of State to AmEmbassy Santiago, "Press Guidance re Visit of Ltc. Lavin"; Vance to Carter, "Evening Report," January 24, 1977; Secretary of State to AmEmbassy Santiago, "Jamie Lavin," January 27, 1977, Chile Declassification Project; AmEmbassy Santiago to Secretary of State, "Jamie Lavin," January 26, 1977, Chile Declassification Project.

17. Secretary of State to AmEmbassy Santiago, "Jamie Lavin," January 27, 1977.

18. Robert Pastor to Arthur Katzman, March 3, 1977, WHCF, CO-33 (Chile), box CO-15, Executive, 1/20/77–1/20/81, JCL; Secretary of State to AmEmbassy Santiago, "Press Guidance re Visit of Ltc. Lavin."

19. Secretary of State to AmEmbassy Santiago, "Jamie Lavin," January 27, 1977.

20. Popper had been named ambassador to Chile by Richard Nixon in February 1974. He stayed in the position throughout the Ford administration until he was replaced by Carter appointee George Landau in May 1977. Secretary of State to AmEmbassy Santiago, "Lavin Affair," February 15, 1977, Chile Declassification Project.

21. Secretary of State to AmEmbassy Santiago, "Ambassador Cauas' Presentation of Credentials to the President," March 24, 1977, Vertical File, box 40, Human Rights-Chile, 6/30/99, JCL.

22. Eduardo Frei was the president of Chile from 1964 to 1970 and a leader in the centrist Christian Democratic Party. Frei was defeated by Allende in the 1970 election and was subsequently critical of the Allende government, seeing it as a communist front that undermined the constitutional rule of law in Chile. The Christian Democrats, including Frei, initially supported the military coup of 1973 but became increasingly critical in the years following the coup and ultimately became the core of the moderate opposition to Pinochet. Frei died in 1982, and an autopsy more than twenty-five years later found that he had been poisoned, likely by the Pinochet regime. Juan Ferero, "Judge Says Chilean Ex-President's 1982 Death Was by Poisoning," *Washington Post*, December 9, 2009, http://www.washingtonpost.com/wp-dyn/content/article/2009/12/08/AR2009120804389.html.

23. George Lister to William Luers, "Frei-Mondale Meeting," May 31, 1977, Declassified Materials, box 1, Lister Papers; North-South Staff to Zbigniew Brzezinski, "Evening Report," May 11, 1977, NLC-10–2–5–7–6, JCL.

24. Robert Pastor to Zbigniew Brzezinski, "Proposed Visit of President Frei," May 13, 1977, WHCF, Country Files, box CO-15, CO-33 Chile, Confidential, JCL.

25. Meeting Memo, May 16, 1977, Vertical File, Human Rights, box 40, Chile 6/30/1999, JCL.

26. Zbigniew Brzezinski to Walter Mondale, "Your Meeting with Eduardo Frei," May 24, 1977, Vertical File, Human Rights, box 40, Chile, 6/30/1999, JCL.

27. North-South Staff to Brzezinski, "Evening Report," May 26, 1977.

28. Memo, "Review of United States Policy toward Latin America," [March 12, 1977], *FRUS 1977–1980*, vol. 24, document 4.

29. Peter Tarnoff to Zbigniew Brzezinski, "Human Rights Policy Impact; Latin America," May 11, 1977, *FRUS 1977–1980*, vol. 24, document 13.

30. "Review of United States Policy toward Latin America."

31. Meeting Memo, May 16, 1977, Vertical File, box 40, Human Rights, Chile 6/30/99, JCL; Department of State Memcon, Chilean Ambassador Jorge Cauas, Deputy Assistant Secretary William H. Luers, ARA, "Forthcoming Visits of Chilean Political Figures to Senior U.S. Officials," May 24, 1977, Vertical File, box 40, Human Rights, Chile 6/30/99, JCL.

32. State Department Memcon, [Frei Visit], May 16, 1977, Vertical File, box 40, Human Rights, Chile, 6/30/99, JCL.

33. Zbigniew Brzezinski to Jimmy Carter, "Report on the Impact of U.S. Human Rights Policy on Latin America," May 16, 1977, NLC-24-55-5-6-4, JCL.

34. North-South to Zbigniew Brzezinski, "Evening Report," March 18, 1977, NLC-10-1-6-34-6, JCL; North-South to Zbigniew Brzezinski, "Evening Report," May 11, 1977, NLC-10-2-5-7-8, JCL.

35. Memcon, Walter Mondale, Zbigniew Brzezinski, Eduardo Frei, Denis Clift, Robert Pastor, "Vice President's Meeting with Former Chilean President Eduardo Frei," May 25, 1977, Vertical File, box 40, Human Rights, Chile, 6/30/99, JCL.

36. For more on the Carter administration's pressure through the UN, see Paul Sigmund, *The United States and Democracy in Chile* (Baltimore: Johns Hopkins University, 1993), 110, 113.

37. Alan Riding, "Vance Takes Theme of Rights to OAS," *New York Times*, June 15, 1977, 7.

38. Terrance Todman to Cyrus Vance, "Your Meeting with Admiral Patricio Carvajal at Grenada," June 3, 1977, Chile Declassification Project; AmEmbassy Santiago to Secretary of State, "Secretary's Bilateral with Chilean Foreign Minister Carvajal as Reported by 'El Mercurio,'" June 18, 1977, Chile Declassification Project.

39. Robert Pastor to Zbigniew Brzezinski, "Frei/Almeyda Visit," May 19, 1977, Vertical File, box 40, Human Rights, Chile 6/30/99, JCL.

40. The report stated, "Although the Foreign Ministry document discusses the option of rejection of U.S. policy as interventionists, its recommendation suggests that a fundamental normalization of relations depends on a Chilean government decision to relax its emergency powers." National Intelligence Daily Cable, "Chile: Human Rights Strategy," June 13, 1977, Chile Declassification Project.

41. DDI Daily Intelligence Briefing, "Reports of Gross Violations of Human Rights in Chile," May 25, 1977, Chile Declassification Project.

42. The Vicaría reported a significant drop in deaths and disappearances in 1977—only 25, as opposed to 139 in 1976. *Report of the Chilean National Commission on Truth and Reconciliation*, 903.

43. "Communiqué of the 28 Relatives of 'Disappeared' Persons on Hunger Strike in Santiago," June 14, 1977, M80-048, box 4, NCCSC, CALA Records.

44. Secretary of State to AmEmbassy Santiago, "Human Rights Demonstrators in UNECLA Headquarters," June 18, 1977, Chile Declassification Project; USMission USUN to Secretary of

State and AmEmbassy Santiago, "Human Rights Protesters in UNECLA Office in Santiago," June 16, 1977, Chile Declassification Project.

45. David Popper stepped down from his position as ambassador in May 1977 and was replaced by George Landau in November, making Boyatt one of the highest-ranking officials at the U.S. embassy at this time.

46. AmEmbassy Santiago to Secretary of State, "Pinochet: ECLA Hunger Strike; Human Rights," June 20, 1977, Chile Declassification Project.

47. See Stern's analysis of "Crisis and Institutionalization" in *Battling for Hearts and Minds*, 138–40.

48. National Coordinating Center for Solidarity with Chile Memo, "New Events in Chile, August–Dec 1977," M82–359, box 2, NCCSC, CALA Records.

49. In a discussion of the PRM on Latin America in March, for example, Todman stressed that the question of human rights "aroused the greatest interest and controversy in Latin America where the U.S. has had a long history of intervention—most recently in the Dominican Republic and Chile. Now we are being accused of intervention on behalf of human rights. The question is: to what extent do we need to intervene?" Minutes of a Policy Review Committee Meeting, "Latin America," March 24, 1977, *FRUS 1977–1980*, vol. 24, document 7. Todman had initially opposed Frei's meeting with the vice president, seeking to lower its profile by proposing to meet with Frei himself. Pastor to Brzezinski, "Frei/Almeyda Visit," May 19, 1977.

50. Robert Pastor to Zbigniew Brzezinski, n.d. [attached to Luigi memo dated May 26, 1977], NSA, Staff Material, North/South Pastor (tab 24), box 9, Chile 2–8/1977, JCL.

51. Robert Pastor to Zbigniew Brzezinski, "Recent Developments, Chile," [July 9, 1977], NSA, Brzezinski Materials, Country Files (tab 6), box 7, Chile, JCL.

52. Pastor to Brzezinski, "U.S. Policy to Chile: An Attempt at Some Consistency," August 9, 1977, NSA, Brzezinski Materials, Country Files (tab 6), box 7, Chile, JCL.

53. Ibid.

54. Ibid. AmEmbassy Santiago to Secretary of State, "'Todman Visit: First Day's Activities in Santiago," August 13, 1977, Chile Declassification Project.

55. AmEmbassy Santiago to Secretary of State, "Pinochet Abolishes National Intelligence Directorate (DINA): Creates National Information Center (CNI)," August 12, 1977, Chile Declassification Project.

56. A U.S. intelligence brief noted that "Chileans have been debating whether the risks of internal subversion are so great that they have to risk jeopardizing their traditional good relations with the US, especially when there is no alternative benefactor." Regional and Political Analysis: Latin America "Focus on Human Rights," August 18, 1977, Chile Declassification Project. Internal documents note that while repressive tactics could still occur under this new arrangement, "It appears that opportunities for repressive practices will be greatly reduced." Regional and Political Analysis: Latin America "Focus on Human Rights," August 18, 1977, Chile Declassification Project. For more on DINA, see Wright, *State Terrorism in Latin America*, 63–68.

57. AmEmbassy Santiago to Secretary of State, "GOC Officials Comment on Changes in DINA: Creation of CNI," August 13, 1977, Chile Declassification Project.

58. "U.S. Official Has Talks in Argentina," *New York Times*, August 16, 1977, 6; see also "A U.S. Official Praises Chile's Action on Police," *New York Times*, August 14, 1977, 46; "Limited Rights Advances Are Reported by Todman," *New York Times*, August 26, 1977; "U.S. Rights Drive Asks Aid of Latin Military," *New York Times*, August 17, 1977, 7.

59. John Dinges, "Visiting U.S. Official Praises Progress on Human Rights in Chile," *Washington Post*, August 14, 1977, box 21, Activities and Organizations—Travel, Assistant Secretary Todman, Periodicals/Articles, August 1977, Lister Papers.

60. "Todman's View of Chilean 'Reality,'" *Chile Legislative Bulletin* 2, no. 2 (October 1977): 2, CALA Records. The administration acknowledged that Todman "has tried to emphasize the readiness of our Government to recognize progress" and "to avoid the development of a sterile adversary relationship." The statement continued that "at no time did he allege that the human rights situation in the Southern Cone countries was satisfactory," although his statement may have given that impression. It reasserted that the State Department "continues to be disappointed with the lack of political freedom in Chile." Quoted in Schoultz, *Human Rights and United States Policy*, 117–18.

61. Eugenio Velasco to Robert Pastor, August 22, 1977, NSA, Staff Materials, North/South Pastor (tab 24), box 9, Chile 2–8/1977, JCL. Italics in original.

62. José Zalaquett, "A Skeptical View of 'Progress' in Chile," *Washington Post*, August 22, 1977, M80–048, box 4, NCCSC, CALA Records.

63. The text initially read, "kept to a minimum and that our relations should be cordial but cool," with the "cordial but" later crossed out. Memo, "Chile—A Tactical Plan," November 15, 1977, Chile Declassification Project. Italics in original.

64. Regional and Political Analysis: Latin America, "Chile Running Hot and Cold," September 1, 1977, Chile Declassification Project.

65. National Intelligence Daily Cable, December 2, 1977, Chile Declassification Project.

66. Anthony Lake to Cyrus Vance, "Country Priorities in Latin America," February 26, 1978, *FRUS 1977–1980*, vol. 24, document 28.

67. "Chile: Still Dreary After All These Years," *Update Latin America* (January/February 1978), Administrative Files, General Management, History, box 30, WOLA Update 1978–81, WOLA Duke Records.

68. John Dinges and Saul Landau, *Assassination on Embassy Row* (New York: Pantheon, 1980), 337–38, 364–66; see also Stern, *Battling for Hearts and Minds*, 432n35.

69. *Report of the Chilean National Commission on Truth and Reconciliation*, 757.

70. Quoted in Stern, *Battling for Hearts and Minds*, 148.

71. CIA Intelligence Evaluation, "Pinochet Plans New Legislation Protecting Human Rights," March 2, 1978, Chile Declassification Project.

72. *Report of the Chilean National Commission on Truth and Reconciliation*, 757.

73. The embassy reported in April that "the price within the military for going along with the amnesty for anti-GOC elements was clearly to provide legal immunity for themselves now that, as demonstrated in the Letelier affair, Pinochet and the executive cannot guarantee protection." AmEmbassy Santiago to Secretary of State, "Chilean Government Declares Broad Amnesty," April 19, 1978, Chile Declassification Project.

74. In April WOLA reported, "While Pinochet has been making concessions to placate his critics, domestic criticism mounts, becoming stronger and more frequent than ever." "Chile: Pinochet under Siege," *Update Latin America* (March/April 1978), Administrative Files, General Management, History, box 30, WOLA Update 1978–81, WOLA Duke Records.

75. *Report of the Chilean National Commission on Truth and Reconciliation*, 756, 761.

76. The report noted that a "careful examination of the amnesty program reveals that the beneficiaries of the government pardon will not be the politically persecuted; instead, amnesty will serve to pardon Junta officials of all crimes of torture, kidnapping, and murder committed during the regime," and it called the effects on the politically persecuted "insignificant." Washington Office on Latin America, "Chile: Justice in the Balance," June 1, 1978, Chile Declassification Project.

77. Chile Legislative Center to Chile Committees and Key Contacts, May 19, 1978, CALA Records.

78. AmEmbassy Santiago to Secretary of State, "Vicariate and Supreme Court Fence over Missing Chileans," January 28, 1977, Chile Declassification Project.

79. Ibid.; AmEmbassy Santiago to Secretary of State, "The Chilean Amnesty and the Disappeared," May 24, 1978, Chile Declassification Project. See also Hilbink, *Judges beyond Politics*.

80. AmEmbassy Santiago to Secretary of State, "Reaction to the Chilean Amnesty," April 26, 1978, Chile Declassification Project; AmEmbassy Santiago to Secretary of State, "More Hunger Strikes by Relatives of Missing Chileans," May 22, 1978, Chile Declassification Project. For more on the hunger strikes and their impact, see Lowden, *Moral Opposition to Authoritarian Rule*, 77–83, and Stern, *Battling for Hearts and Minds*, 149–55.

81. On June 1, one solidarity network bulletin reported sympathy hunger strikes taking place in the Federal Republic of Germany, England, Canada, Sweden, Holland, Venezuela, Italy, Norway, France, Belgium, Austria, Switzerland, Argentina, Mexico, Australia, and Costa Rica, as well as Tucson, Los Angeles, San Francisco, New York City, Boston, Washington, D.C., and Philadelphia. National Chile Center Bulletin, "Urgent Action Update on Hunger Strike," June 1, 1978, M82–359, box 2, NCCSC, CALA Records; Madison Campus Ministry and CALA Bulletin, "Chilean Hunger Strike," June 3, 1978, M82–359, box 2, NCCSC, CALA Records.

82. North-South Staff to Zbigniew Brzezinski, "Evening Report," May 31, 1978, NLC-10–12–1–18–7, JCL.

83. Memcon at AmEmbassy Santiago, Ambassadors of Norway, the Netherlands, and Austria, Chargés of the United Kingdom, Denmark, Sweden, Federal Republic of Germany, and Italy, Father Christian Precht, Vicariate of Solidarity, Abogado Javier Luis Egaña, Vicariate of Solidarity, ADCM Moorhead, "Human Rights; Cardinal's Trip; Disappeared; Hunger Strike," June 1, 1978, Chile Declassification Project.

84. Senator Abourezk received an almost identical letter a week earlier. Hodding Carter to Mr. Gedicks re Hunger Strike, June 29, 1978, M82–359, box 2, Political Prisoners Campaign—Chile, CALA Records; State Department to Senator Abourezk, June 15, 1978, WHCF, CO, box CO-15, CO 33 Chile, Executive Files, JCL.

85. AmEmbassy Santiago to Secretary of State, "The Chilean Amnesty and the Disappeared Problem," May 24, 1978, Chile Declassification Project.

86. AmEmbassy Santiago to Secretary of State, "Overview of Human Rights in Chile: First Third of 1978," May 26, 1978, Chile Declassification Project; Global Issues Staff to Zbigniew Brzezinski, "Evening Report," June 5, 1978, NLC-28–36–6–13–2, JCL.

87. "Chile: Pinochet under Siege," *Update Latin America* (March/April 1978), Administrative Files, General Management, History, box 30, WOLA Update 1978–81, WOLA Duke Records.

88. Cynthia Arnson and Michael Klare, "U.S. Still Equips Chile's Military—Despite Embargo," [January 1978], Geographic Files, Chile, WOLA, box 66, Chile: U.S. Policy, WOLA Duke Records.

89. Bruce Cameron to Members of Congress regarding Foreign Assistance Appropriation Bill, June 14, 1978, M97–135, box 21, folder 17, Legislative Mailings 1978, ADA Records; Bruce Cameron to Interested Senators and Staff, "Security Assistance and Human Rights," May 10, 1978, M97–135, box 21, folder 17, Legislative Mailings 1978, ADA Records; Bruce Cameron to Representatives, May 8, 1978, M97–135, box 21, folder 17, Legislative Mailings 1978, ADA Records, italics in original. HR 12157 authorized the continued operation for the EXIM Bank for the coming fiscal year. The amendment applied the "basic Harkin language" prohibiting financing for all countries engaged in "consistent pattern of gross violations of basic human rights." Cameron to Representatives, May 8, 1978.

90. Of the "no" votes, two were for Chile, three for Argentina, two for Uruguay, and one each for Paraguay and South Yemen. "Report Prepared by the Interagency Group on Human Rights and Foreign Assistance Concerning the Effectiveness of U.S. Human Rights Actions in the

International Financial Institutions," April 30, 1978, *FRUS 1977–1980*, vol. 2, document 139; Mark Schneider to Warren Christopher, "Fraser Amendment on 502B," April 29, 1978, *FRUS 1977–1980*, vol. 2, document 137; Cyrus Vance and Warren Christopher to Jimmy Carter, March 27, 1978, *FRUS 1977–1980*, vol. 2, document 132. See chapter 4 for more on this interpretation.

91. Judith Miller, "U.S. Granting $38 Million Credit to Chilean Farmers," *New York Times*, May 5, 1978, A7.

92. AmEmbassy Santiago to Secretary of State, "Chile and the U.S. Banks III: New Loans," April 7, 1978, Chile Declassification Project.

93. Mark Hertsgaard, "Taking Exception: Response to *Washington Post* Editorial 4/20/1978," mss 1057, box 20, folder 24, Chile-IPS, ADA Records.

94. "Reuss: Rights Policy Not Helped by Loans to Chile from Banks," *Washington Post*, April 13, 1978, A19. The banks named were Bankers Trust of New York, Chemical Bank of New York, the Wells Fargo Bank of San Francisco, Citicorp of New York, Morgan Guaranty Trusty of New York, and First Chicago.

95. David Dlouhy to Ludlow Flower, "Proposed Kennedy-Harkin Banking Amendment," July 25, 1978, Chile Declassification Project.

96. Chile Legislative Center to Chile Committee and Key Contacts, "Current Legislation before the House of Representatives," May 19, 1978, M82–359, box 2, NCCSC, CALA Records.

97. In the memo, the Latin America bureau reported, "Our policy has been to vote against all IFI assistance to Chile. We have discussed in the Department the possibility of shifting to an eventual vote in favor of BHN loans for Chile, but no decision to do so has been made." Robert S. Stevens to John Bushnell, "'Christopher Committee' Policy—Chile," July 5, 1978, Chile Declassification Project.

98. Stephan Oxman to Warren Christopher, "Fraser Amendments," April 28, 1978, *FRUS 1977–1980*, vol. 2, document 136; Mark Schneider to Warren Christopher, "Fraser Amendment on 502B," April 29, 1978, *FRUS 1977–1980*, vol. 2, document 137; Anthony Lake to Warren Christopher, "The Fraser Amendments," April 29, 1978, *FRUS 1977–1980*, vol. 2, document 138.

99. "In effect lending and investment decisions of the private sector have dissipated the impact of USG actions linking economic assistance to human rights—constitutional government improvements." David Dlouhy to Cyrus Vance, "USG Policy on Private Sector Lending to Chile," July 25, 1978, Chile Declassification Project.

100. Stevens to Bushnell, "'Christopher Committee' Policy—Chile," July 5, 1978.

101. Anthony Lake to Warren Christopher, "Human Rights 'Sanctions,'" August 10, 1978, *FRUS 1977–1980*, vol. 2, document 157. Italics in original.

102. Rick Inderfurth to Robert Lipshutz, "Your Meeting with Mrs. Letelier and Mr. Moffitt," February 21, 1978, Chile Declassification Project. For a full account of the investigation from the perspective of Letelier's colleagues at the IPS, see Dinges and Landau, *Assassination on Embassy Row*. For an account from the perspective of the federal investigators, see the book written by the case's chief prosecutor for the federal government, Eugene M. Propper, with Taylor Branch, *Labyrinth* (New York: Viking Press, 1982). See also Alan McPherson, "Letelier Diplomacy: Nonstate Actors and U.S. Chilean Relations," *Diplomatic History* 43, no. 3 (June 2019): 445–68.

103. Michael Townley was an American citizen who had been a DINA agent, involved with the junta from its first days. When passport photos linked him to Moffitt and Letelier's assassination, Townley was living in Santiago. The United States demanded custody of him as a U.S. citizen accused of an act of terrorism. Only after chief investigator Eugene Propper flew to Santiago did the Chilean government admit it had him and release him to U.S. authorities. Townley later offered detailed testimony that implicated the Chilean junta and DINA leadership in the assassination plot that killed Letelier and Moffitt. See Kornbluh, *Pinochet File*, 397.

104. Robert Pastor to Zbigniew Brzezinski, "The Letelier Investigation," April 14, 1978, Chile Declassification Project.

105. CIA, "Chile: Implications of the Letelier Case," May 18, 1978, Chile Declassification Project; AmEmbassy Santiago Chile to Secretary of State, "Survivability of Pinochet: From 'What If' to 'So What?'" April 20, 1978, Chile Declassification Project.

106. AmEmbassy Santiago Chile to Secretary of State, "Survivability of Pinochet: From 'What If' to 'So What?'"

107. Robert Pastor to Zbigniew Brzezinski and David Aaron, "Conversation with our Ambassador to Chile, George Landau," June 28, 1978, NSA, Brzezinski Materials, Country Files (tab 6), box 7, Chile, JCL. In September 1978 a U.S. intelligence report noted the Pinochet government's significant changes to addressing human rights in the past year, yet despite "substantial progress in eliminating egregious human rights violations," Chile had received little attention due to its vacillations between reform and repression. Moreover, the "regime is being haunted by lingering protests over the issue of 'disappeared persons' and by growing controversy over the implications of the Letelier investigation." National Foreign Assessment Center, "Human Rights Performance: January 1977–July 1978," September 1, 1978, Chile Declassification Project.

108. Intelligence Report, "Government Sponsored Propaganda Campaign," May 26, 1978, Chile Declassification Project.

109. For more on the conservatism and degree of independence of the Chilean supreme court during this period, see Hilbink, *Judges beyond Politics*.

110. Intelligence Report, "Strategy of Chilean Government with Respect to Letelier Case, and Impact of Case on Stability of President Pinochet," June 23, 1978, Chile Declassification Project.

111. CIA Latin America Review, "Look Ahead at Letelier Case Developments," August 17, 1978, Chile Declassification Project.

112. Department of State Intelligence Report, "Chile: A Hesitant Momentum for Change," April 16, 1979, Chile Declassification Project. Between 1977 and 1980, economic growth rates ranged between 7.8 and 9.9 percent paired with a significant drop in inflation, although this boom was not shared equally by all in the business community, nor within greater Chilean society. See Stern, *Battling for Hearts and Minds*, 168–69.

113. Stern notes that by 1978 the Pinochet regime had prevailed in the face of mounting pressures at home and abroad. "In the race between crisis and institutionalization, the latter was slowly pulling ahead—and promoting selective erasure of the past." Bolstered by a growing economy, "by 1979–80, the military regime and its supporters were digging in to establish their long-term dominance. The regime had outlasted crisis after crisis. It promoted a memory framework that invited 'forgetting' ugly memory-truths, now defined as inevitable tragedies and excesses of war." Stern, *Battling for Hearts and Minds*, 154, 167.

114. Quoted in Kornbluh, *Pinochet File*, 404.

115. Ibid.

116. Secretary of State to AmEmbassy Santiago, "Text of State Department Spokesman Hodding Carter's Statement of Decision of President of Chilean Supreme Court," May 15, 1979, Chile Declassification Project.

117. Edward Kennedy and Frank Church to Jimmy Carter, May 14, 1979, Chile Declassification Project.

118. Chile Legislative Center to Members of Congress, March 16, 1979, M80–048, box 4, NCCSC, CALA Records.

119. Chile Legislative Center to Chile Committees and Key Contacts, "Important Opportunity for U.S. Chile Solidarity Movement to Press U.S. Government in Letelier/Moffitt Case," April 4, 1979, M80–048, box 4, NCCSC, CALA Records.

120. Quoted in Cable from Secretary of State to AmEmbassy Santiago, "Letelier/Moffitt Case: Public Letter to President Carter Demands Extradition," September 25, 1979, Chile Declassification Project. The letter was signed by more than thirty members of Congress and other notables including John Kenneth Galbraith, Tom Hayden, Jane Fonda, the National Council of Churches, the International Longshoremen's and Warehousemen's Union, and the Chile Legislative Center. U.S. ambassador George Landau and assistant U.S. attorney Eugene Propper, who was prosecuting the case, had lobbied Harkin in May to postpone the resolution. They argued that "a congressional resolution on the case would be seen in Chile as interference in the judicial process and would provide a pretext for denial of extradition on appeal to the body of the Supreme Court." Dinges and Landau, *Assassination on Embassy Row*, 380.

121. "News from Congressman Tom Harkin," October 10, 1979, Chile Declassification Project.

122. Dick Barnebey to Viron Vaky, "Recommended Actions Regarding the Letelier Case," September 6, 1979, Chile Declassification Project. Italics in original.

123. Viron Vaky to Warren Christopher, "Potential Letelier Case Scenarios and Proposed Responses," September 11, 1979, Chile Declassification Project. Vaky had replaced Todman in July 1978 and remained until the end of November 1979. Vaky was a career foreign service officer who had served under Kissinger at the time of the Chilean coup. In 1970, as a member of the National Security Council, he had challenged Kissinger on the plans to destabilize Allende, arguing it was against American principles and policies and would have long-term negative consequences. National Security Archive, "Kissinger and Chile: The Declassified Record," September 11, 2013, https://nsarchive2.gwu.edu/NSAEBB/NSAEBB437/.

124. National Security Archive, "Kissinger and Chile: The Declassified Record."

125. Paul Wilson to CALA, April 20, 1979, M82–359, box 1, General Correspondence, CALA Records.

126. AmEmbassy Santiago to Secretary of State, "Letelier/Moffitt Case—US Bank Lending to Chile," May 20, 1979, Chile Declassification Project.

127. David Dlouhy to Ludlow Flower, "Proposed Kennedy-Harkin Banking Amendment," July 25, 1978, Chile Declassification Project; David Dlouhy to Cyrus Vance, "USG Policy on Private Sector Lending to Chile," July 25, 1978, Chile Declassification Project.

128. George Landau to Cyrus Vance, "Letelier-Moffitt: Economic Sanctions," October 8, 1979, Chile Declassification Project; George Landau to Cyrus Vance, "Letelier/Moffitt Case: Our Response to the Supreme Court Decision," October 8, 1979, Chile Declassification Project.

129. Landau to Vance, "Letelier/Moffitt Case."

130. Ibid.

131. Cyrus Vance to Jimmy Carter, "Letelier/Moffitt Case," October 19, 1979, NSA, Brzezinski Materials, Country Files (tab 6), box 7, Chile, JCL.

132. Ibid.

133. Zbigniew Brzezinski to Cyrus Vance, "Letelier Moffitt Case and U.S. Policy to Chile," November 27, 1979, Brzezinski Materials, Country Files (tab 6), box 7, Chile, JCL; AmEmbassy Santiago to Secretary of State, "Tensions and Nervousness as Pinochet Faces Some Major Political Decisions," December 7, 1979, Chile Declassification Project.

134. Dinges and Landau, *Assassination on Embassy Row*, 380.

135. Peter Weiss to Robert Borsage, Saul Landau, Isabel Letelier, Michael Moffitt, "Off-the-Record Conversation with Robert Pastor about Letelier case," [1980], box 105, Miscellaneous Response to Letelier-Moffitt, IPS Records.

4. Weighing the Costs

1. Inter-American Commission on Human Rights, *Report on the Situation of Human Rights in Argentina* (Washington, D.C.: General Secretariat OAS, 1980).

2. For the longer trajectory of U.S. relations with Argentina that prefaced this diplomacy, see Schmidli, *Fate of Freedom Elsewhere.*

3. See chapters 1 and 2 for more detail on country report response.

4. Lincoln Bloomfield, "The Carter Human Rights Policy: A Preliminary Appraisal," January 11, 1981, Donated Materials, Brzezinski Papers, NSC Accomplishments, Human Rights 1/81, JCL.

5. Alison Brysk, *The Politics of Human Rights in Argentina: Protest, Change, and Democratization* (Stanford: Stanford University Press 1994), 32. For a good overview of political violence in Argentina, see Martin Edwin Andersen, *Dossier Secreto: Argentina's Desaparecidos and the Myth of the "Dirty War"* (Boulder, CO: Westview, 1993), and Wright, *State Terrorism in Latin America*, 95–137.

6. Leftist groups—including the Peronist Montoneros and the Trotskyite Ejército Revolucionario del Pueblo (ERP)—engaged in robbery, kidnapping, and assassinations throughout the country. Beginning in 1974, paramilitary groups began to operate in organized campaigns against a broadly defined left, not just guerrillas. Journalists, unionists, students, and lawyers were targets of these attacks, and an Amnesty International report found that these activities were "more than simply tolerated" by government officials. Amnesty International, *Argentina: The Military Juntas and Human Rights* (London: Amnesty International Publications, 1987), 3.

7. Between 1930 and 1983, Argentina had twenty-six military coups, and of its twenty-four presidents in this period, sixteen had been military officers. Brysk notes that, as a result of its long history of intervention in political affairs, "the military was accepted as a legitimate political actor that regularly intervened in Argentine society in tandem with civilian political forces." Brysk, *Politics of Human Rights*, 23, 27.

8. "The Armed Forces' Decision to Assume the Direction of the State," March 25, 1976, reprinted in Loveman and Davies, *Politics of Antipolitics*, 176.

9. See General Videla's "A Time for Fundamental Reorganization of the Nation," April 5, 1976, reprinted in Loveman and Davies, *Politics of Antipolitics*, 160–63.

10. Quoted in Amnesty International, *Report of an Amnesty International Mission to Argentina, 6–15 November 1976* (London: Amnesty International Publications, 1977).

11. "We will continue fighting," they declared, "without quarter, all forms of subversion, both open and clandestine, and will eradicate all forms of demagoguery. We will tolerate neither corruption nor venality in any form or circumstance, or any transgression against the law, or any opposition to the process of restoration which has been initiated." "Armed Forces' Decision to Assume the Direction of the State," 159. In Argentina the religious element was particularly pronounced. Jeffrey Klaiber observes that "almost all of the top officials, beginning with Videla, were nearly perfect examples of Catholic integralism; all were nationalistic, anticommunist, anti-liberal, and in some cases, anti-Semitic." Jeffrey Klaiber, *The Church, Dictatorships, and Democracy in Latin America* (Maryknoll, NY: Orbis Books, 1998), 75. For more on Argentine's broader anticommunist campaign during this time, see Ariel C. Armony, *Argentina, the United States, and the Anti-Communist Crusade in Central America, 1977–1984* (Athens: Ohio University Center for International Studies, 1997).

12. Comisión Nacional sobre la Desaparición de Personas (CONADEP), *Nunca Más: The Report of the Argentine National Commission on the Disappeared* (New York: Farrar, Straus & Giroux, 1986). For more on the military government's ideology and the dirty war, see Marguerite Feitlowitz, *A Lexicon of Terror: Argentina and the Legacies of Torture* (New York: Oxford University Press, 1999); Donald Clark Hodges, *Argentina's "Dirty War": An Intellectual Biography* (Austin: University of

Texas Press, 1991); Paul H. Lewis, *Guerrillas and Generals: The "Dirty War" in Argentina* (Westport, CT: Praeger, 2002); Frederick M. Nunn, *The Time of the Generals: Latin American Professional Militarism in World Perspective* (Lincoln: University of Nebraska Press, 1992).

13. Brysk notes, for example, that the number of cremations in Buenos Aires's largest cemetery jumped from 13,120 in 1974 to around 30,000 in 1978 and 1979. In contrast to the secrecy surrounding the disappeared and these torture camps, the kidnappings themselves were often an ostentatious show of force; the CONADEP report noted that it was not unusual for several vehicles or helicopters to surround an individual's house during an abduction. A "gang" of people would burst in, threatening the family and neighbors with "weaponry totally disproportionate to the supposed threat posed by the victims" in a deliberate attempt to intimidate and silence any witnesses. Some people were taken off the bus in the middle of the day, or dragged off the street into a waiting car. The military government, when pressed, denied any knowledge of these kidnappings, detention centers, and executions, and the press was explicitly barred from making any mention of kidnappings. Thus state terrorism in Argentina took on a surreal element, pairing the complete denial of any government knowledge of or involvement in the terror with ostentatious displays of its absolute power over its citizens. Brysk, *Politics of Human Rights in Argentina*, 37; CONADEP, *Nunca Más*, 11, 12, 63. See also Amnesty International, *Report of an Amnesty International Mission to Argentina*.

14. In the weeks immediately prior to the coup, Admiral Emilio Massera made overtures to U.S. ambassador Robert Hill, wanting to preempt any negative consequences the advent of a military government might have on relations between the two countries. Hill reported to the State Department that Massera had been actively formulating guidelines to avoid the "sort of problems the Chilean and Uruguayan govts are having with the US over [the] human rights issue." Eight days before the coup, Massera sought out Hill's advice on how to maintain good relations *if* a military government were to take over. Hill relayed to the State Department, "Massera said he did not want to discuss possible intervention as he was sure I would regard it as diplomatically incorrect. However, he said, he did wish to approach me as a friend to say the military was terribly concerned about their public relations in the US should they have to intervene." Massera solicited Hill's advice on finding a good public relations firm in the United States that "might handle the problem for a future military govt." In a meeting at the OAS in Santiago on June 10, 1976, Kissinger and Argentina's foreign minister, César Guzzetti, discussed the growing pressure on human rights abuses in Argentina. Kissinger told Guzzetti that the administration was "aware you are in a difficult period" and "wish[es] the new government well. . . . We will do what we can to help it succeed." AmEmbassy Buenos Aires to Secretary of State, "Military Take Cognizance of Human Rights," February 16, 1976, and AmEmbassy Buenos Aires to Secretary of State, "Ambassador's Conversation with Admiral Massera," March 16, 1976, available at National Security Archive, "On 30th Anniversary of Argentine Coup, New Declassified Details on Repression and U.S. Support for Military Dictatorship," March 23, 2006, http://www.gwu.edu/~nsarchiv/NSAEBB/ NSAEBB185/index.htm; Meeting Memo, July 9, 1976, National Security Archive, "Electronic Briefing Book No. 133: Kissinger to the Argentine Generals in 1976," August 27, 2004, http:// www.gwu.edu/~nsarchiv/NSAEBB/NSAEBB133/index.htm.

15. Memcon, "Secretary's Meeting with Argentine Foreign Minister Guzzetti," October 6, 1976, National Security Archive, "Electronic Briefing Book No. 104: The Dirty War in Argentina," December 4, 2003, http://www.gwu.edu/~nsarchiv/NSAEBB/NSAEBB104/index.htm.

16. In response to ongoing violence and new congressional mandates, U.S. ambassador Hill had begun pressing the military government on human rights issues in the summer of 1976. Guzzetti's triumphant return from his October meeting with Kissinger disturbed Hill, and he wrote a long "bitter complaint" to the State Department. "Guzzetti's remarks both to me and

to the Argentine press since his return are not those of a man who has been impressed with the gravity of the human rights problem as seen from the U.S. . . . Guzzetti went to US fully expecting to hear some strong, firm, direct warning of his [government's] human rights practices. Rather than that, he has returned in a state of jubilation. . . . Based on what Guzzetti is doubtless reporting to the GOA, it must now believe that if it has any problems with the U.S. over human rights, they are confined to certain elements of Congress and what it regards as biased and/or uninformed minor segments of public opinion. While that conviction lasts it will be unrealistic and unbelievable for this embassy to press representations to the [government of Argentina] over human rights violations." Assistant Secretary of State Shlaudeman wrote back, claiming that Guzzetti must have "heard only what he wanted to hear." He assured Hill that the State Department had stressed that a "tranquil and violence-free Argentina" was essential to avoid strains between the two countries. Shlaudeman continued, "[Guzzetti] was told in detail how strongly opinion in this country has reacted against reports of abuses by the security forces in Argentina and the nature of the threat this poses to Argentine interests." AmEmbassy Buenos Aires to Henry Shlaudeman, "Foreign Minister Guzzetti Euphoric over Visit to United States," October 19, 1976, and Henry Shlaudeman to AmEmbassy Buenos Aires, "Guzzetti's Visit to the U.S.," October 22, 1976, National Security Archive, "Electronic Briefing Book No. 104: The Dirty War in Argentina."

17. Good overviews of human rights groups in Argentina during this period include Andersen, *Dossier Secreto*; Brysk, *Politics of Human Rights in Argentina*; Edward L. Cleary, *The Struggle for Human Rights in Latin America* (Westport, CT: Praeger, 1997); Iain Guest, *Behind the Disappearances: Argentina's Dirty War against Human Rights and the United Nations* (Philadelphia: University of Pennsylvania Press, 1990); Klaiber, *Church, Dictatorships, and Democracy*.

18. *Report of an Amnesty International Mission to Argentina.*

19. Fred Rondon to Wayne Smith, "Human Rights in Argentina," January 12, 1977 (4013), Argentina Declassification Project, State Department Collections, U.S. Department of State FOIA Electronic Reading Room (hereafter Argentina Declassification Project).

20. Fred Rondon to Yvonne Thayer, "Human Rights Situation in Argentina," February 11, 1977 (3966), Argentina Declassification Project.

21. Memcon, Emilio Mignone and Fred Rondon, "Military Rule, Human Rights and U.S. Policy," January 28, 1977 (3987), Argentina Declassification Project. See chapter 2 for administration debates over FMS levels in 1977 and more on FMS cuts.

22. AmEmbassy Buenos Aires to Secretary of State Vance, "Argentina Overview," January 28, 1977 (3982), Argentina Declassification Project.

23. Secretary of State to AmEmbassy Buenos Aires, "U.S. Argentine Relations," February 2, 1977 (3982), Argentina Declassification Project; Memcon, "Discussion of Human Rights Issues with Ambassador Aja Espil and General Miro," January 11, 1977 (4016), Argentina Declassification Project; Memcon, Patricia Derian and Members of Argentine Ministry of Foreign Relations, March 30, 1977 (3893), Argentina Declassification Project.

24. Memcon, Emilio Mignone and Fred Rondon, "Military Rule, Human Rights and U.S. Policy."

25. AmEmbassy Buenos Aires to Secretary of State, "Argentine Reactions to Human Rights Issue," March 16, 1977 (3908), Argentina Declassification Project.

26. Ibid. Cox and the *Buenos Aires Herald* occupied a unique position in the Argentine press. Due to self- and state-imposed censorship, most newspapers acted as mouthpieces for the junta's positions, particularly after Jacobo Timerman, the editor of *La Opinión*, was arrested in April 1977. Cox, a U.S. citizen, enjoyed a measure of editorial freedom to express criticism. Although his editorials almost always pointed out the hypocrisy and biases of the U.S. human rights policy, they

also managed to affirm the principle and prod the military leadership for changes in the name of national interests. Still, he and his family faced numerous threats as a result of his work. Cox was detained in 1977 and ultimately left Buenos Aires in 1979. Ibid.

27. AmEmbassy Buenos Aires to Secretary of State, "Argentina Overview," January 28, 1977 (3986), Argentina Declassification Project.

28. Korvadlov explained that "one of the hardest things for him to convey to his American colleagues . . . was that it was in the best interest of Argentina and the Argentine Jewish community to continue to be governed by a moderate military regime." Memcon, Patricia Derian and Jacobo Korvadlov, March 30, 1977 (3982), Argentina Declassification Project.

29. Memcon, Patricia Derian and Dr. Jose Luis de Imaz, March 31, 1977 (3884), Argentina Declassification Project.

30. Memcon, Patricia Derian and Political Left, April 1, 1977 (3880), Argentina Declassification Project.

31. Memcon, Patricia Derian and Papal Nuncio, March 29, 1977 (3894), Argentina Declassification Project.

32. Memcon, Patricia Derian and Bishop Gattinoni, March 31, 1977 (3886), Argentina Declassification Project.

33. Timerman stated that "if he were to be killed by leftists it would merit only a small story in the U.S. press. But if right-wing para-military did him in it would be front page news for weeks." Memcon, Patricia Derian and Jacobo Timerman, March 31, 1977 (3887), Argentina Declassification Project; Fred Rondon to Ken Hill, "Report on Derian's Conversations," April 7, 1977 (3807), Argentina Declassification Project.

34. Fred Rondon to Ken Hill, "Report on Derian's Conversations."

35. WOLA argued, "When the State Department talks of 'cycles of violence,' it should be asked what recourse people have when the armed forces unlawfully seize power." It continued, "granted that there was a popular consensus to end Mrs. Peron's chaotic rule, why could the military not have waited another six months for the scheduled elections (October 1976), instead of intervening once again to impede due electoral process? Popular elections would certainly have resulted in the defeat of the unpopular Mrs. Peron." "Argentina-Armies of the Night—Can It Continue?" *Legislative Update, Latin America* (January/February 1977), box 55, folder 2, Lister Papers.

36. "If the opposition to Videla has coalesced into a non-communist nationalist resistance, then imaginative policy makers should begin to entertain the costs of continued identification with Videla," the article warned. George Lister circulated WOLA's newsletter within the State Department, making special note of its criticism of the human rights report and policy on Argentina. Ibid.

37. WOLA's March newsletter reported, "The administration's position appears to be that keeping military channels open will encourage the Latin American Armed Forces to become more democratic, more professional and consequently more responsive to human rights. Unfortunately, this has often not proven to be the case." "U.S. Military Assistance Programs for Latin America—A Little New but a Lot of the Same," *Legislative Update, Latin America* (March/April 1977), Widener Library.

38. Edward Kennedy to Cyrus Vance, "Human Rights in Argentina," February 28, 1977 (3941), Argentina Declassification Project.

39. Congressman Robert Drinan's Remarks, May 25, 1977, Washington D.C. Office, folder 11, box 5, AIUSA II.1, AIUSA Records.

40. Americans for Democratic Action, "One Hundred Days of the Carter Administration," April 26, 1977, M97–135, box 4, "Carter, Pres Jimmy," ADA Records.

41. State Department Briefing Memo, "United States–Argentine Relations," June 3, 1977 (3726), Argentina Declassification Project.

42. An article in *La Prensa* in June presented international human rights pressures as part of a defamatory campaign by insurgents now operating abroad. "Agentes de al difamación," *La Prensa* (11 June 1977), Colección de Prensa (hereafter Prensa), Archivo de Centro de Estudios Legales y Sociales, Buenos Aires, Argentina (hereafter CELS Archive).

43. Secretary of State to AmEmbassy Buenos Aires, "Human Rights and the IFIs," June 13, 1977 (3719), Argentina Declassification Project; Secretary of State to Secretary of Treasury, "GOA Demarche on Human Rights," June 15, 1977 (3715), Argentina Declassification Project; Cyrus Vance to Terrance Todman, "Argentines Note Human Rights Improvements in Order to Influence US Vote in IFIs," June 16, 1977 (3714), Argentina Declassification Project; Secretary of State to AmEmbassy Buenos Aires, "Human Rights and the IFIs," June 13, 1977 (3719), Argentina Declassification Project; AmEmbassy Buenos Aires to Secretary of State, "GOA Notes Human Rights Improvements," June 22, 1977 (3703), Argentina Declassification Project.

44. AmEmbassy Buenos Aires to Secretary of State, "Argentine Human Rights Situation: A Review," June 14, 1977 (3414), Argentina Declassification Project.

45. AmEmbassy Buenos Aires to Secretary of State, "GOA Notes Human Rights Improvements."

46. AmEmbassy Buenos Aires to Secretary of State, "Argentine Human Rights Situation."

47. Secretary of State to Secretary of Treasury, "GOA Demarche on Human Rights."

48. Zbigniew Brzezinski to Cyrus Vance, July 9, 1977, *FRUS 1977–1980*, vol. 24, document 55.

49. Secretary of State Vance's Delegation to the Department of State, June 16, 1977, *FRUS 1977–1980*, vol. 24, document 54. In a telegram, the State Department instructed the embassy to "approach the GOA at an appropriately senior level and note the considerable interest which the United States has in recently announced GOA steps and inquire whether further information could be provided concerning these steps." The embassy responded that it opted not to invoke the president's name at this time in its démarche as there were "encouraging signs" but also "much that disturbs us." It continued by saying that these mixed signals "[lead] us to hesitate in using a presidential acknowledgement of an improving situation, lest subsequently we discover that human rights gains here were illusory." Zbigniew Brzezinski to Cyrus Vance, "Recognition of Improvements in Human Rights," July 9, 1977, *FRUS 1977–1980*, vol. 24, document 57, n. 3; AmEmbassy Buenos Aires to Secretary of State, "Human Rights Improvements in Argentina," July 18, 1977 (3641), Argentina Declassification Project.

50. AmEmbassy Buenos Aires to Secretary of State, "Argentine Human Rights Situation."

51. Memcon, Patricia Derian and Hipolito Solari Yrigoyen, "Yrigoyen Incarceration," June 28, 1977, Argentina Declassification Project.

52. "Christopher Meets with Exiled Argentine Leader," June 28, 1977, Argentina Declassification Project; Peter Tarnoff to Zbigniew Brzezinski, "Prominent Argentine Senator Writes to the President," June 30, 1977, WHCF, Subject Files, box HU-1, 7/1/77–7/31/77, Executive, JCL.

53. "Argentine Senator Meets with U.S. Government Officials," *Argentine Outreach* (July/August 1977), Lister Papers; "Argentina: Double-Talk 1984," *Legislative Update, Latin America* (May/June 1977), Widener Library. See chapter 3 for more on the Frei meeting.

54. Harris's arrival followed shortly after the departure of Ambassador Hill in May. Hill had been diligent in carrying out his mandate to report on human rights conditions and had often been frustrated with Kissinger and the "double message" coming from Washington. He also, however, had been frequently displeased with the Carter administration's approach to the policy, and after his departure he gave several high-profile interviews to U.S. and Argentine news

outlets criticizing Carter's policy. State Department Briefing Memo, "The Importance of U.S. Argentine Relations," August 1, 1977 (3608), Argentina Declassification Project. See also Schmidli, *Fate of Freedom Elsewhere*, 120–26, 142–47.

55. Some of the more prominent works on Las Madres include Marguerite Guzman Bouvard, *Revolutionizing Motherhood: The Mothers of the Plaza de Mayo* (Wilmington, DE: Scholarly Resources, 1994); Jo Fisher, *Mothers of the Disappeared* (Boston: South End Press, 1989); Marysa Navarro, "The Personal Is Political: Las Madres de Plaza de Mayo," in *Power and Popular Protest: Latin American Social Movements*, ed. Susan Eckstein and Manuel A. Garretón Merino (Berkeley: University of California Press, 2001), 241–58; Matilde Mellibovsky, *Circle of Love over Death: Testimonies of the Mothers of the Plaza De Mayo* (Willimantic, CT: Curbstone Press, 1997); Hebe de Bonafini, *Hebe: La Otra Mujer*, ed. Gabriel Bauducco (Buenos Aires: Asociación Madres de Plaza de Mayo, 2004). See also Kelly, *Sovereign Emergencies*, 208–44.

56. "It was just my thought of, okay, I am going to report on something, it's not in the newspapers, there is no information on it," Harris recalled. His predecessor had been frustrated "because she was reporting on something there was no way to report on." Author interview with F. A. "Tex" Harris, September 12, 2008, McLean, Virginia.

57. Ibid. According to Harris, word got out among foreign reporters in Argentina to "go see this guy Harris at the embassy and buy him lunch and he'll spill his guts." Harris recalled, "These guys would call up and I'd say, 'Absolutely. I look forward to seeing you. Lunch.' So I'd go have a big steak, big bottle of red wine, big salad, lots of french fries," and the writers would be frantically writing across the table from him. Ibid. Harris received some significant resistance on his reporting from his superiors at the embassy. When Harris was tasked with human rights reporting, the embassy gave him "three pages of yellow long legal size paper with names on it and some notes; that is all the human rights files the embassy had." His officer evaluation in April 1978 noted that in the past nine months, Harris had sent more than two hundred cables to Washington. "Officer Evaluation Report of F. Allen Harris, July 31, 1977–April 15, 1978," series 3, box 1, Carter Administration Materials, Memorabilia 3, 1976–1980, Patricia Derian Papers. See Schmidli, *Fate of Freedom Elsewhere*, 121, 144–47.

58. "Officer Evaluation Report of F. Allen Harris," Derian Papers.

59. "Human Rights Evaluation Report: Argentina," July 20, 1977 (3630), Argentina Declassification Project.

60. AmEmbassy Buenos Aires to Cyrus Vance, "Derian Meeting with Argentine Permanent Assembly for Human Rights," September 6, 1977 (3511), Argentina Declassification Project.

61. AmEmbassy Buenos Aires to Warren Christopher and Terrance Todman, "Derian Call on President Videla," August 11, 1977 (3574), Argentina Declassification Project.

62. Secretary of State to AmEmbassy Buenos Aires, "Derian Meeting with Minister of Interior," August 15, 1977 (3568), Argentina Declassification Project; Secretary of State to AmEmbassy Buenos Aires, "Derian Visit with Admiral Massera," August 15, 1977 (3569), Argentina Declassification Project; AmEmbassy Buenos Aires to Warren Christopher and Terrance Todman, "Derian Visit with Economy Minister Martínez de Hoz," August 12, 1977 (3571), Argentina Declassification Project. See also Schmidli, *Fate of Freedom Elsewhere*, 81.

63. AmEmbassy Buenos Aires to Cyrus Vance, "Asst Sec Todman's Meeting with President Videla," August 24, 1977 (3548), Argentina Declassification Project.

64. "Queremos que vean y escuchen, que dialoguen de igual a igual, pero también queremos que sepan que los argentinos no estamos acostumbrados a rendir examen ante nadie y por ningún motivo." The article continued, "No nos asusta y queremos que los ilustres visitantes nos informen sobre los hechos inocultables de violencia generalizada, sobre el uso de drogas alucinógenas y el sostenidos avance de la pornografía" (We are not afraid and want our distinguished visitors to

inform us about the undeniable fact of widespread violence, the use of hallucinogenic drugs and the sustained progress of pornography) in the United States. "¿Y si Argentina investiga lo que pasa en los EE. UU.?" *Clarín*, August 9, 1977, Prensa, CELS Archive. Translations by author unless otherwise noted.

65. "No. La política norteamericana es muy clara al respeto y la posición argentina también creo que está muy clara después de la reunión de la Organización de Estados Americanos en Grenada. Sin embargo, entiendo que el mayor conocimiento por parte de los Estados Unidos de nuestro país y de la realidad actual argentina, que puede concretarse con la visita de Terence Todman y con la posible venida al país del secretario de Estado Cyrus Vance, va a menguar sensiblemente la presión sobre la Argentina por este tema." "Las Guerras Empiezan Donde Fracasa la Diplomática...," *Siete Días Ilustrados*, August 5, 1977, Prensa, CELS Archive.

66. AmEmbassy Buenos Aires to Cyrus Vance, "Recent Human Rights Developments in Argentina," September 13, 1977 (3485), Argentina Declassification Project.

67. Draft Memo, George Lister, "Human Rights Problems in the Southern Cone," Declassified Materials, box 3, Lister Papers.

68. See Schmidli, *Fate of Freedom Elsewhere*, 116.

69. WOLA argued, "This is a critical interlude for U.S.–Latin American policy, as the administration prepares for Act II. And from present indications, the human rights policy is slipping from center stage." The article noted that the administration was giving less attention to human rights in its public statements. "And when they do speak, especially Assistant Secretary Todman and ARA, it is often to cite with satisfaction even the slightest hint that a regime is improving its human rights record." "Latin America Policy: Where to Jimmy," *Legislative Update, Latin America* (September/October 1977), Widener Library. Italics in original.

70. Lofredo took particular exception to Todman's claims that the press was partially at fault for the "distorted view of Argentine reality," noting the extreme personal risk that many foreign and domestic reporters had endured in their attempt to offer uncensored reports of violence perpetrated by the Argentine military. Horacio Lofredo, Argentine Commission for Human Rights to Jimmy Carter, August 31, 1977, NSA, Staff Materials, North/South Pastor (tab 24), box 1, Argentina, JCL.

71. "Latin America Policy: Where to Jimmy."

72. Ibid.

73. "Statement of Cong. Tom Harkin at White House Rally," September 7, 1977, mss 1057, box 47, IPS Records.

74. Memcon, Cyrus Vance and Asamblea Members, "Human Rights Situation in Argentina," November 21, 1977 (3247), Argentina Declassification Project.

75. Memcon, Cyrus Vance and Foreign Minister Montes, "Private Meeting between the Secretary and Foreign Minister Montes," November 21, 1977 (3245), Argentina Declassification Project. The Argentine Commission for Human Rights, for example, sent Mark Schneider a list of political prisoners in advance of Vance's visit. Amnesty International similarly spent a significant amount of time "preparing Vance for his Argentine visit," and Senator Kennedy supporting a request by the CNFMP for Vance to "intervene on behalf of thousands of innocent people who have been kidnapped, detained and tortured." Argentine Commission for Human Rights to Mark Schneider, November 11, 1977 (3292), Argentina Declassification Project; Edward Kennedy to Cyrus Vance, November 15, 1977 (3274), Argentina Declassification Project.

76. Cyrus Vance to White House, "Meeting in Buenos Aires," November 22, 1977, *FRUS 1977–1980*, vol. 24, document 68.

77. AmEmbassy Buenos Aires to Cyrus Vance, "Human Rights Round Up," January 19, 1978 (3035), Argentina Declassification Project. Memorandum for the Record, "ARA/INR/CIA Weekly

Meeting," February 6, 1978, *FRUS 1977–1980*, vol. 24, document 72. A comprehensive evaluation of the administration's human rights policy found that "in Argentina, the rate of disappeared persons remains unchanged, reports of official torture continue to be received, there is convincing evidence that government security personnel continue to operate in vigilante fashion—all of this in the context of a decreasing terrorist threat as a result of successful counter-terrorist action by the government." Paper Prepared in the Bureau of Intelligence and Research, "Progress and Regression in Human Rights in 1977," January 11, 1978, *FRUS 1977–1980*, vol. 2, document 104.

78. Tuchman continued, reporting, "In many countries where bad problems exist, human rights policy is being intensely debated within the responsible government." Memo Jessica Tuchman to David Aaron, "Assessment of Human Rights Accomplishments," January 5, 1978, *FRUS 1977–1980*, vol. 2, document 102.

79. Anthony Lake to Cyrus Vance, "The Human Rights Policy: An Interim Assessment," January 1978, WHCF, Subject, box HU-1, 1/20/77–1/20/81, JCL.

80. Christopher pointed explicitly to Amnesty International's receipt of the Noble Prize, noting that "suddenly Amnesty's reports and letters are being extensively quoted and heavily replied upon by the media and by governments. Amnesty's experience calls to mind the fact" that the administrations' championing of human rights also elevated and legitimized a wide array of organizations that had been long concerned with the issue. A report by the policy planning staff noted, "Once-lonely private activists now find themselves deluged with invitations to conferences. Some who long have been working to advance human rights have taken new hope from the Administration's policies; others doubtless are bandwagon-hopping. But they all contribute to a growing international lobby which combines its influence with our own." Warren Christopher to Jimmy Carter, January 17, 1978, NLC-128–13–4–8–3, JCL; Anthony Lake to Cyrus Vance, "Human Rights Policy: An Interim Assessment."

81. Lake noted that "West European opposition to loans for the Pinochet regime began before ours," but most countries had been otherwise reluctant to use IFIs as an instrument of human rights until recently. Venezuela had joined the U.S. in abstaining on a vote to Chile. Both Britain and Sweden were on record as opposing an IDB loan to Argentina, but the Europeans cast their votes as a regional block, which was collectively in favor of the loan. More broadly, there had been several requests for " 'cooperative exploration' on how to pursue human rights concerns in IFIs," which "may suggest interest in joining us." Anthony Lake to Cyrus Vance, "Human Rights Policy: An Interim Assessment."

82. Ibid.

83. "Admiral Massera's Brand of Human Rights," *Update Latin America* (January/February 1978), Administrative Files, General Management, History, box 30, WOLA Update 1978–81, WOLA Duke Records.

84. William Moorhead to Jimmy Carter, "House Finance Committee Visit to South America," March 16, 1978, WHCF, Subject, box HU-1, 1/20/77–1/20/81, Confidential, JCL.

85. North/South Staff to Zbigniew Brzezinski, "Evening Report," March 17, 1978, NLC-24–53–4–12–0, JCL.

86. Cyrus Vance and Warren Christopher, "Letter from Congressional Group that Recently Visited Latin America," March 27, 1978, NLC-14-20-2-7-5; Zbigniew Brzezinski to Jimmy Carter, "Human Rights," December 3, 1977, NLC-126–10–7–1–2, JCL.

87. Jimmy Carter to William Moorhead, April 12, 1978, WHCF, Subject, box HU-1, 1/20/77–1/20/81, Confidential, JCL.

88. Zbigniew Brzezinski to Cyrus Vance, "Human Rights Reports," May 8, 1978, WHCF, Subject, box HU-1, 1/20/77–1/20/81, Confidential, JCL. See chapter 3 for more on these legislative efforts.

89. Pastor noted that business groups such as the Chamber of Commerce and Council of the Americas had recently criticized the Carter administration's "inflexibility" on human rights decisions. Pastor, pointing to pending legislation on human rights language for the EXIM Bank, "suggested that they direct that criticism to more appropriate places." Daily Activities Report, Robert Pastor to Zbigniew Brzezinski, May 12, 1978, NLC-24-53-6-7-4, JCL.

90. Evening Report, Global Issues Staff to Zbigniew Brzezinski, May 15, 1978, NLC-10-11-5-21-0, JCL.

91. AmEmbassy Buenos Aires to Secretary of State, "Export Import Bank Loans to Argentina," May 16, 1978, Argentina Declassification Project. Raul Castro, former governor of Arizona, took up the post in November 1977 following Hill's resignation in May.

92. Memo to the Files from ECOM, "U.S. Opposition to Argentine Credits from IFIs," April 25, 1978 (2739), Argentina Declassification Project.

93. Zbigniew Brzezinski to Jimmy Carter, "Your Question about the Human Rights Situation in Argentina," July 13, 1978, NSA, Staff Material, North/South Pastor (tab 24), box 1, Argentina, 1–8/78, JCL.

94. At Vance's suggestion to Secretary of Defense Brown, Newsom was joined by Rear Admiral Schuller and Major General Surut. In his meeting with the Argentine leadership, Newsom stressed the Department of Defense's concern with bilateral relations, in particular, stating "in confidence" that his trip had been initiated in part "because Secretary Brown raised with Secretary Vance the implications for the U.S. of a possible termination of military relations with Argentina." Brown had in fact become increasingly impatient over the backlog of arms transfers and feared lasting damage to U.S.-Argentine military relations. Nevertheless, Newsom presented the administration as united on its human rights demands. AmEmbassy Buenos Aires to Secretary of State, "Argentina Human Rights," May 13, 1978 (137311), Argentina Declassification Project; Cyrus Vance to Harold Brown on Newsom Visit, June 3, 1978 (2588), Argentina Declassification Project; Memcon, David Newsom and Jorge Videla, "Human Rights and United States Relations with Argentina," May 24, 1978 (137879), Argentina Declassification Project.

95. Memcon, David Newsom and Orlando Ramón Agosti, "Human Rights and United States Relations with Argentina," May 24, 1978, Argentina Declassification Project.

96. They noted that actual numbers were likely much higher than reported because press censorship and lack of resources prevented families outside the major metropolitan areas from contacting or even being aware of groups such as the Asamblea. Memcon, David Newsom Meeting with Argentine Human Rights Groups, May 25, 1978 (137916), Argentina Declassification Project.

97. Ibid.

98. Ibid.

99. AmEmbassy Buenos Aires to Secretary of State, "Argentine Mood: The Aftermath of the Newsom Visit," June 25, 1978 (137871), Argentina Declassification Project.

100. Memcon, David Newsom and Jorge Videla, "Human Rights and United States Relations with Argentina."

101. Secretary of State to AmEmbassy Buenos Aires, "Human Rights and US Programs in Argentina," June 26, 1978 (2491), Argentina Declassification Project.

102. Jimmy Carter, "Organization of American States Remarks at the Opening Session of the Eighth General Assembly," June 21, 1978, accessed at the American Presidency Project, https://www.presidency.ucsb.edu/node/248850.

103. In a letter to the EXIM chairman, Vance wrote that the administration had hoped to "relax certain restrictions now placed on US aid and trade programs for Argentina," if the government had issued an invitation to the IACHR. However, given that the IACHR did not find the invitation "in a form it can accept," the administration recommended against EXIM financing

of the Allis-Chalmers application for the hydroelectric project at Yacyretá, as well as various aircraft purchases. Cyrus Vance to John Moore, Chairman Export-Import Bank, July 10, 1978 (2440), Argentina Declassification Project. See also Schmidli, *Fate of Freedom Elsewhere*, 147–52; Sikkink, *Mixed Signals*, 133.

104. In response to questions posed by Yatron and Burke, Derian reported that the Argentine government was committing "systematic torture and summary executions." When the committee members questioned the pervasiveness of such tactics, Derian responded that "so much evidence of human rights violation in Argentina has accumulated that to argue about it would be a 'waste of time.'" The Argentine press picked up her statements and the American embassy in Buenos Aires reported that her testimony was perceived by Argentines as "a public and formal accusation by the USG of Argentina." AmEmbassy Buenos Aires to State Department, "Derian Testimony to House Foreign Affairs Committee," August 10, 1978 (2314), Argentina Declassification Project; Secretary of State to AmEmbassy Buenos Aires, "Assistant Secretary Derian Congressional Testimony," August 17, 1978 (2289), Argentina Declassification Project.

105. AmEmbassy Buenos Aires to Secretary of State, "Argentine Distress over Carter OAS Speech," June 27, 1978 (2485), Argentina Declassification Project.

106. AmEmbassy Buenos Aires to Secretary of State, "Continuing Reaction to U.S. Human Rights Sanctions Policy," August 29, 1978 (2249), State-Argentina Project.

107. "Respuesta necesaria," *Clarín*, August 12, 1978, Prensa, CELS Archive; "Una cuestión de política exterior," *La Nación*, August 11, 1978, Prensa, CELS Archive.

108. AmEmbassy Buenos Aires to Secretary of State, "Continuing Reaction to U.S. Human Rights Sanctions Policy"; State Department Memo RC to PD, "Translation of Postcards from Argentina," August 30, 1978 (2243), Argentina Declassification Project.

109. David Rothstein to Robert Pastor, August 1, 1978, NSA, Staff Materials, North/South Pastor (tab 24), box 1, Argentina, 1–8/78, JCL.

110. United Tech to Cyrus Vance, August 24, 1978, NSA, Staff Materials, North/South Pastor (tab 24), box 1, Argentina, 1–8/78, JCL. Pastor responded to Gray's letter sympathetically but noted that the administration had made its decision in compliance with legislative statutes. Robert Pastor to David Rothstein, August 10, 1978, NSA, Staff Materials, North/South Pastor (tab 24), box 1, Argentina, 1–8/78, JCL.

111. Robert Pastor to Zbigniew Brzezinski, "Argentina: Your Questions," August 9, 1978, NSA, Staff Materials, North/South Pastor (tab 24), box 1, Argentina, 1–8/78, JCL.

112. Robert Pastor to Zbigniew Brzezinski, "U.S. Policy to Argentina," August 31, 1978, NSA, Brzezinski Materials, Country Files (tab 6), box 4 Argentina, JCL.

113. Draft Letter, Zbigniew Brzezinski to Cyrus Vance, August 31, 1978, NSA, Brzezinski Materials, Country Files (tab 6), box 4 Argentina, JCL.

114. John Renner to Zbigniew Brzezinski, "US Exports and Human Rights," July 20, 1978, NSA, Brzezinski Materials, Subject (tab 9), box 27, Human Rights, 5/77–11/78, JCL.

115. Draft Letter, Brzezinski to Vance, August 31, 1978; Harold Brown to Cyrus Vance, August 22, 1978, NSA, Brzezinski Materials, Country Files (tab 6), box 4 Argentina, JCL. Brown mentioned specifically Peru, the Beagle Channel dispute, the Rio pact, and relations with the Soviet Bloc as areas where independent Argentine actions could run counter to U.S. interests. Brown suggested the approval of some spare parts whose hold had not been made public and whose release therefore would not appear to be a change of course.

116. Robert Pastor to Zbigniew Brzezinski, "Conversation with Andy Young," August 23, 1978, WHCF, Subject, FO 4–2, 1/20/77–1/20/81, JCL.

117. Pastor to Brzezinski, "Argentina: Your Questions," August 9, 1978. In the memo, Pastor quoted Vance's OAS speech the previous year, stating, "The surest way to defeat terrorism is

to promote justice. . . . Justice that is summary undermines the future it seeks to promote. It produces only more violence."

118. Ibid.; Robert Pastor to Zbigniew Brzezinski, "Human Rights in Argentina," August 28, 1978, *FRUS 1977–1980*, vol. 24, document 88. Kissinger had attended the World Cup soccer tournament held in Argentina that June. During his visit he had met with the Argentine leadership and afterward cautioned the current administration about the unproductive divides between Buenos Aires and Washington. Pastor to Brzezinski, "Argentina: Your Questions," August 9, 1978.

119. Pastor assured Brzezinski he would work with Viron Vaky to regain more stable footing for U.S. policies and mediate between the IACHR and Argentine government "in a way which permits the latter to save face and the former to preserve its institutional integrity." Pastor to Brzezinski, "Argentina: Your Questions," August 9, 1978.

120. Robert Pastor to Zbigniew Brzezinski, August 31, 1978, NSA, Brzezinski Materials, Country Files (tab 6), box 4 Argentina, JCL.

121. Memcon, Jorge Videla and Walter Mondale, September 4, 1978, *FRUS 1977–1980*, vol. 24, document 90.

122. Derian's recent testimony was particularly galling to Videla as he raised it more than once, explaining to Mondale that "Ms. Derian's statements are contributing to a deterioration in our relations." Ibid.

123. Ibid.

124. Raul Castro to Cyrus Vance, "Meeting between the Vice President and President Videla," September 8, 1978 (2190), Argentina Declassification Project.

125. The embassy was careful to note that it didn't "believe that all human rights violations have ceased in Argentina or are about to cease, even though as reported earlier, the number of abuses is down." AmEmbassy Buenos Aires to Secretary of State, "Human Rights: Guarded Optimism," September 28, 1978 (2160), Argentina Declassification Project.

126. Letter from John Moore, Chairman Export-Import Bank, to Jorge Pegoraro, Executive Director Entidad Binacional Yacyretá, "Yacyretá Hydroelectric Project," September 28, 1978, NSA, Staff Materials, North/South Pastor (tab 24), box 1, Argentina 9–12/78, JCL; AmEmbassy Buenos Aires to Secretary of State, "GOA's IACHR Announcement: Background and Fallout," October 18, 1978 (2108), Argentina Declassification Project.

127. Pastor to Brzezinski, "Argentina: Your Questions," August 9, 1978.

128. Zbigniew Brzezinski to Cyrus Vance, "U.S. Policy to Argentina," March 21, 1979, *FRUS 1977–1980*, vol. 24, document 98. See also Kelly, *Sovereign Emergencies*, 245–71; Schmidli, *Fate of Freedom Elsewhere*, 153–55; Sikkink, *Mixed Signals*, 133–34.

129. Pastor to Brzezinski, "U.S. Policy to Argentina," August 31, 1978; Draft Letter, Brzezinski to Vance, August 31, 1978.

130. Jessica Tuchman Mathews to Zbigniew Brzezinski, "Argentina—Human Rights," September 26, 1978, NSA, Staff Materials, North/South Pastor (tab 24), box 1, Argentina, 9–12/1978, JCL.

131. Jessica Tuchman Mathews to Zbigniew Brzezinski, "Thoughts on the Attached," September 25, 1978, NSA, Global Issues (Mathews), Subject File, box 8, HR: Argentina, 8/78–3/79, JCL.

132. Patricia Derian to Warren Christopher and Cyrus Vance, "Next Steps in Argentina," January 26, 1979, Argentina Declassification Project.

133. Viron Vaky to Warren Christopher, "U.S. Initiatives to Effect Human Rights," March 20, 1979 (1728), Argentina Declassification Project.

134. Robert Pastor to Zbigniew Brzezinski, "Daily Activities," September 27, 1978, NLC-24-54-2-16-7, JCL.

135. "WOLA Activity Report: January 1978–October 1978," Administration Files, General Management-History, box 28, Activity Reports 11/78–6/79, WOLA Duke Records.

136. Warren Christopher to Edward Kennedy, October 13, 1978, NSA, Staff Material, North/South Pastor (tab 24), box 1, Argentina 9–12/78, JCL.

137. Les Aspin to John Moore, October 23, 1978, NSA, Staff Material, North/South Pastor (tab 24), box 1, Argentina, 9–12/78, JCL.

138. Harkin had proposed legislation extending binding "gross violator" language to the IMF and the EXIM Bank, both of which had been defeated. "Congress Legislation, Human Rights: The Year in Review," *Update Latin America* (November/December 1978), Administration Files, General Management, History, box 30, 1978–81, WOLA Duke Records.

139. Senator Fritz Hollings to Jimmy Carter, October 17, 1978, NSA, Staff Material, North/South Pastor (tab 24), box 1, Argentina 9–12/78, JCL.

140. Fraser had given up his congressional seat for an unsuccessful bid for the U.S. Senate.

141. Democrats lost fifteen house seats to Republicans in the 1978 midterm elections, retaining the majority but losing the two-thirds supermajority they had held since the 1972 election.

142. Zbigniew Brzezinski to Cyrus Vance, "U.S. Policy to Argentina," March 21, 1979, *FRUS 1977–1980*, vol. 24, document 98. Three days later, Mathews noted that "for better or worse, your memo apparently had an effect," and the State Department had decided to abstain on a World Bank loan vote scheduled for the next day. Global Issues Staff to Zbigniew Brzezinski, "Evening Report," March 26, 1979, NLC-10–19–3–19–7, JCL.

143. Donald Bonkers, who had taken over the committee, held a series of hearings on the administration's human rights policy in the spring and summer of 1979. George Lister to Viron Vaky, "Congressional Human Rights Hearing," May 2, 1979, box 64, folder 1, Vaky, Lister Papers; Warren Christopher, "Implementing the Human Rights Policy," May 2, 1979, box 29, folder 7 Christopher, Lister Papers.

144. Other violators mentioned by name included Nicaragua, the Philippines, South Korea, South Africa, El Salvador, Guatemala, Rhodesia, and Indonesia. Briefing Memo, Patricia Derian to Warren Christopher, "The Non-Governmental Community's Recommendations for Strengthening U.S. Human Rights Policy," *FRUS 1977–1980*, vol. 2, document 187.

145. Jo Marie Griesgraber, "A Critique of the Human Rights Policy toward Latin America," Statement Prepared for Testimony before the U.S. House of Representatives Committee on Foreign Affairs, Subcommittee on International Organizations, June 21, 1979, Administration Files, General Management, History, box 30, Early Docs, WOLA Duke Records.

146. Tom Beard to Tim Kraft, "Leather Goods Industry," August 7, 1979, WHCF, CO-8, Argentina, box CO-10, JCL.

147. Viron Vaky to Cyrus Vance, "Goals for Latin America," August 31, 1979, *FRUS 1977–1980*, vol. 24, document 48.

148. Viron Vaky to Warren Christopher, "U.S. Initiatives to Effect Human Rights," March 20, 1979 (1728), Argentina Declassification Project; Cyrus Vance to USMission USNATO, "Trends in Latin America, March 23, 1978 (1717), Argentina Declassification Project; AmEmbassy Buenos Aires to Secretary of State, "Ambassador Discusses Human Rights with General Viola," March 14, 1979, Argentina Declassification Project.

149. AmEmbassy Buenos Aires to Secretary of State, "Ambassador Discusses Human Rights with General Viola."

150. AmEmbassy Buenos Aires to Secretary of State, "Police Raid Two Human Rights Organizations," August 13, 1979 (1728), Argentina Declassification Project.

151. AmEmbassy Buenos Aires to Latin America Bureau, "Argentine Campaign to Bamboozle IACHR," August 10, 1979 (1376), Argentina Declassification Project.

152. AmEmbassy Buenos Aires to Secretary of State, "IACHR Visit: Not Much Changed?" September 21, 1979 (1209), Argentina Declassification Project.

153. "The First Steps," *Buenos Aires Herald*, September 13, 1979, Prensa, CELS Archive.

154. AmEmbassy Buenos Aires to Secretary of State, "Human Rights in Argentina," October 5, 1979, Argentina Declassification Project.

155. Burton Kaufman and Scott Kaufman note that although many Americans approved of Carter's handling of the various international crises in the summer of 1979, their assessment of the United States' position in the world was much more negative. Carter's speech on January 4, laying out a range of U.S. sanctions in response to Soviet "aggression," including a grain embargo and possible boycott of the 1980 Summer Olympics in Moscow, also received a favorable response from the public. Farber writes that as the crises droned on, "What a large majority of Americans . . . perceived was that in the midst of a runaway inflation, an energy crisis, and what the president himself described as a 'crisis of confidence,' the government was falling apart at the seams." Kaufman and Kaufman, *Presidency of James Earl Carter, Jr.*, 185–86, 197; David Farber, *Taken Hostage: The Iran Hostage Crisis and America's First Encounter with Radical Islam* (Princeton: Princeton University Press, 2005), 34. For more on scholars' assessment of Carter's shift toward Cold War priorities in 1980, see Glad, *Outsider in the White House*, 176–216; Scott Kaufman, *Plans Unraveled*, 201–32; Schmidli, *Fate of Freedom Elsewhere*, 173–79; Sikkink, *Mixed Signals*, 124–25.

156. In an address to the U.S. public on January 4, 1980, Carter announced the suspension of SALT II negotiations and the implementation of a grain embargo on sales to the Soviet Union above the eight-million-ton/five-year agreed minimum level. He also announced new limits on technology exports, curtailment of Soviet fishing privileges in U.S. waters, and a recall of the U.S. ambassador from Moscow. In his memoir Brzezinski wrote, "We had no illusions that sanctions in themselves would force the Soviets out, but we all felt that the Soviet Union had to pay some tangible price for its misconduct." Brzezinski, *Power and Principle*, 430.

157. Zbigniew Brzezinski to Jimmy Carter, "Daily Report," January 14, 1980, NLC-1-13-8-6-2, JCL.

158. Action Memo, John Bushnell to Cyrus Vance, "Human Rights Report for Argentina," January 22, 1980, *FRUS 1977–1980*, vol. 24, document 105. In the margins of the memo noting that State had chosen to approve the Human Rights Bureau's version, Brzezinski wrote, "HO [Henry Owen] get this under control." Bloomfield added, "Henry: I can't recommend any specific changes, nor can Thornton. Any thoughts?" Lincoln Bloomfield to Zbigniew Brzezinski, "Human Rights Report on Argentina," January 30, 1980, NSA, Brzezinski Materials, Country File (tab 6), box 4, Argentina, JCL.

159. Videla complained bitterly about the IACHR and asked for U.S. "help" in the next step of the commission's deliberations. Goodpaster stressed that the United States would not interfere or try to influence an independent commission's findings. Goodpaster also responded to Videla's concerns about the upcoming UN General Assembly by reassuring him that "the U.S. was not interested in Argentina's international censure, but in the improvement in human rights." Cable the Situation Room to Phil Wise for the President, "General Goodpaster's Mission to Argentina: General Report," January 26, 1980, NLC-16-123-2-9-7, JCL.

160. Department of State, "Issue Paper—Argentina," May 12, 1980, *FRUS 1977–1980*, vol. 24, document 109; Vance's instructions to the embassy related that the administration desired cooperation with the Argentine leadership, but "it will be important for them to be able to point to progress on human rights in specific areas. We thus would be interested in discussing specific improvements in human rights as part of these consultations." Vance asserted that ongoing human rights concerns ruled out the weakest option, but "in light of importance of Argentine cooperation with respect to grain sales to [the] Soviets, foregoing should be presented in a

positive way." Secretary of State to AmEmbassy Buenos Aires, "Consultations on Human Rights," February 5, 1980, NLC-16-120-1-21-7, JCL.

161. "US Policy toward Latin America—Post Afghanistan," *Update Latin America* (January/ February 1980), Administrative Files, General Management, History, box 30, WOLA Update 1978–81, WOLA Duke Records.

162. "The Carter Administration and Human Rights," *Update Latin America* (September/ October 1980), Administrative Files, General Management, History, box 30, WOLA Update 1978–81, WOLA Duke Records.

163. ADA Press Release, "ADA Gears Up for 'Draft Kennedy Campaign,'" July 22, 1979, M97–135, box 29, 1980 Presidential Election, ADA Records; National Board Minutes, "1980 Presidential Election," [July 1979], M2001–087, box 1, National Board Minutes, 1979, ADA Records.

164. The National Board Resolution on the 1980 campaign noted that "ADA regrets, but we do not shrink for challenging inadequate Presidential leadership." National Board Minutes, "1980 Presidential Election," [July 1979].

165. "The Candidates: Three Views of the South," *Update Latin America* (July/August 1980), Geographic Files, Argentina, box 45, Argentine Office, WOLA Update, WOLA Duke Records.

166. In a five-page letter to the board members, Arthur Schlesinger, Jr., and Joseph L. Rauh called the endorsement of Carter "an admission of liberal defeat," and they charged that by supporting him, the ADA would call into question its own credibility "as an independent liberal organization." James Loeb to Board Members, September 6, 1980, M97–135, box 29, 1980 Presidential Election, ADA Records; Arthur Schlesinger, Jr., and Joseph L. Rauh to ADA Board Members, September 15, 1980, M97–135, box 29, 1980 Presidential Election, ADA Records.

167. "Foggy Bottom: Foggier than Usual," *Update Latin America* (May/June 1980), Administration Files, General Management, History, box 30, 1979–1981, WOLA Duke Records; Patricia Derian to Warren Christopher, "Problems over the Next Several Weeks and Months," April 30, 1980, *FRUS 1977–1980*, vol. 2, document 200.

168. Special Coordinating Committee Meeting, "Summary of Conclusions: SCC Soviet Grain Policy," May 1, 1980, NLC-132-112-11-3-5, JCL.

169. The State Department's issue paper on Argentina asserted that the Argentine military regime had "no desire to emulate the Soviets or align themselves with the Soviet Union." Department of State Issue Paper—Argentina, May 12, 1980, *FRUS 1977–1980*, vol. 24, document 109; Department of State, "Evolution of Argentine-Soviet Relations," April 23, 1980, NLC-20-32-4-4-6, JCL.

170. The Department of Defense, for example, was the only department to recommend efforts to repeal the Humphrey-Kennedy Amendment. Reviewing its human rights policy in light of the new pressures brought by the grain embargo, the State Department's PRC identified three possible paths forward: a "strong concentration on human rights" that had marked its first two years in office; a moderate effort at strengthening the working relationship between the two countries, offering a "balance in treatment" that recognized improvements but curtailing overt association with the regime through continued restrictions on military supplies and maintaining current voting policy in IFIs; or a decisive move toward normalization of relations, including the resumption of military relationships. In the last scenario, human rights would "remain important to us" and the United States would continue to abstain on international loans. Department of State Issue Paper—Argentina, May 12, 1980.

171. In response to Brzezinski's summary of the meeting, Carter approved the proposals but also noted, "I'm inclined to move faster." Few if any significant new initiatives were outlined in the action memorandum in June. While proposing increased consultative contacts with the Argentine military, all recommendations were carefully couched to abide both by the letter and the sprit of

the Humphrey-Kennedy Amendment, with no intention to modify the statute for the time being. Minutes of a Policy Review Committee Meeting, Argentina, May 14, 1980, *FRUS 1977–1980*, vol. 24, document 110, n. 7; Warren Christopher to Jimmy Carter, "Steps to Improve U.S.-Argentine Relations," June 14, 1980, *FRUS 1977–1980*, vol. 24, document 111.

172. AmEmbassy Buenos Aires to Secretary of State, "Assessment of My Visit to Buenos Aires," March 26, 1980, *FRUS 1977–1980*, vol. 24, document 107.

173. Quoted in ibid., n. 4.

174. Carter noted in the margins, "Ed—Good idea. Same process should be followed with other difficult countries." Christopher to Carter, "Steps to Improve U.S.-Argentine Relations," June 14, 1980, n. 1, n. 11.

175. Kathryn Sikkink to Warren Christopher, May 12, 1981, Geographic, Argentina, box 44, WOLA Letters, Argentina/Official US Executive Branch, WOLA Duke Records; Madison Adams to Kathryn Sikkink, May 22, 1980, Geographic, Argentina, box 44, WOLA Letters, Argentina/Official US Executive Branch, WOLA Duke Records.

176. William Odom to Zbigniew Brzezinski, "Weekly Report," June 5, 1980, NLC-10–29–5–48–2, JCL.

177. Lincoln Bloomfield to Zbigniew Brzezinski, "Human Rights (Argentina)," June 10, 1980, NLC-24–100–8–2–4, JCL.

178. The Department of Defense, for example, had consistently advocated a more robust approach to the Argentine government in response to new security concerns in 1980. Odom to Brzezinski, "Weekly Report," June 5, 1980.

179. Warren Christopher to Jimmy Carter, "Steps to Improve U.S.-Argentine Relations," June 14, 1980; Zbigniew Brzezinski to Jimmy Carter, "Report on US-Argentine Relations," July 3, 1980, *FRUS 1977–1980*, vol. 24, document 112.

180. In late July the State Department reported having evidence of significant Argentine involvement in the Bolivian military coup on July 17, 1980. In response, the administration cancelled a diplomatic visit by Assistant Secretary of State Bill Bowdler, which had been scheduled to coordinate efforts on grain sales, human rights, and nuclear nonproliferation. Edmund Muskie to Jimmy Carter, "Assistant Secretary Bowdler's Visit to Argentina," July 28, 1980, *FRUS 1977–1980*, vol. 24, document 113.

181. "The Carter Administration and Human Rights," *Update Latin America* (September/October 1980), Geographic Files, Argentina, box 45, Argentina Office, WOLA Update, WOLA Duke Records.

182. Jimmy Carter, "Organization of American States Remarks at the 10th Regular Session of the General Assembly," November 11, 1981, https://www.presidency.ucsb.edu/node/250965.

5. The Reagan Reinvention

1. As Michael Schaller observed, "Reagan was another way to respond to problems of Watergate and Vietnam." Michael Schaller, *Ronald Reagan* (New York: Oxford University Press, 2011), 34.

2. Sandra Scanlon argues that Reagan's election reflected "the complex nature of the conservative coalition during the late 1970s and 1980s; and the continuing strength of liberalism which limited conservatives' ability to fully implement their diverse agendas once in power." Sandra Scanlon, "Ronald Reagan and the Conservative Movement," in *A Companion to Ronald Reagan*, ed. Andrew Johns (West Sussex, UK: Wiley-Blackwell, 2015), 586. See also Gil Troy,

Morning in America: How Ronald Reagan Invented the 1980s (Princeton: Princeton University Press, 2005); John Ehrman, *The Rise of Neoconservatism: Intellectuals and Foreign Affairs* (New Haven: Yale University Press, 1995).

3. Although the issue of "strength" made a more frequent appearance than it had in 1976, Carter did not fall back to a simple Cold War framing of military power. Rather, Carter's campaign materials highlighted the importance and centrality of morality and decency, embodied in the administration's human rights diplomacy, to America's ongoing ability to assert its power in the world. Echoing his inaugural address, a 1980 memo for the DNC's platform committee stressed, "The use of American power is necessary as a means of shaping not only a more secure, but also a more decent world. And to shape a decent world, we must pursue objectives that are moral, that make clear our support for the aspirations of mankind and that are rooted in the ideals of the American people." Carter touted his administration's improved relations with the developing world, citing accomplishments such as the Panama Canal Treaties, which identified the United States "with the cause of human rights and democracy" and forged "a more balanced relationship with the nations in the region." Draft Statement, "National Security Policy," June 9, 1980, NSA, Brzezinski Materials, Subject Files (tab 7), box 16, DNC Platform Committee, 06/80, JCL.

4. Jeane Kirkpatrick, "Dictatorships and Double Standards," *Commentary* 68, no. 5 (November 1979): 34–45. Debate briefing materials, citing both Kirkpatrick and Ernest Lefever, affirmed that "human rights should be an important factor in any U.S. foreign policy equation." Reagan's criticisms of Carter's "frequently quixotic human rights policy stem not only from its inconsistencies or its damage to our bilateral relationships but also from the fact that so many other considerations in our overall foreign policy were ignored. Another major criticism of the Administration's human rights policy is that it is not universally applied. As a consequence, the United States is seen as being very hypocritical and following a double standard. Moreover, we sometimes more harshly criticize our friends' human rights record than those of our adversaries. The upshot has been a policy that is neither credible nor sustainable." Briefing Memo, "What Do You Think of the Carter Administration's Human Rights Policy," [1980], Reagan, Ronald: 1980 Campaign Papers, series VI: Debate Files (James Baker), Global Issues, Human Rights, box 239, Ronald Reagan Presidential Library, Simi Valley, California (hereafter RRL).

5. Pamphlet, "Senator Kennedy and President Carter on the Issues Facing America," December 1979, M97–135, box 29, Draft Kennedy, 1980, ADA Records. See chapter 4 for more on Kennedy's primary challenge.

6. Some scholars, such as Kathryn Sikkink, have asserted that Reagan had no human rights policy during his first year and a half in office. Others, such as Joe Renouard, have contended that Reagan embraced human rights from the outset, although with a fundamentally different vision than that of the Carter administration. "First, human rights debates and policies," Renouard writes, "were filtered through the first Reagan administration's obsession with events in Central America . . . and Eastern Europe. . . . Second, the administration did not ignore human rights altogether, but rather interpreted human rights goals to coincide with narrow interests of Cold War anticommunism." Glenn Mower observes, "Whereas most of Carter's tenure in office was marked by intense bureaucratic conflict over the inclusion of human rights in foreign policy considerations, this struggle had virtually ended by the time Reagan assumed the presidency, and human rights had come to be accepted as a legitimate foreign policy element." The debates over human rights in the first year of Reagan's presidency were not primarily whether to keep human rights as an issue but rather what policy objectives it would serve. Sikkink, *Mixed Signals*, 148–49; Joe Renouard, *Human Rights in American Foreign Policy 1960 to the Soviet Collapse* (Philadelphia: University of Pennsylvania Press, 2016), 167–68; A. Glenn Mower, Jr., *Human Rights and American Foreign Policy: The Carter and Reagan Experiences* (New York: Greenwood, 1987), 83. See also Tamar

Jacoby, "The Reagan Turnaround on Human Rights," *Foreign Affairs* 64, no. 5 (Summer 1986): 1066–86.

7. Quoted in Dustin Walcher, "The Reagan Doctrine," in Johns, *Companion to Ronald Reagan*, 345. For more on Reagan's return to Cold War paradigms, see Michael Paulauskas, "Reagan, The Soviet Union and the Cold War, 1981–1985," in Johns, *Companion to Ronald Reagan*, 276–94; Melvyn Leffler, *For the Soul of Mankind* (New York: Hill & Wang, 2007), 339–60; John Lewis Gaddis, *Strategies of Containment* (New York: Oxford University Press, 2005), 349–53; Zelizer, *Arsenal of Democracy*, 303–6.

8. "What Do You Think of the Carter Administration's Human Rights Policy." Patrick Moynihan, for example, supported human rights, but he claimed that "the Carter administration was fouling up its human rights campaign. The administration did not realize that human rights policy was a political weapon to be used in the battle against totalitarianism, and instead treated it as a 'special kind of international social work.'" Carter's human rights constructions "divert our attention from the central political struggle of our time—that between liberal democracy and totalitarian Communist—and focus instead on something else." Quoted in John Ehrman, *The Rise of Neoconservatism: Intellectuals and Foreign Affairs* (New Haven: Yale University Press, 1995), 94.

9. Radio addresses by Ronald Reagan: "Helsinki Pact," December 2, 1979; "Human Rights," January 3, 1979; "Cuba," March 6, 1979, all in Reagan, Ronald: 1980 Campaign Papers, 1965–80, series I: Hannaford/California Headquarters: Ronald Reagan Files, Radio Commentaries/Broadcasts, box 15, RLL; Memo, "International Economics," October 2, 1980, Reagan, Ronald: 1980 Campaign Papers, 1965–80, series IV: Debate Files (James Baker), Global Issues, Human Rights, RRL.

10. Alexander Haig to Ronald Reagan, "Our Policy toward Chile," February 16, 1981, Roger Fontaine Files, Chile, box 4, 1/20/1981–04/26/1981, RRL; Richard Allen to Ronald Reagan, "Secretary Haig's Recommendations on Chile," February 20, 1981, Roger Fontaine Files, Chile, box 4, 1/20/1981–04/26/1981, RRL. See also Morris Morley and Chris McGillion, *Reagan and Pinochet: The Struggle over U.S. Policy toward Chile* (New York: Cambridge University Press, 2015), 13–18, 26–31.

11. John Bushnell, Report of February 23 Interagency Group Meeting on Argentina, February 24, 1981, WHORM, Subject File, CO 008 (Argentine Republic), Begin-017729, RRL.

12. AmEmbassy Santiago to Secretary of State, "Chile/El Salvador," February 27, 1981, Executive Secretariat, NSC: Records, Country File, Chile, box 29, 1/20/81–7/31/84 [5], RRL; AmEmbassy Santiago to Secretary of State, "Argentina/El Salvador," March 2, 1981, Executive Secretariat, NSC: Records, Country File, Chile, box 29, 1/20/81–7/31/84 [5], RRL.

13. Memcon, "Summary of the President's Meeting with Argentine President-designate General Roberto O. Viola," March 17, 1981, Roger Fontaine Files, March 17, 1981—President Viola, box 18 (box 90125), RRL.

14. In Reagan's words, a "real terrorist war had been launched and . . . terrorists felt free in taking human life." Ibid.

15. Ibid.; Secretary of State to AmEmbassy Buenos Aires, "Secretary's Meeting with President-Designate Viola," March 18, 1981, Roger Fontaine Files, Argentina, Mtg w/ President Reagan (5), box 18 (box 90125), RRL.

16. Roger Fontaine to Richard Allen, "The President's Meeting with Roberto Viola, Argentina's President-designate," March 14, 1981, Roger Fontaine Files, Argentina, Mtg w/ President Reagan (2), box 18 (box 90125), RRL. Italics in original.

17. "Excerpts from an Interview with Walter Cronkite of CBS News," March 3, 1981, *Public Papers of the Presidents of the United States, Ronald Reagan, 1981* (Washington, D.C.: Government Printing Office, 1982), 196.

18. Ibid. Italics in original.

19. Similar to resumption of military assistance, the draft argued that multilateral financial institutions "merit continued support because they mobilize additional capital from other donors for developing nations important to U.S. security and economic interests and because they foster the development of market-oriented policies." Ibid.

20. The draft enumerated separately the need for "expanded trade and investment," "access to energy resources," and "economic growth supportive of political and economic objectives outlined above." Ibid.

21. Roger Fontaine to Richard Allen, "South American Speech Outlines," May 18, 1981, Roger Fontaine Files, box 15, Latin America, RRL.

22. Enders warned that Cuba was ruthlessly exploiting and radicalizing internal struggles and dissent with "great subtlety and sophistication," uniting fragmented groups, and training and arming guerrillas in El Salvador, Nicaragua, Guatemala, and Colombia. Thomas Enders, "Tasks for U.S. Policy in the Hemisphere," June 3, 1981, Roger Fontaine Files, box 9, Latin America [June–August 1981], RRL.

23. Enders continued, "I do not see how the interests and hopes implicit in the three tasks I have outlined—for a strengthened prosperity among neighbors, for the defense of strategic interests in the Caribbean and in South America—can be furthered by confrontation or condescension." Ibid.

24. Richard Fairbanks to Jim Courter, "Chile-Kennedy Amendment," May 4, 1981, Chile Declassification Project; State Department Memo, "Rationale for Modifying the Kennedy Amendment Prohibition on Arms Sales and Assistance to Chile," June 18, 1981, Chile Declassification Project; Thomas Enders to Alexander Haig, "Your Meeting with Chilean Foreign Minister René Rojas," June 5, 1981, Chile Declassification Project.

25. The 1977 International Financial Institutions Act required U.S. representatives to MDBs to oppose loans to any country whose "government engages in a consistent pattern of gross violations of internationally recognized human rights." The Carter administration had consistently voted against or abstained on loans to Chile and Argentina that didn't meet basic human needs criteria as part of its human rights strategies, but it had no clear metrics for applying the "gross violator" label. Stephen Palmer, Robert Hormats, Thomas Enders, and Paul Wolfowitz to Alexander Haig, "U.S. Votes on Multilateral Development Bank Loans to Argentina, Chile, and Uruguay," June 27, 1981, Chile Declassification Project.

26. Ibid.

27. "Chile: Back in the Fold," *Update Latin America* (July/August 1981), Geographic Files, Argentina, box 45, Argentina Office, WOLA Update, WOLA Duke Records.

28. "Latin America and the Transition: Taking Aim," *Update Latin America* (January/February 1981), Geographic Files, Argentina, box 45, Argentina Office, WOLA Update, WOLA Duke Records.

29. Letelier-Moffitt Fund to Key Contacts, "Recent State Department Decision to Lift Sanctions against Chile," March 13, 1981, Geographic Files, Chile, WOLA, box 65, Issue, Letelier, WOLA Duke Records; Tom Harkin Press Release, "Harkin Cites Hypocrisy," February 20, 1981, Geographic Files, Chile, WOLA, box 65, Issue, Letelier, WOLA Duke Records; "Statement by Senator Edward M. Kennedy Opposing Administration Actions on Chile," February 20, 1981, Geographic Files, Chile, WOLA, box 65, Issue, Letelier, WOLA Duke Records; "Institute for Policy Studies News Release," February 20, 1981, Geographic Files, Chile, WOLA, box 65, Issue, Letelier, WOLA Duke Records.

30. The arrests included Emilio Mignone and Jose Westerkamp of CELS; Augusto Comte, head of the Asamblea Permanente; and Carmen Lapco of Las Madres. Memo to Nick Meyers,

"Arrests of Key Argentine Human Rights Activists," March 2, 1981, Geographic Files, Argentina, box 45, Argentina Office, WOLA Update, WOLA Duke Records.

31. "A Turn for the Worse in Argentina," and "Human rights Reports: A Valuable Exercise," *Update Latin America* (March/April 1981), Administration Files, General Management, History, box 30, 1978–81, WOLA Duke Records.

32. Ernest Lefever, "The Trivialization of Human Rights," *Policy Review* 3 (1978): 11–26.

33. Ibid. See Ethics and Public Policy Center, *Morality and Foreign Policy: A Symposium on President Carter's Stance*, ed. Ernest Lefever (Washington, D.C.: Georgetown University, 1977).

34. Lefever, "Trivialization of Human Rights," 11–26.

35. "The Worst Yet," *Nation*, February 21, 1981, reprinted in "Summary of News Stories and Commentaries Concerning the Nomination of Ernest W. Lefever for Assistant Secretary of State for Human Rights and Humanitarian Affairs," May 31, 1981, Edwin Meese III Files, OA2408, Meeting on Lefever Nomination, 06/01/1981 (2), RRL.

36. A March 2 *New York Times* editorial, for example, opposed Lefever's nomination on the grounds that he was "dubious of the office he will be administering." "Summary of News Stories and Commentaries Concerning the Nomination of Ernest W. Lefever."

37. The core of the controversy centered on studies about the use of baby formula in the developing world, which critics charged were skewed to please Nestlé, a significant donor to the foundation. Critics charged that not only was the study biased but that it paid *Fortune* magazine an unseemly amount for reprints of an article covering the study, indicating that its findings were favorably skewed as a result of this financial largess. "False Charges against Ernest W. Lefever, Assistant Secretary Designate for Human Rights," March 17, 1981, Council to the Office of the President Files, Appointee Files and Records, Ernest W. Lefever, RRL; Anthony Lewis, "Advice and Consent," *New York Times*, May 21, 1981, reprinted in "Summary of News Stories and Commentaries Concerning the Nomination of Ernest W. Lefever."

38. Before the hearing, Lefever told Percy that opposition was "communist inspired." As a witness, Lefever denied that he used that phrase, and Percy responded, "You did, I heard you." Other senators concurred that Lefever made the same point to them. "Summary of News Stories and Commentaries Concerning the Nomination of Ernest W. Lefever." Lewis, "Advice and Consent."

39. Ibid.

40. A press release by Senators Cranston, Tsongas, and Dodd requested that Lefever withdraw his nomination, warning that if he did not, they "intend to call upon the Chairman . . . to conduct extensive hearings, including sworn public testimony from Lefever, Ambassador Kirkpatrick, from Nestlé Corporation officials and from attorney Thomas J. Ward." "Press Release Issued by Senators Cranston, Tsongas, and Dodd," May 22, 1981, reprinted in "Summary of News Stories and Commentaries Concerning the Nomination of Ernest W. Lefever."

41. Judy Bachrach, "Mr. Lefever's in a Quandary," *Washington Star*, May 25, 1981, reprinted in "Summary of News Stories and Commentaries Concerning the Nomination of Ernest W. Lefever."

42. "Calling Names," *Wall Street Journal*, May 20, 1981, reprinted in "Summary of News Stories and Commentaries Concerning the Nomination of Ernest W. Lefever."

43. "Excerpts from Letters Supporting Dr. Ernest W. Lefever as Assistant Secretary of State for Human Rights and Humanitarian Affairs," April 30, 1981, Counsel to the Office of the President, CFOA 114, [Lefever Nominations—Supporting Letters (Distributed by Senator Hayakawa's Office)], RRL.

44. "Editorial," May 24, 1981, *Washington Post*, reprinted in "Issue #5: General Philosophic Criticisms—News Articles," Counsel to the President's Office, CFOA114, Lefever Nomination-[Issues] (2), RRL.

45. Glenn Mower writes, "For its part, Congress was evidently quite determined to have some say concerning the formulation and implementation of the Reagan administration's human rights policy." Mower, *Human Rights and American Foreign Policy*, 82.

46. His statement explicitly referenced the lifting of EXIM restrictions on Chile, efforts to repeal restrictions on arms sales to Argentina, recent voting instructions for IFIs, and reversal of positions at the UN Human Rights Commission on Chile. U.S. Congress, Committee on Foreign Affairs, Subcommittee on Human Rights and International Organizations, *Implementation of Congressionally Mandated Human Rights Provisions: Hearings before the Subcommittee on Human Rights and International Organizations of the Committee on Foreign Affairs*, 97th Congress, 1st session, July 14 and 30, September 17, 1981 (Washington, D.C.: Government Printing Office, 1982), 2, 3.

47. During the hearing Bonkers stressed, "I have never been consulted. The only thing we have had with respect to our change of policy on international financial institutions is a letter from the Secretary of the Treasury that arrived several days before the policy was changed." Stoessel conceded that the notification could have come earlier, but that the administration was in compliance with the law requiring prior notification, if not consultation. Ibid., 21.

48. Ibid., 26, 22,13.

49. Congressman Leach observed that Stoessel's statement made no explicit mention of the authoritarian-totalitarian distinction and wondered whether this was indicative of a change in the administration's approach. Stoessel noted that debates about the distinction had become a distraction from the real intent of the policy, "which is to be evenhanded about pursuing human rights goals. We still see differences clearly between authoritarian and totalitarian governments." Ibid., 11, 16, 7, 24.

50. Ibid., 98, 93, 25, 31.

51. Ibid., 40.

52. Renouard argues that the defeat of Lefever's nomination was "a triumph of left/liberal vision of human rights policymaking, including the belief that the head of the human rights bureau must be an advocate." Renouard, *Human Rights in American Foreign Policy*, 179. Some scholars, such as Sikkink and Snyder, have pointed to his failed nomination as evidence that the rising status of human rights internationally and within the United States made it impossible for Reagan to jettison the issue from the administration's foreign policy agenda. This is certainly true but also underestimates the ways that Reagan's foreign policy already embraced a new conservative construction of human rights from the first days in office. Sikkink, *Mixed Signals*, 155–56; Sarah B. Snyder, "The Defeat of Ernest Lefever's Nomination: Keeping Human Rights on the United States Foreign Policy Agenda," in *Challenging U.S. Foreign Policy: America and the World in the Long Twentieth Century*, ed. Bevan Sewell and Scott Lucas (London: Palgrave Macmillan, 2011), 136–61.

53. U.S. Congress, *Implementation of Congressionally Mandated Human Rights Provisions*, 33, 16, 38, 47.

54. Ibid., 77, 89.

55. Secretary of State to AmEmbassy Stockholm, "United Nations Human Rights Commission: Final Report on the Thirty-Seventh Session," July 21, 1981, Chile Declassification Project.

56. William Korey notes that Reagan's opposition was represented by a subset of the Republican Party that viewed the Helsinki Accords as a "sell-out to the Soviets." William Korey, *The Promises We Keep: Human Rights, the Helsinki Process, and American Foreign Policy* (New York: St. Martin's Press, 1993), 140. See also Snyder, *Human Rights Activism*, 136, 155. The Madrid CSCE Review Meeting had opened on November 11, 1980, less than a week after Reagan's electoral victory. It concluded in March 1983. See Snyder's definitive work on the Helsinki process, *Human Rights Activism*.

57. Reagan's statement also criticized the Carter administration's "timid" approach to Soviet violations at the Belgrade conference. As William Korey observes, the charge was "inaccurate but fit with idea of inconsistency." Quoted in Korey, *Promises We Keep*, 141. Korey argues, "Significantly, Helsinki activism became Reagan's policy on the eve of the election. He issued a statement on Oct 17, which, after taking note of Madrid prep meetings stressed that the Helsinki Final Act 'involves important commitments to basic human freedoms.' " Ibid., 141.

58. In his memoir, Kampelman recalled that the day after Reagan's election, there was "great uncertainty among our allies with no sense of where our country would go under Reagan." Max M. Kampelman, *Entering New Worlds: The Memoirs of a Private Man in Public Life* (New York: HarperCollins, 1991), 245. Snyder argues that "Reagan's first term support for HR in E. Europe was manifested primarily within the CECE context in Kampelman's vocal and active diplomacy at Madrid." Snyder, *Human Rights Activism*, 143.

59. William Korey, *Human Rights and the Helsinki Accord: Focus on U.S. Policy* (New York: Foreign Policy Association, 1983), 41.

60. Ibid. Kampelman recalled meeting with Richard Allen in December to brief him on the Madrid proceedings. "To my surprise, Allen said he expected President Reagan to ask me to stay on." The day before the inauguration, Haig officially offered him the position. Kampelman, *Entering New Worlds*, 253. Snyder notes that although Kampelman was a Democrat, he was close to many of the neoconservatives shaping Reagan's foreign policy vision, notably Jeane Kirkpatrick. Snyder, *Human Rights Activism*, 137. Both Snyder and Korey believe that Kampelman's appointment led to unexpected consistency between Carter's and Reagan's policies at Helsinki. Snyder writes that Kampelman "established what would become unexpected consistency with Carter's support of the Helsinki process and use of open diplomacy to push for compliance." Ibid.,155. Korey agrees, stating, "What was striking was that American policy at Madrid would not shift at all, even though the new Chief Executive had initially opposed the signing of the Helsinki Final Act and, during the campaign in June 1980, called for a boycott of Madrid." Korey, *Promises We Keep*, 130.

61. Korey, *Promises We Keep*, 132; Snyder, *Human Rights Activism*, 156; Kampelman, *Entering New Worlds*, 279–80.

62. Kampelman wrote, "When Arthur Goldberg insisted—rightly—on the primacy of human rights at the Belgrade meeting in 1977, the NATO allies were hesitant, and this difference in Western approaches caused considerable tensions within the alliance. At Madrid, I was convinced that human rights had to be a part of a combined and coordinated Western policy, and by the end of the meeting, it was. From Madrid onward, the Soviet Union could entertain no further hope of splitting the West over human rights." Ibid., 279. Kampelman deliberately cultivated NATO unity and consultation, creating a formidable Western solidarity at Madrid on human rights, among other issues. Korey, *Human Rights and the Helsinki Accords*, 45–46. Snyder documents that fourteen different countries reported the names of 123 people suffering human rights violations. Snyder, *Human Rights Activism*, 148.

63. Kampelman, *Entering New Worlds*, 258–80; Snyder, *Human Rights Activism*, 144; Korey, *Promises We Keep*, 135. Kampelman logged almost three hundred hours of "off-the-record" discussions with the Soviets at Madrid. Korey argues, "While the dialogue was by no means restricted to human rights, it still enabled the United States to underscore that Washington saw issues of human rights compliance as particularly vital." Korey, *Promises We Keep*, 135.

64. Ronald Reagan to Leonid Brezhnev, April 24, 1981, *FRUS 1981–1988*, vol. 3, *Soviet Union, January 1981–January 1988*, ed. James Graham Wilson (Washington, D.C.: Government Printing Office, 2016), document 47. See also Leonid Brezhnev to Ronald Reagan, March 6, 1981, *FRUS 1981–1988*, vol. 3, document 26; Leonid Brezhnev to Ronald Reagan, May 27, 1981, *FRUS, 1981–*

1988, vol. 3, document 59; Memcon, "Private Meeting between Secretary Haig and Minister Gromyko," September 28, 1981, *FRUS 1981–1988*, vol. 3, document 90.

65. Kampelman explained that one of the United States' primary objectives was "to strengthen the Western alliance by recognizing that our West European friends who share our values were geographically in the forefront of confrontation with the Soviet Union; that they were concerned about a nuclear catastrophe; and that they were therefore in no position to 'ostracize' the Soviet Union." Quoted in Korey, *Promises We Keep*, 104.

66. Ronald Reagan to Leonid Brezhnev, November 17, 1981, *FRUS 1981–1988*, vol. 3, document 103.

67. In his memo, Haig reasoned that the Soviets would be willing to release some dissidents championed by the administration for a softening of U.S. "demands for language on human rights in the concluding document at Madrid. We would thus achieve 'balance': in part by the significant political—and humanitarian symbolism of getting people released. We would meet Congressional concerns that we won't get enough out of Madrid on human rights, and we would demonstrate that the Administration's approach to human rights produces more results that rhetoric." Alexander Haig to Ronald Reagan, "Release of Soviet Dissidents," November 9, 1981, *FRUS 1981–1988*, vol. 3, document 100; Memo for the Record, "Secretary's Debrief on His Meeting with Ambassador Dobrynin, November 11, 1981; 2:45 pm; with Messrs. Eagleburger and Bremer," *FRUS 1981–1988*, vol. 3, document 101.

68. AmEmbassy Santiago to Secretary of State, "Ambassador Kirkpatrick's Visit to Santiago: Overview," August 10, 1981, Chile Declassification Project; John Dinges, "Kirkpatrick Trip Upsets Opposition in Chile," *Washington Post*, August 13, 1981; Kirkpatrick's aide reported making arrangements for human rights materials to be transmitted from the embassy to her office, as well as a report on the meeting, but there is no acknowledgment of her receipt of these materials. Shannon Sorzano to Mike Durkee, "Our Meeting This Morning with Member of the Human Rights Commission of Chile," August 8, 1981, Chile Declassification Project; Department of State Daily Press Briefing, August 13, 1981, Jaqueline Tillman Files, box 90499, Chile, July 1978–11/10/1981, RRL.

69. AmEmbassy Buenos Aires to Secretary of State, "Ambassador Kirkpatrick's Visit to Santiago: Human Rights," August 13, 1981, Chile Declassification Project.

70. Secretary of State to AmEmbassy Santiago, "Noon Briefing on Ambassador Kirkpatrick and Chilean Issues," August 13, 1981, Chile Declassification Project; Secretary of State to AmEmbassy Buenos Aires, "Noon Briefing on Recent Chilean Exiles," August 14, 1981, Chile Declassification Project.

71. AmEmbassy Santiago to Secretary of State, "Foreign Minister's Explanation for Expulsion of Head of Human Rights Commission and Others," August 13, 1981, Chile Declassification Project.

72. John Dinges, "Kirkpatrick Trip Upsets Opposition in Chile," *Washington Post*, August 13, 1981.

73. Press Release, CCHR, August 14, 1981, MSS 1057, box 47, CCHR: Expulsion, IPS Records; Press Release, Council on Hemispheric Affairs, "Reagan Administration's Myopic Chilean Policy Ignores Heightening Levels of Repression," August 17, 1981, MSS 1057, box 47, CCHR: Expulsion, IPS Records.

74. Joe Eldridge to Augusto Pinochet, August 13, 1981, MSS 1057, box 47, CCHR: Expulsion, IPS Records.

75. US Mission USUN New York to Secretary of State, "Ambassador Kirkpatrick's Meeting with Jaime Castillo," September 19, 1981, Chile Declassification Project; US Mission USUN New York to Secretary of State, "Chilean Perm Rep Manuel Trucco's Call on Amb. Kirkpatrick," September 22, 1981, Chile Declassification Project.

76. Thomas Enders to Walter Stoessel, "Your Meeting with Chilean Appointed Ambassador Valenzuela," September 8, 1981, Chile Declassification Project; Memcon, Chilean Appointed Ambassador Enrique Valenzuela and Walter Stoessel, "Kennedy Amendment, Human Rights, Chilean Economy," September 10, 1981, Chile Declassification Project; Tom Enders to Walter Stoessel, "Your Meeting with Chilean Appointed Ambassador Valenzuela," September 8, 1981, Chile Declassification Project; State Department Briefing Memo, "Chile—The Kennedy Amendment," September 11, 1981, Chile Declassification Project.

77. Newsletter, "After Eight Years, Chile's Pinochet More Decisively in Control than Ever," September 5, 1981, Geographic Files, Chile, box 67, NGOs/AFSC, WOLA Duke Records.

78. WOLA, "Human Rights Memo on Chile," September 1981, MSS 1057, box 47, CCHR: Expulsion, IPS Records.

79. U.S. Congress, Committee on Foreign Affairs, Subcommittee on Human Rights and International Organizations, *Implementation of Congressionally Mandated Human Rights Provisions*, 134, 129.

80. Ibid., 166.

81. Ibid., 167, 169, 181.

82. Ibid., 156, 125.

83. Cindy M. Buhl, "A Disappearing Policy: Human Rights and the Reagan Administration," *Coalition Close-Up: Newsletter of the Coalition for a New Foreign and Military Policy* (Fall 1981), M94-371, box 5, Coalition for a New Foreign and Military Policy Close-Up and Updates, 1980+, CALA Records.

84. Ibid.

85. Mower notes, "Congress's capacity to have an impact on an administration's human rights policy is very difficult to determine, [but] it appears that the legislative branch did exert some influence on the Reagan administration." Mower, *Human Rights and U.S. Foreign Policy*, 82.

86. Paul Wolfowitz and Lawrence Eagleburger to Alexander Haig, "Human Rights Policy," October 2, 1981, Chile Declassification Project.

87. Stephen Palmer to Alexander Haig, "Human Rights Opposition to Administration's Foreign Policy," October 9, 1981, Chile Declassification Project.

88. "Excerpt from State Department Memo on Human Rights," November 5, 1981, *New York Times*, A10.

89. Ibid. The earlier draft of the memo from October 2 similarly stated, "Human rights—a somewhat narrow name for our values—gives us the best opportunity to convey what is ultimately at issue in our contest with the Soviet bloc." Wolfowitz and Eagleburger to Haig, "Human Rights Policy."

90. This new language clearly resonated with Reagan personally. In his speech to the British Parliament on June 8, 1982—widely regarded as his seminal human rights speech akin to Carter's Notre Dame address—Reagan used the phrase "human rights" only once (referencing the Universal Declaration of Human Rights). "Freedom," however, made an appearance twenty-two times and "democracy" sixteen. Ronald Reagan, "Address to the Members of the British Parliament," June 8, 1982, http://www.presidency.ucsb.edu/ws/index.php?pid=42614.

91. "Excerpt from State Department Memo on Human Rights."

92. Ibid.

93. Ibid.

94. Abrams worked as assistant counsel for the U.S. Senate Permanent Subcommittee on Investigations in 1975, before becoming special counsel to Jackson from 1975 to 1976. He later became special council and then chief of staff to Moynihan from 1977 to 1979.

95. U.S. Congress, Senate, Committee on Foreign Relations, *Nomination of Elliott Abrams: Hearing before the Committee on Foreign Relations, United States Senate*, 97th Congress, 1st session, November 17, 1981, (Washington, D.C.: Government Printing Office, 1981), 1, 2, 20.

96. Ibid., 2, 12.

97. Abrams cited the statutory obligation to "tell the truth" through country reports, but more importantly he invoked a moral imperative. "We owe it to people everywhere struggling for freedom to weigh our words carefully and to respect the sanctity of their efforts. If we corrupt the language we use to discuss liberty, we commit a grave offense against all those, including tens of thousands of Americans, who have given their lives to preserve it." Ibid., 4.

98. Ibid., 4, 6, 19.

99. Ibid., 21, 15.

100. Ibid., 9.

101. Ibid., 25.

102. "Human Rights Appointment and Memo: A Signal for Change?" *Update Latin America* (November/December 1981), Administrative Files, General Management, History, box 30, 1979–1981, WOLA Duke Records.

103. Robert F. Drinan, "International Human Rights in the 1980s," Annual William H. Leary Lecture, University of Utah Law School, November 19, 1981, M97–135, box 12, folder 6, ADA Speaker's Bureau '81, ADA Records.

104. Ibid.

105. Robert F. Drinan, "The White House Scorns the Aspirations of the Third World," November 20, 1981, M97–135, box 12, folder 6, ADA Speaker's Bureau '81, ADA Records.

106. The session closed with a reaffirmation of the committee's enthusiasm about Abrams's appointment. Percy noted that Abrams's nomination by a republican administration and his service with two Democratic senators "is certainly the spirit of bipartisanship at its best." He promised a speedy and expedited confirmation "so that there will be no question about where we stand with respect to you." U.S. Congress, *Nomination of Elliott Abrams*, 26.

107. Ronald Reagan, "Proclamation 4885—Bill of Rights Day, Human Rights Day and Week, 1981," December 4, 1981, *Public Papers of the President, Ronald Reagan*, 1143.

108. U.S. Congress, "International Human Rights Day—Remarks in House-Observance," December 10, 1981, *Congressional Record*, 97th Congress, 1st session, 30708.

109. Ibid.

110. Ibid.

111. George Lister to Elliott Abrams, "New York January 6 Trip," January 5, 1982, box 2, folder 6 Abrams, Lister Papers.

112. Patricia Rengel to AIUSA Offices, "Off-the-Record Remarks of Elliott Abrams, Carnegie Endowment Dinner," January 19, 1982, AIUSA II.2, box 11, folder 18, Washington Office, 1980–2, AIUSA Records.

113. Ibid.

114. Department of State Memcon, Elliott Abrams and WOLA, February 11, 1982, box 16, folder 16 WOLA, Lister Papers; George Lister to Elliott Abrams, February 11, 1982, box 2, folder 6 Abrams, Lister Papers.

115. Using Chile and El Salvador as examples, Bonkers pressed Abrams to clarify the decision-making process in which the administration incorporated human rights concerns. Abrams declined to discuss specific policy, but he noted that there was a "series of meetings" with various bureaus, but it was not an interagency process like the Christopher Committee as had been the norm under the Carter administration. Amnesty International, "Summary of Human Rights and International Organizations Subcommittee Hearings, 23 February 1982 with Elliott Abrams,

Assistant Secretary for Human Rights and Humanitarian Affairs," February 24, 1982, series II.2, box 11, folder 18, Washington Office, 1980–2, AIUSA Records. The discussion in the following paragraphs comes from this document.

116. Rengel to AIUSA Offices, "Off-the-Record Remarks of Elliott Abrams," January 19, 1982.

117. Reagan, "Address to the Members of the British Parliament."

118. For more on Reagan's democracy promotion projects in his second term, see Evan McCormick, "Braking with Statism? U.S. Democracy Promotion Programs in Latin America, 1984–1988," *Diplomatic History* 42, no. 5 (November 2018): 745–71; Morley and McGillion, *Reagan and Pinochet*; Michael Schmidli and Robert Pee, eds., *The Reagan Administration, the Cold War, and the Transition to Democracy Promotion* (London: Palgrave Macmillan, 2019); Sikkink, *Mixed Signals*, 148–80.

Conclusion

1. In a speech in November 1981, Drinan had wondered, "Will this period be remembered as the Golden Years of Human rights? Or will it be seen as a noble experiment that faded away?" See chapter 5. Robert F. Drinan, "International Human Rights in the 1980s," Annual William H. Leary Lecture, University of Utah Law School, November 19, 1981, M97–135, box 12, folder 6, ADA Speaker's Bureau '81, ADA Records.

2. "The Carter Human Rights Policy: A Provisional Appraisal," January 11, 1981, Donated Materials, Brzezinski, box 34, JCL.

3. Author interview with José Zalaquett, July 2, 2007, Santiago, Chile.

4. Author interview with Joe Eldridge, April 21, 2008, Washington, D.C.

5. LaVoy wrote, "For several years, a group of people concerned about U.S. policy in Latin America—many of whom are present at today's celebration, I'm sure—had been kicking around the idea of a Washington Office." Diane LaVoy to Joe Eldridge, June 11, 1984, Administration Files, General Management-History, box 27, Early History, WOLA Duke Collection.

6. Father J. Bryan Hehir, "The Moral Dimension of Foreign Policy," Seventh Annual Letelier-Moffitt Memorial Human Rights Award Ceremony, September 20, 1983, Geographic Files, Chile, box 65, FSIA/Letelier-Moffitt, WOLA Duke Collection.

Bibliography

Manuscripts and Archival Collections

Amnesty International of the USA, National Office Records (AIUSA Records). Rare Book and Manuscript Library, Columbia University, New York.

Argentina Declassification Project. State Department Collections. U.S. Department of State FOIA Electronic Reading Room.

Arzobispado de Santiago Fundación de Documentación y Archivo de la Vicaría de la Solidaridad (Vicaría Archive). Santiago, Chile.

Archivo de Centro de Estudios Legales y Sociales (CELS). Buenos Aires, Argentina.

Carter, Jimmy. Presidential Library (JCL). Atlanta, Georgia.

Counsel to the President
Hendrik Hertzberg Donated Materials
Office of the Cabinet Secretary, Handwriting File
Records of the Office of the National Security Advisor (NSA)
Robert Lipshutz Files
Vertical File
White House Central Files (WHCF)
Zbigniew Brzezinski Donated Materials

Chile Declassification Project. State Department Collections. U.S. Department of State FOIA Electronic Reading Room.

Derian, Patricia. Papers. Derian Residence, Chapel Hill, North Carolina (subsequently housed at the David M. Rubenstein Rare Book and Manuscript Library, Duke University, Durham, North Carolina).

Ford, Gerald R. Presidential Library (GFL). Ann Arbor, Michigan.

> James Wilson Papers
> Vernon Loen and Charles Leppert Files
> National Security Advisor Files (NSA)
> White House Central Files (WHCF)
> White House Records Office: Legislation Case Files

Lister, George. Papers. Nettie Lee Benson Latin America Collection. University of Texas at Austin.

National Security Archive. George Washington University, Washington, D.C.

Nixon, Richard. Papers. National Archives II, College Park, Maryland.

Reagan, Ronald. Presidential Library (RRL). Simi Valley, California.

> Alfonso Sapia-Bosch Files
> Counsel to the Office of the President Files
> Edwin Meese III Files
> Executive Secretariat, NSC: Records
> National Security Council Files
> Jacqueline Tillman Files
> Ludlow Flower Files
> Roger Fontaine Files
> Ronald Reagan, 1980 Campaign Papers
> Ronald Sable Files
> WHORM Subject Files

National Archives II, College Park, Maryland.

> Chile Declassification Project
> U.S. Department of State Records. Record Group 59 (RG 59)

Washington Office on Latin America. Private Institutional Records (WOLA Private Records). Washington, D.C.

Washington Office on Latin America Records, 1962–2008 (WOLA Duke Records). David M. Rubenstein Rare Book and Manuscript Library, Duke University, Durham, North Carolina.

Wisconsin Historical Society, Madison.

Americans for Democratic Action Records (ADA Records)
Community Action on Latin America (CALA Records)
Institute for Policy Studies Records (IPS Records)

Author Interviews

Eldridge, Joe. Washington, D.C., April 25, 2008, October 7, 2009.
Harris, F. A. "Tex." McLean, Virginia, September 12, 2008.
Zalaquett, José. Santiago, Chile, July 2, 2008.

Published Reports and Documents

Amnesty International. *Argentina: The Military Juntas and Human Rights*. London: Amnesty International Publications, 1987.
———. *Report of an Amnesty International Mission to Argentina, 6–15 November 1976*. London: Amnesty International Publications, 1977.
Brown, Cynthia G. *The Vicaría de la Solidaridad in Chile, an Americas Watch Report*. New York: Americas Watch, 1987.
Comisión Nacional sobre la Desaparición de Personas. *Nunca Más: The Report of the Argentine National Commission on the Disappeared*. New York: Farrar, Straus & Giroux, 1986.
Commission on United States–Latin American Relations. *The United States and Latin America, Next Steps: A Second Report*. New York: Center for Inter-American Relations, 1976.
Crahan, Margaret E. "National Security Ideology and Human Rights." In *Human Rights and Basic Needs*, edited by Margaret E. Crahan, 100–127. Washington, D.C.: Georgetown University Press, 1982.
Department of State Bulletin. Washington, D.C.: Government Printing Office, 1977.
Ethics and Public Policy Center. *Morality and Foreign Policy: A Symposium on President Carter's Stance*. Edited by Ernest Lefever. Washington, D.C.: Georgetown University, 1977.
Foreign Relations of the United States, 1961–1963. Vol. 12: *American Republics*, edited by Edward C. Keefer, Harriet Dashiell Schwar, and W. Taylor Fain III. Washington, D.C.: Government Printing Office, 1996.
Foreign Relations of the United States, 1977–1980. Vol. 1: *Foundations of Foreign Policy*, edited by Kristin L. Ahlberg. Washington, D.C.: Government Printing Office, 2014.

Foreign Relations of the United States, 1977–1980. Vol. 2: *Human Rights and Humanitarian Affairs*, edited by Kristin L. Ahlberg. Washington, D.C.: Government Printing Office, 2013.

Foreign Relations of the United States, 1977–1980. Vol. 24: *South America; Latin America Region*, edited by Sara Berndt. Washington, D.C.: Government Printing Office, 2017.

Foreign Relations of the United States, 1981–1988. Vol. 3: *Soviet Union, January 1981– January 1988*, edited by James Graham Wilson. Washington, D.C.: Government Printing Office, 2016.

Institute for Policy Studies. *The Southern Connection*. Washington, D.C.: Institute for Policy Studies, 1977.

———. *First Harvest: The Institute for Policy Studies, 1963–1983*. New York: Grove Press, 1983.

Inter-American Commission on Human Rights. *Report on the Situation of Human Rights in Argentina*. Washington, D.C.: General Secretariat OAS, 1980.

Letelier, Orlando. *Chile: Economic "Freedom" and Political Repression*. London: Institute of Race Relations, 1976.

Public Papers of the Presidents of the United States: Jimmy Carter, 1977. Washington, D.C.: Government Printing Office, 1978.

Public Papers of the Presidents of the United States: Richard Nixon, 1969. Washington, D.C.: Government Printing Office, 1970.

Public Papers of the Presidents of the United States: Ronald Reagan, 1981. Washington, D.C.: Government Printing Office, 1982.

Report of the Chilean National Commission on Truth and Reconciliation. Translated by Phillip Berryman. Notre Dame: University of Notre Dame Press, 1993.

U.S. Congress. *Covert Action in Chile, 1963–1973: Staff Report of the Select Committee to Study Governmental Operations with Respect to Intelligence Activities, United States Senate*. Washington, D.C.: Government Printing Office, 1975.

———. *International Protection of Human Rights: Hearings before the Subcommittee on International Organizations and Movements of the House Committee on Foreign Affairs*, 93rd Congress, 1st session. Washington, D.C.: Government Printing Office, 1974.

U.S. Congress, House Committee on Foreign Affairs, Subcommittee on Human Rights and International Organizations. *Implementation of Congressionally Mandated Human Rights Provisions: Hearings before the Subcommittee on Human Rights and International Organizations of the Committee on Foreign Affairs*, 97th Congress, 1st session, July 14, July 30, and September 17, 1981. Washington, D.C.: Government Printing Office, 1982.

U.S. Congress, House Committee on Foreign Affairs, Subcommittee on International Organizations and Movements. *Human Rights in the World Community: A Call for U.S. Leadership; Report*. Washington, D.C.: Government Printing Office, 1974.

U.S. Congress, House Committee on International Relations. *Human Rights and U.S. Policy: Argentina, Haiti, Indonesia, Iran, Peru, and the Philippines, Hearings before the House Committee on International Relations, United States House of Representatives*, December 31, 1976. Washington, D.C.: Congressional Printing Office, 1976.

U.S. Congress, Senate Committee on Foreign Relations. *Nomination of Hon. Cyrus R. Vance to Be Secretary of State: Hearing before the Committee on Foreign Relations, United States Senate,* 95th Congress, 1st session, January 11, 1977. Washington, D.C.: Government Printing Office, 1977.

U.S. Department of State. *Human Rights and U.S. Policy: Argentina, Haiti, Indonesia, Iran, Peru, and the Philippines, Reports Submitted to the Committee on International Relations, U.S. House of Representatives by the Department of State, pursuant to Section 502B(c) of the International Security Assistance and Arms Export Act of 1976.* Washington, D.C.: Congressional Printing Office, 1976.

U.S. Senate, Senate Committee on Foreign Relations. *Nomination of Elliott Abrams to Be Assistant Secretary of State for Human Rights and Humanitarian Affairs: Hearing before the Committee on Foreign Relations, United States Senate.* 97th Congress, 1st session, November 17, 1981. Washington, D.C.: Government Printing Office, 1981.

———. *Nomination of Ernest W. Lefever to Be Assistant Secretary of State for Human Rights and Humanitarian Affairs: Hearings before the Committee on Foreign Relations, United States Senate,* 97th Congress, 1st session, May 18, May 19, June 4, and June 5, 1981. Washington, D.C.: Government Printing Office, 1981.

Memoirs

Brzezinski, Zbigniew. *Power and Principle: Memoirs of the National Security Advisor, 1977–1981.* New York: Farrar, Straus & Giroux, 1983.

Carter, Jimmy. *Keeping Faith: Memoirs of a President.* New York: Bantam Books, 1983.

———. *White House Diary.* New York: Farrar, Straus & Giroux, 2010.

Ford, Gerald R. *A Time to Heal: The Autobiography of Gerald R. Ford.* New York: Harper & Row, 1979.

Jordan, Hamilton. *Crisis: The Last Year of the Carter Presidency.* New York: Putnam, 1982.

Kampelman, Max M. *Entering New Worlds: The Memoirs of a Private Man in Public Life.* New York: HarperCollins, 1991.

Kampelman, Max M., and Leonard Sussman. *Three Years at the East-West Divide: The Words of U.S. Ambassador Max M. Kampelman at the Madrid Conference on Security and Human Rights.* New York: Freedom House, 1983.

Kennedy, Edward M. *True Compass: A Memoir.* New York: Twelve, 2009.

Kissinger, Henry. *Years of Renewal.* New York: Simon & Schuster, 1999.

Mellibovsky, Matilde. *Circle of Love over Death: Testimonies of the Mothers of the Plaza de Mayo.* Willimantic, CT: Curbstone Press, 1997.

Salzberg, John P. "A View from the Hill: U.S. Legislation and Human Rights." In *The Diplomacy of Human Rights,* edited by David D. Newsom, 13–20. Lanham, MD: University Press of America, 1986.

Timerman, Jacobo. *Prisoner without a Name, Cell without a Number.* New York: Knopf, 1981.

Vance, Cyrus R. *Hard Choices: Four Critical Years in Managing America's Foreign Policy.* New York: Simon & Schuster, 1983.

Books and Articles

Adler, Paul. "'The Basis of a New Internationalism?' The Institute for Policy Studies and North-South Politics from the NIEO to Neoliberalism." *Diplomatic History* 41, no. 4 (September 2017): 665–93.

Andersen, Martin Edwin. *Dossier Secreto: Argentina's Desaparecidos and the Myth of the "Dirty War."* Boulder, CO: Westview Press, 1993.

Apodaca, Clair. *Understanding U.S. Human Rights Policy: A Paradoxical Legacy.* New York: Routledge, 2006.

Armony, Ariel C. *Argentina, the United States, and the Anti-Communist Crusade in Central America, 1977–1984.* Athens: Ohio University Center for International Studies, 1997.

Berkowitz, Edward D. *Something Happened: A Political and Cultural Overview of the Seventies.* New York: Columbia University Press, 2006.

Bethell, Leslie, and Ian Roxborough. "The Impact of the Cold War on Latin America." In *Origins of the Cold War: An International History,* edited by Melvyn P. Leffler and David S. Painter, 293–316. New York: Routledge, 1994.

Bitzer, Lloyd F. *Carter vs. Ford: The Counterfeit Debates of 1976.* Madison: University of Wisconsin Press, 1980.

Bon Tempo, Carl. "From the Center-Right: Freedom House and Human Rights in the 1970s and 1980s." In Iriye et al., *Human Rights Revolution,* 223–44.

———. *Americans at the Gate.* Princeton: Princeton University Press, 2008.

Borstelmann, Thomas. *The 1970s: A New Global History from Civil Rights to Economic Inequality.* Princeton: Princeton University Press, 2012.

Bouvard, Marguerite Guzman. *Revolutionizing Motherhood: The Mothers of the Plaza de Mayo.* Wilmington, DE: Scholarly Resources Inc, 1994.

Bradley, Mark. *The World Reimagined: Americans and Human Rights in the Twentieth Century.* New York: Cambridge University Press, 2016.

Branch, Taylor, and Eugene M. Propper. *Labyrinth.* New York: Viking Press, 1982.

Brands, Hal. *Latin America's Cold War.* Cambridge, MA: Harvard University Press, 2010.

Brysk, Alison. *The Politics of Human Rights in Argentina: Protest, Change, and Democratization.* Stanford: Stanford University Press, 1994.

Buchanan, Tom. "'The Truth Will Set You Free': The Making of Amnesty International." *Journal of Contemporary History* 37, no. 4 (October 2002): 575–97.

Carouthers, Thomas. *In the Name of Democracy.* Berkeley: University of California Press, 1991.

Clark, Ann Marie. *Diplomacy of Conscience: Amnesty International and Changing Human Rights Norms.* Princeton: Princeton University Press, 2001.

Cleary, Edward L. *The Struggle for Human Rights in Latin America.* Westport, CT: Praeger, 1997.

Clymer, Adam. *Edward M. Kennedy: A Biography.* New York: Morrow, 1999.

Cmiel, Kenneth. "The Emergence of Human Rights Politics in the United States." *Journal of American History* 86, no. 3 (December 1999): 1231–50.

———. "The Recent History of Human Rights." *American Historical Review* 109, no. 1 (February 2004): 117–35.

Constable, Pamela, and Arturo Valenzuela. *A Nation of Enemies: Chile under Pinochet*. New York: Norton, 1993.

Corradi, Juan E., Patricia Weiss Fagen, and Manuel Antonio Garretón, eds. *Fear at the Edge: State Terror and Resistance in Latin America*. Berkeley: University of California, 1992.

Dinges, John, and Saul Landau. *Assassination on Embassy Row*. New York: Pantheon Books, 1980.

Eckel, Jan, and Samuel Moyn. *The Breakthrough: Human Rights in the 1970s*. Philadelphia: University of Pennsylvania Press, 2014.

Ehrman, John. *The Rise of Neoconservatism: Intellectuals and Foreign Affairs*. New Haven: Yale University Press, 1995.

Ensalaco, Mark. *Chile under Pinochet: Recovering the Truth*. Philadelphia: University of Pennsylvania Press, 2000.

Farber, David. *Taken Hostage: The Iran Hostage Crisis and America's First Encounter with Radical Islam*. Princeton: Princeton University Press, 2005.

Feitlowitz, Marguerite. *A Lexicon of Terror: Argentina and the Legacies of Torture*. New York: Oxford University Press, 1999.

Ferguson, Niall, Charles S. Maier, Erez Manela, and Daniel Sargent, eds. *The Shock of the Global: The 1970s in Perspective*. Cambridge, MA: Belknap Press of Harvard University Press, 2010.

Fisher, Jo. *Mothers of the Disappeared*. Boston: South End Press, 1989.

Forsythe, David P. *Human Rights and U.S. Foreign Policy: Congress Reconsidered*. Gainesville: University Press of Florida, 1988.

Friedman, Max Paul. "Retiring the Puppets, Bringing Latin America Back In: Recent Scholarship on United States–Latin American Relations." *Diplomatic History* 25, no. 7 (November 2003): 621–36.

Gaddis, John Lewis. *Strategies of Containment*. New York: Oxford University Press, 2005.

Glad, Betty. *An Outsider in the White House: Jimmy Carter, His Advisors, and the Making of American Foreign Policy*. Ithaca: Cornell University Press, 2009.

Grandin, Greg. *Empire's Workshop: Latin America, the United States, and the Rise of the New Imperialism*. New York: Metropolitan Books, 2006.

———. "The Liberal Traditions in the Americas: Rights, Sovereignty, and the Origins of Liberal Multilateralism." *American Historical Review* 117, no. 1 (2012): 68–91.

Green, James M. *We Cannot Remain Silent: Opposition to the Brazilian Military Dictatorship in the United States*. Durham: Duke University Press, 2010.

Grow, Michael. *U.S. Presidents and Latin American Interventions: Pursuing Regime Change in the Cold War*. Lawrence: University Press of Kansas, 2008.

Guest, Iain. *Behind the Disappearances: Argentina's Dirty War against Human Rights and the United Nations*. Philadelphia: University of Pennsylvania Press, 1990.

Harmer, Tanya. *Allende's Chile and the Inter-American Cold War*. Chapel Hill: University of North Carolina Press, 2011.

Hawkins, Darren G. *International Human Rights and Authoritarian Rule in Chile*. Lincoln: University of Nebraska Press, 2002.

Hilbink, Lisa. *Judges beyond Politics in Democracy and Dictatorship: Lessons from Chile*. New York: Cambridge University Press, 2007.

Hodges, Donald Clark. *Argentina's "Dirty War": An Intellectual Biography*. Austin: University of Texas Press, 1991.

Howison, Jeffrey. *The 1980 Presidential Election: Ronald Reagan and the Shaping of the American Conservative Movement*. New York: Routledge, 2014.

Ignatieff, Michael. *Human Rights as Politics and Idolatry*. Princeton: Princeton University Press, 2001.

Iriye, Akira, Petra Goedde, and William I. Hitchcock, eds. *The Human Rights Revolution: An International History*. New York: Oxford University Press, 2012.

Jacobs, Meg, and Julian E. Zelizer. *Conservatives in Power: The Reagan Years, 1981–1989: A Brief History with Documents*. Boston: Bedford St. Martin's, 2011.

Jacoby, Tamar. "The Reagan Turnaround on Human Rights." *Foreign Affairs* 64, no. 5 (Summer 1986): 1066–86.

Johns, Andrew, ed. *A Companion to Ronald Reagan*. West Sussex, UK: Wiley-Blackwell, 2015.

Johnson, Robert David. *Congress and the Cold War*. New York: Cambridge University Press, 2006.

Joseph, Gilbert, and Daniela Spenser, eds. *In from the Cold: Latin America's New Encounter with the Cold War*. Durham: Duke University Press, 2008.

Kaufman, Burton I., and Scott Kaufman. *The Presidency of James Earl Carter, Jr.* Lawrence: University Press of Kansas, 2006.

Kaufman, Natalie Hevener. *Human Rights Treaties and the Senate: A History of Opposition*. Chapel Hill: University of North Carolina Press, 1990.

Kaufman, Robert G. *Henry M. Jackson: A Life in Politics*. Seattle: University of Washington Press, 2000.

Kaufman, Scott. *Plans Unraveled: The Foreign Policy of the Carter Administration*. Dekalb: Northern Illinois University Press, 2008.

Keck, Margaret E., and Kathryn Sikkink. *Activists beyond Borders: Advocacy Networks in International Politics*. Ithaca: Cornell University Press, 1998.

Kelly, Patrick William. "The 1973 Chilean Coup and the Origins of Transnational Human Rights Activism." *Journal of Global History* 8, no. 1 (March 2013): 165–86.

———. *Sovereign Emergencies: Latin America and the Making of Global Human Rights Politics*. Cambridge: Cambridge University Press, 2018.

Keys, Barbara. "Congress, Kissinger, and the Origins of Human Rights Diplomacy." *Diplomatic History* 34, no. 5 (November 2010): 823–51.

———. "Anti-Torture Politics: Amnesty International, the Greek Junta, and the Origins of the Human Rights 'Boom' in the United States." In Iriye et al., *Human Rights Revolution*, 201–22.

———. *Reclaiming American Virtue: The Human Rights Revolution of the 1970s*. Cambridge, MA: Harvard University Press, 2014.

Kirkpatrick, Jeane. "Dictatorships and Double Standards." *Commentary* 68, no. 5 (November 1979): 34–45.

Klaiber, Jeffrey L. *The Church, Dictatorships, and Democracy in Latin America*. Maryknoll, NY: Orbis Books, 1998.

Korey, William. *Human Rights and the Helsinki Accord: Focus on U.S. Policy*. New York: Foreign Policy Association, 1983.

——. *The Promises We Keep: Human Rights, the Helsinki Process, and American Foreign Policy*. New York: St. Martin's Press, 1993.

Kornbluh, Peter. *The Pinochet File: A Declassified Dossier on Atrocity and Accountability*. New York: New Press, 2003.

Krauss, Gregory. "Impacting Foreign Policy as a Mid-Level Bureaucrat: The Diplomatic Career of George Lister." M.P.Aff., University of Texas at Austin, 2007.

Laber, Jeri. *The Courage of Strangers: Coming of Age with the Human Rights Movement*. New York: Public Affairs, 2002.

LaFeber, Walter. *Inevitable Revolutions: The United States in Central America*. New York: W.W. Norton, 1993.

Lawrence, Mark. "Containing Globalism: The United States and the Developing World in the 1970s." In Ferguson et al., *Shock of the Global*, 205–19.

Leffler, Melvyn. *For the Soul of Mankind: The United States, the Soviet Union, and the Cold War*. New York: Hill & Wang, 2007.

LeoGrande, William M. *Our Own Backyard: The United Sates in Central America, 1977–1992*. Chapel Hill: University of North Carolina Press, 1998.

Lewis, Paul H. *Guerrillas and Generals: The "Dirty War" in Argentina*. Westport, CT: Praeger, 2002.

Loveman, Brian, and Thomas M. Davies, eds. *The Politics of Antipolitics: The Military in Latin America*. Wilmington, DE: Scholarly Resources, 1997.

Lowden, Pamela. *Moral Opposition to Authoritarian Rule in Chile, 1973–90*. New York: Macmillan, 1996.

Markarian, Vania. *Left in Transformation: Uruguayan Exiles and the Latin American Human Rights Networks, 1967–1984*. New York: Routledge, 2005.

Mazower, Mark. "A Strange Triumph of Human Rights." *Historical Journal* 47, no. 2 (June 2004): 379–98.

McCormick, Evan. "Braking with Statism? U.S. Democracy Promotion Programs in Latin America, 1984–1988." *Diplomatic History* 42, no. 5 (November 2018): 745–71.

McLellan, David S. *Cyrus Vance*. Totowa, NJ: Rowman & Allanfeld, 1985.

McPherson, Alan. *Yankee No! Anti-Americanism in U.S.–Latin American Relations*. Cambridge, MA: Harvard University Press, 2003.

——. *Anti-Americanism in Latin America and the Caribbean*. New York: Berghahn, 2006.

——. *A Short History of U.S. Interventions in Latin America and the Caribbean*. Chichester, UK: Wiley-Blackwell, 2016.

——. "Letelier Diplomacy: Nonstate Actors and U.S.-Chilean Relations." *Diplomatic History* 43, no. 3 (June 2019): 445–68.

Mignone, Emilio Fermín. *Witness to the Truth: The Complicity of Church and Dictatorship in Argentina, 1976–1983*. Maryknoll, NY: Orbis Books, 1988.

Mitchell, Nancy. *Jimmy Carter in Africa: Race and the Cold War*. Washington, D.C.: Woodrow Wilson Center Press, 2016.

Morley, Morris, and Chris McGillion. *Reagan and Pinochet: The Struggle over U.S. Policy toward Chile*. New York: Cambridge University Press, 2015.

Mower, Jr., A. Glenn. *Human Rights and American Foreign Policy: The Carter and Reagan Experiences*. New York: Greenwood, 1987.

Moyn, Samuel. *The Last Utopia: Human Rights in History*. Cambridge, MA: Belknap Press of Harvard University Press, 2010.

Mueller, Brian Scott. *Democracy's Think Tank*. Philadelphia: University of Pennsylvania Press, forthcoming.

Navarro, Marysa. "The Personal Is Political: Las Madres de Plaza de Mayo." In *Power and Popular Protest: Latin American Social Movements*, edited by Susan Eckstein and Manuel A. Garretón Merino, 241–58. Berkeley: University of California Press, 2001.

Nguyen, Lien-Hang T. "The Vietnam Decade: The Global Shock of the War." In Ferguson et al., *Shock of the Global*, 159–72.

Nunn, Frederick M. *The Time of the Generals: Latin American Professional Militarism in World Perspective*. Lincoln: University of Nebraska Press, 1992.

Paulauskas, Michael. "Reagan, the Soviet Union and the Cold War, 1981–1985." In Johns, *Companion to Ronald Reagan*, 276–94.

Pee, Robert. *Democracy Promotion, National Security and Strategy: Foreign Policy under the Reagan Administration*. New York: Routledge, 2016.

Power, Margaret. "The U.S. Movement in Solidarity with Chile in the 1970s." *Latin American Perspectives* 36, no. 6 (November 2009): 46–66.

Power, Margaret, and Julie Charlip. "Introduction: On Solidarity." *Latin American Perspectives* 36, no. 6 (November 2009): 3–9.

Prados, John. *The Family Jewels: The CIA, Secrecy, and Presidential Power*. Austin: University of Texas Press, 2013.

Rabe, Stephen. *The Most Dangerous Area in the World: John F. Kennedy Confronts Communist Revolution in Latin America*. Chapel Hill: University of North Carolina Press, 1999.

———. *The Killing Zone: The United States Wages Cold War in Latin America*. New York: Oxford University Press, 2016.

Renouard, Joe. *Human Rights in American Foreign Policy 1960 to the Soviet Collapse*. Philadelphia: University of Pennsylvania Press, 2016.

Risse-Kappen, Thomas, Steve C. Ropp, and Kathryn Sikkink. *The Persistent Power of Human Rights: From Commitment to Compliance*. New York: Cambridge University Press, 2013.

Roniger, Luis, and Mario Sznajder. *The Legacy of Human-Rights Violations in the Southern Cone: Argentina, Chile, and Uruguay*. New York: Oxford University Press, 1999.

Rosenbaum, Herbert D., and Alexej Ugrinsky, eds. *Jimmy Carter: Foreign Policy and Post-Presidential Years*. Westport, CT: Greenwood, 1994.

Rouquié, Alain. *The Military and the State in Latin America*. Berkeley: University of California Press, 1987.

Rozell, Mark. *The Press and the Carter Presidency*. Boulder, CO: Westview Press, 1989.

Sargent, Daniel. *A Superpower Transformed: The Remaking of American Foreign Relations in the 1970s*. New York: Oxford University Press, 2015.

Scanlon, Sandra. "Ronald Reagan and the Conservative Movement." In Johns, *Companion to Ronald Reagan*, 585–607.

Schaller, Michael. *Ronald Reagan*. New York: Oxford University Press, 2011.

Schmidli, William Michael. *The Fate of Freedom Elsewhere: Human Rights and U.S. Cold War Policy toward Argentina*. Ithaca: Cornell University Press, 2013.

Schmidli, William Michael, and Robert Pee, eds. *The Reagan Administration, the Cold War, and the Transition to Democracy Promotion.* London: Palgrave Macmillan, 2019.

Schmitz, David F. "Senator Frank Church, the Ford Administration, and the Challenges of Post-Vietnam Foreign Policy." *Peace and Change* 21, no. 4 (October 1996): 438–64.

———. *Thank God They're on Our Side.* Chapel Hill: University of North Carolina Press, 1999.

———. *The United States and Right-Wing Dictatorships.* New York: Cambridge University Press, 2006.

Schmitz, David F., and Vanessa Walker. "Jimmy Carter and the Foreign Policy of Human Rights: The Development of a Post-Cold War Foreign Policy." *Diplomatic History* 28, no. 1 (January 2004): 113–17.

Schoultz, Lars. *Human Rights and United States Policy toward Latin America.* Princeton: Princeton University Press, 1981.

Schulman, Bruce J., and Julian Zelizer, eds. *Rightward Bound: Making American Conservative in the 1970s.* Cambridge, MA: Harvard University Press, 2008.

Sigmund, Paul. *The United States and Democracy in Chile.* Baltimore: Johns Hopkins University Press, 1993.

Sikkink, Kathryn. *Mixed Signals: U.S. Human Rights Policy and Latin America.* Ithaca: Cornell University Press, 2004.

———. "Reconceptualizing Sovereignty in the Americas." *Houston Journal of International Law* 19, no. 3 (1996–97): 705–24.

———. *Evidence for Hope: Making Human Rights Work in the 21st Century.* Princeton: Princeton University Press, 2017.

Skidmore, David. *Reversing Course: Carter's Foreign Policy, Domestic Politics, and the Failure of Reform.* Nashville: Vanderbilt University Press, 1996.

Smith, Brian H. *The Church and Politics in Chile: Challenges to Modern Catholicism.* Princeton: Princeton University Press, 1982.

Smith, Gaddis. *Morality, Reason, and Power: American Diplomacy in the Carter Years.* New York: Hill & Wang, 1986.

Snyder, Sarah B. "The Defeat of Ernest Lefever's Nomination: Keeping Human Rights on the United States Foreign Policy Agenda." In *Challenging U.S. Foreign Policy: America and the World in the Long Twentieth Century*, edited by Bevan Sewell and Scott Lucas, 136–61. London: Palgrave Macmillan, 2011.

———. *Human Rights Activism and the End of the Cold War: A Transnational History of the Helsinki Network.* New York: Cambridge University Press, 2011.

———. "'A Call for U.S. Leadership': Congressional Activism on Human Rights." *Diplomatic History* 37, no. 2 (April 2013): 372–97.

———. *From Selma to Moscow: How Human Rights Activism Transformed U.S. Foreign Policy.* New York: Columbia University Press, 2018.

Stanley, Timothy. *Kennedy vs. Carter: The 1980 Battle for the Democratic Party's Soul.* Lawrence: University Press of Kansas, 2010.

Stern, Steve J. *Battling for Hearts and Minds: Memory Struggles in Pinochet's Chile, 1973–1988.* Durham: Duke University Press, 2006.

Stites Mor, Jessica, ed. *Human Rights and Transnational Solidarity in Cold War Latin America*. Madison: University of Wisconsin Press, 2013.

Stuckey, Mary E. *Jimmy Carter, Human Rights, and the National Agenda*. College Station: Texas A&M University Press, 2008.

Suri, Jeremi. *Henry Kissinger and the American Century*. Cambridge, MA: Belknap Press of Harvard University Press, 2007.

Troy, Gil. *Morning in America: How Ronald Reagan Invented the 1980s*. Princeton: Princeton University Press, 2005.

Valenzuela, Arturo. *The Breakdown of Democratic Regimes: Chile*. Baltimore: Johns Hopkins University Press, 1978.

Walcher, Dustin. "The Reagan Doctrine." In Johns, *Companion to Ronald Reagan*, 339–58.

Walker, Vanessa. "The Paradoxes of Human Rights Diplomacy: The Institute for Policy Studies and U.S.–Latin American Relations in the Carter Administration." MA thesis, University of Wisconsin–Madison, 2004.

———. "At the End of Influence: The Letelier Assassination, Human Rights, and Rethinking Intervention in U.S. Latin American Relations." *Journal of Contemporary History* 46, no. 1 (2011): 109–35.

Westad, Odd Arne. *The Global Cold War: Third World Interventions and the Making of Our Times*. New York: Cambridge University Press, 2007.

Wright, Thomas C. *Latin America in the Era of the Cuban Revolution*. New York: Praeger, 1991.

———. *State Terrorism in Latin America: Chile, Argentina, and International Human Rights*. Lanham, MD: Rowman & Littlefield, 2007.

Wright, Thomas C., and Rody Oñate, eds. *Flight from Chile: Voices of Exile*. Albuquerque: University of New Mexico Press, 1998.

Wu, Judy Tzu-Chun. *Radicals on the Road: Internationalism, Orientalism, and Feminism during the Vietnam War*. Ithaca: Cornell University Press, 2013.

Youngers, Coletta. *Thirty Years of Advocacy for Human Rights, Democracy and Social Justice*. Washington, D.C.: Washington Office on Latin America, 2006.

Zaretsky, Natasha. "Restraint of Retreat? The Debate over the Panama Canal Treaties and U.S. Nationalism after Vietnam." *Diplomatic History* 35, no. 1 (June 2011): 535–62.

Zelizer, Julian. *Arsenal of Democracy*. New York: Basic Books, 2010.

———. *Jimmy Carter*. New York: Times Books, Henry Holt, 2010.

Index

Page numbers in *italic* refer to figures.